One Nation, Underprivileged

ONE NATION,
UNDERPRIVILEGED

Why American Poverty

Affects Us All

Mark Robert Rank

OXFORD
UNIVERSITY PRESS

2004

OXFORD

UNIVERSITY PRESS

Oxford   New York
Auckland   Bangkok   Buenos Aires   Cape Town   Chennai
Dar es Salaam   Delhi   Hong Kong   Istanbul   Karachi   Kolkata
Kuala Lumpur   Madrid   Melbourne   Mexico City   Mumbai   Nairobi
São Paulo   Shanghai   Taipei   Tokyo   Toronto

Copyright © 2004 by Mark Robert Rank

Published by Oxford University Press, Inc.
198 Madison Avenue, New York, New York 10016

www.oup.com

Oxford is a registered trademark of Oxford University Press

Library of Congress Cataloging-in-Publication Data
Rank, Mark R.
One nation, underprivileged : why American poverty affects us all /
Mark Robert Rank.
p. cm.
ISBN 0-19-510168-5
1. Poverty—United States.   2. Poor—United States.
3. Poor—Government policy—United States.   I. Title.
HV91 .R363   2004
339.4'6—dc21   2003011312

9 8 7 6 5 4 3 2 1

Printed in the United States of America
on acid-free paper

Preface

FOR QUITE SOME TIME I have felt the
need for a book that would address
American poverty in a very different
fashion from the way it has typically been
approached. Although there have been
countless books and articles written on the
subject, something fundamental seemed to
be missing from many of them. Much of
this work simply reinforced the view that
poverty could be understood through the
inadequacies of the poor. Whether these
shortcomings were a lack of motivation, low
levels of education, insufficient skills, or
single parenthood, they all pointed their
fingers at the poor themselves. Yet this
struck me as deeply amiss, for it seemed to
capture only a small slice of the scope and
meaning of poverty in this country. As a
result, the arguments laid out in these pages
are an attempt to introduce a new way of
thinking about American poverty.

In the process, I have come to fully appreciate an old saying—"The more you know, the
less you know." As I researched and wrote this
book, the meaning of this expression has
become both painfully and delightfully apparent. The pain has resulted from realizing that

the topics I have written about in *One Nation, Underprivileged* require considerably more depth in order for us to fully appreciate their meaning and nuance. The delight has arisen from being able to explore and develop material typically not found in the standard treatments of poverty.

One example will suffice. In the chapter entitled "True to Values," I consider how the values of liberty, equality, and justice are undermined by the presence of poverty. Obviously, one could spend an entire life's work exploring the meaning behind any one of these concepts (and, indeed, many have). Yet in spite of such warnings, I devote only a handful of pages in order to make sense of these concepts. It is clear that much more needs to be written about the relationship of these concepts to poverty.

However, to ignore these issues on the grounds of not being able to explore all of their nuances strikes me as equally inadequate. The delight has thus come from being able to think and write about some extremely interesting, innovative, and pertinent areas that are generally not brought together in standard academic treatises on poverty. I have felt a bit like the kid in the proverbial candy store. With a multitude of unexplored angles and approaches, the choosing has been exciting and challenging.

As a result, I have gained a greater appreciation of the array of research and disciplines that touch upon the condition of poverty. Areas such as sociology, economics, politics, history, health, philosophy, social work, anthropology, theology, law, psychology, and others are essential if we are to grasp the fuller meaning of impoverishment in America.

In experiencing this broadening of my individual perspective, I have also come to understand the process by which academics narrow their focus and become more specialized in their fields of research. Given the volumes of information generated these days surrounding virtually any subject, one's area of expertise is often narrowed by necessity. That is, a researcher can claim precision over any one topic, only when the subject matter has become extremely restricted. In the process, something important has been lost.

Perhaps the adage about losing sight of the forest as one gazes at the individual trees is most apt. Those of us in academic disciplines have too often lost sight of the forest. We can describe in detail various snippets of the social order, but we experience enormous difficulty in telling others why such snippets are important and how they might fit into the larger meaning of things. As one narrows one's focus, such a renaissance perspective becomes increasingly rare. Although we often nod our heads approvingly when the notion of interdisciplinary research is raised, in my opinion, too many of us have become overly provincial in our outlooks.

And yet, to view the forest without an understanding of the individual trees is also a danger. Such an approach is marked by abstract reasoning or, worse, rhetorical claims, without a grounding in reality. Clearly a balance is in order. In this book I have sought not only to locate a number of the obvious and less than obvious trees in the forest but also to understand their position relative to the overall whole.

Perhaps most exciting has been the attempt to develop a new way of thinking about American poverty. As I argue in the pages ahead, I believe that the manner in which we have traditionally thought about poverty has been misguided. This outlook has led to exceptionally high rates of poverty and our overall acceptance of the status quo. The purpose of this book is to outline a new and, I hope, more insightful perspective on the issue of poverty than one typically encounters. Developing this perspective has been both challenging and rewarding. The ultimate test will reside in how it stands up in the minds of you, the reader. That is the task at hand.

In attempting to accomplish this task, I have been helped by many along the way. First, the dean of the George Warren Brown School of Social Work at Washington University, Shanti Khinduka, has been exceptionally supportive of this project. He has provided the moral encouragement and institutional assistance that have been pivotal to the completion of this book. Perhaps most important, he has served as an inspiration to continually challenge oneself and to always reach a bit further.

A number of scholars and friends have provided valuable written insights and suggestions on earlier versions of this manuscript. They include Matthew Howard, Ed Kain, Tim McBride, Joel Myerson, Ann Nichols-Casebolt, Alice O'Connor, Karen Seccombe, Margaret Sherraden, David Stewart, John Robertson, Tom Shapiro, and Nancy Vosler. I am extremely grateful for their enormous generosity and wisdom. Over the years, I have also discussed the ideas in this book with a number of colleagues here at Washington University, including John Bricout, David Cronin, Jack Knight, Curtis McMillen, Larry May, Robert Pollack, Shirley Porterfield, Michael Sherraden, James Herbert Williams, and Gautam Yadama. My thanks to all of them for allowing me to bend their ears.

The life course analysis of poverty and welfare found in chapters 3 and 4 and appendix B is the result of a long collaboration with my very good friend and colleague at Cornell University, Thomas A. Hirschl. Tom and I have worked over the past several years on a series of articles that examine the life course risk of economic deprivation in America. The research reported in this book represents a small piece of that work.

Portions of the life table analyses in chapter 4 have appeared in *Social Work* (vol. 44, no. 3, 1999; vol. 47, no. 3, 2002), and parts of appendix B were published in *Journal of Marriage and the Family* (vol. 61, no. 4, 1999) and *Journal of Gerontology* (vol. 54B, no. 4, 1999). In addition, an earlier version of chapter 2 appeared in *Handbook of Family Diversity*, edited by David H. Demo, Katherine R. Allen, and Mark A. Fine (Oxford University Press, 2000). Verses of "This Land Is Your Land" found in chapter 1 are used by permission, words and music by Woody Guthrie, TRO © copyright 1956 (renewed, 1958 [renewed], 1970 [renewed]), Ludlow Music, Inc., New York, NY.

Several students have lent their valuable assistance to this project. Hong-Sik Yoon provided computational help in estimating tables 3.1, 3.2, and 3.3, while Walt Paquin tracked down several research studies and materials. The students in my classes have been a constant source of enlightenment. In particular, I have had the pleasure of being able to exchange and bounce ideas off those enrolled in my course on American poverty and inequality. Steve Brodbeck, Amanda Moore McBride, Connie Probst, Will Rainford, and April Shaw, all former students, have continued to remain important sounding boards for the ideas in this book.

The editorial staff at Oxford University Press has been superb. My original editor, Gioia Stevens, provided the encouragement and impetus at the beginnings of this project, while Joan Bossert has lent her invaluable guidance and support during its completion. In addition, Jeri Famighetti, Stacey Hamilton, Maura Roessner, and Lisa Stallings have all been instrumental in guiding this book to publication.

My family has provided the emotional foundation and support so important in life. My daughters, Libby and Katie, and my wife, Anne, have all given me their encouragement and inspiration during the writing of this book.

Finally, I would like to acknowledge the unsung efforts of those striving to alleviate the pain and injustice of poverty. I have been very fortunate to have met some of these individuals during the course of my work. From the volunteer in a homeless shelter, to the inspirational teacher in a school strapped for resources, to the organizer lobbying for a living wage, there are literally millions of fair-minded Americans who are working in various ways to reduce the pain of poverty. If this book can contribute in some small way to highlighting the importance and urgency of these struggles, my time will have been well spent.

Contents

The Nature of

American Poverty

I

Disturbing Contrasts

1

The test of our progress is not whether we add more to the abundance of those who have much; it is whether we provide enough for those who have too little.

Franklin D. Roosevelt

POVERTY IN AMERICA. The words themselves seem to clash with one another. The United States symbolizes a land of opportunity, bread-basket to the world, home of the American Dream, not a producer of poverty. It is a country of overwhelming resources, materials, and skills. Poverty in America? Surely an oxymoron.

Unfortunately, poverty in America is not an oxymoron but a reality. It is as American as the free-market system that underlies it. Its face is found in every corner of this affluent nation. It stretches along busy intersections and down deserted back roads. Ultimately, as this book will show, poverty casts its shadow upon a majority of our citizens at some point during their lives.

Perhaps what is most troubling about this issue is precisely the contrast between our considerable wealth as a nation and the impoverishment of a significant percentage of our people. It is one thing for a country to be mixed in poverty but to lack the resources to change the conditions. It is quite another to have the capital and assets but consistently fail to do much about it. It is the latter that characterizes the United States. As a result, we are left with a multitude of disturbing contrasts.

Such contrasts have become particularly harsh in recent years. The homeless man dying on a park bench while joggers whisk by in oblivion.[1] The single mother struggling to survive on one of the least generous systems of public assistance in the Western world as politicians continue to slash the social safety net, arguing that they are helping such women by doing so. The preschool child who goes to bed hungry yet sleeps in a town where grain is stockpiled in warehouses. In short, the contrasts are sharp, penetrating, and disturbing.

These paradoxes are found in every state, city, and village across America.[2] In my current hometown of St. Louis, one encounters a striking visual contrast early on. As you approach St. Louis traveling east to west, the Gateway Arch begins to rise alongside the Mississippi River. Built as a monument to America's westward expansion, it symbolizes the hopes and strengths of our people. Its curving stainless steel contour and size are truly an architectural marvel.

Yet as the Arch comes closer in to view, so too does one of the most depressed and impoverished cities in the United States—East St. Louis. Its architectural themes include schools with boarded-up windows, sewer systems that back up, and houses on the verge of collapse. Jonathan Kozol has written powerfully about the squalid conditions found on the east bank of the Mississippi, in the shadows of the Arch. Kozol recalls the remarks of a local reporter:

> The ultimate terror for white people . . . is to leave the highway
> by mistake and find themselves in East St. Louis. People speak of
> getting lost in East St. Louis as a nightmare. The nightmare to
> me is that they never leave that highway so they never know what
> life is like for all the children here. They *ought* to get off that
> highway. The nightmare isn't in their heads. It's a real place.
> There are children living here. (1991: 18)

This contradiction between abundant resources on the one hand and poverty on the other is equally ironic in what has become one of our unofficial national anthems—"This Land Is Your Land," by Woody Guthrie. Each year, millions of schoolchildren (including those in East St. Louis) sing the words to "This Land." The verses evoke an uplifting spirit of America—the endless skyway and golden valley; the redwood forests and Gulf Stream waters. As the title of the song implies, this spirit and vision belong to us all.

Yet as with many of Guthrie's ballads, the song is also about the hardships, struggles, and desires of folks who are down on their luck and looking to find a better life elsewhere. It is about Dust Bowl families uprooted in the 1930s and moving west in search of the Promised Land. The Okie walking "that ribbon of highway" finds himself stopped by the police at the California border and is told to turn around. His reply? "This land is your land, this land is my land . . ."

This context provides the backdrop for two additional verses Guthrie wrote that most parents are unaware of, since they rarely appear in their children's song books.

> Was a big high wall there, that tried to stop me.
> Was a great big sign that said Private Property.
> But on the other side, it didn't say nothin'.
> That side was made for you and me.

> One bright sunny morning, in the shadow of the steeple,
> By the relief office, I saw my people.
> As they stood there hungry, I stood there wondering, if
> This land was made for you and me.

It is ironic indeed that within this most American of songs, hidden away, are the darker sides of our country—inequality, injustice, and poverty. According to Guthrie, this too "was made for you and me."[3]

In many ways, this side of America has become worse since Woody Guthrie penned these words in 1940. From the early 1970s to the present, wages and income have stagnated, the gap between rich and poor has widened, increasing numbers of working families fall below the poverty line, inner cities and rural areas have become ever more economically isolated, and so on down the list. Roughly one-fifth of our population is either in poverty or precariously close to falling into poverty at any point in time. In fact, the United States has far and away the highest rates of poverty and income inequality among Western industrialized countries, in spite of being the wealthiest nation in the world. And so we are left again with both a disturbing contrast and a critical question—Why should this be?

The argument and premise of this book is that much of the answer to this question lies in the manner in which poverty has typically been viewed and acted on in the United States—that poverty is the result of individual inadequacies, that poverty lies outside the mainstream American experience, and therefore that poverty is not a national priority.

This book is intended to provide a radically different perspective on American poverty. It will be argued and empirically demonstrated that poverty is the result of systemic failings within the U.S. economic and social structures, that a majority of Americans experience poverty during their adult lifetimes, and that poverty is an issue of vital national concern. In short, the purpose of this book is to lay out and detail a paradigm for thinking about U.S. poverty that is entirely different from the manner in which we have traditionally thought about this issue. Such a paradigm shift is essential to constructing lasting and effective changes that will reduce the severity, magnitude, and injustice of American poverty.

Beginnings

The intellectual beginnings of this book can be traced back to my earlier work, *Living on the Edge: The Realities of Welfare in America*. In conducting the research for *Living on the Edge*, I set out to learn from the true experts—those on welfare—what it was like to be poor and to survive on public assistance programs in this country. What I heard and saw was in sharp contrast with the typical image of the welfare recipient.

Rather than the stereotype of people too lazy to work, these were families that sounded remarkably like the families one might encounter in the grocery store or down the street. They wanted to get ahead in their lives, wished the best for their children, and were willing to put in the effort to accomplish it.

The words of Denise Turner, a thirty-seven-year-old mother of four children, were characteristic of many of the recipients I talked to:

> I always try to be positive in life. 'Cause I know it takes a positive
> mental attitude to be successful. So I said, "Well, hey, I may not
> have a lot of things, and I'm still on assistance, but I think I have

a goal. I might not ever reach it, but at least I have a goal. Somewhere, something that I'm trying to accomplish." And I want to try to get as close to it as I can. And it's for that reason I'm positive . . . about my future, and my children. Their future is theirs.

And that's another good thing about this country. . . . The avenues for success . . . are not limited to . . . just a few. I think the avenues for success are open up . . . to the majority of people in this country. Now, success to different people means different things. I don't mean to be a Howard Hughes . . . success. But I mean success in the respect that I'm able to stand on my own two feet and take care of my family. That's the kind of success that I think is open to me, and open to everybody in this country. With a little bit of sacrifice, and a little bit of struggle. I think that everybody can accomplish that. (1994: 96–97)

Once again, we find a startling contrast. Denise Turner had been on and off public assistance for fourteen years, working at low-wage jobs most of the time. Denise had every reason to feel dispirited, and I certainly would not have blamed her had she said so. Yet remarkably, here was a woman who talked about the open avenues of success in America and about her goals and aspirations, which she hoped would lead her down those avenues.

The predicament for Denise and for many of the families I spoke with was not that their attitudes or motivations were holding them back but rather that their poverty and economic vulnerability created sizable roadblocks in their lives. As Denise characterized her family life:

The only thing I can say, is that . . . it can be summarized in one word, and that's survival. That's what we're tryin' to do. We're tryin' to survive. And . . . I talk to a lot of people, and they say, "Well, hey, if you went to Ethiopia, you know, survival would be one thing. And that's . . . eating." But, damn it, I'm not in Ethiopia! You know. So I want a little bit more than just . . . having some food. Having a coupla meals. So, if I can just summarize it, in one word, it would be we're tryin' to survive. We're tryin' to stay together. That's my major concern, keepin' all my family together, my children together. And to survive. (1994: 88)

I began to think further. If these families were basically in the same ballpark as many of their fellow Americans in terms of their outlooks and motivations, why were they in the positions they were in? After all, if you work hard in America, shouldn't you expect to earn a decent living without fear of impoverishment?

Further questions began to unfold. How many other families like Denise's would fall into poverty in the years ahead? Where did the causes lie? Why does the United States offer so little assistance to the poor compared to other Western industrialized countries? Who should bear the responsibility for the condition of poverty? These and many other questions began to take form, eventually planting the seeds for the current work.

In a very real sense, this book begins where *Living on the Edge* left off. As I wrote in the final chapter of *Living on the Edge*, the question for us to ask ourselves is whether we will continue down the path we have taken—that of castigating the poor without a careful reading of the evidence or whether we will begin to explore an alternative path, one that involves a serious reexamination of the issue of poverty, as well as a conscientious look at the role that we and our society should play in addressing poverty. The purpose of *One Nation, Underprivileged* is to provide that reexamination, based on a careful reading of the evidence.

Design and Strategy

The overall design of the book addresses three fundamental questions. First, what are the conditions of poverty and the reasons that underlie it? Second, why is poverty an issue of vital concern to America? And third, how can we effectively reduce the extent of poverty in the United States? Each section is intended to build upon the evidence and arguments presented in prior chapters.

We begin by examining the conditions and causes of American poverty. As the current chapter points out, one of the striking aspects of America is the contrast between the magnitude of wealth and the extent and depth of economic deprivation. Chapter 2 provides a more detailed look at the landscape of American poverty, including the manner in which poverty is measured, lessons learned with respect to the patterns and features of U.S. poverty, the extent of poverty in the United States compared with poverty in other Western industrialized countries, and an understanding of the human meaning and pain associated with poverty.

Chapter 3 turns to the question of why poverty exists at such high rates in the United States. Much of the focus in the past has been upon explaining poverty in terms of individual characteristics and personal deficits. This chapter argues that such an approach misses the underlying causes and mechanisms that produce poverty. To use an analogy, previous work has focused on who loses out in the overall economic game, rather than on the fact that the game ensures that there will be losers in the first place. I argue that the fundamental causes of poverty are to be found in the economic, political, and social failings of society, and develop the concept of structural vulnerability as a new way of understanding American poverty.

The second third of the book focuses upon a question that most social scientists have failed to address—Why should poverty be a cause for national concern? Chapters 4, 5, and 6 develop an overall argument detailing the reasons. Chapter 4 builds a case on self-interest. Poverty drains us both individually and as a community and society. Each of us directly and indirectly pays a high price for allowing poverty to walk in our midst. In addition, I discuss a set of analyses that demonstrates for the first time the fact that a majority of Americans experience poverty at some point during their lives. Unbeknownst to many, poverty touches us in our own backyard. This chapter demonstrates such a connection.

Chapter 5 takes up the issue of values. The goal of reducing poverty is consistent, and in fact critical, to the realization of two core sets of values held in high esteem by the majority of Americans. These include the Judeo-Christian ethic and the American civic values that have shaped this country (liberty, justice, equality, and democracy). The argument developed here is that if we examine these sets of values carefully, we find that attitudes of apathy toward the poor contradict their very core. In order to remain consistent with our principles, a concerted attempt to reduce poverty is necessary. Certainly there is room for disagreement regarding the causes and solutions to impoverishment. But there can be no disagreement about the imperative to confront this issue if one professes allegiance to either the Judeo-Christian ethic or the founding values on which this country was built.

Chapter 6 develops a third argument for why Americans should care about poverty—active involvement and concern for those experiencing misfortune is an important (but often neglected) aspect of citizenship. As members of communities larger than simply ourselves as individuals, we share an obligation and responsibility to alleviate grievous ills, such as poverty, that befall other members of our community. This position is based on the assertion that the concept of citizenship necessitates a sense of shared responsibility and stewardship. Such obligations become particularly binding when it can be demonstrated that a specific problem is largely the product of structural inequities. Part of our civic responsibility lies in addressing such inequities. In addition, by alleviating the blight of poverty, we are exerting wise stewardship over our communities. I argue that such stewardship is also an essential component of the concept of citizenship.

A three-pronged argument is therefore made in this section, asserting that a substantial reduction in poverty is in our self-interest, is consistent with many of our most important values, and is a part of our shared responsibility. These concepts represent a foundation for constructing a bridge from the nonpoor to the poor and back again. Such a bridge has been largely absent in our discussions of poverty but is absolutely vital to creating positive social change.

The final section of the book explores the directions we should take in order to significantly reduce the extent and severity of poverty. Chapter 7 argues that the first step on the road to positive change is a national shift in how we think about poverty. While the prior chapters lay out the foundation for such a shift, chapter 7 explores this new paradigm and the implications that derive from it. It represents a sharp departure from the old and tired ways of viewing poverty. A new conceptualization of poverty represents the beginning point of creating a dramatic and positive change in American society.

Chapter 8 discusses a set of policies and politically feasible strategies that have the potential to significantly reduce the likelihood and severity of impoverishment. These strategies flow from the new paradigm and are linked to the diagnoses of poverty found in the preceding chapters. They include the creation of adequately paying jobs, increasing the accessibility of several key public goods, buffering the economic consequences of family change, building individual and community assets, and providing a sensible safety net. In combination, they are designed to reduce both the short- and longer-term risk of poverty.

The final chapter pulls together several concluding observations, themes, and thoughts. In particular, I discuss the ways in which one person can make an important difference in helping to create the fundamental changes necessary if this country is to once and for all effectively combat the injustice of poverty.

I turn to a wide range of information and research during the course of the book in order to build my arguments. Sources include analyses I have conducted with various national data sets; information from the U.S. Census Bureau and other government sources; discussions and interviews I have had with those who are living in poverty as well as with individuals who are working on the front lines of poverty; historical material; and the vast array of previous research and writings on this subject.

The plan is to construct a strong and convincing case based upon a solid body of evidence and reasoning. Although values are a critical component of my argument, there is a danger of becoming overly polemic or ideological, straying too far from the evidence at hand. The arguments developed in this book should be judged upon the weight of the evidence presented. I leave it to you, the reader, to make those judgments.

This book is ultimately about rethinking and reconceptualizing poverty in a fundamentally new way. For much of our recent history, we have looked at poverty as the domain of the individual. The causes of poverty have been routinely reduced to individual inadequacies, and the impact of such poverty has been localized to the individual's household or perhaps the immediate neighborhood. This viewpoint has helped to maintain the status quo of severe economic deprivation in America, and, perhaps worse, to justify rolling back the protections provided by a safety net and other social programs. As will be shown throughout this book, such a perspective is both incorrect and short sighted. Poverty indeed affects us all, and we must awaken to this fact of life.

The Challenge

The challenge, of course, is getting people to see poverty in such a new light. It remains an uphill struggle because of several uniquely American factors that have worked against a grasping of the true nature and scope of poverty. I touch upon these at various points in the ensuing chapters, but several of the more important ones are worth mentioning here.

America has historically been marked by a strong sense of individualism. As Herbert Gans begins his book *Middle American Individualism*:

America has often been seen—and has seen itself—as constantly in flux. Still, as anyone who has ever read de Tocqueville's *Democracy in America* knows after just a few pages, there are many ways in which the United States has changed only slightly in over 150 years, and one of the stable elements is the continued pursuit of individualism by virtually all sectors of the population. (1988: 1)

This individualism has tended to work against a sense of community and caring for others. In his assessment of American values, Lawrence Mitchell notes that "individualism has taken pride of place in constructing our image of our nation and ourselves with a strength that drowns out our ethic of care" (1998: 11). It has also worked against seeing the societal and economic sources of various problems within this country. The tendency has been to individualize social problems such as poverty.

Strongly connected with individualism has been the historical importance of self-reliance. The ability to take care of oneself and one's family without depending on others has been a strong ideal from our frontier past to the present. As Ben Franklin wrote in *Poor Richard's Almanac*, "God helps them that help themselves." Individuals have been seen as responsible for their own well-being, including getting out of poverty.

A third hurdle to grasping the reality of poverty has been the widely shared belief that the United States is a land where opportunities exist for all who are willing to strive for them and that virtue, talent, and hard work can overshadow the constraints of disadvantage. That with enough individual effort, literally anything is possible. In short, that the American dream is alive and well in this land of opportunity.[4] Given this belief, poverty is often viewed as the result of individual failings that can be overcome only by individual effort.

Finally, the heterogenous nature of our society has also worked against seeing our connections with others and their problems. One of the defining characteristics of the United States has been its multiracial and ethnic composition. Research has shown that communities with greater variations in terms of race and ethnicity tend to display less empathy and concern toward the plight of the disadvantaged (who are often the minority members of a community).

Although all of these characteristics have particular strengths and advantages, they also undercut our ability as a nation to view the systemic nature of particular social and economic problems. Taken together, they present a sizable hurdle to viewing the structural nature of poverty along with our shared connections and responsibility to the issue of poverty. America was founded on the belief of vast opportunities for those who are willing to work for them—that with enough sacrifice and effort the newly arrived immigrant could climb the ladder of opportunity, going from rags to riches. According to this vision, those who remain poor in this country have no one but themselves to blame. Unfortunately, such myths blind us to the harsher realities found in this book. As John F. Kennedy observed in his 1962 commencement address at Yale University, "The great enemy of the truth is very often not the lie—deliberate, contrived and dishonest—but the myth—persistent, persuasive and unrealistic."

Consequently, rather than look to our economic, social, or political structures for answers, and rather than recognize our shared responsibility and concern for poverty, we point to each other with accusatory fingers. In the process, we redirect society's ills upon easy targets, turning them into scapegoats. Such scapegoats are often our least powerful citizens—welfare recipients, minority groups, immigrants, single women with children, the homeless, and so on down the list.[5]

Our debates become dominated by discussions of welfare dependency, the underclass, criminal behavior, illegitimacy, or deadbeat vagrants in the streets. The words *poverty* and *inequality* have been replaced by diatribes about a host of counterproductive behaviors and characterizations. Although these are assuredly critical issues, I believe they have led us down a back road. In many ways they are the consequences rather than the causes of poverty and inequality. They represent a smoke screen that blinds us to the real issues. Instead of wandering down these side roads, we will be traveling upon what I consider to be the main highway, getting off at many points along the way.

There are two additional roadblocks that often arise on such a journey. These are the questions surrounding the cost of attacking poverty and our ability to do so. What I argue in the pages ahead is that we are already paying a tremendous economic and social price by having the Western world's highest rates of impoverishment. Poverty leads to rising health care expenditures, a less effective work force, and scores of other direct and indirect costs that affect us all. Our current path of apathy is a far more expensive road to take than one that aggressively reduces the extent of poverty.

But do we have the means to do so? The answer is unequivocally yes. This country clearly has the financial ability and resources to substantially reduce the scourge of poverty. As outlined in chapter 8, there are a number of specific and effective steps to be taken that will dramatically reduce the extent and severity of poverty. The question is, do we have the desire to do so? Providing such motivation is what this book is all about.

One final contrast and challenge is well-suited to conclude this chapter. More than four decades have come and gone since Michael Harrington wrote his classic exposé of poverty, *The Other America*. It was truly one of those remarkable books that fundamentally changed the nature of the debate. At its conclusion, Harrington wrote,

> The means are at hand to fulfill the age-old dream: poverty can now be abolished. How long shall we ignore this underdeveloped nation in our midst? How long shall we look the other way while our fellow human beings suffer? How long? (1962: 184)

Twenty-seven years later I had the good fortune to hear Michael Harrington give what turned out to be one of his final formal addresses.[6] Innumerable changes had occurred in this country since the writing of *The Other America*. Yet the question remained—How long? Harrington spoke that morning with passion and insight. He talked about the changes that were occurring in America—the widening gap in inequality and the increasing numbers of working poor families.

That night, several colleagues and I had dinner with Harrington. It was quite clear that he was suffering from a painful illness and that his days were numbered. Yet the flame was still there, the insights intact. The question still burned—How long? Four months later he was gone.

I have often thought about that encounter. What struck me then as now was not so much what Harrington said that day but how he said it—with passion and concern, in spite of the formidable odds and pain working against him. Why?

My sense was that, in spite of the serious problems plaguing him and America on that day, Harrington strongly believed in this country and was convinced that solid evidence and arguments could make a positive difference despite the powerful forces working against such an approach. He felt that dialogue and an exchange of ideas was essential to our democracy, and that positive improvement was possible through an understanding of the dynamic changes occurring in our society and through grassroots organizing to confront those changes. Harrington concluded his talk with the following question:

> Is it possible for people at the base, for ordinary men and
> women, to take control of this process of radical change and turn
> it to the advantage of human freedom? That's why you have to
> care. Because that is a fundamental question that is posed to this
> generation.[7]

Such has been true of many of this country's directional changes and revolutions. For example, the civil rights movement represented a dramatic case of raising the level of consciousness in order to facilitate change. Through a series of protests and demonstrations, Dr. Martin Luther King, Jr., was able to vividly reveal the racial hypocrisy of America. As a result, many white Americans began to change their views about the legitimacy and urgency of black Americans' demands for equality and justice. This, in turn, helped to precipitate the important legal and policy changes aimed at reducing racial inequality in America.

King's focus was also very much on altering the collective perceptions of poverty. In his final book, *Where Do We Go from Here*, he noted:

> A true revolution of value will soon cause us to question the
> fairness and justice of many of our past and present policies. We
> are called to play the Good Samaritan on life's roadside; but that
> will be only an initial act. One day the whole Jericho road must
> be transformed so that men and women will not be beaten and
> robbed as they make their journey through life. True compassion
> is more than flinging a coin to a beggar; it understands that an
> edifice which produces beggars needs restructuring. A true
> revolution of values will soon look uneasily on the glaring
> contrast of poverty and wealth. (1967a: 187–188)

Lasting change must begin with the realization that the status quo of widespread poverty within our borders is unwise, unjust, and intolerable. The purpose of this book is to carefully and convincingly present this point of view. Ultimately, I would like *One Nation, Underprivileged* to touch not only the minds, but also the hearts and souls of my readers. The most persuasive arguments move us on all levels. In order to construct positive social change, we must have the correct description and diagnosis, we must have the concern and passion, and we must have effective remedies to follow through. Only then will we be able to confront the disturbing contrast between the promise of America and the shadow of poverty that underprivileges us all.

Below
the Line

2

Who are the poor? The facts would shock most Americans.

Michael Harrington

HAVING ENDED the previous chapter with a description of a memorable encounter, let me begin this chapter by describing a somewhat different encounter. It was one of those moments that lingers in your memory for a long time. I had been asked by a national family planning organization to take part in a symposium on Capitol Hill. The purpose was to explore the relationship between welfare and illegitimacy. On the panel were several social scientists, including Charles Murray.

Over the past two decades, Murray has garnered considerable attention regarding his views on poverty. His influential book *Losing Ground* argues that the welfare system has destroyed the poor's incentives to build strong families and work histories and therefore should be abolished. Even more controversial, *The Bell Curve* examines the impact of intelligence on life outcomes. According to Murray and his coauthor, Richard Herrnstein, poverty and welfare use are largely the result of lower intelligence among those who inhabit its ranks.

Six months prior to the symposium, Murray had written a commentary in the *Wall Street Journal* that was widely circulated. In it he suggested that the United States reconsider orphanages as a way of rearing out-of-wedlock children born to mothers who are no longer economically self-sufficient. His argument was that our society must enforce penalties upon women who have illegitimate births in order to reduce their numbers. Furthermore, "Those who prattle about the importance of keeping children with their biological mothers may wish to spend some time in a patrol car or with a social worker seeing what the reality of life with welfare-dependent biological mothers can be like" (Murray, 1993).

The panelists had finished their introductory statements, and questions were being posed by the audience. A woman rose to the microphone and remarked that she was puzzled by Murray's position advocating orphanages as a safety net. Noting that he had stressed the importance of families in his introductory comments, she wondered "if two parents are preferable to one, why isn't one parent preferable to none?" Murray began, "There is a dirty little secret about the problem of out-of-wedlock births to poor women. The dirty little secret is that very large numbers of them are rotten mothers." He then paused to clear his throat and went on:

And by rotten mothers I don't mean all of them, obviously. But I do mean that there are very large numbers of children who are being left alone, all day and into the night, not because the mother is out searching for a job, but because she's partying. That there is a very widespread problem of children being simply treated as objects, not talked to. When I say it's a dirty little secret, what I mean is this. If you go out and talk to cops, and if you go out and talk to social workers, they run into things everyday that make the story about the Chicago incident a couple months ago with the nineteen kids not a big deal. The number of kids was a big deal, but that type of neglect and abuse is not unusual. Nobody likes to say it. It's blaming the victim, I know, and all this. In the meantime, we have lots and lots of children who are growing up in the most wretched kinds of circumstances.

What he was referring to was a well-publicized story about nineteen children who were living in a two-bedroom Chicago apartment in what could only be described as hellish conditions. Believing that the location was a crack house, the police raided the apartment and found instead the youngsters, most of whom were under the age of ten, with little food, scant clothing, and no shortage of filth. Meanwhile, the children's six mothers were collecting $4,500 a month from welfare, little of which was apparently going to their kids (Shryer, 1994). Murray continued,

> I used the word *orphanage* in the *Wall Street Journal* article because I'm so unhappy with the foster care system. The foster care system is also a farce and a tragedy. I'll tell you the weird thing about that. The orphanage business was not a major theme in the article, but what happened thereafter was not just that some people went off the wall saying, "How can this guy be talking about orphanages, Dickens, etc., etc." But I'd say, "Well, I wasn't just talking about Dickens but how about Boys Town?" And then the next thing that happened was I started getting all these letters from people who had either grown up in orphanages themselves or who had parents who had grown up, saying, "Well, you know, it wasn't as good as being with the real family, loving parents and so forth, but it was a stable, nurturing environment where they taught me a lot and sent me on the road, and it's about time we started talking about this again."[1]

As I sat there listening to Charles Murray, it was his sentence "The dirty little secret is that very large numbers of them are rotten mothers" that I found so hard to let go of. Yet here was a portrait of the poor, encompassed in those few words, that many Americans would in fact agree with—the poor as unfit and abusive parents; the poor as looking to "party" rather than finding jobs; the poor as addicted to welfare; the poor as highly deserving of the blame for their failures. One does not have to look far to find such a portrait. It can be heard in the passing comments of a neighbor down the street, in the vast array of survey data detailing American attitudes toward poverty and welfare, or in the rhetoric reverberating off the congressional halls I was in. It is a perspective that views the poor as essentially different from the rest of us, and different in a quite negative manner.

As we look at the conditions of poverty in this and the next chapter, a fundamental question to be asked is, How close to reality is such a perspective? One of the unspoken advantages and appeals of such a perspective is that it lets us all off the hook. In other words, it serves to relieve us of any responsibility regarding poverty. Although I may feel sorry or distressed about the plight of the poor, I bear no accountability for their situation or their troubles. In fact, my active engagement may only make the situation worse.

It is no coincidence that such a perspective lies at the heart of the think tanks, such as the American Enterprise Institute, that have funded Charles Murray's research. Their purpose has largely been to provide quasi-scientific support for their conservative political agenda.[2] That agenda has been to promote unfettered free-market capitalism and individual responsibility as the sole solutions to poverty, while governmental social programs and safety nets have been derided as abject failures. Throughout the next several chapters, we will see that this perspective largely represents political ideology, rather than empirical reality. In fact, the evidence suggests that free-market capitalism leaves in its wake millions of impoverished households, while governmental actions and supports can effectively reduce the extent of poverty.

We begin our examination with an overview of poverty's terrain as it affects American households. Several questions are examined: (1) How is poverty measured? (2) What lessons have been learned with respect to the characteristics of American poverty? (3) How do U.S. levels of poverty compare to those of other countries? and (4) What is the human meaning of poverty?

Measuring Poverty

In 1964, President Lyndon Johnson declared his famous war on poverty. Delivering his State of the Union address to Congress and the American people, the president announced,

> This Administration today, here and now, declares unconditional
> war on poverty in America, and I urge this Congress and all
> Americans to join with me in that effort. It will not be a short or
> easy struggle, no single weapon or strategy will suffice, but we
> shall not rest until that war is won. The richest nation on earth
> can afford to win it. We cannot afford to lose it. (Johnson, 1965a)

Yet as the administration was to learn on both the domestic and foreign battlefields, a country marching off to war must have a credible estimate of the enemy's size and strength. Surprisingly, up until this point in our nation's history, we had no official measure of poverty and therefore no statistics on its scope, shape, or changing nature. The task was therefore to come up with a way of measuring how many people in America were poor.[3]

In doing so, two questions are critical. First, how does one define poverty? Second, how does one go about measuring it? Both questions are pivotal and should involve a series of well-informed judgments and decisions. Nevertheless, in the final analysis, poverty and its measurement involve a degree of subjectivity. That is, despite the importance of well-grounded thinking, poverty is partially in the eye of the beholder.

Furthermore, although we may be able to achieve a general consensus upon a broad definition of poverty, as the old saying goes, the devil lies in the details. Take for example the time-honored description of poverty that was stated more than 200 years ago by Adam Smith in his treatise, *Wealth of Nations* (1776). Smith defined poverty as a lack of those necessities that "the custom of the country renders it indecent for creditable people, even of the lowest order, to be without." This type of definition is known as an absolute approach. One defines a minimum threshold for living conditions, and individuals who fall below that threshold are considered poor.

On its surface, many of us would probably agree with Smith's description. However, our consensus would begin to break down over what such necessities encompass. Certainly most of us would include items such as food, clothing, and shelter, but what kind of food, clothing, and shelter? Further, what additional items might we include—a car, a telephone, health insurance, child care, and so on?

Perhaps, then, poverty might be better measured in a relative sense. For example, individuals who fall into the bottom 20 percent of the income distribution might be considered poor. Alternatively, the poor could be defined as those whose incomes fall below 50 percent of the population's median income. Using such a definition eliminates the need to come up with a subjective basket of goods deemed necessary for a minimal existence. Such a measure also has the advantage of allowing for relatively easy comparisons across countries.

Yet such demarcations are equally subjective. For example, why not choose a 10 percent rather than a 20 percent cutoff? This measure also has the disadvantage of holding constant the percentage of people who are poor over time, making it difficult to gauge how well we are doing as a nation in confronting poverty. Finally, this type of definition conveys little about the overall standard of living for those who are defined as poor. It simply says that such households fall at the bottom of the overall income distribution.

Still another alternative for defining poverty is to survey the population in order to gauge general perceptions regarding the level of income felt to be minimally needed for survival and then to use this level in order to categorize the poor. This has the advantage of tapping into the overall sentiments of the population to guide the process. Nevertheless, such an approach is also problematic. For example, the manner in which the survey questions are worded has been found to have a dramatic impact on the types and levels of responses given.

Finally, some might argue that poverty involves more than just a minimum level of material resources. A definition of poverty could take into account certain kinds of "destructive" or "antisocial" behaviors. Many of the discussions and definitions surrounding the underclass implicitly incorporate such factors. Yet once again, such a definition raises the specter of subjectivity.

All of these approaches have been and continue to be discussed in policy circles (for an extended discussion on various ways of measuring poverty see Brady, 2003; Glennerster, 2002; Institute for Research on Poverty, 1998; National Research Council, 1995; Ruggles, 1990, 1992; Sycheva, 1997; U.S. Census Bureau, 1999a). At the time of President Johnson's declared war on poverty, any one of these approaches could have been taken to assess the federal government's efforts. The task fell upon Molly Orshansky, an economist working for the Social Security Administration, to devise the country's yardstick for measuring poverty (see Fischer, 1992, and Orshansky, 1965, for a descriptive history of her method).

The approach that Orshansky took was consistent with Adam Smith's definition two hundred years earlier. That is, poverty was conceptualized as a failure to have the income necessary to purchase a basic basket of goods and services that allows for a minimally decent level of existence.

The way that this was (and still is) calculated is straightforward. One begins by estimating the household costs of obtaining a minimally adequate diet during the course of the year.[4] For example, a family of four would need to spend $6,130.67 to purchase such a diet in 2002. This figure is then multiplied by three (in the sample case $6,130.67 \times 3 = \$18,392$), which constitutes the official poverty line for a family of four (using the weighted average). The reason for using three as a multiplier is that Orshansky relied upon a 1955 Department of Agriculture survey showing that families with three or more persons spent approximately one-third of their income on food and the remaining two-thirds on other items such as clothing, housing, and heating. Thus, the logic in the example is that if $6,131 will purchase a subsistence diet for a family of four, then the remaining $12,261 should provide enough income to purchase the other basic necessities needed for a minimal level of existence.

Several other points are important regarding the measurement of poverty. Each year the poverty levels are adjusted to take into account inflation. Obviously it costs more to purchase a basic basket of goods today than it did forty years ago. Second, the measuring stick to determine whether individuals fall above or below the poverty threshold is household income. Household income is based on annual gross income before taxes or Social Security payments are taken out. It also does not include in-kind program benefits such as Medicaid or Food Stamps. Third, the actual estimates of how many Americans fall below the poverty line are derived from the Census Bureau's annual Current Population Survey, which consists of approximately 60,000 households (see appendix A). Fourth, the levels of poverty established each year do not distinguish among the cost of living differences found in various parts of the country. Finally, the monetary amount necessary for a small family's basic needs will obviously differ from those of a larger family, and therefore the poverty levels are adjusted for family size. For example, in 2002 the poverty level for a family of one was $9,183, while that of a family of nine or more was $37,062.[5]

To illustrate what these numbers mean in a day-to-day sense, let us take the poverty level for a family of four—$18,392. Using the one-third/two-thirds split, our hypothetical family would have $6,131 available for food during the year. This comes out to $118 a week, $16.86 a day, or $4.22 a day for each member of that family. Assuming that family members eat three meals per day, this works out to $1.41 per person per meal per day. Taking the remaining two-thirds of the poverty line's threshold—$12,261—provides our family with $236 per week for other expenses. For example, the average fair-market rent for a two-bedroom apartment (which would represent fairly tight quarters for such a family) across 130 major metropolitan areas was around $600, or $150 per week (Harkness et al., 2002). This leaves our family of four with $86 a week for all other expenses, including transportation, clothing, child care, utilities, medical costs, and the various additional expenditures that a family might have. Bringing the poverty line down to this level allows for a more meaningful sense of what these numbers represent in terms of people's lives.[6] As we shall see later in this chapter, to live below the poverty line embodies physical hardship.[7]

In addition, it is important to keep in mind that this example captures poverty at its most opulent level; families fall to varying degrees below the poverty line. In 2002, 41 percent of all poor persons were living in households where the income fell below one-half of their respective poverty thresholds (U.S. Bureau of the Census, 2003a). If we take 50 percent of the poverty threshold for a family of four, this works out to $59 per week for food, and $118 per week for all other expenses.

Yet another way of translating the meaning of poverty into one's own life can be illustrated with the following statistic. In 2001, the median income for a family of four in the United States was $63,278. On the other hand, the poverty threshold for such a family in 2001 was $18,104 (U.S. Bureau of the Census, 2002a; 2002b; 2003b). Consequently, the income for a family of four at the edge of poverty was just 29 percent of the overall median income for such a family.[8]

Some of you reading this book may be near the median in terms of your family income. A number of you (as I do) may occasionally find it difficult to keep up with various household expenses and needs. Now imagine that, instead of the income you currently have coming in for this month, next month you will be receiving only 29 percent of your income. The other 71 percent is suddenly gone. That 71 percent is the distance between your current standard of living and the standard of living for those at the edge of poverty. Yet as noted, this represents poverty at its most opulent level. Forty-one percent of poor individuals have incomes less than one-half of the poverty line. For a family of four this would be $9,052, or 14 percent of the national median income.

Finally, in an important respect, today's poverty is harsher than it was forty years ago. In 1947 the poverty threshold for a family of four stood at 69 percent of the median four-person family income. When we began counting the numbers of poor Americans in 1959, it had dropped to just below 50 percent of the median. In 1980, it was 35 percent; by 2000, the poverty threshold had fallen to 28 percent. Being categorized today as poor means living farther from the economic midpoint than in the past.[9] If we were to apply in 2001 the economic distance that families in poverty were from the median income found in 1959, the poverty threshold for a family of four would rise from $18,104 to $31,639. As Howard Glennerster notes:

> Very few American voters can realize that the measure of poverty that dominates political discussion has been getting more and more mean as the years pass. . . . If the present rate of income growth continues and the poverty line remains unchanged, the poverty line will soon be equivalent not to half of median earnings, as it was when Mollie Orshansky invented the number, but to a quarter of median earnings. That would be twice as harsh a measure as other countries in the world adopt. (2002: 90)

In this sense, poverty has become more severe today than it was forty years ago.

Currently, there are 34.6 million Americans, or 12.1 percent of the population, who fall below the poverty line. Using 1.25 of the poverty line (in other words, increasing the poverty level by 25 percent) results in a rate of 16.5 percent, or 47.1 million Americans, while 61.1 million Americans (or 21.4 percent) live below 1.50 of the poverty line (U.S. Census Bureau, 2002a). Consequently, in addition to the 34.6 million Americans in poverty, a further 12.5 to 26.5 million Americans live precariously close to the poverty line.

Lessons Learned

Over the past four decades, an extensive amount of information has been collected pertaining to the overall patterns and features of U.S. poverty. This body of knowledge has laid the groundwork for three important lessons learned.

The Key Success and Failure across Time

The first lesson is an understanding of the major American success story (the elderly) and failure (children) in terms of averting poverty over time. In 1959, the elderly had the highest poverty rates of any age group, standing at

35.2 percent. The rate for children in 1959 was 27.3 percent, while the over-all rate stood at 22.4 percent (see figure 2.1). Since that time we can see that there has been a remarkable reduction in the risk of poverty among the elderly. Their rate fell substantially during the 1960s and 1970s and continued to fall during the 1980s and 1990s. It currently stands at 10.4 percent, which is slightly below the 12.1 percent overall rate of poverty. The reduction of poverty within the elderly population represents a major American success story in terms of poverty alleviation over the past four decades.

On the other hand, the story of American children constitutes a major social policy failure. As with the elderly, children's poverty rates fell during the 1960s; however, unlike those for the elderly, we can see that they began to rise during the 1970s and then rose much more sharply during the early 1980s. Although their levels of poverty came down somewhat in the late 1990s, children are currently the age group most at risk of impoverishment in the United States. The relative positions of these two groups have thus made a dramatic reversal over the course of four decades.

There are several reasons why such changes have occurred. In the elderly's case, their substantial reduction in the risk of poverty is directly

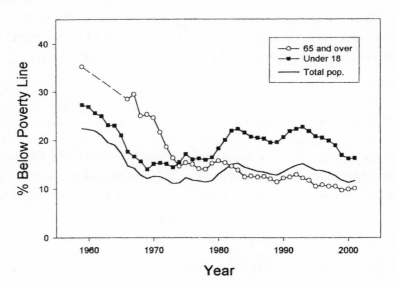

FIGURE 2.1. Percentage of children, the elderly, and the total population below the poverty line. *Source*: U.S. Bureau of the Census, Current Population Reports, Series P60-219, 2002, and Historical Poverty Tables—Current Population Survey.

attributed to the increasing generosity of the Social Security program, as well as the introduction of Medicare in 1965 and the Supplemental Security Income program in 1974. During the 1960s and 1970s, Social Security benefits were substantially increased and indexed to inflation, which helped many of the elderly get above the poverty line. It is estimated today that without the Social Security program, the poverty rate for the elderly would be close to 50 percent. Put another way, Social Security is responsible for getting 80 percent of the elderly above the poverty line who would be poor in its absence.[10]

In the case of children, three reasons stand to explain why the risk of poverty has increased since 1969. At the same time that the social safety net for the elderly was becoming stronger, that for the nation's children was beginning to unravel (Ozawa and Kim, 1998; Preston, 1984). From the early 1970s on, social welfare programs to assist low-income children have lost ground to inflation, resulting in more children falling below the poverty line (U.S. House of Representatives, 2000).

Second, the annual earnings of young (under age 30) heads of household with children have dropped significantly over the past three decades. Their median annual earnings fell an average of 44 percent from 1973 to 1990, regardless of differences in family structure, race, and levels of education (Edelman, 1992). As a result, young children have faced an increasing risk of poverty.

Third, there have been dramatic changes in family structure since the mid-1960s. As a result of the increasing rates of divorce and out-of-wedlock childbearing, more youngsters have been spending periods of their childhood in female-headed families. The risk of poverty in female-headed families is substantially greater than that in married couple families, which has put more children in a precarious position vis-à-vis poverty and which is reflected in the changes found in the overall rates of child poverty shown in figure 2.1.

This point is illustrated in figure 2.2, which plots the percent of female-headed families (with children under age 18) below the poverty line. What is readily apparent is the dramatic shift in the household living arrangements of children in poverty. In 1959, one out of four white families and one out of three black families below the poverty line were female headed. From 1964 to 1978, a rapid growth took place in the percentage of poor families that were female headed; by 1978, one out of two white families, four out of five

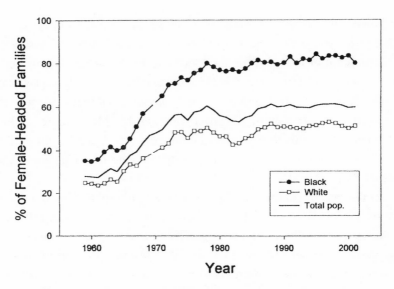

FIGURE 2.2. Percentage of families below the poverty line (with children under 18) that are female headed. *Source*: U.S. Bureau of the Census, Current Population Reports, Series P60-219, 2002, and Historical Poverty Tables—Current Population Survey.

black families, and three out of five overall families with poor children were female headed. These percentages dipped somewhat during the early 1980s but have since returned to their previous high levels.[11]

The Length and Frequency of Poverty

A second lesson that has been learned over the past two decades pertains to the length of time that people spend in poverty. It had frequently been assumed that most who experienced poverty did so for extended periods of time. It turns out that this image was incorrect. Several large, longitudinal data sets were begun in the 1970s and 1980s that have tracked individuals and families across a number of years (e.g., the Panel Study of Income Dynamics; the National Survey of Youth; the Survey of Income and Program Participation). By following the same households over time, one can observe the length of time that families are in poverty, as well as the extent of their income mobility. Several broad conclusions can be drawn from these data.

First, most spells of poverty are of fairly modest length. The typical pattern is that households are impoverished for one or two years and then manage to get above the poverty line (Bane and Ellwood, 1986; Blank, 1997; Duncan, 1984; Stevens, 1994). They may stay there for a period of time, only to experience an additional fall into poverty at some later point in their lives (Stevens, 1999).[12]

In contrast, a much smaller number of households experience chronic poverty for years at a time. These are the cases that one generally thinks of when the term *underclass* is used. Typically they have characteristics that put them at a severe disadvantage vis-à-vis the labor market (e.g., individuals with serious work disabilities, female-headed families with large numbers of children, racial minorities living in inner-city areas). Their prospects for getting out of poverty for any significant period of time are diminished.

This body of research has also shown that periods of poverty are frequently triggered as a result of unfavorable events that occur to households, with employment difficulties being the most important. Using the Panel Study of Income Dynamics data, Greg Duncan and colleagues (1995) found that two-thirds of all entries into poverty were associated with either a reduction in work (48 percent) or the loss of work (18 percent). In addition, divorce and separation were associated with approximately 10 percent of all spells of poverty. Factors of employment were much more likely to trigger spells of poverty in the United States than they were in countries such as France, Germany, or the Netherlands. In addition, the advent of ill health has been shown to initiate periods of poverty (Schiller, 2004).

Rebecca Blank (1997) also found that employment and family structure changes were influential in ending spells of poverty. Two-thirds of those below the poverty line escaped impoverishment as a result of increases in the individual earnings of family members or increases from other sources of income, while the remaining third had their spells of poverty end as a result of changes in family structure (such as marriage or a child leaving the household).

The picture of poverty that emerges from this body of research is thus characterized by fluidity. Individuals and households tend to weave their way in and out of poverty depending on the occurrence or nonoccurrence of detrimental events (e.g., job loss, family disruption, ill health). Of course, the amount by which individuals find themselves above the poverty line is often quite modest, so that future detrimental events can throw them back below the poverty line. Similar findings have been found with respect to the longitudinal patterns of welfare use (Bane and Ellwood, 1994; Blank, 1997; Duncan, 1984; Rank, 1994).

Characteristics Associated with Poverty

A third lesson to be gleaned from earlier research is that poverty is not randomly distributed within the population but rather is associated with particular characteristics that place individuals and families at a disadvantage in terms of their ability to compete in the labor market. Table 2.1 contains recent Census Bureau data with respect to a small number of demographic characteristics (U.S. Bureau of the Census, 2003a). What is readily apparent from the first column in table 2.1 is that racial and ethnic minorities, children, women, female-headed families, those in the South, in central cities, or in rural areas, and individuals with less education or who suffer from disabilities all experience elevated risks of poverty.

What these characteristics have in common is that they tend to increase the vulnerability of individuals vis-à-vis the labor market. This concept is discussed more fully in chapter 3, but suffice it to say here that the risk of poverty for specific individuals can be understood largely in terms of their economic vulnerability. As mentioned, individuals move into poverty largely due to detrimental events such as the loss of work, a reduction in earnings, or the breakup of a family. Those with less advantageous characteristics (for example, those who lack education) are more likely to experience such events and to be more fully exposed to the negative brunt of such events. This results in a greater likelihood that they will fall below the poverty line for some amount of time until they can get back on their feet. Consequently, minorities, children and young adults, women, female heads of household, residents of central cities or economically depressed neighborhoods, and individuals with little education or a disability all face greater risks of poverty. These relationships have held steady across decades of cross-sectional yearly poverty data.

A slightly different picture emerges if one looks at the overall demographic composition of the poverty population (found in the second column of table 2.1). While some groups exhibit a low rate of poverty, they may constitute a majority of the poor if their overall proportion within the general population is large. Race is an illustration of this. The poverty rate for whites

TABLE 2.1. Poverty Rates and Demographic Composition of the Poor and Overall Populations, 2002

Household Characteristics	Poverty Rate	Percent of Poor Population	Percent of Overall Population
Total	12.1	100.0	100.0
Race			
White	10.2	67.9	80.7
Not of Hispanic Origin	8.0	45.0	68.0
Black	24.1	24.9	12.5
Hispanic	21.8	24.7	13.7
Asian	10.1	3.4	4.0
Age			
Under 18	16.7	35.1	25.5
18 to 24	16.5	13.1	9.6
25 to 34	11.9	13.5	13.8
35 to 44	9.3	11.8	15.4
45 to 54	7.5	8.7	14.1
55 to 64	9.4	7.4	9.6
65 and over	10.4	10.3	12.0
Gender (18 and over)			
Women	12.3	60.2	51.8
Men	8.7	39.8	48.2
Household Status			
Married Couple Household	6.1	32.3	64.3
with Children under 18	7.5	24.7	39.9
Female Headed Household	28.8	33.7	14.2
with Children under 18	35.2	30.6	10.5
Unrelated Individual	20.4	27.8	16.5
Region			
South	13.8	40.6	35.6
Northeast	10.9	17.0	18.9
Midwest	10.3	19.1	22.6
West	12.4	23.3	22.9
Residence			
In Metropolitan Areas	11.6	78.4	81.6
In Central Cities	16.7	39.9	29.0
Outside Central Cities	8.9	38.5	52.6
Outside Metropolitan Areas	14.2	21.6	18.4
Education (25 and over)			
Less than 12	23.3	37.2	15.4
12	10.3	34.0	32.0
13 to 15	7.0	18.3	25.3
16 or more	3.8	10.6	27.2
Disability Status (25 to 64)[1]			
No Disability	8.3	62.3	81.0
Disability	21.4	37.7	19.0
Severe Disability	27.9	30.9	12.0

Source: U.S. Bureau of the Census, Current Population Reports, Series P60-222, 2003, and Detailed Poverty Tables (P60 Package).
[1]From U.S. Bureau of the Census, Current Population Reports, Series P70-73, 2001. Data are from the Survey of Income and Program Participation for 1997.

is 10.2 percent. Yet they make up 67.9 percent of the total poor population, since their overall percentage of the general population is 80.7 percent. Conversely, while the black poverty rate is more than twice that of whites (24.1 percent), blacks make up much less of the poor population (24.9 percent) than whites because their total proportion of the overall population is only 12.5 percent.[13]

What characterizes the demographic composition of the poor?

- Two-thirds of the poor are white (45 percent if Hispanics are counted separately).[14]
- Blacks make up one-quarter of the poor population, with Hispanics making up an additional quarter.
- More than one-third of the poor are children, and nearly two-thirds of the poor are below age 35.
- Women make up three-fifths of the poverty population over the age of eighteen.
- One-third of those below the poverty line live in female-headed families, one-third in married-couple families; 27.8 percent are living on their own without relatives.
- Forty-one percent of the poor live in the South.
- Three-quarters of the poor reside in metropolitan areas, with 39.9 percent living in central cities, 38.5 percent in suburban areas, and 21.6 percent in rural areas.
- Only 9.7 percent of the poor live in neighborhoods characterized by extreme poverty (neighborhoods with poverty levels of 40 percent of more, not shown here).[15]
- More than one out of three of the poor (age 25 and over) do not have a high school diploma.
- Thirty-eight percent of the poor (ages 25–64) are plagued with a disability, and 31 percent have a severe disability.[16]

The picture that emerges when one focuses on the composition of the poverty population is a slightly different one from that for the rates of poverty. Nevertheless, what is noticeably apparent is that the poor are characterized by less advantageous labor market attributes. As a result, it is a population that is economically vulnerable when events such as the loss of employment occur.

International Comparisons

How do the rates of poverty in the United States compare with those of other industrialized countries? Asking this question allows us to gauge whether our rates of poverty are high or low with respect to a number of countries that we often compare ourselves to.

Several problems have made such comparisons difficult. First and foremost has been the lack of comparable data sets to allow for such an analysis. Fortunately this obstacle has been largely overcome with the Luxembourg Income Study (LIS). Begun in the 1980s, the LIS contains income and demographic information on households in more than twenty-five different nations from 1967 to the present (see Luxembourg Income Study, 2000, for a detailed description). By standardizing variables across seventy data sets, it allows one to conduct cross-national analyses regarding poverty and income inequality.

Table 2.2 draws upon an analysis by Timothy Smeeding, Lee Rainwater, and Gary Burtless (2000) that uses the LIS to compare the rates of poverty across eighteen developed nations. A relative measure of poverty is employed in the first three columns—the percentage of persons living with incomes below half of the median income. In the case of the United States, this works out to approximately 125 percent of the current poverty thresholds discussed earlier.[17]

What we find is that U.S. poverty rates are substantially higher than those found in any of the other eighteen nations.[18] The overall U.S. rate using this measure stands at 17.8 percent. The next closest country to the United States is Italy, at 13.9 percent, followed by the United Kingdom, Canada, Spain, and Israel, with the Scandinavian and Benelux countries falling near the bottom. The average for all seventeen nations is 8.6 percent.

Looking at the rates for children and the elderly, we can see the same patterns. The United States again leads all nations in having the highest rates of child poverty at 22.3 percent, with the overall average standing at 9.9 percent.[19] Only in the case of the elderly does the United States not lead the developed world. Here the U.S. poverty rate of 20.7 percent is second from the top, falling behind only Australia's, with the overall average being 11.6.

The final column in table 2.2 estimates the overall poverty rates for a subset of these nations using an absolute measure. One critique that could be leveled at columns one to three is that while the United States has

TABLE 2.2. Extent of Poverty across 18 Developed Countries

Country	Percent of Population Below 50% of Median Income			Percent of Population Below U.S. Poverty Line
	Overall	*Children*	*Elderly*	*Overall*
United States (1997)	17.8	22.3	20.7	13.6*
Italy (1995)	13.9	18.9	12.4	—
United Kingdom (1995)	13.2	20.1	13.9	15.7
Canada (1994)	11.4	15.3	4.7	7.4
Spain (1990)	10.4	12.8	11.4	—
Israel (1992)	10.2	11.6	17.2	—
Netherlands (1994)	7.9	7.9	6.2	7.1
Germany (1994)	7.5	10.6	7.0	7.3
France (1994)	7.4	6.7	10.2	9.9
Denmark (1992)	7.1	4.8	11.1	—
Norway (1995)	6.9	3.9	14.5	4.3
Switzerland (1992)	6.9	7.5	7.4	—
Australia (1994)	6.7	15.0	28.9	17.6
Austria (1992)	6.7	5.9	17.4	—
Sweden (1992)	6.5	2.6	2.6	6.3
Belgium (1992)	5.5	4.4	11.9	—
Finland (1995)	5.0	4.1	5.1	4.8
Luxembourg (1994)	3.9	4.4	6.7	0.3
Overall Average	8.6	9.9	11.6	8.6

Source: Smeeding, Rainwater, and Burtless, LIS Working Paper #244, 2000.
*Data for the United States in this column are for 1994.

extremely high rates of relative poverty, the standard of living that poor Americans experience is potentially greater than that of the poor or near-poor in many of the comparison countries, since the overall levels of income are higher. Consequently, column four calculates the rates of poverty by applying the official U.S. poverty line (which was discussed earlier) to eleven countries for which the data allow such comparisons.

Using this measure, the United States is again near the top in terms of having the highest absolute rates of poverty. Australia and the United Kingdom have greater levels of absolute poverty at 17.6 percent and 15.7 percent, followed by the United States at 13.6 percent. The overall average for the 11 countries is 8.6 percent. Consequently, even when differences in the standard of living are taken into account, the United States' level of absolute poverty remains among the highest in the industrialized world.

Further analyses show that the purchasing power of U.S. households at the 10th percentile of the income distribution is far below that of comparable households in other Western countries. Among 12 major industrialized countries, only the poor in Australia and the United Kingdom had less purchasing power than their U.S. counterparts (Smeeding and Rainwater, 2001; see also Jencks, 2002). On the other hand, the purchasing power of wealthy Americans at the 90th percentile of the income distribution far surpassed their counterparts in all other countries. A similar story can be told with respect to children (Rainwater and Smeeding, 2003; Smeeding, 2002).

What makes the high absolute rate of U.S. poverty particularly glaring is that each country in table 2.2, with the exception of Luxembourg, has a per-capita income level well below that of the United States. These range from 67 percent of the United States level for the United Kingdom to 86 percent for Norway. Thus, even though the United States is considerably wealthier than each of the comparison nations, it has a higher rate of absolute poverty than nearly all the comparison countries.

To summarize, when analyzing poverty as the number of persons who fall below 50 percent of a country's median income, we find that the United States has far and away the highest overall poverty rate in this group of eighteen developed nations. It is also near the top in terms of an absolute measure of poverty.[20] At the same time, the United States is arguably the wealthiest nation in the world.

This paradox is revealed in additional LIS analyses that have examined how well children and adults from the lower, middle, and upper ends of the income scale do. Not surprisingly, the United States has the highest standards of living at the middle and upper ends of the income distribution scale; yet, for children at the lower end, their standards of living fall behind most other industrialized nations. The conclusion to be drawn from these divergent patterns regarding American children is stated succinctly by Rainwater and Smeeding:

> In other words, while the United States has a higher real level of income than most of our comparison countries it is the high and middle income children who reap the benefits (and much more the former than the latter). Low income American children suffer in both absolute and relative terms. The average low income child in the other 17 countries is at least one-third better off than is the average low-income American child. (1995: 9)

The reasons for such a discrepancy are twofold. First, the social safety net in the United States is much weaker than those in virtually every other country listed in table 2.2. Second, the United States is plagued by relatively low wages at the bottom of the income distribution scale when compared to other developed countries (Smeeding, 1997b; Smeeding, Rainwater, and Burtless, 2001). These factors contribute to the relative and absolute depths of U.S. poverty in comparison to poverty in other industrialized nations (which is discussed at much greater length in the next chapter).[21]

The Human Meaning of Poverty

Up to this point we have surveyed the statistical landscape of poverty. Yet what constitutes the human condition of American poverty? Unfortunately, the discourse coming out of Washington over the past twenty-five years has been marked by a remarkable lack of perception regarding the daily lives of struggling Americans. Nowhere is this more apparent than when it comes to the poor, particularly the poor who turn to welfare assistance. Rather than being guided by insight and wisdom, the debate surrounding welfare reform is routinely couched in ignorance, callousness, stereotypes, and political oneupmanship.

A low point in this debate came during the discussions that preceded the 1996 welfare reform bill signed by President Clinton. Two House members on the congressional floor argued that a potential cut of $69 billion in public assistance programs was justified on the grounds that the use of welfare by recipients is analogous to the unnatural feeding of dangerous animals. Representative John Mica, of Florida, held up a sign that read, "DON'T FEED THE ALLIGATORS." He went on to say, "We post these warnings because unnatural feeding and artificial care create dependency. When dependency sets in, these otherwise able alligators can no longer survive on their own." Later in the day, and not to be outdone, Wyoming Representative Barbara Cubin continued this line of argument with the following analogy:

> The Federal government introduced wolves into the State of Wyoming, and they put them in pens, and they brought elk and venison to them every day. This is what I call the wolf welfare program. The Federal Government provided everything that the wolves need for their existence. But guess what? They opened the gates and let the wolves out, and now the wolves won't go. Just

like any animal in the species, any mammal, when you take away their freedom and their dignity and their ability, they can't provide for themselves. (Pear, 1995)

Perhaps if Representatives Mica and Cubin had educated themselves about the difficulties and struggles that face welfare recipients, they would not have been so quick to draw comparisons to alligators and wolves and might have realized that living on welfare is hardly analogous to wolves being "brought elk and venison every day."

Such an appreciation certainly does not mean that one should gloss over the problems that face the poor or glorify the downtrodden. What it does mean is that we need a fuller and more realistic sense of the complexity and issues involved in people's lives. This complexity is too often absent in our discussions regarding welfare recipients. Rather, they are routinely reduced to the caricature of the lazy, Cadillac-driving welfare freeloader, or worse, to alligators or wolves.

However, an additional element is noticeably absent in our policy and general debates regarding the poor. It is an appreciation of the pain and suffering caused by poverty. For a host of reasons, we tend to shy away from such discussions.[22] Yet they are essential in appreciating the deeper meaning and human costs of impoverishment. Behind each of the numbers presented in this chapter are literally millions of lives and stories. Embedded within those lives is an untold pain caused by poverty. The familiar saying that statistics represent faces with the tears wiped off is certainly apropos.

It is essential to appreciate this human dimension of poverty. Without such a connection, we lose sight of that which we are trying to rectify. As Martha Nussbaum writes in her book *Poetic Justice*, "the ability to imagine vividly, and then to assess judicially, another person's pain, to participate in it and then to ask about its significance, is a powerful way of learning what the human facts are and of acquiring a motivation to alter them" (1995: 91).

Although many experiences are associated with poverty, there are three that I believe capture the essence of the American experience of poverty in individuals' and families' lives—having to make significant compromises regarding the daily necessities in life; enduring elevated levels of stress as a result of such insufficiencies; and experiencing a stunting of one's development and potential as a result of impoverishment.[23] These are the painful and all too human costs of what it means to be poor in an American context of plenty. Each is explored in the following sections.

Doing Without

By its very definition, poverty represents a lack or absence of essential resources. Webster's (1996) defines poverty in three ways: "1. the state or condition of having little or no money, goods, or means of support; 2. deficiency of necessary or desirable ingredients, qualities, etc.; 3. scantiness; insufficiency." The experience of poverty is epitomized by having to do without.

This having to do without includes compromises involving basic resources such as food, clothing, shelter, health care, and transportation. It also entails not having other items and services that many of us take for granted, from the convenience of writing a check to the small pleasure of going out for lunch. And as noted earlier, the purchasing power of poor Americans is far less than the purchasing power of their counterparts in many other industrialized countries. In short, poverty embodies a "deficiency of necessary or desirable ingredients" that most Americans possess. I discuss several of these.

Living in poverty often means having to do without a sufficiently balanced diet and adequate intake of calories (McGovern, 2001; Poppendieck, 1997, 1998; Schwartz-Nobel, 2002). Several large-scale studies have indicated that those in poverty routinely have bouts of hunger, undernutrition, and/ or a detrimental altering of the diet at some point during the month. The U.S. Department of Agriculture determined that 45.5 percent of all children below the poverty line were in households that experienced food insecurity in 2002 (Nord et al., 2003).[24] Furthermore, 23.3 million people received emergency food aid from America's Second Harvest (the nation's largest organization of emergency food providers) in 2001, while the median household income for these individuals was 71 percent of the federal poverty level (Kim et al., 2001). The risk of hunger and food insecurity affects both children and adults (Alaimo et al., 2001), as well as the elderly (Lee and Frongillo, 2001).

For example, an elderly woman I interviewed in *Living on the Edge* described how she could not afford a balanced diet, which then compounded her health problems:

Toward the end of the month, we just live on toast and stuff. Toast and eggs or something like that. I'm supposed to eat green vegetables. I'm supposed to be on a special diet because I'm a diabetic. But there's a lotta things that I'm supposed to eat that I can't afford. Because the fruit and vegetables are terribly high in the store. It's ridiculous! I was out to Cedar's grocery, they're chargin' fifty-nine cents for one grapefruit. I'm supposed to eat grapefruit, but who's gonna pay fifty-nine cents for one grape-fruit when you don't have much money? But my doctor says that that's one thing that's important, is to eat the right foods when you're a diabetic. But I eat what I can afford. And if I can't afford it, I can't eat it. So that's why my blood sugar's high because lots of times I should have certain things to eat and I just can't pay. I can't afford it. (1994: 59)

Having enough food on the table is a constant battle for families in poverty. As Dan Glickman, the former secretary of agriculture, aptly noted, "One in three of our kids live in families that do constant battle with hunger—whether it's missed meals the last few days before a paycheck, or skipped medical appointments in favor of putting food on the table. These kids are at constant risk of malnutrition and the lifetime of chronic illness that can accompany it" (1997).

This leads to a second area where families in poverty often have to do without—good health. One of the most consistent findings in epidemiology is that the quality of an individual's health is negatively affected by lower socioeconomic status, particularly impoverishment (Kawachi, Kennedy, and Wilkinson, 1999; Mullahy and Wolfe, 2001). Poverty is associated with a host of health risks, including elevated rates of heart disease, diabetes, hypertension, cancer, infant mortality, mental illness, undernutrition, lead poisoning, asthma, and dental problems (Klerman and Parker, 1991; Leidenfrost, 1993; Lichter and Crowley, 2002; Mullahy and Wolfe, 2001; Sherman, 1994; Williams and Collins, 1995). The result is a death rate for the poverty-stricken between the ages of 25 and 64 that is approximately three times higher than that for the affluent within the same age range (Pappas et al., 1993), and a life expectancy that is considerably shorter (Geronimus et al., 2001). For example, Americans in the top 5 percent of the income distribution can expect to live approximately 9 years longer than those in the bottom 10 percent (Jencks, 2002). As Nancy Leidenfrost writes in her review of the literature, "Health disparities between the poor and those with higher incomes are almost universal for all dimensions of health" (1993: 1).

Furthermore, poverty often exerts a negative effect upon children's health status, which in turn affects their well-being as adults (Korenman and Miller, 1997). According to Bradley Schiller,

> A child born to a poverty-stricken mother is likely to be under-nourished both before and after birth. Furthermore, the child is less likely to receive proper postnatal care, to be immunized against disease, or even to have his or her eyes and teeth examined. As a result, the child is likely to grow up prone to illness and poverty, and, in the most insidious of cases, be impaired by organic brain damage. (2004: 122)

The connection between poverty and ill health exists for several reasons, including the lack of an adequate diet, reduced access to medical care, residence in unhealthy and stressful physical and mental environments, and lowered educational awareness regarding health issues. The result is an increase in pain and suffering at the doorsteps of the poor.[25]

Although Medicaid and Medicare have helped to increase the poor's access to health care, nevertheless when use of health services is compared to need for services, low-income households have the lowest rate (Mullahy and Wolfe, 2001). Furthermore, a number of the poor and near-poor have no insurance whatsoever—approximately 30 percent of those below the poverty line were uninsured for the entire year of 2002 (U.S. Census Bureau, 2003d). And when these families have insurance, it is often restrictive in terms of what is covered.

Just as good health is often compromised as a result of poverty, so too is living in a safe and decent neighborhood. Although it is true that most of the poor do not live in neighborhoods that are characterized as impoverished inner-city areas, poverty nevertheless limits the choices available in terms of the overall quality of life in a neighborhood. For example, a poverty-stricken mother of two teenagers described her neighborhood as follows:

> The territory is horrible. Across the street is the place that's been hitting the news lately. And it's really bad, 'cause when you go away, on weekends, we go down to my older son sometimes.

And you really don't know what you're gonna have left when you come back. Because the apartment next door has been broken into twice. And it's bad. You can never be comfortable at night 'cause ya can never leave your windows open. You have to lock everything up, because you never know. But I guess if you want reasonable, cheap rent, you have to. (Rank, 2000: 136)

Racial discrimination in the housing market further restricts the options available to minorities, particularly African Americans (Feagin, 2000; Jargowsky, 1997; Massey and Denton, 1993; Yinger, 1995).

Being confined to a low-income neighborhood, coupled with transportation problems, often means that the poor pay more for and spend more time acquiring basic necessities (Caplovitz, 1963). This includes paying higher prices for food at the local grocery store (Chung and Myers, 1999; Kaufman, 1999), not being able to buy in bulk or to take advantage of items on sales (Lichter and Crowley, 2002), facing a scarcity of neighborhood retail outlets (Allwitt and Donley, 1997), and having limited access to financial institutions and therefore being exposed to predatory lending practices at check-cashing stores and pawnshops (Andreason, 1993; Caskey, 1994). Take the case of a single mother I talked to who was living in a highly segregated, low-income black neighborhood.[26]

I normally try to catch a ride with somebody or save a couple dollars and buy somebody some gas to take me somewhere. You know, you can go on the bus, but if you're grocery shoppin' it's hard to get back home. Usually I haveta grocery shop right around here where I can walk to. And then I'll have the kids meet me, and they'll help me bring the groceries back. I couldn't afford to pay somebody to go to the grocery store. I'd like to go to other places— you'd probably catch more bargains, but if you don't have no way to get there, then you have to shop where you can shop.

She went on to note,

I'm rentin' a washin' machine for 42 dollars a month. For two years I gotta pay that. It's a lotta money for a washin' machine. But I don't have a car to go to the laundromat, and I don't have the cash to pay cash for a washin' machine, so I don't have any choice. I'm stuck with one of those rent-to-own places.

Doing without adequate transportation affects the ability to compete and hold a job, as much of the research on moving welfare recipients to work has found (Card and Blank, 2002; Duncan and Chase-Lansdale, 2002; Gueron and Pauly, 1991; Pugh, 1998; Raphael and Stoll, 2000). For those who do have a job, not having reliable transportation also causes difficulties, as was clear in a conversation I had with a thirty-seven-year-old, never-married mother who was working part time as a cashier while also attending school. She was asked whether not having a car caused her any difficulty.

> That's a great difficulty. I use my bicycle to go to work during the winter. As long as there's a clear spot, I went on ice. With a bicycle. People told me I was crazy. But I mean, I had to do it. And I did it. And I will be doing it again this year. If there's one little patch that's been cleared, I don't care if it's in January, I will be on that bike.

What is perhaps most bitter regarding all of these hardships is that they take place within a context of abundance. Most Americans have plenty to eat or clothes to wear, experience good health and safe neighborhoods, are not forced to ride a bicycle across icy streets to work, and so on. This message of abundance is seen daily from the shopping malls to television programming. The result is that poverty in America has an especially bitter taste. It imprints upon the poor a strong sense of relative deprivation and failure.[27]

In short, living in poverty is epitomized by the struggle to acquire, and at times, the need to forgo, the daily necessities and resources that most Americans take for granted. It is the paradox and humiliation of having to do without in a land of plenty.

The Stressful Weight of Poverty

A consequence of the struggles described is that impoverishment puts a heavy weight upon the shoulders of most who walk in its ranks. In essence, poverty acts to amplify the stress found in everyday life and its relationships. The struggle of having to juggle and balance expenses on an ongoing basis places a stressful burden upon the poverty-stricken and their families (Shirk et al., 1999). This is illustrated in the worries a working mother conveyed to me:

My biggest worry is running out of money. You know, my kids cannot understand and I wish they could, and some day they will. But right now, every time I go shopping or even if we're sitting there and lookin' at TV—"Mom, I want this. Mom can I get this? Mom, you owe me so much for allowance. Mom can you give us so much money?" And I'm beginning to realize what my husband went through sometimes, when I said, "Gee, I wish I could have . . ." and knowing that he may wanted to have gotten it for me, but knowing he couldn't afford it. It's just frustrating.

Rather than being able to afford the items her children yearned for, this mother of three must try and juggle her ever-present array of bills within the constraints of a slightly higher-than-minimum-wage full-time income.

I want to go to bed at night thinking, all the bills are paid up, I'm on the up and up with everybody and I don't have to worry about things. That's not the worry I want to have. But like last night, I got hold of the phone bill. I saw when it was due, like on the 17th. And I knew that if I didn't do something about it right away, then I wouldn't have a phone. So I went ahead and paid it and called them up today to let them know that it was in the mail so I wouldn't get one of those polite little notices. But our gas bill, that was due . . . I think it is coming due. I'm gonna have to hold that over until my next check and just pay the late charge, as much as I hate doing that. But they will still get paid. I wish that I were able to just go ahead and pay like I should.

Perhaps the most well-known juggling act is what has been called the "heat-or-eat" dilemma. As heating bills climb in the winter, impoverished families may be forced into the hard decision of choosing between purchasing food and paying for heat. Bhattacharya and colleagues (2002) have empirically documented that poor families do indeed lower their food expenditures during cold-weather periods (in addition, see Kim et al., 2001).

Such ongoing frustrations are commonplace. They intensify the stress and tension within individuals and, by extension, their relationships. Take the marital relationship. Research has consistently found that poverty and lower income are associated with a greater risk of separation and divorce, as well as spousal and child violence (Drake and Pandey, 1996; Gelles, 1993; Sedlak and Broadhurst, 1996; U.S. Bureau of the Census, 1992; White and Rogers, 2000).

What frequently happens is that unemployment precipitates a fall into poverty (as mentioned earlier), which results in a tremendous strain upon a marriage. Research has indeed shown that the impact of unemployment upon marital relationships is quite deleterious (Cottle, 2001; Vosler, 1996). When blended with poverty, it creates a particularly destructive combination (Voydanoff, 1990).

For example, an out-of-work husband in Lillian Rubin's *Families on the Faultline* described his feelings as follows:

> It's hard enough being out of work, but then my wife gets on my case, yakking all the time about how we're going to be on the street if I don't get off my butt, like it's my fault or something that there's no work out there. When she starts up like that, I swear I want to hit her, anything just to shut her mouth. (1994: 115–116)

As Rubin writes, "the stress and conflict in families where father loses his job can give rise to the kind of interaction described here, a dynamic that all too frequently ends in physical assaults against women and children" (1994: 116).

In many ways, the stress of poverty is even greater for female-headed families. For these women, there is no partner to turn to for a helping hand during the routine crises and struggles outlined earlier. Furthermore, most female heads of households work at two full-time jobs (within the labor force and at home). The result is often stress, frustration, and exhaustion, which in turn influence women's ability to care for and raise their children (Berrick, 1995; McLanahan and Sandefur, 1994; Seccombe, 1999; Sidel, 1996).

For single men and women in poverty, impoverishment also exerts a stressful weight upon their shoulders. In many such cases, this pressure is exacerbated by a physical or mental disability. For example, in my study of welfare recipients (Rank, 1994), many of the single men and women who were receiving some form of public assistance also had physical and mental disabilities, which, in combination with poverty, created significant levels of stress in their lives.

In short, the daily trials and tribulations of living in poverty put a heavy strain upon the backs of the poor. These anxieties then spill over into relationships with family and friends. Yet it is not the case that such individuals are intrinsically "rotten mothers or fathers," to paraphrase Charles Murray. Rather, they battle head-first against the formidable pressures exerted by poverty, and they come up scarred.

Stunted Growth

Having to do without, combined with the stress of living in poverty, often produces a stunting of growth. A simple analogy is to a tree. If one denies a tree the proper nutrients, while at the same time creating stressful environmental conditions, it will fail to develop to its full potential. Often there will be a noticeable stunting of growth and deformity of its trunk and branches.

So it is with individuals who live in poverty for sustained periods of time. A lack of proper food, shelter, education, and other essential resources, coupled with the stress of impoverishment, results in stunted individual development. Sometimes this stunting is visibly apparent; often times it lies underneath the surface. Moreover, the longer the duration of poverty and the greater the depth of poverty, the larger the negative impact.

This process is perhaps most salient in poverty's stunting effects upon young children's physical and mental growth. Poor infants and young children in the United States are likely to have far lower levels of physical and mental growth (as measured in a variety of ways) than their nonpoor counterparts (Duncan and Brooks-Gunn, 1997; Korenman and Miller, 1997; Smith et al., 1997).

Furthermore, both the duration and the depth of poverty intensify these negative outcomes. For example, in their research on poverty's effects upon young children's cognitive and verbal ability and early school achievement, Judith Smith and colleagues report, "Duration of poverty has very negative effects on children's IQ, verbal ability, and achievement scores. Children who lived in persistently poor families scored 6–9 points lower on the various assessments than children who were never poor. In addition, the negative effects of persistent poverty seem to get stronger as the child gets older" (1997: 164). They also found that "The effects of family poverty varied dramatically depending on whether a family was very poor (family income below 50 percent of the poverty level), poor, or near poor. Children in the very poor group had scores 7–12 points lower than did children in the near-poor group" (1997: 164).

In a study that looked at the impact of the duration of poverty upon children's mental health, Jane McLeod and Michael Shanahan found that "The length of time spent in poverty is an important predictor of children's mental health, even after current poverty status is taken into account. As the length of time spent in poverty increases, so too do children's feelings of unhappiness, anxiety, and dependence" (1993: 360).

As children grow older and if they continue to reside in poverty, the disadvantages of growing up poor multiply. These disadvantages include attendance at inferior schools (Kahlenberg, 2001), problems associated with disadvantaged neighborhoods (Brooks-Gunn, Duncan, and Aber, 1997), less educationally stimulating home environments (Mayer, 1997), unmet health needs (Sherman, 1994), and a host of other disadvantages.

One simple but telling example of this involved a single mother of four children, ages 14, 12, 10, and 8. She told me that she was not able to provide the kinds of educational and social experiences for her children that she would have liked to. Her inability to afford a summer program was one example.

> They were in a program at the elementary school. Which was five dollars per child. My one daughter was in a science program, chemistry program. And that was a three-week program. That was just five dollars. But there were a lot of other programs that I didn't want to spend money for, but they weren't that much. Five or ten dollars, or maybe twenty-five. They had a summer camp, which was for four days. That was twenty-five dollars through the park district. But I wasn't able to do that. For two children, that would've been fifty dollars. I did it for one child last year. But I had two. And I couldn't send one and not the other. But I mean what's twenty-five dollars? It's a lot if you don't have it.

> They kept 'em from eight to three. They had a camp-out. And they had swimming. And they roasted marshmallows. And they had arts and crafts. It woulda been a nice program. But I just don't have it. . . . And there's a lot of other additional programs that maybe I could've looked into had I the money.

This represented just one instance of how poverty diminished in a relatively small way the potential growth of two young children. Yet multiplied over hundreds of such events for these children, the effect becomes profound. This is expressed in the feelings of a mother who had been out of work for two years and who could not adequately provide for the needs of her children.

> After two years it gets to the point where you can just about start
> pulling out your hair. Because there is so much that you want to
> do, and you see your kids growing up around you, and you can't
> do a damn thing to help 'em out. And oooooh. It really drives you
> nuts.

As children continue to grow up, the disadvantages of poverty or near-poverty multiply. By the time they reach their early twenties, they may be at a significant disadvantage in terms of their ability to compete effectively within the labor market, which in turn increases their risk of experiencing poverty as adults.

As adults age, the stunting effects of poverty become less pronounced but are nevertheless still quite real. These effects include poor physical and mental health, lower productivity as workers, and reduced participation in civic activities as well as in other aspects of life (Rank, 1997).

Living in poverty also takes its toll in other ways. For example, individuals may develop strategies for coping with the stress of poverty. Some of these can be helpful, such as cultivating support networks. Unfortunately, others, such as the use of alcohol or drugs, are self-destructive.

Suffice it to say that a third bitter taste of poverty involves not being able to achieve the full development of one's potential and one's children's potential. This is perhaps the most painful pill to swallow. It is poverty's knack of being able to undercut the capabilities that are found in all of us. It is not an exaggeration to call this a tragedy, for that is precisely what the loss of such human potential is.

I have chosen in this section to focus on what in my view is the essence of poverty in people's lives—having to make major compromises concerning the daily necessities that most of us take for granted; enduring significant levels of stress as a result of such insufficiencies; and experiencing the stunting of one's own development and one's children's development. These can be summarized in Alexander Chase's observation that "The rich man may never get into heaven, but the pauper is already serving his term in hell." This is the painful and all too human cost of what it means to be poor in a land of plenty.

The concern throughout this book is with the condition of poverty and its impact upon individuals, families, and society. It is therefore important to highlight the distinction between the condition of poverty and the poor themselves. Too often we look at the issues discussed in this section and blame the poor for bringing these on themselves, while losing sight of the fact that it is the condition of poverty that results in much of the stress and frustrations that we have seen. As stated earlier, poverty represents a state of extreme economic and social deprivation. The poor, on the other hand, are individuals and families who for some period of time occupy such a state. The condition of poverty, and the amelioration of its deleterious effects, is where our concern and efforts should lie.

Finally, it must be emphasized that in spite of these very serious components of poverty, research has repeatedly demonstrated that those who fall below the poverty line essentially hold the same fundamental aspirations, beliefs, and hopes as most other Americans. For example, throughout my book *Living on the Edge*, it is clear that those in poverty and on public assistance repeatedly express support for and try to fulfill the mainstream goals of wanting to get ahead in life, working hard, struggling to provide the best for their children, and persevering despite the many obstacles laid in their path. The example of Denise Turner, to whom I referred in the first chapter, exemplifies those beliefs. Despite the odds against her, she and many others hold onto the faith that they and their children will eventually get ahead. When we understand the formidable dimensions of poverty that have been outlined in this section, such adherence to this dominant set of American personal values and beliefs becomes all the more remarkable.

Yet this raises a critical question. If the poor basically endorse and reflect the mainstream values of work and perseverance, why does poverty occur in the first place? Having sketched the boundaries and parameters of poverty, let us now turn to the causes of American poverty.

Poverty as
a Structural
Failing

3

The trouble with the profit system has
always been that it was highly unprofitable
to most people.

E. B. White

FEW QUESTIONS HAVE GENERATED as much
discussion across time as those pertaining to
the causes of human impoverishment. As the
historian R. M. Hartwell notes, "The causes of
poverty, its relief and cure, have been a matter
of serious concern to theologians, statesmen,
civil servants, intellectuals, tax-payers and
humanitarians since the Middle Ages" (1986:
16). The question of causality has found itself at
the heart of most debates surrounding poverty
and the poor.[1]

Within the United States, the dominant
perspective has been that of poverty as an
individual failing. From Ben Franklin's *Poor
Richard's Almanac* to the recent welfare reform
changes, poverty has been conceptualized
primarily as a consequence of individual
failings and deficiencies. Social surveys asking
about the causes of poverty have consistently
found that Americans tend to rank individual
reasons (such as laziness, lack of effort, and low
ability) as the most important factors related to

poverty, while structural reasons such as unemployment or discrimination are typically viewed as less important (Feagin, 1975; Gilens, 1999; Kluegel and Smith, 1986; Smith and Stone, 1989).

The emphasis on individual attributes as the primary cause of poverty has been reinforced by social scientists engaged in poverty research (O'Connor, 2001). As the social survey has become the dominant methodological approach during the past fifty years, with multivariate modeling being the preferred statistical approach, the research emphasis has increasingly fallen on understanding poverty and welfare dependency in terms of individual attributes. The unit of analysis in these studies is by definition the individual, rather than the wider social or economic structures, resulting in statistical models of individual characteristics that predict individual behavior. Consequently, the longstanding tension between structural and individual approaches to explaining poverty has largely been tilted within the empirical poverty research community toward that of the individual. As Alice O'Connor writes,

> That this tension has more often been resolved in favor of the
> individualist interpretation can be seen in several oft-noted
> features in poverty research. One is the virtual absence of class as
> an analytic category, at least as compared with more individual-
> ized measures of status such as family background and human
> capital. A similar individualizing tendency can be seen in the
> reduction of race and gender to little more than demographic,
> rather than structurally constituted, categories. (2001: 9)

The argument in this chapter is that such an emphasis is misplaced and misdirected. By focusing on individual attributes as the cause of poverty, we have largely missed the underlying dynamic of American impoverishment. Poverty researchers and social commentators have in effect focused on who loses out at the economic game, rather than addressing the fact that the game produces losers in the first place. An analysis of this underlying dynamic is critical to advancing our state of knowledge regarding American poverty.

Three lines of evidence are provided to suggest that U.S. poverty is largely the result of structural failings at the economic, political, and social levels. These include an analysis of the lack of adequately paying jobs in the economy that would allow wage earners to raise their families out of poverty or near-poverty; a comparative examination of the ineffectiveness of the social safety net in preventing poverty; and the systemic nature of poverty as indicated by the life-course risk of impoverishment experienced by a majority of Americans (which is explored in greater detail in chapter 4).

I will then outline a conceptual model that allows us to reinterpret the dynamic of American poverty. It incorporates the importance of human capital characteristics in determining who loses out at the economic game, within the broader structural nature of American poverty that ensures the existence of economic losers in the first place. I refer to this as a structural vulnerability explanation of poverty. Let me begin by briefly reviewing the current approach toward understanding U.S. poverty.

The Current Approach:
Individual Attributes and Poverty

The mainstream research emphasis has by and large focused on the individual attributes and demographic characteristics of the poor. These, in turn, have been used to explain why particular individuals and households experience poverty.

As we saw in the previous chapter, annual cross-sectional surveys such as the Current Population Survey have indicated that the likelihood of poverty varies sharply with respect to age, race, gender, family structure, and residence. For example, the U.S. Census Bureau (2003a) reports that while the overall U.S. poverty rate in 2002 was 12.1 percent, it was 14.2 percent for those who resided in rural areas, 16.7 percent for children, 24.1 percent for African Americans, and 35.2 percent for female-headed households with children under the age of eighteen. Other demographic characteristics closely associated with the risk of poverty include giving birth out of wedlock, being in a family with a large number of children, and having children at an early age (Maynard, 1997).

Cross-sectional research has also shown a close association between human capital characteristics and an individual's risk of poverty—those lacking in human capital are much more likely to become impoverished. Lower levels of education, lack of marketable skills, and a physical disability are all highly correlated with poverty (Blank, 1997; Schiller, 2004). On the other hand, research comparing the attitudes and motivation of the poor and the nonpoor have found relatively few differences between these two groups

(Goodwin, 1972; 1983; Lichter and Crowley, 2002; Rank, 1994; Seccombe, 1999) and little to suggest that they are a causal factor that leads to poverty (Duncan, 1984; Edwards et al., 2001).

Longitudinal studies have addressed the length of time and factors related to households that experience a spell of poverty. As indicated in chapter 2, this body of work has revealed that most spells of poverty are of modest length. The typical pattern is that households are impoverished for one, two, or three years and then manage to get above the poverty line. They may stay there for a period of time, only to experience another fall into poverty at some later point. Since their economic distance above the poverty threshold is often narrow, a detrimental economic or social event can push a household back below the poverty line. Longitudinal research has also focused on the nature of these events and the individual changes that result in a spell of poverty. The most important of these have been the loss of employment and earnings, changes in family structure, and health problems.

A substantial body of work has also examined the dynamics of welfare use and dependency. This research has shown that individuals who utilize public assistance programs and who experience longer spells of welfare use often have characteristics that place them at a distinct disadvantage vis-à-vis the labor market (Bane and Ellwood, 1994; Boisjoly et al., 1998; Card and Blank, 2002; Duncan et al., 2000; Harris, 1996; Moffitt, 1992; Rank, 1988; Sandefur and Cook, 1998). Consequently, those with work disabilities, poor educations, many children, or who live in inner-city areas are more likely to utilize the welfare system extensively. The results from these studies largely mirror the findings that have been gathered regarding the length and duration of poverty spells.

To summarize, the current research approach to understanding U.S. poverty has examined the impact that individual and family characteristics exert upon the likelihood that Americans will experience poverty and/or welfare use. It has established that particular attributes and characteristics (specifically those that place individuals at a disadvantage in terms of competing in the labor market) are critical in predicting who is more likely to experience poverty.

This body of work has provided an important understanding into who the economic losers are in American society. At the same time it has failed to address the question of why there are economic losers in the first place.

The premise of this chapter is that in order to answer this question, it is essential to analyze specific failings at the structural level.

The Structural Nature of Poverty:
Evidence and Arguments

I will discuss three lines of evidence in order to illustrate the structural nature of American poverty: (1) the inability of the U.S. labor market to provide enough decent-paying jobs for all families to avoid poverty or near-poverty; (2) the ineffectiveness of American public policy in reducing levels of poverty via the social safety net; and (3) the fact that the majority of Americans will experience poverty during their adult lifetimes, which suggests the systemic nature of U.S. poverty. Each of these patterns empirically illustrates that the high rates of American poverty are by and large the result of structural failures and processes.

The Inability of the Labor Market
to Support All Families

Several of the pioneering large-scale empirical studies of poverty in England and the United States conducted at the end of the nineteenth and beginning of the twentieth century focused heavily on the importance of labor market failings to explain poverty. The work of Charles Booth (1892), Seebohm Rowntree (1901), researchers at Hull House (1895), Robert Hunter (1904), and W. E. B. Du Bois (1899) all emphasized the importance of inadequate wages, lack of jobs, and unstable working conditions as primary causes of poverty. For example, Rowntree (1901) estimated that approximately 57 percent of individuals in poverty were there as a direct result of labor market failures (low wages, unemployment, irregularity of work).

By the 1960s, the emphasis had shifted from a critique of the economic structure as a primary cause of poverty to an analysis of individual deficiencies (e.g., the lack of human capital) as the underlying reason for poverty. Timothy Bartik (2001) notes that U.S. antipoverty policy has increasingly focused on labor supply policies (e.g., raising individuals' human capital or incentives to work through welfare reform), rather than labor demand policies (increasing the number and quality of jobs). As mentioned earlier, social scientific research has reinforced this policy approach by focusing on individual deficiencies in order to explain individual poverty.

However, it can be clearly demonstrated that irrespective of the specific characteristics that Americans possess, there simply are not enough well-paying jobs to support all of those (and their families) who are looking for work. During the past twenty-five years the American economy has increasingly produced larger numbers of low-paying jobs, jobs that are part-time, and jobs that are lacking in benefits (Seccombe, 2000). The Census Bureau reports that the median hourly earnings of workers who were paid hourly wages in 2000 was $9.91, while at the same time approximately three million Americans were working part-time as a result of the lack of sufficient full-time work (U.S. Census Bureau, 2002d). In addition, 43.6 million Americans were lacking in health insurance, largely because their employer did not provide such benefits (U.S. Census Bureau, 2003d).

Studies analyzing the percentage of the U.S. workforce that falls into the low-wage sector have shown that far more American workers fall into this category than do their counterparts in other developed countries. For example, in the Smeeding, Rainwater, and Burtless (2000) study mentioned in chapter 2, the authors found that 25 percent of all U.S. full-time workers could be classified as employed in low-wage work (defined as earning less than 65 percent of the national median earnings for full-time jobs). This was by far the highest percentage of the countries analyzed; the average was 12.9 percent.

Beyond the low wages, the part-time work, and the lack of benefits, there is also a mismatch between the number of available jobs and the number of those who need them. Economists frequently discuss what is known as a natural unemployment rate; in order for free market economies to effectively function, a certain percentage of laborers must be out of work. Full employment would, for example, impede the ability of employers to attract and hire workers, particularly within the low-wage sector. Consequently, a certain degree of unemployment is systemic within a market economy, irrespective of the individual characteristics possessed by those who participate in that economy.

During the past forty years, U.S. monthly unemployment rates have averaged between 4 and 10 percent (U.S. Census Bureau, 2002d). These percentages represent individuals who are out of work but actively seeking employment. In the year 2001, this translated into nearly 7 million people unemployed at any particular point in time, while more than fifteen million people experienced unemployment at some point during the year (Schiller, 2004). Certainly some of these individuals had voluntarily left their jobs in order to locate other jobs (known as frictional unemployment), while in other cases the unemployed may have included individuals whose families were not dependent on their earnings for their economic survival (e.g., teenagers looking for summer work). Nevertheless, a good proportion of unemployment is involuntary and results from layoffs and downsizing, which directly affect millions of heads of households.[2]

Bartik (2001, 2002) used several different approaches and assumptions to estimate the number of jobs that would be needed to significantly address the issue of poverty in the United States. His conclusion? Even in the booming U.S. economy of the late 1990s, between five and nine million more jobs were needed in order to meet the needs of the poor and disadvantaged.

Similarly, Philip Harvey notes,

> . . . a number of job vacancy surveys have been conducted in
> various parts of the country over the past several decades, and
> their results paint a consistent portrait of U.S. labor markets.
> The surveys show that in periods of relative prosperity as well as
> during recessions, the number of job seekers generally exceeds—
> usually by a wide margin—the number of job vacancies in the
> labor markets surveyed. (2000: 706)

The structural failing of the labor market to support the pool of labor that currently exists can be further illustrated through the Survey of Income and Program Participation (SIPP). The SIPP is a large, ongoing longitudinal study that interviews households every four months over rolling periods of three to four years. It gathers detailed monthly information regarding individuals' employment and income during these periods of time, enabling one to map the patterns of labor force participation for a large nationally representative sample (for further detail, see appendix A).

This data set can empirically illustrate the mismatch between the number of jobs in the labor market that allow families to subsist above the threshold of poverty, and the number of heads of families in need of such jobs. Tables 3.1, 3.2, and 3.3 are based upon the jobs and work behavior of family heads across all twelve months of 1999. This allows us to estimate the annual number of hours worked, the annual amount of pay received, and whether such earnings were sufficient to raise a family above the poverty line. The analysis is confined to heads of families who are between the ages of eighteen and sixty-four.[3]

Tables 3.1 and 3.2 examine whether the jobs that household heads were working at during the year were able to get their families out of poverty. Three poverty thresholds are examined—below 1.00 (the official poverty line); below 1.25 of the poverty line (the official poverty line raised by 25 percent); and below 1.50 of the poverty line (the official poverty line raised by 50 percent). To illustrate, the poverty line for a family of 4 in 1999 was $17,029. Consequently, the 1.25 poverty threshold for this family would be $21,286, while the 1.50 poverty threshold would be $25,544. These thresholds provide us with several alternative levels of poverty and near-poverty.

Are the jobs that family heads found themselves employed at during the year capable of getting their families out of poverty? The separate panels in tables 3.1 and 3.2 examine this question for three different populations of family heads who were in the labor market. The top panel includes only those heads of households who were working full-time throughout the year (defined here as averaging thirty-five or more hours per week across the fifty-two weeks of the year). The second panel contains those working full-time as well as those who were working at least half-time throughout the year (defined as working an average of twenty or more hours per week across fifty-two weeks). The third panel includes all heads of families in the labor market (defined as someone who either worked at some point during the year or who actively looked for work).

For those employed full-time throughout the year (top panel of table 3.1), 9.4 percent were working at jobs in which their annual earnings could not pull their families above the poverty line, 15.3 percent were at jobs in which their earnings would not get their families above 1.25 of the poverty line, and 22.0 percent were employed at jobs that could not raise their families above 1.50 of the poverty line. We can clearly see that the jobs that one-parent family heads were working at were much less able to sustain families above the level of poverty than were the jobs held by heads of all types of families combined. On the other hand, single men and women were more likely to be able to lift themselves out of poverty through their work. Married couples fell in between these two family types.[4]

If we include all family heads who were working half-time or more throughout the year (the middle panel of table 3.1), nearly 15 percent were

TABLE 3.1. Inability of the Labor Market to Support Various Family Structures above Poverty Threshold Levels

	Current Family Status			
Poverty Threshold	All Families	One-Parent Families	Single Families	Married-Couple Families
Heads of Families Working Full-Time				
Below 1.00	9.4	16.9	3.2	9.9
Below 1.25	15.3	26.4	6.6	16.0
Below 1.50	22.0	36.6	10.2	23.0
Heads of Families Working Half-Time or More				
Below 1.00	14.9	27.7	9.5	13.5
Below 1.25	21.4	37.0	14.3	19.8
Below 1.50	28.0	46.5	18.3	26.7
Heads of Families in the Labor Market				
Below 1.00	20.3	36.8	15.8	17.1
Below 1.25	26.5	44.9	20.4	23.3
Below 1.50	32.7	53.4	24.2	30.0

Source: Survey of Income and Program Participation, Rank and Yoon computations.

employed at jobs in which their incomes would not raise their families above the poverty line, 21.4 percent were at jobs that would not get their families over 1.25 of the poverty line, and 28 percent were at jobs that fell below 1.50 of the poverty line.

The bottom panel includes all household heads who were in the labor market at some point during the year. Here we can see that the percentages for the three poverty thresholds were 20.3, 26.5, and 32.7.

Consequently, depending on the level of poverty and the size of the pool of labor, the failure of the labor market to raise families out of poverty ranges from 9.4 percent (utilizing the official poverty line for those working full-time) to 32.7 percent (applying 1.50 of the poverty line for all who are in the labor market). To use an analogy that will be developed later, the balance between the supply of decent-paying jobs and the demand for labor might be thought of as an ongoing game of musical chairs. There is a finite number of jobs available in the labor market that pay enough to support a family above the threshold of poverty (which might be thought of as the chairs in this analogy). On the other hand, the amount of labor, as represented by the number of family heads in the labor market (and hence the players in the game), is far greater than the number of adequately paying jobs. As indicated in table 3.1, this imbalance ranges from 9.4 percent to 32.7 percent.

The structure of the labor market basically ensures that some families will lose out at this musical-chairs game of finding a decent-paying job capable of lifting a family above the poverty threshold.

Table 3.2 illustrates this in a slightly different fashion. Here we estimate the earnings capacity of jobs held by family heads to support various hypothetical household sizes at levels above our three different thresholds of poverty. For the pool of family heads who are working full-time, the jobs they are employed at are quite able to support a one- or two-person family above the official poverty line. For example, only 2.4 percent are in full-time jobs in which their earnings would not raise a one-person family above the official poverty line; 4.7 percent of family heads are working at jobs that would not raise a family of two above the poverty line.

However, as we look at the ability of such jobs to lift larger-size families above the thresholds of poverty, we can see their increasing failure to do so. Fifteen percent of these jobs will not raise a family of four above 1.00 of the poverty line. At the 1.25 level, the figure is 25.1 percent, and at the 1.50 level, it is 36 percent. The current supply of full-time jobs in the labor market appears able to lift most one- or two-person families out of poverty, but that supply becomes much less effective in raising moderate-size families

TABLE 3.2. Inability of the Labor Market to Support Various Family Sizes above Poverty Threshold Levels

Poverty Threshold	Hypothetical Family Size					
	1- Person Family	2- Person Family	3- Person Family	4- Person Family	5- Person Family	6- Person Family
Heads of Families Working Full-Time						
Below 1.00	2.4	4.7	7.6	15.0	22.3	29.0
Below 1.25	4.3	8.9	14.0	25.1	35.0	42.4
Below 1.50	7.2	14.5	21.8	36.0	46.3	54.6
Heads of Families Working Half-Time or More						
Below 1.00	6.3	10.2	13.8	21.6	28.9	35.3
Below 1.25	9.6	15.2	20.6	31.6	41.0	47.9
Below 1.50	13.2	21.1	28.3	42.0	51.6	59.3
Heads of Families in the Labor Market						
Below 1.00	12.0	15.8	19.3	26.9	33.7	39.7
Below 1.25	15.3	20.8	25.9	36.3	45.0	51.5
Below 1.50	18.8	26.4	33.2	46.0	54.9	62.1

Source: Survey of Income and Program Participation, Rank and Yoon computations.

out of poverty. As we include household heads who are working at least half-time (the middle panel of table 3.2) or who are in the labor market (the bottom panel of table 3.2), the percentages who are unable to get out of poverty rise significantly.

Finally, table 3.3 illustrates in yet another fashion why this is the case. The annual average hourly wages are calculated for heads of families and for all individuals who worked at some point during the year. The table indicates that 12.1 percent of family heads were working at jobs that paid an average of less than $6 an hour, 21.2 percent worked at jobs paying less than $8 an hour, and 31.7 percent worked at jobs paying less than $10 an hour. In 1999, in order to raise a family of three above the official poverty line, one would have to be working full-time (defined as averaging thirty-five hours per week across the fifty-two weeks of the year) at $7.30 an hour; for a family of four, the figure would be $9.36 an hour. Table 3.3 indicates that nearly a third of family heads were working at jobs paying less than $10 an hour, which puts them at a significant risk of poverty. For all individuals in the labor market, 43.3 percent were earning less than $10 an hour.

To summarize, the data presented in this section indicate that a major factor leading to poverty in the United States is a failure of the economic structure to provide sufficient opportunities for all who are participating in that system. The labor market simply does not provide enough decent-paying jobs for all who need them. As a result, millions of families find

TABLE 3.3. Cumulative Percent of the
American Population Working below Various
Hourly Wage Levels

Annual Average Hourly Wage	Heads of Families	All Individuals
Less than:		
$6.00	12.1	19.8
$8.00	21.2	31.8
$10.00	31.7	43.3
$12.00	42.7	53.9
$14.00	52.1	62.4
$16.00	60.7	69.8
$18.00	68.0	75.9
$20.00	74.1	80.6

Source: Survey of Income and Program Participation,
Rank and Yoon computations.

themselves struggling below or precariously close to the poverty line (see Munger, 2002, for various ethnographies describing these conditions; Ehrenreich, 2001, for a firsthand account; or Appelbaum, Bernhardt, and Murnane, 2003, for an examination of low income industries).

The Ineffectiveness of the Social Safety Net in Preventing Poverty

A second major structural failure is found at the political level. Despite the popular rhetoric about vast amounts of tax dollars being spent on public assistance, the American welfare state, and particularly its social safety net, can be more accurately described in minimalist terms. Compared to other Western industrialized countries, the United States devotes far fewer re-sources to programs aimed at assisting the economically vulnerable (Orga-nization for Economic Cooperation and Development, 1999). In fact, the United States allocates a smaller proportion of its GDP to social welfare programs than any other industrialized country except Japan (Gilens, 1999). As Charles Noble writes, "The U.S. welfare state is striking precisely because it is so limited in scope and ambition" (1997: 3).

In contrast, most European countries provide a wide range of social and insurance programs that largely prevent families from falling into poverty. These include substantial family or children's allowances, which are de-signed to transfer cash assistance to families with children. Unemployment assistance is far more generous in these countries than in the United States, often providing support for more than a year following the loss of a job. Furthermore, universal health coverage is routinely provided, along with considerable support for child care.

The result of these social policy differences is that they substantially reduce the extent of poverty in Europe and Canada, while American social policy exerts only a small impact upon poverty reduction. As Rebecca Blank notes, "the national choice in the United States to provide relatively less generous transfers to low-income families has meant higher relative pov-erty rates in the country. While low-income families in the United States work more than in many other countries, they are not able to make up for lower governmental income support relative to their European counterparts" (Blank, 1997: 141–142).

This effect can be clearly seen in table 3.4. The data in this table are based upon an analysis of the Luxembourg Income Study (discussed in the previous chapter) conducted by Veli-Matti Ritakallio (2001). For a household, poverty is defined as having disposable income of less than one-half of the country's median annual income. Eight European countries and Canada are compared to the United States in terms of their pretransfer and posttransfer rates of poverty. The pretransfer rates (column one) indicate what the level of poverty would be in each country in the absence of any governmental income transfers such as welfare payments, unemployment compensation, or social security payments. The posttransfer rates (column two) represent the level of poverty after governmental transfers are included (which is how poverty is officially measured in the United States and many other countries). Comparing these two levels of poverty (column three) reveals how effective (or ineffective) governmental policy is in reducing the overall extent of poverty in a country.

Looking first at the rates of pretransfer poverty, we can see that the United States is on the low end of the scale. Norway's pretransfer poverty rate is 27 percent, followed by the United States, Canada, and Germany at 29 percent. The Netherlands' pretransfer rate is 30 percent; Finland stands at 33 percent, Sweden at 36 percent, the United Kingdom at 38 percent. France possesses the highest level of pretransfer poverty at 39 percent.

When we examine the posttransfer rates of poverty, listed in column two, we see a dramatic reversal in terms of where the United States stands vis-à-

TABLE 3.4. Comparative Analysis of Governmental Effectiveness in Reducing Poverty across Selected Countries

Country	Pretransfer Poverty Rates	Posttransfer Poverty Rates	Reduction Factor (percentage)
Canada (1994)	29	10	66
Finland (1995)	33	4	88
France (1994)	39	8	79
Germany (1994)	29	7	76
Netherlands (1994)	30	7	77
Norway (1995)	27	4	85
Sweden (1995)	36	3	92
United Kingdom (1995)	38	13	66
United States (1994)	29	18	38

Source: Luxembourg Income Study, adapted from Ritakallio (2001) computations.

vis the comparison countries. The average posttransfer poverty rate for the eight comparison countries in table 3.4 is 7 percent, whereas the United States' posttransfer poverty rate stands at 18 percent. As a result of their more active social policies, Canada and Europe are able to significantly cut their overall rates of poverty. For example, Sweden is able to reduce the number of people who would be poor in the absence of any governmental help by 92 percent as a result of social policies. The overall average reduction factor for the eight countries is 79 percent. In contrast, the United States poverty reduction factor is only 38 percent (with much of this being the result of Social Security).

Table 3.4 clearly illustrates a second major structural failing leading to the high rates of U.S. poverty. It is a failure at the political and policy level. Specifically, social and economic programs directed to economically vulnerable populations in the United States are minimal in their ability to raise families out of poverty. While America has always been a "reluctant welfare state," the past twenty-five years have witnessed an overall retrenchment and reduction in the social safety net. These reductions have included both a scaling back of the amount of benefits being transferred and a tightening of program eligibility (Katz, 2001; Noble, 1997; Patterson, 2000). The United States has also failed to offer the type of universal coverage for child care, medical insurance, or child allowances that most other developed countries routinely provide. As a result, the overall U.S. poverty rates remain at high levels.[5]

This failure has virtually nothing to do with the individual. Rather, it is emblematic of a failure at the structural level. By focusing on individual characteristics, we lose sight of the fact that governments can and do exert a sizable impact on the extent of poverty within their jurisdictions. In the analysis presented here, Canada and Europe are able to lift a significant percentage of their economically vulnerable above the threshold of poverty through governmental transfer and assistance policies. In contrast, the United States provides substantially less support through its social safety net, resulting in poverty rates that are currently among the highest in the industrialized world.[6]

The Widespread Life Course Risk of Poverty

A third approach that reveals the structural nature of American poverty can be found in a life-course analysis of poverty. Previous work on poverty has looked at the cross-sectional and spell dynamic risk. Yet there is another way in which the incidence of poverty can be examined. Such an approach places the risk of poverty within the context of the American life course and thereby reveals the systematic nature of American poverty (this technique and the wider array of findings are discussed at much greater length in chapter 4).

Table 3.5 is constructed through the merging of twenty-five years of information gathered by the nationally representative Panel Study of Income Dynamics. A series of life tables have been generated that calculate the cumulative percentage of the American population that will experience poverty at some point during adulthood. As in tables 3.1 and 3.2, we examine the likelihood of falling below three different poverty thresholds—1.00 (the official poverty line); 1.25 (the poverty line raised by 25 percent); and 1.50 (the poverty line raised by 50 percent).

Table 3.5 provides us with an approximation of the percentage of Americans who will experience at least one year of poverty by the time they reach a particular age. At age 20 (the starting point of the analysis), we can see that 10.6 percent of Americans fall below the poverty line (which is similar to the cross-sectional rate of poverty for twenty-year-olds), with 15 percent falling below the 1.25 threshold and 19.1 percent falling below the 1.50 threshold. By age 35, the percent of Americans experiencing poverty has increased sharply—31.4 percent of Americans have experienced at least one year below the poverty line; 39 percent have experienced at least one year below 1.25 of the poverty line; and 46.9 percent have experienced a year below 1.50 of the poverty line. At age 55, the percentages stand at 45.0, 52.8, and 61.0, and by age 75, they have risen to 58.5, 68, and 76.

TABLE 3.5. The Cumulative Percent of Americans Experiencing Poverty across Adulthood

	Level of Poverty		
Age	Below 1.00 Poverty Line	Below 1.25 Poverty Line	Below 1.50 Poverty Line
20	10.6	15.0	19.1
35	31.4	39.0	46.9
55	45.0	52.8	61.0
75	58.5	68.0	76.0

Source: Panel Study of Income Dynamics, Rank and Hirschl computations.

What these percentages indicate is that a clear majority of Americans will experience poverty at some point during their lifetimes. Rather than an isolated event that occurs only among what has been labeled the "underclass," poverty is an experience that the majority of Americans will encounter firsthand during adulthood.

Such patterns illustrate the systematic characteristic of American poverty, which in turn points to the structural nature of poverty. We can occasionally see widespread examples of this. Consider the economic collapse during the Great Depression of the 1930s. Given the enormity of the collapse, it became clear to many Americans that their neighbors were not directly responsible for the dire economic situation in which they found themselves. This awareness helped provide much of the impetus and justification for the New Deal.

The existence of the "other" America, as noted by Michael Harrington (1962) during the early 1960s, pointed again to the widespread nature of U.S. poverty. The other America was represented by the extremely high rates of poverty found in economically depressed areas such as rural Appalachia and the urban inner city. The War on Poverty during the 1960s was an attempt to address these large-scale structural pockets of poverty amid plenty.

The analysis in this section (dealt with much more extensively in chapter 4) indicates that poverty is as widespread and systematic today as in these examples. Yet we have been unable to see this as a result of not looking in the right direction. By focusing on the life-course risks, the prevalent nature of American poverty is revealed. At some point during adulthood, the majority of Americans will face impoverishment. The approach of emphasizing individual failings or attributes as the primary cause of poverty loses much of its explanatory power in the face of such patterns. Rather, given the widespread occurrence of economic vulnerability, a lifespan analysis points to a third line of evidence, indicating that poverty is more appropriately viewed as a structural failing of American society. As C. Wright Mills observes with respect to unemployment,

> When, in a city of 100,000, only one man is unemployed, that is his personal trouble, and for its relief we properly look to the character of the man, his skills, and his immediate opportunities. But when in a nation of 50 million employees, 15 million men are unemployed, that is an issue, and we may not hope to find its

solution within the range of opportunities open to any one individual. The very structure of opportunities has collapsed. Both the correct statement of the problem and the range of possible solutions require us to consider the economic and political institutions of the society, and not merely the personal situation and character of a scatter of individuals. (1959: 9)

To summarize, three lines of evidence presented here suggest that American poverty is primarily the result of structural inadequacies. These include the lack of adequately paying jobs in the labor market, the ineffectiveness of America's social safety net as a means to pull individuals and families out of poverty, and the fact that a clear majority of Americans will experience poverty at some point during their adulthood years. Other structural failings could have been explored as well (e.g., the inequities in educational quality in the United States, the systematic lack of political power of the economically disenfranchised, or the widespread patterns of racial residential segregation). Nevertheless, the three areas of research discussed here appear critical as we unveil the structural nature of American poverty.

A Structural Vulnerability Explanation of Poverty

Given that poverty is largely rooted in the structure of American society, how might we better understand the specific patterns of poverty and how they play themselves out on a daily basis? In order to answer this question, I turn to what I have earlier referred to as a structural vulnerability explanation of poverty. This perspective has developed out of my prior work examining the lives of welfare recipients (Rank, 1994). It is intended to provide a framework for understanding who loses out at the economic game, while emphasizing that the game itself is structured in a way that ultimately produces economic losers. In this sense, it brings together the prior research on individual human capital and demographic characteristics and my view of the structural roots of poverty, discussed earlier.

There are three basic premises underlying the structural vulnerability perspective. The first is that particular characteristics, such as the lack of human capital, tend to place individuals in a vulnerable state when detrimental events and crises occur. The incidence of these events (e.g., the loss of a job, family breakup, ill health) often result in poverty. A lack of human capital also increases the likelihood that such events will occur (particularly those related to the labor market). In this sense, human capital characteristics help to explain who in the population is likely to encounter poverty more frequently and for longer periods of time.

Second, the acquisition of human capital is strongly influenced by the impact of social class on this process. Those who grow up in working-class or lower-income homes face greater obstacles in their attempts to acquire marketable educations and skills during their lifetime. Additional background characteristics also play a role in the acquisition of human capital, including race, gender, and particular innate abilities.

Finally, while individual characteristics help to explain who loses out at the economic game, the structural forces described earlier ensure that there will be losers in the first place. The dynamic of poverty can be described as a game of musical chairs in which those with the least advantageous characteristics are likely to find themselves without a chair and therefore left standing, with a heightened risk of economic vulnerability. Each of these components is discussed in the following sections.

Economic Vulnerability and Human Capital

Essential to an initial understanding of poverty is the concept of economic vulnerability and an awareness of the importance of the lack of human capital in accentuating such vulnerability. Individuals who are more likely to experience poverty tend to have attributes that put them at a disadvantage in terms of their earnings ability within the labor market.

These attributes can be thought of largely in terms of human capital, or that basket of skills, education, and qualifications that individuals bring with them into the economy (Becker, 1981, 1993). Those who do well in the labor market often do so as a result of the human capital they have acquired (in particular, they possess marketable skills and training). As a result, they are in greater demand by employers and enjoy brighter job and earnings prospects.

On the other hand, those who face an elevated risk of poverty tend to have acquired less valuable human capital. Their educations may be truncated or of an inferior quality, while their job experience and skills may be less marketable. As a result, they are less attractive in the job market. Additional attributes can also limit their ability to compete effectively in the labor market. Households that reside in inner cities or in remote rural areas often face diminished job prospects. Single mothers with young children experience reduced flexibility in their ability to take a job as a result of having to arrange child care. In addition, employers may use factors such as race and gender to screen and/or limit the promotion of potential employees. In short, those who experience poverty are more likely to have attributes that place them at a disadvantage in terms of competing in the labor market.

However, these factors alone do not directly cause poverty. If they were solely responsible, how might we explain the fluid movements of people in and out of poverty, as indicated by the research into the longitudinal dynamics of poverty? As we saw earlier, the typical pattern is that individuals may be poor for one or two years and then get themselves above the poverty line, perhaps experiencing an additional spell of poverty in the future. Furthermore, the life-course patterns of poverty (see chapter 4) also suggest the frequency of short but recurring periods of impoverishment. For many people, their personal characteristics have remained constant, while their poverty status has not. An explanation that focuses solely on human capital cannot in and of itself account for such transitions.

What is argued here is that, because some individuals lack human capital, they experience certain life crises more often and with greater intensity than do others. This appears particularly true in the case of labor market difficulties. Those with less human capital are more likely to experience job instability, longer periods of unemployment, lower wages, and part-time work. Each of these, in turn, is associated with an elevated risk of poverty (as we saw earlier in the section detailing the failings of the labor market).

The lack of human capital also places individuals in a more economically vulnerable position when faced with the loss of employment, changes in family status, illness and incapacitation, and so on. Individuals and families who are marginalized in terms of their ability to participate in the free market system will have a more difficult time weathering such storms. It will take them longer to find jobs, or earn enough to tide them through the breakup of a family. When such events take place, they often throw individuals into poverty for a period of time until they are able to get back on their feet.

A lack of human capital therefore increases the likelihood that particular detrimental economic events will occur (e.g., not having a job that can sustain a family) and also makes it more difficult to weather such events when they do occur. As a result, those who are lacking in human capital might be thought of as walking a very fine line. If nothing out of the ordinary happens, many of these families are able to just get by. However, should a crisis, such as the loss of a job, an unanticipated medical problem, or a costly but needed repair of an automobile, occur, it generally sends the household into an economic tailspin.

Many of the families that I interviewed for my book *Living on the Edge* were straddling the borderline between self-sufficiency and dependence. One wrong step, and they were likely to land back in poverty and on welfare. They simply did not have the resources and assets necessary to tide them over for more than several weeks. For example, I asked Cindy and Jeff Franklin, a married couple with two children, to describe these types of situations,

> Cindy: Well, I think it's running out of money. (Sighs) If something comes up—a car repair or (pause) our refrigerator's on the fritz . . . we have enough money for a nice, adequate, simple lifestyle as long as nothing happens. If something happens, then we really get thrown in a tizzy. And I'd say that's the worst—that's the worst.

> Jeff: Yeah, 'cause just recently, in the last month, the car that we had was about to rust apart. Sort of literally. And so we had to switch cars. And my parents had this car that we've got now, sitting around. They gave it to us for free, but we had to put about two hundred dollars into it just to get it in safe enough condition so that we don't have to constantly be wondering if something's gonna break on it.

> Cindy: I think that sense of having to choose—the car is a real good example of it—having to choose between letting things go—in a situation that's unsafe, or destituting ourselves in order to fix it. Having to make that kind of choice is really hard. (1994: 57)

The phrase "one paycheck away from poverty" is particularly apt in describing the situations for most of these households.

Other work has revealed parallel findings. Studies of blue-collar or working-class families have found a similar dynamic (Halle, 1984; Howell, 1972; Rubin, 1992). Because they have fewer marketable skills and less education, people in these households experience a heightened vulnerability to economic deprivation and poverty. The title of Lillian Rubin's book *Families on the Faultline* exemplifies this notion with regard to working-class families. As Rubin writes,

> These are the men and women, by far the largest part of the American work force, who work at the lower levels of the manufacturing and service sectors of the economy; workers whose education is limited, whose mobility options are severely restricted, and who usually work for an hourly rather than a weekly wage. . . . They go to work every day to provide for their families, often at jobs they hate. But they live on the edge. Any unexpected event—a child's illness, an accident on the job, a brief layoff—threatens to throw them into the abyss. (1994: 30–31)

The first factor, therefore, in understanding the occurrence of poverty is the concept of economic vulnerability and the role that the lack of human capital plays in accentuating such vulnerability. People who have fewer skills and education or who possess other attributes that put them at a disadvantage as they compete in the labor market (such as single parenthood) are more likely to experience detrimental economic events and to be more adversely affected when they occur. These episodes often push individuals and families below the poverty line.

The Impact of Social Class upon Human Capital Acquisition

Given that skills and education bear upon poverty (by causing varying degrees of vulnerability), why are individuals lacking these in the first place? A major reason, often neglected in such discussions, is social class. This is the second component of the structural vulnerability framework.

Analyses of the American system of stratification have shown that, while some amount of social mobility does occur, social class as a whole tends to reproduce itself (Beeghley, 2000; Fischer et al., 1996). Those with working-class or lower-class parents are likely to remain working or lower class themselves. Similarly, those whose parents are affluent are likely to remain affluent. Why? The reason is that parents' class differences result in significant differences in the resources and opportunities available to their children. These differences in turn affect children's future life chances and outcomes, including the accumulation of skills and education. While it is certainly possible for someone to rise from rags to riches, that tends to be much more the exception than the rule. Again turning to Lillian Rubin's analysis,

> Our denial notwithstanding, then, class inequalities not only exist in our society, they're handed down from parents to children in the same way that wealth is passed along in the upper class. True, American society has always had a less rigid and clearly defined class structure than many other nations. Poor people climb up; wealthy ones fall. These often well-publicized figures help to fuel the myth about equality of opportunity. But they're not the norm. Nor is the perpetuation of our class structure accidental. The economy, the polity, and the educational system all play their part in ensuring the continuity and stability of our social classes. (1994: 36)

Differences in income and social class transmitted from one generation to the next are critical in explaining the differences in human capital and skill that exist in today's society.

A game analogy illustrates this process. Imagine three players beginning a game of Monopoly. Normally, each player is given $1,500 at the start of the game. The playing field is in effect level, with each of the players' outcomes determined by the roll of the dice and by their own skills and judgments.

Now let us imagine a modified game of Monopoly, in which the players start out with quite different advantages and disadvantages, much as they would in life. Player 1 begins with $5,000 and several Monopoly properties on which houses have already been built. Player 2 starts out with the standard $1,500 and no properties. Finally, player 3 begins the game with only $250.

Who will be the winners and losers in this modified game of Monopoly? Both luck and skill are still involved, but given the differing sets of resources and assets that each player begins with, these become much less important in predicting the game's outcome. Certainly, it is possible for player 1, with $5,000, to lose, and for player 3, with $250, to win, but that is unlikely given the unequal allocation of money at the start of the game. Moreover, while player 3 may win in any individual game, over the course of hundreds of games, the odds are that player 1 will win considerably more often, even if player 3 is much luckier and more skilled.

In addition, the way each of the three individuals is able to play the game will vary considerably. Player 1 is able to take greater chances and risks. If he or she makes several tactical mistakes, these probably will not matter much in the larger scheme of things. If Player 3 makes one such mistake, it may very well result in disaster. Player 1 will also be easily able to purchase assets in the form of properties and houses that Player 3 is largely locked out of. These assets, in turn, will generate further income later in the game for Player 1 and in all likelihood will result in the bankrupting of Player 3.

This analogy illustrates the concept that Americans are not beginning their lives at the same starting point. Differences in parental incomes and resources exert a major influence over children's ability to acquire valuable skills and education. These differences in human capital will, in turn, strongly influence how well such children are able to compete in the labor market and therefore determine the extent of their economic vulnerability during the course of their lives.

The argument that the economic race is run as an altered game of Monopoly has been confirmed in an array of empirical work. Research over the past fifteen years has revealed a sizable correlation between father's and son's incomes, averaging around .4 (Aughinbaugh, 2000; Corcoran et al., 1992; Mulligan, 1997; Solon, 1989, 1992, Zimmerman, 1992). To illustrate what this means, if a father has a level of income that falls in the bottom 5 percent of the income distribution, 42 percent of the sons of such a father will wind up in the bottom quintile of the income distribution when they grow up, while only 5 percent will reach the top quintile. On the other hand, if a father has an income in the top 5 percent of the income distribution, 42 percent of his sons will earn incomes in the top quintitle of the income distribution, while only 5 percent will fall into the bottom quintile (Solon, 1989, 1992).

Another way of conceptualizing this association is that a correlation of .4 is approximately the correlation between fathers' and sons' heights. Thus, "if people's incomes were represented by their heights, the similarity in income between generations would resemble the similarity observed in the heights of fathers and sons" (Krueger, 2002). Recent studies have found even higher correlations. For example, using Social Security records for fathers' and sons' earnings, Bhashkar Mazumder (2001) reported an intergenerational correlation of .6.[7]

Research on the transmission of occupational status has also found a strong connection between parents and children. For example, Daniel McMurrer and Isabel Sawhill report that children of professionals are "significantly more likely to become professionals as adults, and children of blue collar workers significantly more likely to work in blue collar occupations. . . . Men with white collar origins are almost twice as likely as those with blue collar origins to end up in upper white collar jobs" (1997: 2).

If one looks at the transmission of wealth, a similar pattern emerges. William Gale and John Scholz (1994) estimate that intended family transfers and bequests account for 51 percent of current U.S. wealth, while an additional 12 percent is acquired through the payment of college expenses by parents. Consequently, approximately two-thirds of the net worth that individuals acquire comes through family transfers. Parents with considerable wealth are able to pass on these assets and advantages to their children. As a result, it is estimated that "children of the very rich have roughly 40 times better odds of being very rich than do the children of the poor" (Gokhale and Kotlikoff, 2002: 268).

Additional work has focused on the impact that growing up in poverty has upon one's later economic well-being (Duncan et al., 1998; Corcoran, 2002; Gottschalk, McLanahan, and Sandfur, 1994; Rank and Cheng, 1995). In our Monopoly example, this might represent the player who begins the game with $250. Joan Rodgers (1995) has found that of those who experienced poverty as an adult, 50 percent had experienced poverty as a child, while an additional 38 percent had grown up in homes that were defined as near-poor (below 2.00 of the poverty line). Once again, we see that the social class in which a child is reared has a profound impact on that child's later economic well-being and outcomes. In summarizing this body of research, Mary Corcoran writes,

These studies strongly support the economic resources model:
Parental economic resources consistently predict children's adult
attainments. They predict all outcomes and have large impacts
on men's labor supply, wages and earnings. Furthermore,
parental income effects on labor market outcomes are nonlinear:
Being poor matters a lot. (1995: 261)

This is not to say that economic movement is nonexistent. Individuals do move up and down the economic ladder across adulthood (Duncan, 1988; McMurrer and Sawhill, 1998; Rank and Hirschl, 2001c). However, when such movement does happen, people often do not move far from their economic origins. In fact, contrary to popular myth, the United States tends to have somewhat less intergenerational mobility than a number of other developed countries (Kangas, 2000). The empirical evidence clearly points to the fact that children from lower-class backgrounds face a much greater risk of economic vulnerability in their adult lives than do children from wealthier families.

The reason for this is that children from working-class backgrounds simply do not have the range and depth of opportunities that children from middle- or upper-class backgrounds enjoy. This affects the quantity and quality of human capital they are able to acquire. The discussion in chapter 2 regarding the impact of poverty upon children's development illustrates this point. Likewise, the vast differences in educational quality according to residence and income illuminate the magnitude of these opportunity differences.

The work of Thomas Shapiro (Shapiro, 2004; Shapiro and Johnson, 2000) illustrates the manner in which wealthier families are able to utilize their assets (a significant portion of which have been received through inheritance and/or gifts from parents) in order to acquire high-quality primary and secondary educations for their children. This is accomplished either by purchasing a home in an affluent school district or by sending their children to private schools. In-depth interviews conducted with scores of parents in Boston, St. Louis, and Los Angeles made this point abundantly clear. As Shapiro and Johnson note, "By accessing quality school systems parents ensure specific kinds of schooling for their children and in this way help to pass their own social position along to the next generation" (2000: 2).

And, of course, this process continues with higher education. Children from wealthier families are often able to attend elite private universities, children from middle-class backgrounds enroll at state public universities, while children from lower-class backgrounds will probably not continue on to college, and, if they do, they will likely attend a community or two-year college. As McMurrer and Sawhill note,

> family background has a significant and increasing effect on who goes to college, where, and for how long. With the rewards for going to college greater than ever, and family background now a

stronger influence over who reaps those rewards, the United States is at risk of becoming more class stratified in coming decades. (1998: 69)

Beyond social class, there are several other factors that clearly play a role in the acquisition of human capital. A sizable amount of research over the years has established that race exerts a powerful effect upon the life chances of children apart from social class (Duncan, 1968; Feagin, 2000; Jencks, 1979; Moss and Tilly, 2001; Oliver and Shapiro, 1995; Rank and Hirschl, 2001b).[8] For example, patterns of racial residential segregation ensure that more black children find themselves in schools that are severely segregated and that lack resources than do white children from similar social class backgrounds (Massey and Denton, 1993; Orfield and Yun, 1999). These patterns, albeit to a lesser extent, also apply to Latino children. Gender has also been shown to impact upon the acquisition of human capital. Throughout their schooling, girls are more likely to be steered into less lucrative career paths (Blau et al., 2002). Finally, differences in innate abilities such as cognitive reasoning can play a role in the acquisition of human capital.[9] All of these factors influence the ability of children to acquire human capital and compete effectively in the labor market.

Consequently, where one begins one's life exerts a powerful effect throughout the life course. This process was succinctly described by Howard Wachtel:

> If you are black, female, have parents with low socioeconomic status, and [are] dependent upon labor income, there is a high probability that you will have relatively low levels of human capital which will slot you into low-paying jobs, in low wage industries, in low wage markets. With this initial placement, the individual is placed in a high risk category, destined to end up poor sometime during her working and nonworking years. She may earn her poverty by working fulltime. Or she may suffer either sporadic or long periods of unemployment. Or she may become disabled, thereby reducing her earning power even further. Or when she retires, social security payments will place her in poverty even if she escaped this fate throughout her working years. With little savings, wealth, or private pension income, the retiree will be poor. (1971: 6)

Thus, in order to understand why people are lacking in skills and education in the first place, it is important to look at the economic status of the families in which they grew up. It is a process often neglected in political and policy discussions, but unfortunately the class you are born into has wide ranging implications upon your life course.[10] As Billie Holiday sang more than fifty years ago, "Them that's got shall get, them that's not shall lose. So the Bible says, and it still is news."

Two Levels of Understanding Poverty

A third component of the structural vulnerability perspective is the realization that there are two levels to understanding impoverishment. On one hand, we can identify who is more likely to experience poverty by understanding the impact that human capital has on individual economic vulnerability, as discussed earlier. On the other hand, we can ascertain why poverty occurs in the first place by looking at the structural failings discussed in the first half of this chapter. To illustrate these two levels, we can use another analogy—that of musical chairs. The key is whether one chooses to analyze the losers of the game or the game itself.

Let us imagine eight chairs and ten players. The players begin to circle around the chairs until the music stops. Who fails to find a chair? If we focus on the winners and losers of the game, we will find that some combination of luck and skill will be involved. In all likelihood, the losers will be those in an unfavorable position when the music stops, those who are somewhat slower, less agile, and so on. In one sense, these are appropriately cited as the reasons for losing the game.

However, if we focus on the game itself, then it is quite clear that, given only eight chairs, two players are bound to lose. Even if every player were suddenly to double his or her speed and agility, there would still be two losers. From this broader context, it really does not matter what the loser's characteristics are, given that two are destined to lose.

I would argue that this musical-chairs analogy can be applied to what has occurred in America economically, socially, and politically. Given that there is unemployment that translates into a shortage of jobs; given that we are producing more and more low-paying jobs that lack benefits; given that countless inner-city and rural communities have been devastated by economic restructuring; given the weak safety net in place to provide economic protection to the vulnerable; given that there is a scarcity of decent-quality, affordable child care; given that there are few provisions to care for those who can no longer participate in the economy because of illness—someone is going to lose at this game.

The losers will generally be those who are lacking in skills, education, and training and who therefore cannot compete as effectively as and are more vulnerable than their counterparts who have acquired greater skills and education. In one sense, we can focus on these deficits as the reasons for why individuals are at a greater risk of becoming poor.

Yet if we focus on the game itself, then the causes of poverty change from the individual's lack of skills or education to the fact that the economy produces unemployment, creates low-paying jobs, bypasses low-income communities, offers few social supports and protection, lacks affordable child care, and does not provide for those who can no longer participate economically due to illness. These then become the fundamental reasons that people are poor in this country. The discussion in the first half of this chapter provided empirical evidence about the magnitude of these structural failings, illustrating the mismatch between the number of opportunities and the number of Americans in need of such opportunities.

The degree and intensity of these structural failings may certainly vary over time. In our musical-chairs analogy, there may be nine chairs for every ten players, or only six or seven. Likewise, the circumstances surrounding the economic game can and do change, in turn affecting the overall number of losers. Such changes result from a variety of factors, including economic conditions, public policy initiatives and changes, and demographic shifts in the population. The number of losers produced by the economic, social and political systems in this country is therefore not written in stone.

For example, during the 1930s, the Great Depression resulted in a dramatic reduction in the number of economic opportunities, resulting in widespread unemployment and poverty. During this period of time, the number of available chairs for the participants in the game was significantly reduced. On the other hand, the 1960s saw a booming economy coupled with federal initiatives to address poverty. The result was a dramatic increase in the number of chairs available and a significant drop in the overall rates of poverty during the decade. Nevertheless, while the ratio of opportunities to participants fluctuates over time, at any given point there tends to be a significant number of losers produced by the overall game.

What this means is that when we focus solely on personal characteristics, such as education, we can shuffle individual people up or down in terms of their being more likely to find a job, but we are still going to have somebody lose out if there are not enough decent-paying jobs to go around. In short, we are playing a game of musical chairs in this country with ten players but only eight chairs.

Many examples of this mismatch exist in today's society. Perhaps the most important is the earlier mentioned imbalance between the number of jobs that can support a family in the current economy and the number of families in need of such jobs. In his study of long-term unemployment, Thomas Cottle talked with one man who had worked for twenty-five years for the same company, only to be downsized. After two and a half years of searching, he eventually found a job at a much lower pay, but felt fortunate to have such a job, nonetheless. He referred to his job search using the musical chairs analogy:

> The musical chairs of work still have me in the game. The music
> plays, we run around, the music stops and I dive for a chair.
> Took me two and half years to find this last one, I don't want the
> music to stop again. I'm only fifty-two, but pretty soon they'll
> take all the chairs away. Then what? That's the part I don't want
> to think about. (2001: 216)

Or take the mismatch between the number of people in economically depressed geographical areas and the number of opportunities in such areas. This is particularly apparent for those who reside in urban inner cities or in remote rural regions. Such areas are not hard to find—the rural Mississippi Delta; metropolitan Cleveland or Detroit; American Indian reservations across the Southwest; the Appalachian mountain region. In these cases, economic opportunities have largely moved away (or were never there in the first place), leaving many scrambling for the few chairs that are left. William Julius Wilson documents this process in his study of inner-city Chicago residents, aptly titled *When Work Disappears* (1996). Wilson states, "The increasing suburbanization of employment has accompanied industrial restructuring and has further exacerbated the problems of inner-city joblessness and restricted access to jobs" (1996: 37).[11] Illustrative of this is Katherine Newman's ethnography of jobs and economic conditions in central Harlem during the mid-1990s, in which she found that there were as many as fourteen applicants for each fast-food job offered (1999).

Similarly, Dwight Billings and Kathleen Blee (2000) describe the process of diminishing jobs and opportunities in rural Appalachia, with thousands left behind who must compete with one another for the dwindling number of viable economic opportunities. As Cynthia Duncan notes,

> There are so few jobs available in these communities, and so many who need work, that people seek fast-food and other part-time retail work in order to support their families. But the jobs are set up for those who do not need them to offer a living wage. When household heads do get these jobs, their hours are always uncertain and unpredictable, always subject to change. (1992: 120)[12]

In these cases it is relatively easy to visualize the mismatch between the number of players and the number of chairs. Yet such a mismatch is operating nationally, as was demonstrated in the first half of this chapter. This mismatch illustrates the third point of the structural vulnerability explanation of poverty—given the structural failures, a certain percentage of the American population will experience economic vulnerability regardless of its characteristics. As in the musical-chairs analogy, the game is structured so that some of the players are bound to lose. As Cindy Franklin, who discussed earlier her problems with unanticipated expenses, put it,

> There are only so many good-paying jobs that exist in this society, and there are tons and tons of minimum wage jobs. And as long as we expect people to work them, there are gonna be people who can't make it without help. There's only so many people can rise to the top, and then no more can. (Rank, 1994: 127)

Increasing everyone's human capital will do little to alter the fact that there are only a limited number of decent-paying jobs available. In such a case, employers will simply raise the bar in terms of their employee qualifications, leaving behind a more qualified percentage of the population at risk of economic deprivation. Consequently, although understanding the role of human capital helps us to see who the losers of the economic game are likely to be, the structural components of our economic, social, and political systems explain why there are losers in the first place.

Pulling It Together

As noted at the beginning of this chapter, researchers and social commentators who investigate poverty have largely focused on individual deficiencies and demographic attributes in order to explain the occurrence of poverty in America. In doing so, they have reinforced the mainstream American predilection for interpreting social problems as primarily the result of individual failings. In contrast, this chapter has argued that the dynamic of poverty can be better grasped through a perspective of structural vulnerability.

This framework is illustrated in figure 3.1. It suggests that there are two ways of understanding individual vulnerability to poverty. Paths A and B deal with the question of *who* is at risk of poverty in America, while paths C and D focus on the question of *why* poverty exists in America.

The bulk of the empirical research pertaining to American poverty has focused on path A. Economists, sociologists, and demographers have concerned themselves with understanding the individual attributes that are associated with a greater risk of impoverishment. As we have discussed earlier, these attributes can largely be understood in terms of their role in limiting an individual's ability to compete in the labor market. Those with less education, fewer job skills, health problems, single mothers, or minorities living in inner cities, will face a heightened vulnerability to poverty.

Path B suggests that several background characteristics largely determine which Americans are more likely to be lacking in such human capital. The most important of these is social class. Those who grow up in lower- or working-class families are more likely to have their acquisition of human capital assets truncated. Race, gender, and differences in innate abilities can also play a role in influencing the acquisition of human capital.

Paths A and B therefore explain who in America faces the greatest risk of experiencing poverty during their lives. The critical mistake has been the following: poverty analysts have confused the question of *who* is at risk of poverty with the question of *why* poverty exists. They have stopped at Path A in their explanation of poverty. According to mainstream research, the question of why poverty exists is typically answered by noting that the poor are lacking in education, skills, and so on and that these are the reasons for impoverishment. We can see in figure 3.1 that this is an incomplete and misleading account.

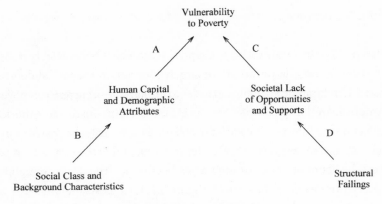

FIGURE 3.1. Structural vulnerability model of poverty.

The right side of the structural vulnerability model presents paths C and D. These explain why so many Americans are at an elevated risk of poverty. Path C suggests that the lack of opportunities and social supports is a critical reason for this risk. As discussed earlier, there is a mismatch between the number of jobs that will adequately support a family and the number of families in need of such jobs. Likewise, American society has failed to provide the necessary supports for those in need—U.S. social policy has been marked by a tattered safety net, inadequate child care assistance, lack of health care coverage, a dearth of affordable low-cost housing, and so on. This lack of economic opportunities and social supports has significantly raised the number of Americans vulnerable to the risk of poverty.

The shortage of opportunities and adequate supports has been produced by structural failings at the economic and political levels (path D). The tendency of our free-market economy has been to produce a growing number of jobs that will no longer support a family.[13] In addition, the basic nature of capitalism ensures that unemployment exists at modest levels. Both of these directly result in a shortage of economic opportunities in American society. On the other hand, the absence of social supports stems from failings at the political and policy levels. The United States has traditionally lacked the political desire to put in place effective policies and programs to support the economically vulnerable. Structural failings at both the economic and the political levels have therefore produced a lack of opportunities and supports, resulting in high rates of American poverty.[14]

We can think of the dynamic of poverty as a large-scale game of musical chairs. For every ten American households, there are good jobs and opportunities at any point in time to adequately support roughly eight of those ten. The remaining two households will be shut out of such opportunities, often resulting in poverty or near-poverty. Individuals who experience such economic deprivation are likely to have characteristics that put them at a disadvantage in terms of competing in the economy (e.g., less education, fewer skills, head of a single-parent family, illness or incapacitation, member of a racial or ethnic minority residing in an inner city). These characteristics help to explain why particular individuals and households are at a greater risk of poverty.

Yet given the earlier discussed structural failures, a certain percentage of the American population will experience economic vulnerability regardless of their characteristics. The structure of the American economy, along with its weak social safety net and the inadequacy of public policies directed toward the economically vulnerable, ensures that millions of Americans will experience impoverishment at any point in time and that a much larger number will experience poverty over the course of a lifetime. The fact that three-quarters of Americans will experience poverty or near-poverty (at the 1.50 level) during their adulthoods is emblematic of these structural-level failings.

In summary, the approach taken in this chapter is intended to provide a new framework for understanding the dynamics of American poverty.[15] Previous work has generally placed this dynamic within the framework of individual deficiencies. I have argued here that such a perspective is misdirected. Whereas individual attributes (such as human capital) help to explain who faces a greater risk of experiencing poverty at any point in time, the fact that substantial poverty exists on a national level can be understood only through an analysis of the structural dynamics of American society.

Understanding the reasons behind poverty is essential not only for appreciating the nature of poverty, but also for building our individual and societal responses to the condition of American poverty. If poverty is viewed as affecting a small proportion of the population that is plagued by moral failings and individual inadequacies, our individual and societal response will likely follow the familiar course we have taken in the past. That direction has been to assume relatively little collective responsibility for the problem of poverty, while continually focusing on welfare reform initiatives that attempt to strengthen the work and family incentives for the poor. This approach has accomplished very little in terms of alleviating poverty.

On the other hand, if poverty is viewed as a failing at the structural level, this suggests a very different approach for building an effective response to the issue (taken up in chapters 7–9). It also implies the need for a reexamination of our individual and personal connections to the issue of poverty. We now embark on such an exploration.

A Cause for Concern

II

In Our
Self-Interest

Your own property is at stake when your neighbor's house is on fire.

Horace

4

DURING MY YEARS IN the classroom as an undergraduate and then a graduate student, I was introduced to various social issues and problems. Yet throughout this training, my social science background was noticeably silent on one critical question—Why care? Perhaps this was viewed as the territory of political activism, philosophy, or religious studies. In hindsight, such an omission was a mistake. If one of the principal goals of the social sciences is to improve the human condition, then we are taking necessary but insufficient steps toward that realization by describing a problem's dynamic. Unquestionably, these are important steps to take—indeed, the first third of this book deals precisely with this issue. However, we must also provide convincing arguments regarding the importance of rectifying a problem. Only then will we be in a strong position to advocate for solutions. The next three chapters attempt to provide the impetus needed to foster a desire to address the condition of poverty.

Such an impetus was not always so noticeably lacking. In its infancy, the social sciences had much more to say about such issues. Twenty years after the founding of the American Social Science Association (which existed from 1865 to 1909), Frank Sanborn noted that its purpose was "To learn patiently what is—and to promote diligently what should be—this is the double duty of all the social sciences" (quoted in Pickering, 1988).

Throughout the past one hundred years, the social scientific disciplines have moved away from incorporating ethical or pragmatic issues into their discussions.[1] We are then left with this situation: no matter how sound the description, causal analysis, and potential strategies for addressing a problem, if people really do not give a damn, it is, as they say, an academic exercise.

The result has been a noticeable gap between the analysis of an issue and a researcher's claim that a particular issue should be of concern to most Americans. For example, much has been researched and written regarding the rising tide of income inequality in the United States. Yet social scientists have offered little to explain why Americans should concern themselves with these trends and patterns.

Such a gap is unfortunately present in the vast majority of social scientific writing on societal problems. Perhaps we (as social scientists) assume that because these are important issues in our own minds (after all, we spend most of our lives examining a handful of topics), others should feel the same. However, unless I can convince you of the validity and urgency of the problem, my analyses stand a good chance of sitting on the shelf gathering dust.

The next three chapters discuss why poverty is a pressing issue for America. These chapters clarify some of the reasons the current nonpoor should be concerned about the poor. Establishing such a connection is vital in demonstrating who and what is at stake if we allow poverty to walk in our midst. Lasting progress in the reduction of poverty will be made when a sizable number of citizens feel an imperative to do so and are willing to work toward such a goal. The first step down that road occurs within the minds and consciousness of people. Such a process starts when we are challenged to look critically at our own ideas, beliefs, and values. This is where the seeds of change begin.

Many of this country's directional changes and revolutions have started here. For example, John Adams wrote in 1815 to Thomas Jefferson regarding the American Revolution, "What do we mean by the revolution? The war? That was no part of the revolution; it was only an effect and consequence of it. The revolution was in the minds of the people, and this was effected from 1760 to 1775, in the course of fifteen years, before a drop of blood was shed at Lexington" (Platt, 1989: 304). Adams went on to write several years later, "The Revolution was in the minds and hearts of the people; a change in their religious sentiments of their duties and obligations. . . . This radical change in the principles, opinions, sentiments and affections of the people, was the real American Revolution" (Andrews, 1993: 785). In the years leading up to 1776, many colonists had come to the realization that the status quo was unwise, unjust, and intolerable. This state of consciousness, as Adams points out, set the stage for the American Revolution.

Today, as was the case for the colonists more than two centuries ago, I believe we must conclude that the status quo of widespread poverty within our borders is also unwise, unjust, and intolerable. The purpose of these chapters is to carefully and convincingly present this point of view.

I argue this point on three grounds. First, it is in the self-interest of Americans to do so. Poverty drains us both individually and as a community and society. Each of us directly and indirectly pays a high price for allowing poverty to walk in our midst. In addition, given the precarious economic position occupied by a growing number of Americans, it is in our individual self-interest to ensure that society provides reasonable protections against the ravages of poverty (since there but for the grace of God go I). In fact, as touched upon in the prior chapter, I will demonstrate that a majority of Americans will at some point in their lives experience at least one year lived below the poverty line.

Second, the goal of reducing poverty is consistent with two core sets of values held in high esteem by the majority of Americans. These are the Judeo-Christian ethic and the founding civic values that have shaped this country. If we truly believe in such values and principles, then the reduction of poverty is highly consistent with, and in fact critical, to their realization.

Third, as members of communities larger than simply ourselves, we have a shared obligation and responsibility to alleviate grievous ills, such as poverty, that befall other members of our community. This position is based on the assertion that the concept of citizenship necessitates a sense of shared responsibility and stewardship. Such obligations become particularly binding when it can be demonstrated that a specific problem, such as poverty, is largely the product of structural inequities within our system.

Thus, I will make a three-pronged argument, asserting that a substantial reduction in poverty is in our self-interest, is consistent with many of our most important values, and is our shared responsibility. Each of these lines of thinking will be developed in detail.

Ultimately, this section of the book is about building bridges. The bridges I am constructing are from the nonpoor to the poor, and back again, creating a more accessible route for traveling from one side to the other. As discussed earlier, part of the problem in our thinking about poverty is that we have not constructed such bridges. As a result, we fail to notice the poor, or we view them with distant compassion, or perhaps with hostility. Too rarely do we see the poor as part of the community in which we live. Rarer still do we understand the implications that poverty has for us all. I believe that in order for positive action to take place, we must begin to see poverty in this new and different light.

I begin with the issue of self-interest. Of the criteria I am asking readers to consider, this is arguably the most powerful. Although we are motivated by various concerns during our lives, self-interest is undoubtedly close to the top for many of us. As the Australian prime minister Gough Whitlam wrote in the London *Daily Telegraph*, "The punters know that the horse named Morality rarely gets past the post, whereas the nag named Self-Interest always runs a good race" (Andrews, 1993: 824).

The Risk of Poverty across the American Life Course

There is a very direct way of thinking about poverty in terms of self-interest: what are the chances that an average American will face poverty during his or her adulthood? The answer to this question can reveal the extent to which addressing poverty is in our own direct self-interest.

As touched upon in chapter 3, the notion of poverty as an economic risk in the lives of Americans is a qualitatively different paradigm from that which has existed in this country. The public has historically viewed poverty as something that happens outside the mainstream American experience, often to marginalized groups (Gans, 1995; Wolfe, 1998). Yet to what extent is this true? In this section we explore the life-course risk of poverty and the use of welfare across the American life span.

Poverty as a Life-Course Event

The research findings that were discussed in chapter 2 have added much to our knowledge regarding the nature and dynamics of poverty. They have provided insights into the yearly rates of poverty, as well as the average length of time that individuals are poor. Yet there is a very different way of thinking about and gauging the impact of poverty. It is an approach that places poverty within the context of the entire adult life course. Impoverishment is then analyzed as a life-course event that may or may not occur across adulthood.

Various questions come to mind. To what extent is poverty a "normal" life-course event? How likely is it that an American will encounter a relatively short spell of poverty, rather than a much longer spell? What impact do one's race, gender, and education have on one's odds of experiencing poverty during adulthood? Is it possible that a majority of the American population will rely upon a welfare program at some point during their lives? These and many other questions can be analyzed through a life-course approach, which are directly relevant to the question of self-interest.

The concept of the life course has had a long and distinguished history within the social sciences (Settersten and Mayer, 1997). It has proven to be an extremely helpful tool in thinking about the manner in which individual lives unfold (Elder, 1996). The term itself refers to "social processes extending over the individual lifespan or over significant portions of it, especially [with regard to] the family cycle, educational and training histories, and employment and occupational careers" (Mayer and Tuma, 1990: 3). In addition, as Settersten and Mayer argue, "While these dimensions describe the primary activities across life, a more complete picture of the life course must also include more marginal periods and events—such as brief periods of training, second or part-time jobs, periods of unemployment or sickness" (1997: 252). Poverty should certainly be included in this list as well.

Interestingly, some of the earliest social scientific work on poverty attempted to place it within a life-course framework. Seebohm Rowntree's (1901) description of 11,560 working-class families in the English city of York is illustrative. For each family, Rowntree estimated the likelihood of falling below the poverty line at various stages of the life course (on the basis of their household economic conditions in 1899). His calculations were limited in that they were projected from only one point in time. Nevertheless,

Rowntree's work was seminal in the development of the concept of the life cycle. His research indicated that working-class families were more likely to experience poverty at certain economically vulnerable stages along the life cycle (e.g., while starting a new family or during retirement). In addition, Rowntree's analysis demonstrated that a life-course perspective could more fully reveal the widespread nature of poverty than a point-in-time approach. As he wrote, "The proportion of the community who at one period or another of their lives suffer from poverty to the point of physical privation is therefore much greater, and the injurious effects of such a condition are much more widespread than would appear from a consideration of the number who can be shown to be below the poverty line at any given moment" (1901: 172).

Likewise, Robert Hunter, in his book *Poverty* (1904), attempted to place impoverishment within the context of the life course. Poverty was viewed as a critical life event that tended to occur for working-class families at several points during their life cycle.

In spite of these early writings, poverty as a potential life-course event has been largely overlooked in the research and policy communities during the twentieth century. As Ralf Dahrendorf notes,

> Arguably the most exciting dimension of social analysis is time.
> Yet it has long been neglected by mainstream sociology. Much of
> the study of social stratification, even of mobility, is static, based
> on snapshots which ignore the place of such moments in
> people's life histories. (1999: ix)

The difficulty, of course, has been finding a way to measure events across a prolonged period of time such as thirty, forty, or even fifty years. Retrospective or life history data may be gathered from older individuals, but they are plagued with problems of reliability and are confined to a cohort of the population that has been shaped by very specific historical experiences, making it difficult to generalize results to the rest of the population. The problem of finding a suitable methodological approach and data for this type of analysis is daunting.

In order to resolve these issues, I turn to an extremely valuable and unique data set that has been utilized in a number of the earlier mentioned studies. The Panel Study of Income Dynamics (or PSID) is an ongoing study that has followed the same individuals and households each year from 1968 to the present.[2] It constitutes the longest-running panel data set in the world. It was specifically designed to track income dynamics over time and is therefore ideally suited for the purpose at hand. In addition, because of its large, representative sample, results can be generalized to the U.S. population as a whole.

The PSID initially interviewed approximately 4,800 U.S. households in 1968, obtaining detailed information on roughly 18,000 individuals in those households. These individuals have been tracked annually, including children and adults who eventually broke off from their original households to form new households (for example, children who left home; adults after separation or divorce). Those who dropped out of the study were replaced with individuals with similar characteristics. Thus, the PSID was designed so that in any given year the sample would be representative of the entire nonimmigrant U.S. population.

The tables in this section are built from information that spans the years 1968–1997.[3] Taken together, there are thirty waves of longitudinal information embedded in the analysis, which translates into roughly 300,000 person-years of information. The analytical strategy is to use the household income and demographic information on individuals throughout this thirty-year period in order to construct several life tables that estimate the risk of poverty and welfare use across the adult lifespan.

The life table is a technique that demographers and medical researchers frequently use. For example, when we say that an individual born during the past year has an average life expectancy of seventy-eight years, such an estimate is derived from a life table analysis. The life table examines the extent to which specific events occur across intervals of time. In the analysis presented here, our time intervals are each year an individual ages. During those years, we can calculate the probability that an event will occur (in this case poverty) for those who have yet to experience the event. Furthermore, on the basis of these age-specific probabilities, the cumulative probabilities that an event will occur across the life span can be calculated. These cumulative probabilities and percentages represent the core of the analysis (for a more extended discussion of the methodology involved, see appendix A).

The life table thus allows us to understand the concepts of time and risk very differently from the way we typically think of them. It enables us to envision poverty as a potential risk within the context of a lifetime. We now examine that risk.[4]

The Likelihood of Poverty

Our first table provides the cumulative percentage of the American population that will experience at least one year of poverty across the adult years (for additional life tables analyzing the risk of poverty to children and the elderly, see appendix B). These are shown at five-year intervals. The likelihood of falling below the official poverty line, 125 percent of the poverty line, 150 percent of the poverty line, and 50 percent of the poverty line are included.

Looking at the 1.00 level, we can see that at age 20 (the start of the analysis), 10.6 percent of the population are below the official poverty line. By age 40, 35.6 percent of Americans have experienced at least one year of poverty during their early adulthood. By age 60, the percentage has risen to 48.2. By the time Americans have reached age 75, 58.5 percent of the population have passed a year in poverty.[5]

As mentioned in the prior chapter, what these percentages strikingly reveal is that rather than being an event occurring among a small minority of the U.S. population, poverty is an experience that touches a clear majority of Americans at some point during their adult lifetimes. The life table approach offers a very different perspective on the nature of poverty than either the cross-sectional snapshots provided by surveys such as the U.S. Census Bureau's or the earlier cited studies of length of time in poverty.

The third and fourth columns of table 4.1 show the percentage of Americans who fall below 125 and 150 percent of the poverty line at some point during their adulthood. These capture the experience of poverty and near-poverty conditions. At age 20, 15 percent of the population fall below 1.25 of the poverty line, while 19.1 percent fall below 1.50 of poverty line. By age 40, the percentages are 43.6 and 51.7 percent; by age 60, 56.1 and 64.2 percent; and by age 75, 68 and 76 percent.

Finally, the far left column of table 4.1 contains the estimates for experiencing dire poverty, as measured by falling below one-half of the official poverty line. Here we can see that at age 20, 3.1 percent of Americans fall below this level. By age 40, 18.4 percent of Americans have experienced a year in extreme poverty; by age 60, 28.4 percent; and by age 75, 32.9 percent. The likelihood of experiencing dire poverty is therefore substantially less than that of falling below the official poverty line, but, nevertheless, one-third of the U.S. population between ages 20 and 75 have experienced such dire need.

TABLE 4.1. The Cumulative Percent of Americans Who Experience Poverty across Adulthood

	Level of Poverty			
Age	Below .50 Poverty Line	Below 1.00 Poverty Line	Below 1.25 Poverty Line	Below 1.50 Poverty Line
20	3.1	10.6	15.0	19.1
25	9.7	21.6	27.8	34.3
30	13.2	27.1	34.1	41.3
35	16.1	31.4	39.0	46.9
40	18.4	35.6	43.6	51.7
45	21.2	38.8	46.7	55.0
50	23.2	41.8	49.6	57.9
55	25.9	45.0	52.8	61.0
60	28.4	48.2	56.1	64.2
65	30.2	51.4	59.7	67.5
70	31.3	55.0	63.6	71.8
75	32.9	58.5	68.0	76.0

Source: Panel Study of Income Dynamics, Rank and Hirschl computations.

In sum, this table indicates that poverty is an event that touches a surprisingly high percentage of Americans at some point during their adult years. By age 75, 32.9 percent of Americans have experienced poverty at the .50 level, 58.5 percent of Americans have spent at least one year of their adulthood below the poverty line, 68 percent have encountered poverty at the 1.25 level, and 76 percent of the adult population have fallen below 1.50 of the poverty line.

Table 4.2 extends this analysis by looking at the likelihood that one will spend a longer period of time below the poverty line. This is examined in two different ways. The upper panel of table 4.2 shows the cumulative percentages of Americans who encounter shorter versus longer spells of poverty during adulthood. This reveals the risk of encountering one, two, three, four, and five or more consecutive years below the poverty line. The lower panel provides the total number of years poverty is experienced across the life course (regardless of whether the years experienced are consecutive). This is calculated for one, two, three, four, and five or more total years. The first column in both panels is identical to that found in column two in table 4.1.

Looking at the figures for consecutive years, it is clear that the chances of experiencing long periods of time below the poverty line are fairly low. By the age of forty, 35.6 percent of the population will have encountered one

TABLE 4.2. The Cumulative Percent of Americans Who Experience Various Years in Poverty across Adulthood

	Years				
Age	1 or More	2 or More	3 or More	4 or More	5 or More
Consecutive Years Experienced					
20	10.6	—	—	—	—
25	21.6	9.5	5.2	2.1	1.2
30	27.1	12.5	7.4	3.3	2.0
35	31.4	15.4	9.8	4.6	2.8
40	35.6	17.9	11.4	5.7	3.5
45	38.8	20.0	12.9	6.7	4.2
50	41.8	21.8	14.3	7.6	4.7
55	45.0	23.7	15.9	8.7	5.5
60	48.2	26.1	17.5	9.8	6.1
65	51.4	27.9	19.0	10.7	6.8
70	55.0	30.6	21.4	12.0	7.7
75	58.5	33.7	24.0	13.9	9.2
Total Years Experienced					
20	10.6	—	—	—	—
25	21.6	12.2	6.8	4.5	2.6
30	27.1	17.0	11.0	8.4	6.6
35	31.4	21.7	15.2	12.1	9.7
40	35.6	25.1	18.1	15.2	12.4
45	38.8	28.2	20.9	17.5	14.2
50	41.8	30.8	23.3	19.5	16.2
55	45.0	33.2	25.9	21.8	18.6
60	48.2	36.3	28.7	24.2	20.6
65	51.4	38.7	31.4	26.8	23.1
70	55.0	42.0	34.8	29.9	25.9
75	58.5	45.7	38.6	33.9	29.9

Source: Panel Study of Income Dynamics, Rank and Hirschl computations.

or more consecutive years of poverty, 17.9 percent two or more consecutive years, 11.4 percent three or more consecutive years, 5.7 percent four or more consecutive years, and 3.5 percent have experienced five or more years of poverty in a row. By age 60, the percentages are 48.2 percent, 26.1 percent, 17.5 percent, 9.8 percent, and 6.1 percent. Finally, by age 75, while 58.5 percent of Americans have spent at least one year below the poverty line, 33.7 percent of Americans have experienced a poverty spell of two or more years, 24 percent for three or more years, 13.9 percent four or more years, and 9.2 percent five or more years. These numbers indicate that the risk of experiencing long spells of poverty, decreases sharply with increases in the time period considered.

The lower panel of table 4.2 tells a somewhat different story. This panel reveals that once poverty occurs in people's lives, it is quite likely to occur at another point(s) in their lives. Of those who experience poverty, 78.1 percent (45.7/58.5) will undergo at least one additional year of poverty, while 51.1 percent (29.9/58.5) of those who encounter poverty will do so for five or more years across adulthood. Thus, four out of five people who encounter poverty in America do so more than once, while slightly more than half of the poverty-stricken will pass five or more years below the poverty line.

The total number of years that Americans encounter poverty during their adulthood is substantially higher than that found in the upper panel. By age 75, 58.5 percent of Americans have encountered at least one year of poverty, whereas 45.7 percent of Americans have experienced two or more years, 38.6 percent three or more years, 33.9 percent four or more years, and 29.9 percent of Americans five or more years of poverty during their lifespan. The fact that nearly 30 percent of the American population experiences five or more years of poverty during adulthood is eye opening.

These findings are consistent with the earlier mentioned research on poverty-spell dynamics. Most Americans who encounter poverty experience a short-term spell of impoverishment, while only a small minority experience poverty for an extended period. Yet once poverty strikes, it is likely to strike again at some point. Table 4.2 has placed the likelihood of these events within the course of the entire adult life cycle.

The Impact of Race, Education, and Gender

Our next two tables examine the impact of three key attributes on the long-term risk of poverty—race, education, and gender. Prior research has repeatedly demonstrated that these three factors exert considerable influence on patterns of income inequality, social stratification, and economic life chances within the United States (Beeghley, 2000). As we have seen in chapter 2, nonwhites, those with lower levels of education, and women all fare considerably worse in terms of poverty and economic vulnerability than their white, better educated, male counterparts. Yet how do these variables influence the lifetime risk of poverty?

Table 4.3 indicates that at age 20, 29.7 percent of African Americans have experienced poverty. By age 40, the figure is two-thirds, and by age 60, 81.9 percent of blacks have spent some period of time below the poverty

TABLE 4.3. The Cumulative Percent of Americans Who
Experience Poverty by Race, Education, and Gender

	Race		Education		Gender	
Age	Black	White	< 12	≥ 12	Female	Male
20	29.7	6.9	12.4	8.6	11.3	9.8
25	48.1	16.6	24.9	20.7	21.4	21.3
30	56.1	21.7	34.1	25.4	26.9	26.6
35	61.6	25.6	41.5	29.1	31.8	29.9
40	66.3	29.7	47.8	32.8	36.2	33.7
45	72.0	32.2	52.1	35.2	39.3	36.6
50	76.1	35.0	56.7	37.0	42.4	39.4
55	79.3	38.3	60.5	39.2	46.0	41.9
60	81.9	41.8	64.2	41.7	49.2	45.0
65	84.4	45.3	68.0	43.5	52.4	48.0
70	88.4	48.8	72.0	45.4	55.7	51.9
75	91.0	52.6	75.3	48.0	59.0	55.5

Source: Panel Study of Income Dynamics, Rank and Hirschl computations.

line. Of black Americans who reach age 75, 91 percent have been touched by the experience of poverty (in addition, it is important to keep in mind that we are not including the risk of poverty during the first nineteen years of life or the risk beyond age 75). While this figure is startling, it becomes less surprising when one considers that, on average, in any given year, approximately 25 to 30 percent of the black population lives below the poverty line (U.S. Bureau of the Census, 2003a). Now consider that table 4.3 is looking over the course of fifty-six years. The result is that nine out of every ten black Americans who live out a normal lifespan will encounter poverty at some point during their prime working-age adult years.

Such an experience overshadows that found in the white (non-Hispanic) population. Here we find that by age 40, 29.7 percent of whites have encountered poverty; by age 75, more than half (52.6 percent) of white Americans have spent one or more of their adult years living below the poverty line. The fact that one out of two white Americans is eventually touched by poverty is significant indeed. Nevertheless, it pales in comparison to the enormity of poverty's grasp within the black population.

Another way of viewing this contrast is in the following manner. By age 28 (see Rank and Hirschl, 1999a), the black population will have exceeded the cumulative level of lifetime poverty that the white population reaches by age 75. In other words, blacks have experienced in nine years the same risk of poverty that whites face in fifty-six years.

The middle columns focus on a second critical variable that has been shown to directly impact the likelihood of poverty—education. Here we find an equally powerful story. The gap between individuals who have fewer than twelve years of education and those who have twelve or more years is fairly narrow for those in their twenties, but for those in their thirties and older, the gap widens considerably. The importance of education in avoiding a first bout of poverty builds over the course of the life cycle. By age 30, 34.1 percent of those with fewer than twelve years of education versus 25.4 percent of those with twelve or more years of education have experienced poverty; by age 40, the figures are 47.8 percent and 32.8 percent; by age 50, 56.7 percent and 37 percent; by age 60, 64.2 percent and 41.7 percent; and by age 75, 75.3 percent and 48 percent. It is not until age 60 that education becomes cumulatively more important than being white for avoiding poverty.

The relationship between race and education is of particular interest. Among those with a lower risk, individuals with twelve or more years of education and individuals who are white have fairly similar odds of encountering poverty. However, for those with the greatest risk of poverty, African Americans are considerably more likely to experience poverty than are those with fewer than twelve years of education. In other words, being black appears to be a unique disadvantage when it comes to experiencing poverty across the adult life course.

The two right columns of table 4.3 estimate the adult risk of poverty for women and men. Here we see a story very different than that for race and education. Gender appears to exert only a slight effect on the odds that women, compared to men, will be more likely to experience poverty. By age 40, 36.2 percent of women and 33.7 percent of men have experienced poverty; by age 60, 49.2 percent and 45 percent; and by age 75, 59 percent and 55.5 percent. The effect of gender on the probability of experiencing poverty for the first time is actually quite small.

Why should this be? If we were to focus more narrowly on female-headed families with young children, our cumulative poverty percentages would be exceedingly high (see appendix B). However, most women at any point during the course of the fifty-six years of observation are not in such a household arrangement. For example, using age-specific marriage rates for 1980 (which represents roughly the midpoint of our time frame), Sweet and

Bumpass (1986) estimate that men spend twenty-eight years in marriage between the ages of twenty and fifty-nine, whereas for women the number is twenty-seven years. Consequently, women and men experience identical odds of poverty during roughly 70 percent of the time between the ages of twenty and fifty-nine. This results in a dramatic narrowing of gender differences and partially accounts for why gender as a whole does not exert a stronger influence on the risk of ever experiencing poverty. The long-term patterns of marriage serve to soften the impact that gender exerts upon the lifespan risk of economic vulnerability.

In order to simultaneously assess the impact of race, education, and gender on the cumulative risk of poverty, a multivariate life table was built that allows us to compare the risk of poverty for individuals with various combinations of characteristics found in table 4.3. Table 4.4 is arranged such that those with the least likelihood of experiencing poverty are in the upper left portions of the table, while those with the greatest likelihood of experiencing poverty are located in the lower right portions of the table.

Several patterns are apparent. first, the risk of poverty is dramatically altered by the various combinations of characteristics. For example, 25.6 percent of white men with twelve or more years of education experience poverty between the ages of 20 and 40, whereas 83.8 percent of black women with fewer than twelve years of education are touched by poverty during the same span.

Second, race remains the most influential of the three characteristics in affecting the probability of poverty. By comparing individuals with similar gender and educational backgrounds, we can see the magnitude of this racial effect. For example, comparing fifty-year-old black and white men who have completed twelve or more years of education, we find that 29.1 percent of whites experience poverty between ages 20 and 50, compared with 73 percent of blacks. Likewise, for men with fewer than twelve years of education, the figures are 42.4 percent versus 87.8 percent; for women with twelve or more years education, 33.1 percent versus 77.3 percent; and for women with fewer than twelve years of education, 50 percent versus 91.9 percent.

Third, the impact of gender upon the lifespan incidence of poverty is again quite modest. For fifty-year-old whites with twelve or more years of education, 29.1 percent of men experience poverty between the ages of twenty and fifty, compared with 33.1 percent of women. Likewise, for whites with fewer than twelve years of education, the figures are 42.4 percent and 50 percent; for blacks with twelve or more years of education, 73 percent

TABLE 4.4. The Cumulative Percent of Americans
Who Experience Poverty by Various Combinations of
Race, Education, and Gender

Age	White		Black	
	≥ 12	< 12	≥ 12	< 12
Male				
20	5.2	7.6	23.5	31.7
25	15.8	18.2	49.5	55.4
30	19.8	25.8	57.2	68.0
35	22.4	30.6	61.1	73.8
40	25.6	35.6	65.2	78.7
45	27.5	38.9	70.2	84.1
50	29.1	42.4	73.0	87.8
55	30.7	45.7	74.7	89.8
60	33.1	49.8	76.4	91.7
65	34.7	53.7	77.9	93.2
70	36.6	58.1	80.6	95.8
75	39.2	62.1	83.0	97.1
Female				
20	6.0	8.8	26.5	35.3
25	16.3	19.0	50.6	57.0
30	20.9	27.8	58.9	70.3
35	25.1	35.3	65.0	78.7
40	29.1	41.6	69.8	83.8
45	31.3	44.2	74.7	88.6
50	33.1	50.0	77.3	91.9
55	36.0	55.3	80.1	94.2
60	38.9	59.9	82.3	95.6
65	41.0	64.7	83.8	96.8
70	42.9	68.7	86.2	98.2
75	45.8	72.2	88.2	98.8

Source: Panel Study of Income Dynamics, Rank and Hirschl
computations.

and 77.3 percent; and for blacks with fewer than twelve years of education,
87.8 percent and 91.9 percent.

Several important implications regarding the significance of race, education, and gender upon the life-course risk of poverty follow from these
two tables. First, being black in America is virtually synonymous with experiencing poverty at some point during one's adult lifetime. This substantial
racial effect is undoubtedly related to a complex set of historical, institutional,
and social forces associated with educational and occupational disadvantage,
labor market discrimination, and residential segregation (Charles, 2003;

Jaynes and Williams, 1989; Feagin, 2000; Massey and Denton, 1993; Oliver and Shapiro, 1995). This set of structural forces appear to be relatively stable in the context of the socioeconomic changes currently at work in the world. Although progress was made toward racial equality in the decades following World War II, there is still a long way to go, as noted by Reynolds Farley:

> From the 1940s through the 1970s . . . black-white gaps narrowed with regard to death rates, the earnings of men and women, family incomes, and poverty. But a continuation of those favorable trends that would have brought us much closer to racial parity slowed or stopped in the mid-1970s. It is not so much that blacks have fallen further behind whites on these important indicators. They have not. But the unambiguous thirty-five year trend toward declining black-white differences ended when the economy entered a new era in the mid-1970s. (1996: 262)

The thrust of this section's racial findings leads us back to W. E. B. Du Bois's (1983, originally published in 1935) classical formulation that in American society, the dynamics of race and class are organically interrelated. The fact that virtually all African Americans will experience poverty at some point during their adulthood speaks volumes about the economic meaning of being black in America. A life-course approach fully reveals the lifetime economic insecurities faced by black individuals and their families in the United States.

Failing to graduate from high school is also strongly associated with encountering poverty during one's lifetime. As was discussed in chapter 3, human capital, and particularly education, has been shown to have a profound impact upon economic wellbeing (Danziger and Gottschalk, 1995; Schiller, 2004). What has been demonstrated here is the long-term impact of education on the ability to avoid poverty. The importance of education in protecting specific individuals from poverty tends to build across the life course.

The results also shed an interesting light on the feminization-of-poverty literature. This body of work has established that women are at a significantly greater risk of poverty, primarily because of the increased prevalence of female-headed families (McLanahan et al., 1989; Pearce, 1978; Sidel, 1996). Yet in looking at the total female population across the adult life course, we find that as a group, women's risk of poverty is only slightly higher than that for men. Why? The answer lies in the fact that throughout much of the life course, women and men experience identical odds of poverty as a consequence of being married. This results in a dramatic narrowing of gender differences. As Lieberson (1994) has argued, marriage tends to mitigate the effects of gender in terms of economic stratification.[6]

The Question of Welfare Use

Having established that a majority of the U.S. population will experience poverty, to what extent do Americans rely upon the social safety net in order to help them navigate through these periods of economic distress? This represents a second line of thinking with respect to the argument that the alleviation of poverty is in our direct self-interest. If a majority of Americans end up using welfare assistance at some point during the life course, the viability of such a safety net is of direct concern.

The conventional image of welfare use is one of social deviance. Few behaviors are as stigmatized in American society as that of using welfare. Survey research has repeatedly documented the public's considerable animosity toward welfare programs and its participants (Gilens, 1999; Horan and Austin, 1974; Kluegel and Smith, 1986; MacLeod and Speer, 1999; Tropman, 1998). At the heart of this opposition is the belief that welfare recipients are largely undeserving of such assistance. As Gilens writes,

> While no one factor can fully account for the public's opposition
> to welfare, the most important single component is this wide-
> spread belief that most welfare recipients would rather sit home
> and collect benefits than work hard themselves. In large measure
> Americans hate welfare because they view it as a program that
> rewards the undeserving poor. (1999: 2–3)

Accentuating this belief is the pervasive image that those who rely on welfare are predominately minorities, often plagued by alcohol or drug problems, with large numbers of children, who remain on the dole for years at a time (Gans, 1995). The visual portrait is of someone quite alien to mainstream America. In short, many Americans perceive welfare use as something that happens to someone else and welfare recipients as atypical of the American experience.

How accurate is this assumption? To what extent will Americans find themselves economically strapped and having to rely on government assistance in order to alleviate their needs? Put a slightly different way, to what extent does the welfare system touch the lives of American citizens? We have seen that a majority of Americans will face the experience of poverty. Here we explore whether such patterns also characterize the use of America's social welfare programs.

Our focus is on the major means-tested programs in the United States. In order to qualify for these programs, households must fall below certain income levels (for example, in order to receive Food Stamps, families must generally be at or below 130 percent of the official poverty line). In addition, public assistance programs do not allow households to hold assets beyond a certain monetary level. In general, these are set quite low. The result is that, in order to receive public assistance, individuals and families must be either below or not far removed from the poverty line, with a minimum accumulation of assets. The specific income and asset guidelines vary from program to program and, in some cases, from state to state within the jurisdiction of a program.

Welfare assistance in the United States consists of either in-kind or cash. In-kind programs provide specific resources such as food, housing, and medical assistance to meet particular needs. Major in-kind programs include the Food Stamp, Medicaid, and Housing Assistance programs. Cash programs include those that provide the recipient with a monthly check, such as Aid to Families with Dependent Children (AFDC), which has been replaced by the 1996 Temporary Assistance to Needy Families program (TANF), Supplemental Security Income (SSI), and General Assistance. Persons may receive help from one program (for example, just Food Stamps) or from various combinations of programs (e.g., SSI, Medicaid, and Food Stamp simultaneously).[7]

Welfare use is measured by PSID interviewers through a series of questions concerning whether the household has received any cash or in-kind public assistance program at some point during the prior year. During the time period 1967–1996, Medicaid, Food Stamps, and AFDC were available in the United States (although the PSID began to ask specific questions about Medicaid receipt only from 1977 on). SSI was available from 1975 on. If a household received any public assistance, the individuals within the household were counted as receiving welfare.

The percentages of the U.S. population receiving welfare between the ages of twenty and sixty-five are found in table 4.5. I have divided the analysis into the probabilities of receiving a cash program, an in-kind program, and any welfare program (cash and/or in-kind). We can see that for twenty-year-olds, 8.3 percent of the population participated in a cash welfare program, 12.6 percent received help from an in-kind program, and 14.2 percent received assistance from a cash and/or in-kind program (which is roughly equivalent to the average cross-sectional participation rates reported by the U.S. Census Bureau). By the time Americans reach age 35, 22.4 percent have received help from a cash program, 38.1 percent from an in-kind program, and 38.7 percent from either type of program. For those age 50, the percentages rise to 30.1 percent, 50 percent, and 50.9 percent; by age 65, 37.6 percent of Americans have used a cash welfare program at some point during their adult years, 64.2 percent have used an in-kind program, and 65 percent have received support from a cash and/or in-kind program.

These percentages indicate that Americans are much more likely to receive help from an in-kind program during the life course than from a cash program. Virtually every American who receives welfare receives support from at least one in-kind program. Put a slightly different way, of the two-thirds of Americans who received help from a public assistance program in table 4.5, 63 percent received Medicaid, 52 percent received Food Stamps,

TABLE 4.5. The Cumulative Percent of
Americans Who Participate in Welfare Programs
across Adulthood

	Type of Welfare Program		
Age	Cash Program	In-Kind Program	Any Program
20	8.3	12.6	14.2
25	15.3	25.7	26.6
30	19.5	32.7	33.3
35	22.4	38.1	38.7
40	25.1	43.0	43.7
45	27.7	46.4	47.2
50	30.1	50.0	50.9
55	32.4	53.6	54.6
60	35.0	57.4	58.4
65	37.6	64.2	65.0

Source: Panel Study of Income Dynamics, Rank and
Hirschl computations.

13 percent received AFDC, 10 percent received SSI, and 14 percent received funds from some other cash welfare program. As noted earlier, individuals can receive support from several programs at once or from only one program. Medicaid and Food Stamps clearly have the farthest reach in terms of usage across the adult life course. Rather than being targeted to one category of the population (for example, SSI to the disabled, or AFDC to female-headed families), these programs are more widely available because they have fewer eligibility restrictions. This, in turn, results in greater usage across the adult years. In addition, those who receive AFDC or SSI automatically receive Medicaid, as well.

The numbers in table 4.5 reveal that the majority of Americans utilize a public assistance program at least once during their adulthood. Two-thirds of adults turn to a means-tested program in order to receive some type of assistance between the ages of twenty and sixty-five. These findings are consistent with the earlier tables that address the likelihood of living in poverty across the life course; these reveal that the majority of Americans experience poverty or near-poverty at some point during their adulthood. The fact that two-thirds of adult Americans utilize a welfare program is emblematic of these life-course patterns of poverty and economic vulnerability.

Table 4.6 details the amount of time that individuals experience welfare recipiency. As in table 4.2, this is examined both in terms of the number of consecutive years that a person receives welfare and the total number of years that an individual receives welfare (regardless of whether the years are consecutive).

Between the ages of twenty and thirty-five, 38.7 percent of Americans received welfare in at least one year, 23.3 percent in two or more consecutive years, 16.8 percent for three or more years, 11.3 percent for four or more years, and 8.5 percent for five or more years. By age 50, the percentages are 50.9 percent, 31.3 percent, 23.2 percent, 15.8 percent, and 12 percent. Finally, by age 65, the corresponding percentages are 65 percent, 41.4 percent, 31.8 percent, 21.1 percent, and 15.9 percent. The top panel of table 4.6 reveals that, although the likelihood of experiencing one or two consecutive years of welfare use across the adult life course is considerable, people are far less likely to experience a higher number of consecutive years of welfare use.

The bottom panel of table 4.6 tells us a story similar to that which we found in table 4.2. Here we can see that the total number of years in which

TABLE 4.6. The Cumulative Percent of Americans Who Experience Various Years of Welfare Receipt across Adulthood

	Length of Spell				
Age	1 or More Years	2 or More Years	3 or More Years	4 or More Years	5 or More Years
Consecutive Years Experienced					
20	14.2	—	—	—	—
25	26.6	14.9	9.9	6.2	4.5
30	33.3	20.0	14.0	9.3	7.1
35	38.7	23.3	16.8	11.3	8.5
40	43.7	26.2	19.1	13.0	9.8
45	47.2	28.6	21.1	14.5	10.9
50	50.9	31.3	23.2	15.8	12.0
55	54.6	33.9	25.6	17.4	13.2
60	58.4	37.3	28.5	18.8	14.4
65	65.0	41.4	31.8	21.1	15.9
Total Years Experienced					
20	14.2	—	—	—	—
25	26.6	18.9	13.9	9.8	6.7
30	33.3	26.5	22.3	17.9	14.2
35	38.7	31.9	27.4	23.3	18.1
40	43.7	36.5	32.4	27.8	21.9
45	47.2	40.6	36.5	31.4	25.3
50	50.9	44.2	40.5	35.2	29.2
55	54.6	48.2	44.1	38.8	32.2
60	58.4	52.7	48.4	42.6	35.5
65	65.0	58.7	54.2	48.0	40.3

Source: Panel Study of Income Dynamics, Rank and Hirschl computations.

welfare will be accessed across the adulthood years is considerably greater than the number of consecutive years it is received. By age 65, 65 percent of the population have received welfare in at least one year, 58.7 percent in at least two different years, 54.2 percent in three different years, 48 percent in four different years, and 40.3 percent in five or more different years. While the upper panel tells us that the number of consecutive years that welfare is used is generally quite short, the bottom panel informs us that such periods tend to reoccur across the span of adulthood. Put a slightly different way, once individuals utilize welfare, they are quite likely to do so again in the future. Accordingly, 90 percent (58.7/65.0) of those who use welfare once will do so at least once more during their adulthood.

Tables 4.5 and 4.6 appear to cast considerable doubt on the notion that the use of welfare falls outside the mainstream American experience. In fact, two-thirds of all Americans between the ages of twenty and sixty-five at some point turn to a public assistance program, while 40 percent of the population access a welfare program in five or more years during their adulthood. Such assistance is often in the form of in-kind programs, such as Medicaid or Food Stamps, although 38 percent of the population receive some type of cash assistance, as well. It should also be noted that had we carried out our analysis to age 80 or 85, these percentages would be even higher. From age 65 on, there is an increased likelihood that individuals will receive Medicaid and/or SSI.

Implications

The findings presented here point to a powerful argument for viewing poverty as a cause for concern. It is an argument that until now has not been fully revealed. For the majority of Americans, it is in their direct self-interest to alleviate and/or be able to access protection from the ravages of poverty.

Poverty has often been perceived by the American public as something that occurs to others (Gans, 1995; Katz, 1989). Yet by looking across the adult life span, we have demonstrated that poverty and the use of the social safety net touch a clear majority of Americans. Even among white Americans, poverty is an event that eventually touches more than half the population. For those who believe that poverty is a risk only among African Americans in this country, these numbers clearly contradict such a position. Poverty is a "mainstream" event experienced by the dominant racial group and not something that can be easily dismissed as a condition of marginalized groups.

Assuming that most Americans would rather avoid this experience, it is in their self-interest to ensure that we reduce poverty and/or that a safety net is in place in order to soften its blows. Such a perspective can be referred to as a risk-sharing argument (Blank, 1997) and has been elaborated most notably by John Rawls (1971, 1993, 2001).

The argument here is similar to the argument in favor of automobile insurance. No one plans to have a car accident. Yet drivers are willing to invest in automobile insurance because they recognize that at some point they may be involved in a serious traffic accident that could result in sizable expenses. Hence, we are willing to pay for automobile insurance today in order to minimize the risks in the future.

Rather than a traffic risk, poverty can be thought of as an economic risk that accompanies our economic system. If an individual loses a job, becomes ill, sees her family split up, or encounters countless other circumstances, she runs a risk of dwindling income, resulting in eventual poverty. Just as automobile insurance is a form of protection against an unforeseen accident, the social safety net is a form of insurance against the accidents that occur around the rough edges of the free-market system.

In spite of this, many Americans undoubtedly believe that their chance of encountering poverty is remote, and therefore they fail to perceive the benefits of an antipoverty policy or of a social safety net in terms of their own self-interest. The research findings in this chapter directly challenge such beliefs. In doing so, they provide a vital piece for making a self-interest argument—most Americans will in fact be directly touched by poverty and will rely upon the social safety net.

The findings in this chapter contain an additional implication to be drawn with regard to making an effective case for poverty as a cause for concern (which is discussed in greater length in chapter 6 and was also discussed in chapter 3). Much of the general public's resistance toward assisting the poor and particularly those on welfare is that they are perceived to be undeserving of such assistance (Katz, 1989). Their poverty is seen as the result of a lack of motivation, of questionable morals, and so on. In short, the poor are viewed as fundamentally different from the rest of us and therefore as not warranting sacrifices on our part. Yet the analysis in this and the prior chapter suggests that poverty appears endemic to our economic structure. In short, we have met the enemy, and they are us.

Such a realization can cause a paradigm shift in thinking. By focusing on the lifespan risks, the prevalent nature of American poverty is revealed. At some point during our adult lives, the bulk of Americans will face the bitterness of poverty. Consequently, unless we are willing to argue that the majority of us are undeserving, the tactic of using character flaws and individual failings as a justification for doing as little as possible to address poverty loses much of its credibility. The ability to break down this barrier with effective arguments and evidence is a significant step toward increasing social and political support for the alleviation of poverty.

The findings regarding welfare use also appear to have several important ramifications. Contrary to much of the popular rhetoric, the reliance upon America's social safety net is widespread and mainstream. Although the users of public assistance are routinely vilified and portrayed as members of marginalized groups, in fact most Americans encounter the welfare system at some point during their adult years. While it is true that the more disadvantaged members of our society interact to a greater extent with poverty and the welfare system, the relevancy of a social safety net is extremely widespread. Such a finding should cause us to seriously reflect upon the scapegoating that often surrounds the welfare issue. The saying about letting "he who is without sin cast the first stone" appears particularly apt.

It is interesting to consider these patterns in view of the fact that the American welfare state, and specifically its social safety net, have often been described in minimalist terms (Esping-Andersen, 1990). While the U.S. welfare state may be minimalist in terms of the scope and level of benefits it offers to the economically vulnerable and consequently in its effectiveness in reducing poverty (as we saw in Chapter 3), it is far from minimalist in the extent to which it is eventually relied upon by the general population. This fact has gone largely unnoticed until now. The importance and relevancy of the welfare state should be perceived as a mainstream issue that affects the lives of millions of Americans. Too often this issue has been framed as something outside the normal American experience. A life table approach has shown that this perception is incorrect.

A second important implication derived from our analysis is the fact that most life-course spells of welfare utilization are relatively short in duration, which implies that the welfare state largely operates as an insurance policy against sporadic periods of economic need that occur across the life cycle. Although some individuals do use public assistance for long periods of time, the majority of Americans rely on welfare programs to provide short-term assistance. This suggests that the welfare state is operating to a large extent as most Americans indicate they would like it to operate (Gilens, 1999).

Yet it is also true that the total number of years across the life course in which Americans receive welfare assistance is quite high. The data reveal that approximately 40 percent of the population uses a welfare program in five or more separate years between the ages of twenty and sixty-five. It should be noted that we are measuring only whether welfare is used at any point during the year, rather than looking at use across all months of the year. Nevertheless, the fact that two out of five Americans utilize a social safety net program in at least five different years during their working-age adulthood is startling.

Finally, the life-course patterns of welfare use clearly underscore the existence of economic vulnerability in America. This is consistent with and builds on the findings that approximately three out of four Americans experience poverty or near-poverty (households that fall below 150 percent of the poverty line). Taken together, these results imply that our free-market economic structure brings periods of economic uncertainty to the lives of its participants (discussed in chapter 3). The majority of Americans turn to some form of public assistance in order to help them through such periods of economic turmoil. By utilizing a life-course perspective, we have revealed both the long-term economic risks and the importance of a social safety net for ameliorating such risks.

It should be noted that embedded within these life course calculations. poverty can take on different meanings. For some, poverty is a one-time or infrequent occurrence that takes place as a result of a particular event or set of circumstances. It represents an aberration from their typical life course pattern. For others, poverty is an ever-present possibility looming on the horizon. It is the embodiment of an ongoing threat. As discussed in chapter 3, and indicated in tables 4.3 and 4.4, those falling into the latter category are more likely to have characteristics putting them at a disadvantage in terms of competing in the labor market. Yet what has not been generally understood until now is that the experience of poverty, in one way or another, directly touches a very wide segment of the population.

By conceptualizing and measuring impoverishment over the adult life cycle, a set of proportions have been calculated that cast a new light on the subject of poverty in the United States. For the majority of American adults, the question is not whether they will experience poverty, but when. This strongly suggests that the condition of poverty is of direct self-interest for the majority of Americans. Such a reality should cause us to seriously reevaluate the very nature, scope, and meaning of poverty in America.

The Societal Costs of Poverty

There is a second major way of thinking about poverty within the context of self-interest. As we have seen in chapter 2, poverty exacts a heavy toll from those who fall within its grasp. What we have failed to recognize is that poverty also places enormous economic, social, and psychological costs on the nonpoor, as well. These costs affect us both individually and as a nation, although we have been slow to recognize them. Too often the attitude has been, "I don't see how I'm affected, so why worry about it?"

Yet the issues that many Americans are in fact deeply concerned about, such as crime, access to and affordability of health care, race relations, and worker productivity, to name but a few, are directly affected and exacerbated by the condition of poverty. As a result, the general public winds up paying a heavy price for allowing poverty to walk in our midst. A report by the Children's Defense Fund on the costs of childhood poverty makes this strikingly clear:

> The children who suffer poverty's effects are not its only victims. When children do not succeed as adults, all of society pays the price: businesses are able to find fewer good workers, consumers pay more for their goods, hospitals and health insurers spend more treating preventable illnesses, teachers spend more time on remediation and special education, private citizens feel less safe on the streets, governors hire more prison guards, mayors must pay to shelter homeless families, judges must hear more criminal, domestic, and other cases, taxpayers pay for problems that could have been prevented, fire and medical workers must respond to emergencies that never should have happened, and funeral directors must bury children who never should have died. (Sherman, 1994: 99)

When we speak of homeland security, these are the issues that truly undermine us and our security as a nation.

This sense of a broad awareness of the costs of poverty can be referred to as enlightened self-interest. In other words, by becoming aware of the various costs associated with poverty or, conversely, the various benefits associated with the reduction of poverty, we begin to realize that it is in our own self-interest to combat the condition of poverty.

Alexis de Tocqueville referred to this in his treatise on America as self-interest properly understood. In fact, the full title of the chapter from his *Democracy in America* is "How the Americans Combat Individualism by the Doctrine of Self-Interest Properly Understood." His basic premise was that "one sees that by serving his fellows, man serves himself and that doing good is to his private advantage" (1988: 525).

This awareness is often achieved through education, since the connections are frequently not self-evident. The case of poverty is a good example. For most Americans, poverty is seen as an individualized condition that affects exclusively the poor, their families, and perhaps their neighborhoods. Rarely do we conceptualize a stranger's poverty as having a direct or indirect effect upon our own well-being. By becoming aware of such impacts through informed knowledge, we begin to understand that reducing poverty is very much in our enlightened self-interest.

Yet the ability to estimate the magnitude of the costs surrounding an issue such as poverty is exceedingly complex. Arriving at a dollar amount and claiming precision is wishful thinking at best. Although countless studies have demonstrated that the costs of poverty to society are both real and consequential, it is virtually impossible to factor in all the nuances and relevant components that affect society.

My approach here is a simpler one. I focus on three substantive areas that Americans describe as being extremely important to them and on which federal, state, and local governments expend considerable amounts of taxpayers' money and resources—health, education, and crime. In each of these examples, my argument is that the existence of deep and widespread poverty causes us to spend considerably more than we would if poverty were reduced, and with considerably less effectiveness. Such examples will hopefully illustrate that reducing poverty is not only in the interest of the current poor but in a very real sense in the interest of the nonpoor as well.

Health

As a nation, we expend an enormous amount of resources on health care. The United States spends more per capita on health care than any other country in the world (Mullahy and Wolfe, 2001). In 2000, total expenditures for health care were $1.3 billion, or $4,481 per person annually (U.S. Census Bureau, 2002d). Clearly, this is an area that exerts a strong impact upon the "average" American.

One way to reduce the overall cost of health care is to improve people's general well-being, and one way to accomplish that goal is to reduce the number of people living in poverty. Indeed, professionals in the field of public health consistently contend that one of the most critical factors in improving the overall health of the American population is to reduce the rate of poverty.

As was made clear in chapter 2, the condition of poverty often damages the medical well-being of individuals. Poverty and low income are associated with elevated rates of heart disease, diabetes, hypertension, cancer, infant mortality, mental illness, undernutrition, lead poisoning, asthma, dental problems, and a host of other ailments and diseases. What is often not appreciated in discussions of poverty and health is that, although these maladies have an impact on the poor directly, they also put a strain on the cost of health care for us all. Several examples illustrate the ways in which this process operates.

Women in poverty are significantly more likely to bear children who are either premature or underweight. Such a connection exists because poverty is associated with a greater risk of inadequate nutrition, substance abuse, and a lack of prenatal care during pregnancy (National Commission to Prevent Infant Mortality, 1992). These conditions dramatically increase the likelihood of bearing a low-birthweight or premature baby.

The health costs of a severely underweight or premature infant are enormous. For example, it has been estimated that the median treatment cost of delivery for a very-low-birthweight infant is approximately $50,000 over a median length of stay of forty-nine days in the hospital (Avruch and Cackley, 1995; Rogowski, 1999). The lifetime medical costs for a premature baby have been estimated conservatively at $500,000 (March of Dimes, 2002). These expenses are absorbed by us all because hospitals and insurance companies pass on their costs in various ways, ultimately resulting in higher insurance premiums paid by everyone. In addition, low-birthweight babies face twice the risk of experiencing learning problems (learning disability, hyperactivity, emotional problems, and mental illness), have a much greater chance of neurodevelopmental problems (seizures, epilepsy, water on the brain, cerebral palsy, and mental retardation), and are more likely to have a loss of eyesight or hearing (McCormick et al., 1992). All of these conditions put further pressure on existing health care resources, again resulting in increased health care costs for us all.

Lead poisoning is a second condition that illustrates the connection between poverty and escalated health care costs. Although the incidence of lead poisoning has dropped significantly over the past twenty years, in 1998 an estimated 7.6 percent of preschool children still had elevated levels of lead in their bloodstreams, with those in poverty disproportionally represented (Centers for Disease Control and Prevention, 2000). Lead poisoning is closely allied with impoverishment; poor children are more likely to be exposed to hazardous levels of lead by ingesting peeling or fallen lead-paint chips found in deteriorating housing or by breathing leaded paint dust (Needleman, 1994; Richardson, 2002). Furthermore, poverty is closely associated with iron deficiency, making the effects of lead poisoning even more potent (U.S. Public Health Service, 1988). Lead poisoning in children is associated with stunted growth, hearing loss, damage to the brain and central nervous system, and impaired blood production and kidney development.

These conditions result in higher medical care expenses as well as additional costs associated with lead poisoning (such as a diminished ability to learn). In a cost-benefit analysis conducted by the Centers for Disease Control and Prevention in Atlanta, it was conservatively estimated that the nation would save $28 billion beyond the cost of removing lead from children's homes (*New York Times*, March 21, 1995). These savings would be achieved through the reduced need for medical care and special education, as well as through the increase in wages (and therefore greater tax revenue) that typically accompanies a higher I.Q.[8]

A third example of the link between poverty and elevated health care costs is the overreliance upon emergency room visits by the poor. This overreliance occurs for several reasons. Due to limited access to medical care, coupled with lower levels of education, the poor are more likely to let health problems fester until they become extremely problematic, requiring emergency measures (Leidenfrost, 1993). Second, because of restricted access to conventional health care, the poor tend to use emergency room visits as a way of accessing the medical care system for situations that would normally be considered routine (Olson, 1994; Shah-Canning et al., 1996). In both cases, the result is an increased financial burden on hospitals. This expense gets passed on throughout the entire health care system, eventually resulting in higher payments for us all.

These examples illustrate but a few of the ways in which poverty is associated with heightened medical problems and costs. Ultimately, such costs are paid by us all through higher health care premiums. Reducing poverty is therefore in all Americans' self-interest. By alleviating the detrimental effects of poverty, we all benefit through health care dollar savings.

Education

Education represents a second area in which our nation expends a sizable amount of resources, yet at the same time fails to get the biggest bang for its buck as a result of poverty. In 2001, total school expenditures on public elementary and secondary schools was estimated at $392 billion (U.S. Census Bureau, 2002d). The premise here is that by reducing poverty, each of us will receive a greater benefit from the dollars we are already spending on education.

Research has demonstrated that the educational quality received by lower-income children is substantially below that of their middle-or upper-class counterparts (Phillips and Chin, 2003). However, my argument rests on a process that occurs beyond this obvious gap. Poor children are often unable to take full advantage of the education they do receive as a consequence of poverty. This is the result of several factors.

First, poverty is closely tied to hunger and undernutrition among children (Alaimo et al., 2001a), which can affect the overall ability of such children to learn (Alaimo, Olson, and Frongillo, 2001; Brown and Pollitt, 1996; Reid, 2000). For example, a study conducted by the U.S. Department of Education found that more than half of the principals in the poorest schools under the Chapter 1 compensatory education program believed that poor nutrition and a lack of rest were moderate or serious problems for their students (Millsap, Moss, and Gamse, 1993). This in turn has an impact on youngsters' ability to concentrate and to learn in the classroom. Children who attend school on an empty stomach are at a distinct disadvantage in their ability to absorb and comprehend classroom material.

Second, as discussed earlier, poverty is associated with health problems beyond undernutrition. These problems can affect children's ability to learn. The earlier example of lead poisoning illustrates this. Elevated levels of lead have been shown to significantly impair children's cognitive abilities. As Nancy Rothman and colleagues note,

> Lead poisoning in children has been associated with reduced
> intelligence, shortened memory, slowed reaction times, poor
> hand-eye coordination, and antisocial behavior. The cost to
> society includes not only medical treatment and special educa-

tion but also higher high-school drop-out rates, which are associated with crime and low earning potential. (2002: 739)

Third, poverty has a detrimental impact on children's education because family resources are often not available to augment and enhance a child's learning. Studies have shown that children in poor families have access to fewer books in the household, fewer computing resources, and fewer learning opportunities beyond the classroom (Mayer, 1997).

Finally, as documented earlier, the condition of poverty can create a stressful home and neighborhood environment. Children are often caught square in the middle of extreme family stress, which can seriously impair their ability to learn. Likewise, neighborhood problems such as crime or violence can make the process of learning more difficult.

All of these effects increase the likelihood that an impoverished child's cognitive ability will be stunted. Just as poverty can stunt a child's physical growth, so too can it stunt a child's educational growth. The result of this process is obviously tragic for the child in question, but it is also tragic for society as a whole. In a relatively short period of time, these children will become part of our country's workforce. Their levels of productivity and creativity will affect the well-being of the country. If a significant percentage of our workforce does not have the cognitive tools to compete in a global economy, then we will all surely pay the price.

In an attempt to measure what such a price might be, the Children's Defense Fund (1994) pulled together several sets of economic assessments to estimate the monetary cost of poverty. The estimates focused on the overall loss of economic productivity as a result of poverty's effect in truncating children's education. The numbers ranged from a low of $36 billion annually to a high of $177 billion.[9] As the report notes,

> No matter which approach is used, the costs of poverty are
> enormous. It is no surprise that the results differ from each
> other somewhat, because each looks at children who have
> different age ranges and other characteristics; therefore, each
> measures slightly different things. None of these four estimates
> is definitive. Instead, each reinforces the others and supports the
> finding that child poverty is acting as a costly brake on the U.S.
> economy. (Sherman, 1994: 102)

Crime

Few issues garner as much concern among Americans as that of crime. Americans consistently rank the occurrence of crime as one of our most pressing social problems (Maguire and Pastore, 2001). These anxieties are matched by the amount we spend each year in attempting to combat crime. In 1999 the United States spent $147 billion on justice expenditures, including police protection, corrections, and judicial and legal activities (U.S. Department of Justice, 2002). These expenses have increased more than 300 percent since 1982 (or 145 percent in constant dollars). For example, prison construction is rapidly becoming one the biggest line items in many state governments' budgets (U.S. Bureau of the Census, 2002d). Since 1982, more than 600 state and more than fifty federal correctional facilities have been opened (Maguire and Pastore, 2001).

Yet crime takes a much bigger economic toll upon society if we factor in the myriad other costs that result from the occurrence of particular crimes. For example, in a study sponsored by the National Institute of Justice, Mark Cohen and colleagues (1996) attempted to measure the cost to society of crimes such as robbery, murder, rape, child abuse, and domestic violence. They calculated a number of out-of-pocket costs associated with these offenses, such as legal fees, lost work time, police work, mental health care problems and reduced quality of life for victims, and so on. Their eye-opening estimate was that the overall cost of crime was approximately $450 billion a year. By comparison, the Defense Department's budget in 2001 was $329 billion (U.S. Bureau of the Census, 2002d).[10] It is certainly not an exaggeration to argue that we are spending an immense amount of resources either directly or indirectly as a result of criminal activity.[11]

Yet in spite of the costs, concerns, and expenditures, our society is treading water in terms of reducing the magnitude and cost of crime. If anything, we appear to be spending more, with less to show for our efforts. While it is certainly true that the rates for some types of crime dropped during the 1990s (Federal Bureau of Investigation, 2001), this is partially the result of the fact that the United States has the highest incarceration rate of any country in the world (Maguire and Pastore, 2001; Short, 1997; Walmsley, 2003). The total number of state and federal inmates grew from 319,598 in 1980 to 1,361,258 in 2002 (U.S. Department of Justice, 2003a). In addition, the number of local jail inmates increased from 182,288 in 1980 to 665,475 in

2002; adults on probation increased from 1.1 million to 4 million; and those on parole rose from 220,438 to 753,141 (U.S. Census Bureau, 2002d; U.S. Department of Justice, 2003b) As a result, nearly 1 percent of the adult U.S. population is currently incarcerated, while 3 percent are either incarcerated, on parole, or on probation.[12] We have been putting greater numbers of people behind bars during the past twenty years, at an exorbitant price tag, yet without a major reduction in the rate of crime. Why?

I believe a fundamental reason lies in the fact that we have failed to deal with one of the root causes of crime—the conditions of dire poverty.[13] A substantial body of research indicates that, although crime occurs for a variety of reasons, and although there are clear class and racial biases in the rates of arrest and sentencing (Smith, 1991; Tonry, 1995; Turk, 1969), long-term poverty and economic inequality are nevertheless critical sources for the crime that occurs in society (Currie, 1985; Fowles and Merva, 1996; Hagan and Peterson, 1995; Martinez, 1996; Parker, 1989; Rosenfeld, 2002; Short, 1997; Western, Kleykamp, and Rosenfeld, 2003; Williams, 1984). This is particularly true with regard to property and violent crimes. The National Research Council, in reporting on adolescents in high-risk settings, concludes that "data from the Centers for Disease Control indicate that personal and neighborhood income are the strongest predictors of violent crime" (1993: 156). Likewise, the President's Commission on Law Enforcement and Administration of Justice wrote more than thirty-five years ago, "The offender at the end of road in prison is likely to be a member of the lowest social and economic groups in the country" (1967: 44).[14]

Why should this be? One reason is that the surrounding conditions of long-term poverty (inadequate education, lack of resources, family instability, unemployment) negatively impact upon an individual's access to legitimate opportunities for economic success. Such blocked opportunities may then intensify the perception that one's legitimate means for accomplishing economic success are bleak (Blau and Blau, 1982; Cloward and Ohlin, 1960; Cohen, 1955; Freeman, 1996; Merton, 1938). This becomes particularly instrumental in fostering crime within a society such as the United States, where a strong emphasis is placed on the value of material success (Bourgois, 1995; Jankowski, 1995). A report by the American Psychological Association stresses the importance of this factor in understanding youth violence:

But beyond mere income level, it is the socioeconomic inequality of the poor—their sense of relative deprivation and their lack of opportunity to ameliorate their life circumstances—that facilitates higher rates of violence. . . . Not only do the poor in America lack basic necessities, but they are aware that they do not have those things most other Americans have and that they lack other opportunities needed to obtain them in the future. (Commission on Violence and Youth, 1993: 23–24)

In addition, we have seen earlier how the daily necessities that most of us take for granted are much harder to come by for those living in poverty. The poor are routinely put into the position of having to make hard choices among essential items such as food, shelter, and heat, and face difficulties in acquiring them (Edin and Lein, 1997; Seccombe, 1999; Shirk et al., 1999). Coupled with this, economically depressed neighborhoods often suffer from significant levels of community disorganization (Sampson and Wilson, 1995). Finally, research indicates that much of the violent crime in the United States and elsewhere is triggered by intense feelings of anger. The conditions of poverty often provide the breeding grounds in which such feelings fester.

These conditions increase the attractiveness while reducing the perceived costs of engaging in illegitimate means to obtain goods that are normally acquired through legitimate means. For example, Jeffrey Reiman, in his book *The Rich Get Rich and the Poor Get Prison*, observes, "We know that poverty increases the pressures to commit crimes in pursuit of property, and that crimes to obtain property account for about 90 percent of the crime rate—and yet we do little to improve the conditions of our impoverished inner-city neighborhoods beyond clicking our tongues over the strange coincidence that these are also the neighborhoods with the highest crime rates" (2001: 20). Although it must be emphasized that the vast majority of the poor do not engage in criminal activity (Blank, 1997), nevertheless, poverty at both the neighborhood and the individual levels significantly increases the probability that a crime will occur.

Severe economic deprivation, poverty, and a sense of injustice can also lead to more widespread forms of violence, such as riots. Regardless of the place or time—East St. Louis, 1917; Detroit, 1967; Los Angeles, 1992—the conditions that lead to mass destruction and violence are largely parallel. In announcing the formation of the Kerner Commission to investigate the rioting in major U.S. cities throughout the mid-1960s, President Johnson observed,

> The only genuine, long-range solution for what has happened
> lies in an attack—mounted at every level—upon the conditions
> that breed despair and violence. All of us know what those
> conditions are: ignorance, discrimination, slums, poverty,
> disease, not enough jobs. . . . We should attack these condi-
> tions—not because we are frightened by conflict, but because we
> are fired by conscience. We should attack them because there is
> simply no other way to achieve a decent and orderly society in
> America. (Harris and Wilkins, 1988: 3–4)

Thus, the conditions that foster crime and violence on an individual level can also lead to destructive behavior on a group level.[15] As Aristotle noted some two millennia ago, "Poverty is the parent of revolution and crime."[16] Or as George Bernard Shaw wrote in his preface to *Major Barbara*, "Security, the chief pretence of civilization, cannot exist where the worst of dangers, the danger of poverty, hangs over everyone's head."

One of the most effective long-term policy measures for reducing crime and its cost to society is to alleviate the dire conditions of long-term poverty, particularly in economically depressed inner-city neighborhoods. As Reiman points out, "The elimination of poverty is the most promising crime-fighting strategy there is, and, in the long run, the most cost-effective" (2001: 191). And, as Reiman notes, it is not poverty in and of itself but what often accompanies poverty that fuels the higher rates of crime. By combating poverty, we begin to alleviate these conditions.

> The truth is that it is not poverty as such that breeds crime, but
> the things that poverty brings with it in a modern, free, and free-
> enterprise society like ours: lack of good education (because
> schools are financed primarily out of local property taxes), lack of
> parental authority (because unemployed parents easily lose their
> children's respect), lack of cohesive local community (because
> those who can, escape the poor inner cities as quickly as pos-
> sible), and so on. It is these things, rather than lack of money
> itself, that lead to crime. Investing in our inner cities and

providing high-quality education, job-training, and jobs for the unemployed will give us more productive citizens with a stake in playing by the rules. And it will be cheaper than paying for police and prisons to house those who break the rules. (2001: 191–192)

Indeed, a study by Mark Cohen (1998) estimates that preventing a high-risk youth from engaging in a criminal career saves on average between $1.7 and 2.3 million in lifetime social costs.[17]

Furthermore, there is a gain to be had by reducing the psychological costs associated with crime. Crime is an issue that genuinely frightens many Americans. It affects our behavior in various ways; we avoid particular neighborhoods, invest in security systems, worry about family members, and so on. Thirty-five percent of all Americans said that there are places within a mile of their home where they are afraid to walk alone at night (Gallup, 2003), while 88 percent of high school seniors reported that they worry about crime and violence "sometimes" or "often" (Bachman et al., 1991). By making our physical environment safer through poverty reduction, we lessen the psychological stress that affects millions of Americans in a manner that is difficult to measure economically but that is nevertheless quite real (Skogan, 1990; Skogan and Maxfield, 1981).

For each of the issues I have discussed in this section—health, education, and crime—my argument has been that poverty is closely interconnected with the high costs that each imposes on society. By allowing poverty to persist at acute levels, we wind up spending considerably more in these areas than if poverty were substantially reduced. Impoverishment breeds serious health problems, inadequately educated children, and higher rates of criminal activity.[18] As a result, we pay more for health care, we produce less-productive workers, and we divert needed resources into the building and maintaining of correctional facilities. In each of these cases, we are spending our money on the back end of the problem of poverty rather than on the front end, which is almost always a more expensive approach to take.

There are many other social issues associated with poverty in which the same argument could be made. For example, low income (and particularly poverty) has been shown to be strongly related to teenage childbearing (U.S. Bureau of the Census, 2002d). In turn, the economic costs of teenagers having children are exceedingly high. One study estimated that the cost to taxpayers of adolescent childbearing (as a result of increased social problems) was $7 billion a year (Maynard, 1997). By reducing poverty, which in turn would reduce teenage childbearing, we would reduce our social costs in the future.

In the earlier-mentioned analysis of children's poverty, the Children's Defense Fund estimated both the costs and the benefits of eliminating poverty among children. Their conclusion was that, "When long-term benefits and costs are compared, ending child poverty appears highly affordable. In fact, it may result in a large net financial gain for society over time—even when only a limited portion of the benefits of ending child poverty are considered" (Sherman, 1994: 119).

The old saying "An ounce of prevention is worth a pound of cure" is certainly apropos. As I have demonstrated, it is not a question of paying or not paying. Rather, it is a question of how we want to pay, which then affects the amount we end up spending. I prefer to use my money in a smart and efficient way. That is precisely what I am advocating when I argue for making poverty a priority issue. In making an investment up front to alleviate poverty, the evidence suggests that we will be repaid many times over by lowering the costs associated with a host of social problems.

Yet it is also true that we will not recoup these lower costs overnight. It will take time for the savings to become apparent. And therein lies part of the problem. Too often we base our policy decisions on the short-term rather than the long-term gains. Congressional and presidential terms of two or four years tend to drive the policy process. Nevertheless, it is the long-term savings that can produce the greatest benefits over time.

Finally, I believe that there is an important psychological benefit to investing our resources in ways that avoid or substantially reduce social problems in the first place, rather than spending our resources on the negative fallout from such problems. Such a benefit is extremely difficult to measure financially, but ask yourself what kind of community you would prefer to live in—one in which we spend our money building prisons, or one in which we invest in people and their neighborhoods so that they do not eventually wind up in prisons. I believe that most people intrinsically feel better about communities that are characterized by the latter, rather than the former.[19] In short, reducing poverty is in our psychological self-interest, as well as in our economic and social self-interest.

True
to Values

5

> I tremble for my country when I reflect that
> God is just, that his justice cannot sleep forever.
> *Thomas Jefferson*

AS A RESULT OF our unique history and geography, America is marked by its diversity. We are a nation whose people have brought distinctive cultures and experiences onto the American landscape. Although the nation is often described as a melting pot, a patchwork quilt is perhaps the more appropriate analogy.[1]

Moreover, as Michael Walzer (1990, 1992) has noted, there is in actuality no country called America. Rather, we live in the United States of America. The nation was not named after an ethnic group but rather a federation of states. Typically, one hears our country referred to outside its borders as simply "the States."

Yet binding us together as *Americans* are several fundamental sets of beliefs shared by most. Throughout our history, two of the most important have been the Judeo-Christian ethic and what might be referred to as the founding American civic values (liberty, justice, equality, and democracy). The vast majority of Americans have held and continue to hold these two sets of values in high esteem (e.g., Gans, 1988; Wolfe, 1998).

The argument developed in this chapter is that if we examine these sets of values carefully, we find that attitudes of apathy toward the poor contradict their very core. In order to remain consistent with these principles, a concerted attempt to reduce poverty is necessary. Certainly there is room for disagreement regarding the solutions to impoverishment. But there can be no disagreement about the imperative to confront this issue, given that one professes allegiance to the Judeo-Christian ethic and/or to the founding political values on which this country was based.

The Judeo-Christian Ethic

Discussions of ethics, theology, or religious texts are generally not found in social science examinations of poverty. This is uncomfortable territory for the empirically trained social scientist to venture into. Nevertheless, religious and ethical bodies of thinking have had much to say regarding the role of the community and its members in addressing poverty. Millions of Americans turn to these bodies of wisdom in seeking out a moral direction for their lives. To build an argument regarding the importance of poverty as a social issue and at the same time avoid the ethical and religious basis on which such an argument can be made appears to overlook an important dimension.

Although virtually all of the world's major religions and creeds are practiced in the United States, it has been the Judeo-Christian ethic that most Americans have associated themselves with. The cornerstone of the Judeo-Christian ethic are the books found in the texts of Judaism (commonly called the Old Testament among Christians, of which the first five represent the Torah, with most of the remaining books constituting the Jewish Bible) and those of the New Testament (which taken together with the Old Testament constitute the Catholic, Orthodox, and Protestant Bibles).[2] These writings are the foundation for both Judaism and Christianity, and together contain what we commonly refer to as the Judeo-Christian ethic. The Judeo-Christian ethic has provided a set of religious and moral guidelines on how individuals ought to structure their lives and communities.

The writings themselves stretch over at least a thousand year period, covering a vast array of topics. In addition, they include a variety of stylistic approaches. As Wayne Meeks notes,

Anyone who looks carefully at the Bible will be struck by the immense variety of its contents. Here we have prose and poetry, expansive narratives and short stories, legal codes embedded in historical reports, hymns and prayers, quoted archival documents, quasi-mythic accounts of things that happened "in the beginning" or in God's court in heaven, collections of proverbs, maxims, aphorisms, and riddles, letters to various groups, and reports of mysterious revelations interpreted by heavenly figures. (1993: xviii)

Given this diversity, one sails into treacherous waters when turning to the Old and/or New Testament to justify a particular ideology or stance. The danger is that by pulling out isolated passages from the Bible to support a particular position, one misses the deeper and more encompassing message found throughout. It would be analogous to sampling 500 respondents but choosing only one individual to represent the entire group.

In order to judiciously examine what the Old and New Testaments have to say regarding poverty, it is necessary to read the works carefully in their entirety. By doing so, one begins to grasp the fuller and more encompassing themes dealing with poverty, the downtrodden, and the poor. Although the themes found in the Old and New Testament are discussed separately, there is considerable overlap between the two.[3] Taken as a whole, the message is strong and clear. Whether one interprets the Judeo-Christian ethic from a religious perspective or from an ethical perspective, there is a direct imperative to help the poor. In fact, this message lies at the heart of the Judeo-Christian ethic.

The Texts of Judaism (The Old Testament)

Several interconnected themes are found in the Old Testament regarding the poor.[4] To begin, there is a strong sense that it is God's will for those in a community to help the poor. For example, the book of Deuteronomy narrates God's laws as derived through Moses. The role that individuals and communities should play towards the impoverished is detailed.

If there is among you anyone in need, a member of your community in any of your towns within the land that the Lord your God is giving you, do not be hard-hearted or tight-fisted toward your needy neighbor. You should rather open your hand, willingly lending enough to meet the need, whatever it may be . . . Give liberally and be ungrudging when you do so, for on this account the Lord your God will bless you in all your work and in all that you undertake. Since there will never cease to be some in need on earth, I therefore command you, "Open your hand to the poor and needy neighbor in your land." (Deuteronomy 15.7–8, 15.10–11)

Moses goes on to describe the various ways this can be accomplished, such as sharing the harvest of the land, granting remission of debts every seventh year, not withholding wages, redistributing land at the time of the jubilee year, and so on.

One finds this theme reoccurring throughout the Old Testament (Exodus 22.21–24; Deuteronomy 10.17–19; Zechariah 7.8–10; Tobit 4.5–11, 4.16–17, 12.6–10). For example, the book of Tobit is exemplified by the passage, "Do not turn your face away from anyone who is poor, and the face of God will not be turned away from you" (Tobit 4.7).

As the National Conference of Catholic Bishops notes in its pastoral letter, "Economic Justice for All," the overarching theme in the Old Testament is that God is a God of justice and of righteousness, particularly in terms of the downtrodden. Individuals, communities, and rulers are judged on the basis of how well they treat these groups.

Central to the biblical presentation of justice is that the justice of a community is measured by its treatment of the powerless in society, most often described as the widow, the orphan, the poor, and the stranger (non-Israelite) in the land. The Law, the Prophets, and the Wisdom literature of the Old Testament all show deep concerns for the proper treatment of such people. What these groups of people have in common is their vulnerability and lack of power. They are often alone and have no protector or advocate. Therefore, it is God who hears their cries, and the king who is God's anointed is commanded to have special concern for them. (1986: 21)

There are a number of passages in the Old Testament that detail the obligations and responsibilities of a good and just ruler toward the poor. Such a ruler is seen as reflecting God's position as an advocate for the poor (Proverbs 29.14, 31.4–9; Ecclesiastes 5.8–9; Isaiah 3.13–15, 10.1–4, 11.3–5, 32.1–8; Sirach 7.4–7). For example, Psalm 72 is entitled "Prayer for Guidance and Support for the King."

> May he defend the cause of the
> poor of the people,
> give deliverance to the needy,
> and crush the oppressor.

It goes on:

> For he delivers the needy when
> they call,
> the poor and those who have
> no helper.
> He has pity on the weak and the
> needy,
> and saves the lives of the
> needy.
> From oppression and violence he
> redeems their life;
> and precious is their blood in
> his sight.

The Old Testament thus makes it clear that those who assist the poor, whether king or subject, follow in God's footsteps. It is they who will be rewarded and blessed (Job 20.10, 29.11–17; Psalms 111.9; Isaiah 58.6–9; Sirach 7.32–36). The beginning of Psalm 41, "Assurance of God's Help and a Plea for Healing," reflects this sentiment:

> Happy are those who consider
> the poor;
> the Lord delivers them in the
> day of trouble.
> The Lord protects them and
> keeps them alive;
> they are called happy in the
> land. (41.1–2)

Conversely, those who fail to help the poor shall fall from God's grace and suffer His wrath (2 Samuel 12.1–6; Proverbs 14.31, 29.7; Amos 2.6–8, 4.1–3, 5.10–13, 8.4–14; Malachi 3.1–5). Two passages from Proverbs (17.5, 21.13) are typical:

> Those who mock the poor insult
> their Maker;
> those who are glad at calamity
> will not go unpunished.

> If you close your ear to the cry of
> the poor,
> you will cry out and not be
> heard.

The Old Testament further suggests that it is the wealthy who tend to close their "ear to the cry of the poor," that wealth does not open the doors of heaven, and that wealth can often lead to the exploitation of the poor (Psalms 49.1–20; Proverbs 10.15, 13.7–8, 14.20–21, 22.2, 22.16). This is reiterated throughout the Wisdom of Sirach:

> A rich person does wrong, and
> even adds insults;
> a poor person suffers wrong,
> and must add apologies.
> A rich person will exploit you if
> you can be of use to him,
> but if you are in need he will
> abandon you. (Sirach 13.3–4)

Finally, the poor are seen as blessed in the eyes of God, and hence they will receive their just rewards (1 Samuel 2.7–8; Job 5.15–16; Psalms 9.18, 11.5–6, 14.6, 37.14–15, 113.5–9; Proverbs 28.6; Isaiah 25.4, 41.17). There is the concept that the last shall become first and the first become last (also found in the New Testament, Matthew 19.30; Mark 10.31). The well-known passage about the meek inheriting the earth (also found in the New Testament, Matthew 5.4), is characteristic of this theme:

> Yet a little while, and the wicked
> will be no more;

though you look diligently for
their place, they will not
be there.
But the meek shall inherit the
land,
and delight themselves in
abundant prosperity. (Psalms 37.10–11)

The New Testament

The New Testament echoes many of the same themes found in the Old Testament. However, God's words and wisdom, rather than coming from the prophets, come through Jesus and through Jesus' disciples (primarily Paul). Interestingly, Jesus comes to this world not as a king or wealthy businessman but in poverty and humility, a carpenter by trade. He ministers largely to the poor, bringing them the "Good News." Rather than economically rich, the Son of God is materially impoverished. Why?

The reason is that it is quite consistent with the overall message regarding the poor—that they are blessed in the eyes of the Lord (Matthew 5.1–5.12; Luke 4.16–19, 6.17–49, 9.46–48; 1 Corinthians 1.26–31; 2 Corinthians 6.9–10). In his Sermon on the Mount and Sermon on the Plain, Jesus reiterates the Old Testament theme that it is the poor, the hungry, the meek, and the merciful who will one day reap the rewards that God offers.

Furthermore, each of us will be judged on the basis of how we have treated the least powerful and most vulnerable in our midst. Jesus tells his disciples the manner in which God will make his final judgement on us all:

Then the king will say to those at his right hand, "Come, you that are blessed by my Father, inherit the kingdom prepared for you from the foundation of the world; for I was hungry and you gave me food, I was thirsty and you gave me something to drink, I was a stranger and you welcomed me, I was naked and you gave me clothing, I was sick and you took care of me, I was in prison and you visited me." Then the righteous will answer him, "Lord, when was it that we saw you hungry and gave you food, or thirsty and gave you something to drink? And when was it that we saw you a stranger and welcomed you, or naked and gave you clothing? And when was it that we saw you sick or in prison and visited you?" And the king will answer them, "Truly I tell you, just as you did it to one of the least of these who are members of my family you did it to me." (Matthew 25.34–40)

The Letter of James further elaborates this message, drawing the distinction between faith and works. To simply believe in God and Jesus is not enough. One must also show such belief through one's actions and deeds.

What good is it, my brothers and sisters, if you say you have faith but do not have works? Can faith save you? If a brother or sister is naked and lacks daily food, and one of you says to them, "Go in peace; keep warm and eat your fill," and yet you do not supply their bodily needs, what is the good of that? So faith by itself, if it has no works, is dead. (James 2.14–17)

The showing of kindness, relief, and mercy to others is consistent with a second major theme in the New Testament—love your neighbor as yourself (Matthew 22.34–40; Mark 12–28–34; Romans 13.8–10). Likewise, do unto others as you would have them do unto you (Matthew 7.12).[5] One should thus treat the poor and vulnerable as one would wish to be treated.[6]

As a result, one is instructed to be generous in their help and assistance to the poor. This is conveyed throughout the New Testament (Matthew 6.2–4, 19.16–30; Mark 10.17–31, 12.41–44; Luke 10.25–37, 11.37–41, 12.32–34, 14.7–24, 18.18–30, 19.1–10, 21.1–4; Romans 15.25–27; 2 Corinthians 8.1–15, 9.1–15; Galatians 2.10). The parable that Jesus tells of the Good Samaritan, his story of the widow's offering, and the story of Zacchaeus all reflect this sentiment. This theme continues later in the New Testament as well. For example, during his journeys, Paul speaks to the elders of a newly established church: "In all this I have given you an example that by such work we must support the weak, remembering the words of the Lord Jesus, for he himself said, 'It is more blessed to give than to receive'" (Acts 20.35).[7]

Finally, the teachings of Jesus reinforce the Old Testament theme regarding the dangers of wealth (Matthew 13.22; Luke 1.51–53; 16.19–31; James 1.9–11, 2.1–7, 5.1–6). Jesus proclaims, "You cannot serve God and wealth" (Matthew 6.24). Later, the First Letter to Timothy states, "The love of money is a root of all kinds of evil" (1 Timothy 6.10).

As an illustration of this, Jesus tells the story of the rich man/rich ruler, recounted in three of the four Gospels. The rich ruler asks what he must do to inherit eternal life. Jesus says first to follow the commandments. The ruler says he has done this.

> When Jesus heard this, he said to him, "There is still one thing lacking. Sell all that you own and distribute the money to the poor, and you will have treasure in heaven; then come, follow me." But when he heard this, he became sad; for he was very rich. Jesus looked at him and said, "How hard it is for those who have wealth to enter the kingdom of God! Indeed, it is easier for a camel to go through the eye of a needle than for someone who is rich to enter the kingdom of God." (Luke 18.22–25)

Taken as a whole, the theological and ethical message conveyed in both the Old and New Testaments is one of mercy, generosity, and urgency in helping the poor. This perspective spans the period from Moses, to Jesus, to Paul. It is an issue that has been and remains central to both Judaism and Christianity. As Warren Copeland writes,

> To be specific about the issues of poverty within the Christian tradition, there can be no doubt about its religious status. Indeed, of all contemporary public issues, historically the Christian Scriptures and Christian churches have been most clear that poverty is a religious issue. In the Hebrew Scriptures, kings were judged on how the poor fared under their rule; prophets focused on the gap between the rich and the poor as a reason for God's judgment. In the Gospels, Jesus associated himself with the poor and offered little comfort to the rich. The early churches raised funds to aid the poor among them. Again and again ever since, official and unofficial ethical statements by churches have centered on the issue of poverty. The overall thrust of this tradition is to place God's presence with the poor and God's judgment upon the affluent who misuse or ignore the needs of the poor. (1994: 125–126)

To disregard the plight of the poor and at the same time profess allegiance to Judeo-Christian values is simply an oxymoron. As the Catholic bishops wrote in their pastoral letter, "No one may claim the name Christian and be comfortable in the face of the hunger, homelessness, insecurity, and injustice found in this country and the world" (National Conference of Catholic Bishops, 1986: 13). And, in fact, virtually all of the major religions worldwide express a deep concern and urgency regarding the plight of the poor.

The underlying lessons pertaining to the poor capture the very essence of what the Judeo-Christian ethic teaches us regarding our everyday interactions with one another. It serves as a blueprint for organizing a just and compassionate society. The barometer for such a society is our treatment of the poor and vulnerable. In short, we are morally only as strong as our weakest link.[8]

American Civic Principles

The political and philosophical principles on which America was founded represent a second set of values that has shaped this country profoundly and that a vast majority of Americans continue to hold in high esteem. Among the most important are the concepts of liberty, justice, equality, and democracy. If we examine America's most revered political documents—the Declaration of Independence, the Constitution, the Bill of Rights, the Gettysburg Address, the Pledge of Allegiance—all stress the centrality of these four concepts.

Within these documents are embedded the most familiar sentences in our collective consciousness. They in turn reflect the principles of liberty, justice, equality, and democracy. For example, the Declaration of Independence proclaims, "We hold these truths to be self-evident, that all men are created equal, that they are endowed by their Creator with certain unalienable Rights, that among these are Life, Liberty, and the pursuit of Happiness."

The Constitution of the United States begins with the following sentence: "We the People of the United States, in Order to form a more perfect Union, establish Justice, insure domestic Tranquility, provide for the common defense, promote the general Welfare, and secure the Blessings of Liberty to ourselves and our Posterity, do ordain and establish this Constitution for the United States of America."

Abraham Lincoln began his Gettysburg Address with the well-known words "Fourscore and seven years ago our fathers brought forth, on this continent, a new nation, conceived in Liberty, and dedicated to the proposition that all men are created equal." Lincoln ended with the declaration that those who died at Gettysburg "shall not have died in vain—that this nation, under God, shall have a new birth of freedom—and that government of the people, by the people, for the people, shall not perish from the Earth."

Finally, in America's classrooms each day, school children recite the familiar "I pledge allegiance to the Flag of the United States of America, and to the Republic for which it stands, one Nation under God, indivisible, with liberty and justice for all."

All of these statements, and the documents of which they are a part, reflect the general concepts of liberty, justice, equality, and/or democracy. They are arguably our most important political ideals and constitute the guiding principles that we as Americans expect our government to reflect and protect.[9]

My thesis in this section is that each of these principles is undermined by the existence of poverty. Just as the condition of slavery grossly compromised such principles during the country's first hundred years, the condition of poverty undercuts their realization today. These four political values are juxtaposed with the condition of poverty in order to illustrate this point.

Liberty

The first definition of liberty in Webster's Dictionary is "the quality or state of being free: (a) the power to do as one pleases; (b) freedom from physical restraint; (c) freedom from arbitrary or despotic control; (d) the positive enjoyment of various social, political, or economic rights and privileges; (e) the power of choice."

If we think about the condition of poverty as described in chapter 2, it is clear that impoverishment infringes upon each of these subdefinitions of liberty. The poor do not have the power to do as they please; they do not have freedom from physical restraint; they are not free from arbitrary control; they are limited in their enjoyment of various social, political, or economic rights and privileges; and their power of choice is constrained.[10]

These restraints are exemplified in the words of Mary Summers, whom I interviewed for my book *Living on the Edge*. She was asked to summarize what her life was like in poverty and on welfare:

This is probably about the lowest point in my life, and I hope I never reach it again. Because this where you're just up against a wall. You can't make a move. You can't buy anything that you want for your home. You can't go on a vacation. You can't take a weekend off and go and see things because it costs too much. And it's just such a waste of life. (1994: 52)

Her comment "You can't make a move" perfectly captures in five words the effect of poverty upon liberty.

Poverty severely constrains people's choices, power, and ability to act. This is precisely what Mary Summers was describing in her personal life. The poor in America are not able to benefit from the social blessings of liberty to the extent that their economically better-off counterparts can. This is one of the overriding characteristics of what it means to be poor in America.

As should be clear from chapter 2, it is not a matter of being unable to purchase a flat-screen television or a sport utility vehicle. Rather, it is a question of being unable to afford the basic necessities of life in order to function at a level that most Americans would say is minimally acceptable. It is a question of being unable to reach a reasonable facsimile of "life, liberty, and the pursuit of happiness." Any trip to an impoverished urban or rural area in the United States will make it poignantly clear that these goals are significantly compromised within such an environment. It is in this sense that Amartya Sen argues the central meaning of impoverishment is captured by "poverty as lack of freedom" (1992: 152).[11]

Occasionally, the nation has recognized this. During the 1940s, the idea that poverty served to undermine freedom was explicitly recognized. On the eve of America's entrance into World War II, President Roosevelt introduced the concept of the Four Freedoms in his State of the Union Address on January 6, 1941. According to Roosevelt, they represented the freedoms that America and the free world stood for—freedom of speech, freedom of worship, freedom from want, and freedom from fear. *Freedom from want* expressed the idea that Americans should be free from the type of poverty we have described, and, as Eric Foner notes, this freedom seemed to "strike the deepest chord in a nation just emerging from the Great Depression" (1998: 225). Once the United States entered the war, the Four Freedoms quickly became one of Roosevelt's most important criteria for distinguishing between the Allies and the Axis, while Norman

Rockwell's paintings of the Four Freedoms were an enormously popular portrayal on the home front.[12]

Twenty years later, President Lyndon B. Johnson would return to this theme with his Great Society initiatives. As he explained to the Democratic National Convention in 1964, "the man who is hungry, who cannot find work or educate his children, who is bowed by want, that man is not fully free."

Up to this point, I have been focusing on the constraints of poverty that diminish liberty in an economic and social sense. However, these constraints also diminish liberty in a more civic sense. The federal and state governments, along with our judicial systems, have traditionally been viewed as the guardians and protectors of specific freedoms that are entitlements of all citizens. The Bill of Rights, for example, specifies some of these, including freedom of speech, freedom to assemble peaceably, and so on. Liberty is often interpreted as the freedom to engage in such activities and rights. In this sense, liberty is similar to that of Webster's earlier fourth subdefinition.

A fundamental point regarding this interpretation of liberty is that, although certain rights are guaranteed by the Constitution and by the Bill of Rights, if economic deprivation reduces an individual's ability to fully partake of those rights, liberty has been curtailed, even though it is still guaranteed under the law.

Take the judicial right to be assumed innocent until proven guilty. A strong argument can be made that the ability to fully benefit from this right is directly affected by the financial resources one is able to bring to bear upon the legal system.[13] Assume a hypothetical case of two individuals—Sam, who is wealthy and lives in a suburban setting, and Ned, who is impoverished and lives in an inner city. Both are accused of an identical crime, with incriminating circumstances surrounding their cases, yet both are innocent. The question is, Who has the greater likelihood of receiving a verdict of not guilty?

Sam will be able to hire an eminently qualified and experienced lawyer, or perhaps a team of expert trial lawyers. The lawyer(s) will be able to devote considerable time, energy, and resources to the case, since Sam can afford for them to do so. Ned, in all likelihood, will have to depend upon the public defender, who will be burdened with a heavy caseload that has already stretched him or her to the limit. By necessity, far less time and energy will be spent preparing for Ned's defense.

These factors, along with many others related to economic class, increase the odds that Sam will receive the proper verdict of not guilty, while they decrease the odds that Ned will receive the same verdict. Certainly there are many times when individuals in Ned's position receive a verdict of not guilty, and times when individuals in Sam's position receive a verdict of guilty. However, if we were to repeat this experiment over and over, it is quite probable that, on the whole, individuals in Sam's situation would receive not guilty verdicts significantly more often than those in Ned's situation.[14]

As Derek Bok further points out, a case such as Ned's may not even reach the point of trial. Bok uses the right to an attorney to illustrate how economic reality infringes upon guaranteed liberties:

> Surely there is no other nation where the nature of individual freedom has been elaborated in such detail, or any other society that is so well organized to ensure that essential liberties are defended and preserved. At the same time, freedom in the United States may be more limited by other forces than it is abroad. For example, the government in America often makes less effort than others to make sure that all or most Americans have the means to exercise important rights they formally possess. To choose but one example, it is impressive to grant everyone accused of a serious crime the right to qualified counsel, but the right may not be worth much in practice if the lawyers assigned turn out to have so little time that they can scarcely do more than hastily agree to exchange a guilty plea for a slightly reduced sentence. Yet this is the situation that exists in many jurisdictions of this country. (1996: 311)

Many other rights can also be seen in this light. For example, it is legally guaranteed that anyone who meets several basic qualifications such as age and residency can run for public office. Yet in reality, economics has a profound impact on the ability to mount a campaign for office, and even more on the ability to win. Who is it that can afford to take time off from work to run for office? Generally, it is those who are either independently well off or who have jobs that allow them the luxury of doing so. Consequently, individuals with the fewest economic resources are the least likely to avail themselves of such a right.

Or take the basic right to vote. Although all citizens have the right to vote, in reality, economics plays a role in influencing overall voter participation rates. The fact that the United States conducts its elections on Tuesdays rather than on weekends, combined with our cumbersome registration procedures, tends to create barriers for the poor. Leonard Beeghley notes,

> In sum, while any individual can presumably go to the polls, the structure of voting means that middle-class and rich people dominate this form of participation. The poor and working class are least capable of voting on a working day, getting registered, coping with voting procedures, and overcoming the problem posed by separate and frequent elections. These facts exist externally to individuals, decisively influencing rates of participation. Thus, for those at the lower end of the stratification hierarchy, the pluralist system may seem open but it is closed in fact. (2000: 143)

These examples illustrate the more general point I am making regarding liberty in the sense of rights guaranteed under the law. Although in principle such rights apply to all, in reality, economics, and particularly poverty, can infringe upon the full realization of those rights.[15]

Justice

As with each of the values discussed, volumes have been written about the meaning of justice. In a nutshell, justice within the context of the United States has come to imply a sense of fairness and deservedness. When someone works hard and plays by the rules, we often hope that the person will receive his or her "just rewards." Or, when a crime is committed, justice is seen as being served if the criminal is sentenced to a punishment that fits the nature and the severity of the crime. On the other hand, if an individual commits a serious crime and is neither apprehended nor punished, the feeling is that an injustice has occurred.

In cases where individuals experience outcomes and consequences that are congruent with their prior actions and behaviors, the world is seen as just. Conversely, in situations where individuals experience outcomes and consequences that are incongruent with their prior actions and behaviors, the world is perceived as unjust.

This concept of balance is visually represented in the symbol of justice found from local courtrooms to the U.S. Capitol—that of Themis, or Lady Justice. Here one finds a woman, often blindfolded, holding a measuring scale in one hand and a sword in the other. Justice is portrayed as being impartial and not beholden to special interests (hence the blindfold). The fact that she is holding the scales has a double meaning. They imply that evidence should be weighed carefully in deciding how justice will be delivered. But they also suggest that justice is served by balance. That is, prior actions and future consequences should be in balance and congruent with each other. Furthermore, the sword gripped in her right hand represents the strength and authority of justice and acts as a balance to the judgement derived from the scales held in her left hand.[16]

If we think of justice in terms of balance and congruence, one can ask whether the condition of poverty is just. Poverty is clearly a negative condition that very few people would wish upon themselves. Consequently, the critical question becomes whether such poverty is deserved because of prior negative actions and behaviors. If the answer is yes, justice in the sense I have described is served. If the answer is no, an injustice has occurred.[17]

Interestingly, this has been the criterion used over the centuries, particularly since the English Poor Laws of 1601, to divide the poor into the categories of deserving and undeserving. The deserving poor are individuals deemed worthy of our compassion and assistance because they find themselves in poverty through little fault of their own. Thus, an injustice has occurred. Such persons include those who suffer from an unavoidable illness or accident, children, widows, and so on. On the other hand, individuals who fall into the category of the undeserving poor are seen as meriting neither our compassion nor our assistance. Such poverty is perceived as the result of laziness, immorality, or some other failing, and therefore impoverishment is a just or deserving consequence of prior behavior.

Using the concept of justice I have described, to what extent is poverty just? My argument is that, for the vast majority of individuals in poverty, the condition is quite unmerited and therefore unjust. If we simply examine the composition of the poverty population (see chapter 2), we quickly discover that 35 percent of the poor are under age 18. I challenge anyone to make the argument that an eight-year-old child deserves to live in poverty as a result of his or her prior actions. That argument simply cannot be made.

An additional 10 percent of the poor are over age 65, a category that we generally feel is deserving of some kind of assistance. A further 31 percent of the poor are between the ages of twenty-five and sixty-four and suffer from some type of severe disability. Therefore, simply looking at the demographics, we see that approximately three quarters of the poverty population fall into categories that most people would argue in no way serve justice.

The remaining quarter of the poor are men and women between the ages of eighteen and sixty-four who do not have a work disability. To what extent do they deserve their fate of poverty? Or, put another way, to what extent is their poverty a result of immorality and/or laziness? As we have seen in prior chapters, there are various situations and circumstances that can lead to poverty. However, as argued in chapter 3, many of these situations are the result of structural failings and conditions that lie beyond the control of the individual. These include the involuntary loss of a job, difficulty in finding work because of economic conditions, families that split up against a partner's wishes, jobs that do not pay a living wage, racial and/or gender discrimination, and so on down the list.

If we combine these cases with the previously discussed categories, we come to an overall conclusion that, for the vast majority of the poor, impoverishment cannot be justified in terms of prior negative actions. In short, justice is simply not being served.

The discussion of justice up to this point has focused on individuals and groups. However, there is another way of thinking about justice, and that is on a societal level. Let us consider an economically poor country such as Ethiopia. If one were to hear that the vast majority of the poor in Ethiopia were in situations where their poverty was undeserved, one's reaction might well be sympathy. However, it is also likely that we would view their poverty within the larger context of the entire country's poverty. That is, although the Ethiopian government may want to make a concerted effort to reduce poverty, that goal would be extremely difficult to accomplish given the country's limited resources and low GDP.

This is clearly not the case in the United States. We are a wealthy country. Despite the ongoing concerns about the federal debt, we have the ability to prioritize our goals in order to make a vigorous effort to reduce poverty. However, we choose not to do so. As a result, we live in a society where an injustice is occurring for the vast majority of the poor; yet collectively we choose to look the other way.

As I noted at the beginning of this book, such injustice can be observed all around us. It is most apparent if we contrast the wealth and comfortable standard of living that many Americans experience with the poverty and suffering found among the bottom 20 percent of the population. This was precisely the contrast that President Johnson was referring to in his inaugural address of 1965, when he spoke about the meaning of America:

> Conceived in justice, written in liberty, bound in union, it was meant one day to inspire the hopes of all mankind. And it binds us still. If we keep its terms, we shall flourish. First, justice was the promise that all who made the journey would share in the fruits of the land. In a land of great wealth, families must not live in hopeless poverty. In a land rich in harvest, children just must not go hungry. In a land of healing miracles, neighbors must not suffer and die unattended. In a great land of learning and scholars, young people must be taught to read and write. (Johnson, 1965b)

To allow such situations to exist on a societal level is not only a moral outrage but violates one of our most fundamental principles—that of justice.

Equality

The concept of equality in America is an interesting one. It has seldom been thought of in the sense that every American should experience equality of outcomes.[18] Rather, it has meant that there should be equality in terms of access to opportunities.[19] Every citizen has the right to an education and a means to a livelihood. No one should be denied these on the basis of race, gender, class, religion, or other extraneous factors.

Furthermore, equality of opportunity includes the notion that individuals should be judged and rewarded on the basis of their abilities. Robert Haveman notes, in his book *Starting Even*, that "it has to do with having the same chance to run the race for economic success as others with similar talents and drives. Equality of opportunity exists if a black youth and a white youth have the same access to education, training, jobs, earnings, and incomes, according to their abilities" (1988: 30).

Using these definitions, I argue that poverty dramatically infringes on the concept of equal access to opportunity. For example, education has long been viewed in the United States as an important means for achieving opportunities such as economic success. Public education began in the nineteenth century as a way of ensuring that all children would have access to this important tool. Yet in order to effectively compete for economic opportunities, the quality and quantity of education are critical. On both counts, poverty stunts the educational process (Schiller, 2004). Public education is funded largely through local real estate taxes. Those who grow up in poor households are likely to be living in lower-income areas. These communities, in turn, are limited in the amount of financial resources that they can devote to their school systems (because they have limited tax bases). The ability of a poor school district to purchase state-of-the-art educational resources (e.g., computers, lab equipment, library materials) and to attract highly qualified teachers (by paying competitive salaries) is fundamentally compromised. This results in a reduction in the quality of education that each pupil receives. One has only to compare the physical facilities at any inner-city public school with those at an affluent public suburban school or private school to observe the process I am describing. Furthermore, the ability to go on to college, let alone a prestigious college, is severely constrained by poverty. Low-income eighteen-year-olds often do not have the resources, time, expectations, or educational preparation (because of the limitations described) to pursue such a goal.

These realities illustrate that while all children have access to education, the type of education they wind up with is strongly influenced by their family's socioeconomic standing. This, in turn, constrains their ability to compete for future opportunities in the marketplace. Seen in this light, equal access to opportunities becomes less fact than fiction.

The manner in which poverty restricts access to opportunities can be witnessed in other areas as well. Take the case of health. In order to effectively compete in the labor market, one must have reasonably good health. As we saw in chapters 2 and 4, poverty has a negative impact on health status. Adults who are poor are more likely to have higher rates of heart disease, cancer, diabetes, and virtually every other major illness and cause of death. Children in poverty are also more likely to suffer from various health ailments, such as lead poisoning, asthma, and injury from accidents and violence. These illnesses and conditions are less likely to be attended to through the health care system. As a result, health deteriorates, again leading to reduced opportunities.

In short, the American ideal of equal access to opportunities is undermined by the existence of poverty. As illustrated in our examples, the poor simply do not have the same chance that others in our society do to compete for opportunities. This is particularly troubling in that America has prided itself on being the land of the American Dream, where individuals can freely travel from "rags to riches" upon the ladder of opportunity. The Statue of Liberty beckons:

> Give me your tired, your poor,
> Your huddled masses yearning to breathe free,
> The wretched refuse of your teeming shore.
> Send these, the homeless, tempest-tost to me,
> I lift my lamp beside the golden door!

Yet despite Liberty's invitation, the golden door of opportunity is simply not open to the same extent for all Americans.

Democracy

A fourth key American value has been the belief in democracy, that is, the belief that government should be "of the people, by the people, for the people." By its very definition, democracy implies that all citizens and groups have equal access to the democratic process. The true nature of a democracy is attained through such access and participation.

This process can be thought of in terms of a level playing field. As Thomas Simon writes,

> All definitions of democracy have a common presupposition. All
> presuppose a level playing field. The phrase "a level playing field"
> serves as a convenient metaphor for saying that a democracy,
> defined anyplace along the spectrum, presupposes the absence of
> a wide disparity in the participatory capabilities of the citizenry.
> Widespread participatory disparity, especially among groups,
> undermines democracy. (1995: 145)

If particular groups tend to be excluded from or underrepresented in democratic processes (for whatever reasons other than voluntary), there is a structural flaw in the democracy.

Poverty, I argue, reflects one of those structural flaws. Impoverishment significantly impacts on the poor's ability to fully participate in the democratic process. I discussed earlier how the acts of voting and running for office are systematically made more difficult for the poor. Although these rights exist for all, economic deprivation disproportionally blocks their full realization for those who fall within poverty's ranks.

Other aspects of democratic participation are also made more difficult for those in poverty. For example, the ability to lobby and exert influence on the appropriate players is often critical in the democratic decision-making process in today's America. Such lobbying efforts are highly dependent on financial resources, of which the poor by definition have few. The poor's "special interests" are rarely lobbied for in the same manner and with the same economic clout that other special-interest groups are able to bring to bear. As a result, the concerns and needs of the poverty-stricken are often given short shrift in the public arena.

Likewise, being well informed regarding pertinent issues is an important component of democracy. Wise decision making, both individual and collective, depends on citizens' ability to understand the various dimensions of particular topics and then to act on such knowledge. Poverty compromises the ability of low-income households to achieve such an understanding, which in turn affects the quality of their participation. Hobbled by poor education and facing ongoing concerns with economic survival, the poor are often less informed than the rest of society regarding public issues.

As a result of these circumstances, the poor are often invisible to the democratic process. A poignant expression of this was voiced in 1790 by John Adams:

> The poor man's conscience is clear; yet he is ashamed. . . . He
> feels himself out of the sight of others, groping in the dark.
> Mankind takes no notice of him. He rambles and wanders
> unheeded. In the midst of a crowd, at church, in the market . . .
> he is in as much obscurity as he would be in a garret or a cellar.
> He is not disapproved, censured, or reproached; he is only not
> seen. (Arendt, 1963: 63–64)

This sense of darkness and obscurity captures the essence of the poverty stricken who are left out of the democratic process.

In short, the democratic process is undermined by the existence of poverty. Economic deprivation infringes upon the ability of the poor to participate in the process in roughly the same manner as others within society (Gaffaney, 2000; Verba, 2001). Such disparities should raise a red flag among those who believe in the importance of democracy. As Simon argues, "It does not make any sense for a nation to proclaim itself a democracy if there is widespread and structural participatory disparity within the nation. A nation that strives for democracy must make a commitment to alleviate the plight of disadvantaged groups" (1995: 170–171).

Concluding Note

There are obviously other conditions beyond poverty that undermine the principles of liberty, justice, equality, and democracy. Some of these are discrimination, ignorance, and intolerance. They, along with poverty, prevent all citizens from sharing in the benefits of our American ideals.

But the key word here is *all*. The Pledge of Allegiance ends not with the words "liberty and justice for some" or "liberty and justice for most" but "liberty and justice for all." If the principles of liberty, justice, equality, and democracy are to fulfill their true meaning, they must apply to all. The fact that a significant percentage of our citizens live in circumstances that infringe on this goal should be cause for concern. In short, poverty tarnishes our legitimacy as the standard-bearer of these principles. I can think of no stronger *American* reason than this to motivate our fellow citizens.

A very simple way to visualize the points I have been making is to do the following. Take a moment and ask yourself what it is that you think America should represent. Many things will come to mind. Each of us will have our own set of principles that we would like to see the United States epitomize. However, I think it is quite safe to say that very few individuals would conceptualize poverty as part of their image of what America should be about. In fact, most people, if they were asked to include poverty in their idealized image of what America should strive for, would suggest that the idea is completely absurd and un-American. And that is precisely my point.

Essence of
Citizenship

6

What counts is that a wrong has been committed. . . . As citizens we must prevent wrong-doing since the world we all share, wrong-doer, wrong-sufferer and spectator, is at stake.

Hannah Arendt

MORE THAN TWO MILLENNIA have passed since the Greek philosophers debated the nature and meaning of community and citizenship. Athenian discussions revolved around several fundamental civic questions—Does citizenship imply certain obligations regarding the well-being of others? Under what conditions were such obligations more binding? To what extent should citizens be held responsible for the maintenance and well-being of their communities? These questions and their resolution were vital to the construction of ancient Greek society, and they have helped to lay the civic foundations of modern civilization.

More recently, the idea of the social contract has taken prominence in our discussions of the obligations and responsibilities that we have to each other and to the wider community. From Jean-Jacques Rousseau's *On the Social Contract,* written in 1695, to Robert Putnam's more recent *Bowling Alone* (2000), political philosophers have attempted to inform us as to the manner and scope of our civic obligations.

In this chapter, I argue that the concept of community and citizenship represents a third significant link between Americans and the issue of poverty. As members of communities larger than ourselves, we carry a civic obligation to alleviate serious harms that befall community members, particularly when such hardships are caused by conditions largely beyond the immediate control of any one individual.[1] Poverty is such a condition.

Exerting wise stewardship within our communities is also an important civic obligation. We have recently begun to understand the importance of such an obligation with respect to the physical environment. This has involved a fundamental shift in thinking about the consequences of our actions within the framework of an ecological system. I argue later in this chapter that we must begin to understand poverty in a similar light, one that considers the impact of poverty and rising inequality upon the sustainability and health of our social system.

In many ways I argue that we must live up to the expression "I am my brother's keeper." The ability to do so is in the finest sense of what it means to be human. Indeed, the word *humane*, whose root is *human*, is "marked or motivated by concern with the alleviation of suffering" (American Heritage College Dictionary, 1993). Such empathy occurs within a group context, since a distinguishing feature of humanity is that it is organized around the concept of community and society. As Alan Wolfe writes in his book *Whose Keeper?*

> Society does not carry out our obligations to others for us, but instead creates the possibility that we can carry those obligations out ourselves. If we choose not to do so, we deny what is social about us and are left only with something resembling the state of nature. (1989: 23)

Or, as Jean-Jacques Rousseau wrote much earlier,

> Why are kings without pity for their subjects? It is because they count on never being human beings. Why are the rich so harsh to the poor? It is because they do not have fear of becoming poor. Why does a noble have such contempt for a peasant? It is

because he never will be a peasant. . . . It is the weakness of the human being that makes it sociable, it is our common sufferings that carry our hearts to humanity; we would owe it nothing if we were not humans. Every attachment is a sign of insufficiency. . . . Thus from our weakness itself, our fragile happiness is born. (*Emile*, bk. 4)

Obviously, we are each distinct individuals, and that individuality is an essential component of our characters. Yet all of us are also members of communities much larger than ourselves.[2] These communities include our families, places of work, neighborhoods, and so on. As such, we have a role to play within this larger group and community context. In this chapter I discuss that role as it relates to poverty.

I begin with the issue of responsibility. Specifically, to what extent do the nonpoor bear a shared responsibility for addressing poverty, and if they do have such a responsibility, why? The issue of responsibility has been at the heart of the historic and contemporary debate surrounding poverty. Is the responsibility for poverty to be found within the individual who finds him- or herself poor; is it to be found in the broader structures of society; or is it to be found in some combination of individual and societal influences? The manner in which we answer these questions is fundamental to understanding what our individual and collective responses to poverty should be.

Suppose, for example, that I believe the poor have no one but themselves to blame—that their poverty is a result of personal inadequacies such as a lack of motivation or bad judgment. In this case, my individual and collective obligation to those impoverished will be weak to nonexistent. In fact, I may very well feel that such folks "got what they deserved."

On the other hand, assume that my view of poverty is that it stems from events and forces beyond the control or responsibility of any single individual—an economy that produces low-wage jobs or an educational structure that fails to adequately prepare poor children. Here, I will be much more likely to feel a personal and/or collective imperative to assist those in need, since such individuals find themselves in poverty through little fault of their own.

The issue of responsibility is therefore intimately connected to the issue of causality. I should point out that in our earlier discussions involving self-interest and values (in chapters 4 and 5), the causes of poverty were relatively unimportant—it is still in our self-interest to attack the condition of poverty whatever the reasons may be. A similar position applies to the question of values (i.e., the imperative to help the poor within the Judeo-Christian ethic basically stands, regardless of the causes underlying poverty).

In the case of responsibility, however, the issue of causality is critical. If the cause of poverty is perceived as lying beyond the control of the individual, we generally will not hold such persons responsible for their condition and will therefore be more willing to extend a helping hand. On the other hand, if poverty can be traced to the deliberate actions of individuals, we will then hold such individuals responsible for their fate and consequently be less willing to help. The issue of individual responsibility, and by extension that of shared responsibility, is intimately connected to that of causality.[3]

The concept of responsibility also underlies the longstanding distinction between what has been called the deserving and the undeserving poor. Since the English Poor Laws of 1601, such a distinction has served to divide the poor into the categories of worthy and unworthy recipients of our compassion and assistance. Those perceived as falling into poverty through no fault of their own (e.g., because of unavoidable illness, death of a spouse) were often viewed as deserving of society's compassion and help. On the other hand, those characterized as the able-bodied poor were seen as undeserving of such assistance. Responsibility has therefore been central to the debates surrounding the extent of our collective obligations to the poor.

And it continues to this day. The recent U.S. welfare reform debate culminated in the Personal Responsibility and Work Opportunity Reconciliation Act of 1996. It is no coincidence that the word *responsibility* is featured prominently in the title of this act. Much of the emphasis in this bill and its reauthorization has been to encourage individual responsibility with regard to welfare, work, and family. The concept of responsibility remains fundamental to the ideological and political debates that surround the issue of poverty.

I have argued that the high levels of U.S. poverty are primarily the result of structural conditions, rather than individual inadequacies. These include a shortage of decent-paying jobs and a lack of adequate social supports. As a result, the premise of this chapter is that we all bear responsibility for the existence and alleviation of poverty. It is one of the obligations that accompany the privilege of being an American citizen. The connections among responsibility, reciprocity, citizenship, and poverty are examined in the following sections.

Responsibility, Reciprocity, and Citizenship

One formal dimension of membership in a community is citizenship. For example, we are citizens of municipalities, counties, and states, as well as citizens of the country. This formal aspect of what it means to be a member of society carries both a legal and civic status.

Fundamental to the civic component of citizenship is responsibility. The term *citizenship* as defined by Webster's consists of two interrelated parts— "the state of being vested with the rights, privileges, and duties of a citizen" and "the character of an individual viewed as a member of society; behavior in terms of the duties, obligations, and functions of a citizen" (*Webster's Encyclopedic Unabridged Dictionary of the English Languages*, 1996). In other words, citizenship bestows certain rights and privileges upon its members but asks in return that individuals reciprocate by actively engaging in various duties, obligations, and functions (in other words, responsibilities), which in turn benefit the community or society as a whole. That is the essence of citizenship.

Take the example of trial by jury. As Americans, we expect that if accused of a crime, we will be tried by a jury of our peers. This is a fundamental right that as citizens of the United States we are entitled to. Yet paradoxically, many of us are reluctant to serve on such juries.[4] We justify this reluctance by arguing that our time is too short or too valuable, that we have other more pressing responsibilities, that someone else can be found to take our place, and so on down the list. Nevertheless, on an intuitive level, many of us would agree that this reluctance is not a component of good citizenship. Why?

The reason lies in the concept of reciprocity. In order to call oneself a good citizen, one cannot simply take (in this case the benefit of a trial by jury), without at the same time giving something in return (such as jury service).[5] This concept of reciprocity is what ensures that responsibility is a vital component of citizenship.

Citizenship thus involves not just reaping the benefits that accrue to us from being citizens in the community but also accepting the responsibility to help maintain the common good. Such responsibility is twofold: individual responsibility, and shared responsibility, which is not as familiar but is equally important. Each is discussed in the following sections.

Individual Responsibility

Within the context of citizenship, what constitutes individual responsibility, and why is it important? I suggest that individual responsibility lies in the ability to manage one's own affairs in a socially accountable manner. What might this entail? Although any list is open to subjectivity, there is a set of behaviors that many of us would undoubtedly agree belong on such a list. For example, living within the boundaries of well-established laws such as not robbing one's neighbor, paying one's taxes, and participating and voting in elections, along with countless other behaviors, are consistent with individual responsibility.

Those who violate such laws and standards of behavior are generally not considered models of good citizenship. Why? By failing to meet these accepted standards, individuals often place an undue burden on their fellow citizens, as well as the broader community. The example of taxes will suffice. Those who refuse to pay their taxes yet at the same time share in the benefits paid for by taxation cause other citizen's taxes to go up and/or the quality of their services to go down. Such individuals are taking without giving in return. This behavior is inconsistent with the principle of reciprocity that underlies good citizenship.

Beyond compliance with established laws and regulations, individual responsibility also entails a willingness to take care of oneself and one's immediate family to the best of one's own abilities. It was in this context that Teddy Roosevelt noted, "The first requisite of a good citizen in this republic of ours is that he shall be able and willing to pull his weight" (Andrews, 1993: 154).

This component of individual responsibility revolves once again around the concept of reciprocity. The status of *citizen* endows individuals with certain rights and privileges. In return, individuals have a responsibility not to economically burden their fellow citizens if they can avoid it. Citizenship involves being able to pull your own weight to the best of your abilities.

It is within this context that Americans often assert that those who are poor are not fulfilling their end of the bargain. They point to the fact that poor households utilize low-income government assistance programs to meet their daily needs, demonstrating that they are not fully supporting themselves or their families.[6] In addition, the perception is often that they have brought this situation on themselves. This position leads one to ask, "Is this not an abdication of the poor's responsibility, and if so, why should we as citizens bear any responsibility for alleviating the situation?"

This question is critical to resolving what our collective obligations are regarding the issue of poverty. What I have argued in chapter 3 is that the condition of poverty is primarily the result of structural failings within the U.S. economic and political systems, rather than the result of individuals' unwillingness to pull their own weight. Although most of the poor are trying their best under adverse conditions, trying their best is not enough to eradicate the condition of poverty. Does this absolve the poor from any individual responsibility? Assuredly not. What it does suggest, however, is that the scope of their responsibility must be understood within the context of these constraints.

Beyond the empirical case built in chapter 3, there are several other lines of evidence that illustrate why much of the responsibility for poverty is not to be found within the poor themselves. First, as discussed in chapter 5, a substantial percentage of the U.S. poor at any point in time fall into categories that many of us would agree should not be held responsible for their economic condition—35 percent of the current poor in America are children under age 18, while 10 percent are 65 or older (U.S. Bureau of the Census, 2003a). Consequently, nearly half of the poor population in the United States consists of either children or the elderly, two age categories that many Americans would undoubtedly maintain should not be seen as responsible for or deserving of their poverty. Nearly one-third (31 percent) of the poor between ages 25 and 64 also suffer from some type of severe disability, again placing them in a category that few would say are deserving of their poverty.

For those of working age, a substantial body of survey and ethnographic work has shown that the poor tend to strongly affirm the importance of hard work and of independently supporting oneself and one's family as important life goals, coupled with a disdain of welfare (Rank, 1994). The life patterns of employment also reveal that the vast majority of the poor have worked in the past and will work in the future. Consequently, the behaviors and attitudes of the poor largely mirror those of mainstream America in

terms of their willingness to abide by the rules of the game, again suggest-
ing that individuals are not shirking their individual responsibilities.

In addition, as we saw in chapters 2, 3, and 4, the patterns of poverty
and welfare use are short term. Those who fall into poverty do so temporarily and are able to get back on their feet fairly quickly. This implies that
for a good portion of their lives, those who experience poverty are not drawing on welfare funds but rather have been contributing to various safety net
programs through federal and state taxes that they have paid out across the
life course. This again suggests that individuals who do experience poverty
are largely abiding by their individual responsibilities.

Finally, as demonstrated in chapter 4, two-thirds of the American population will utilize a welfare program sometime between the ages of 20 and
65. Rather than an aberrant behavior that occurs among a small slice of the
population, reliance on the safety net for some period of time occurs among
a clear majority of Americans. Instead of viewing this behavior as "not pulling one's weight," we might more appropriately interpret it as a common
life-course event triggered by periods of economic vulnerability during adulthood. For all of these reasons, I argue that much of the responsibility for
addressing poverty must be shared by all of us.[7]

Poverty as a Shared Responsibility

We now come to a second type of responsibility essential to citizenship
and community membership, that of shared responsibility. In other words,
what are my obligations, beyond those to myself and my immediate family, to my fellow citizens? Or, put another way, to what degree am I my
brother's keeper? These and similar questions reflect the basic concept of
shared responsibility.

As I argued earlier, the essence of citizenship is reciprocity. Just as individual responsibility is a component of such reciprocity, so too is shared
responsibility. As citizens of the United States we receive a number of benefits derived from the larger community and its well-being. But as part of the
bargain of citizenship, we also have a shared responsibility for the maintenance of that community. Such maintenance involves, among other things,
addressing various injuries and wrongs that befall our communities and its
members. As Larry May writes in his book *Sharing Responsibility*,

As members of communities . . . we derive various benefits, which change the scope of our responsibilities. The shared responsibility we should feel for the harms perpetrated within our communities is precisely the cost we incur by being members of those communities. But because we rarely think about responsibility in communal terms, it is difficult for most of us to accept these responsibilities. (1992: 183)

I argue further that the concept of shared responsibility becomes particularly relevant when such wrongs and injuries are the result of factors generated not at the individual level but at the group or societal level. In this case, responsibility shifts from a personal obligation to a shared responsibility. Where egregious conditions are clearly beyond the control of the individuals directly affected, all members of the community must share in the responsibility and alleviation of those circumstances.[8]

Take the case of unemployment. As mentioned in chapter 3, most economists argue that within capitalist economies, there exists what is called a natural unemployment rate. This represents the level of unemployment necessary for the smooth functioning of a free-market economy. As unemployment falls below such a level, the costs of producing goods rise because employers must offer greater financial incentives to attract qualified workers; these costs are passed on to the consumer, resulting in inflation.

A consequence of this (referred to as the Phillips Curve problem) is that conscious decisions are made, particularly by the Federal Reserve Board, to ensure that unemployment will not fall below a level of approximately 4 percent. As a result, those of us who are currently employed enjoy the benefits of low rates of inflation. However, this comes at the expense of those currently out of work, whose lack of gainful employment is ultimately the result of policies and dynamics that guarantee that at any point in time there will not be enough jobs available to all who want one.

Likewise, when wages are driven down through various mechanisms such as global competition, we benefit because the prices of consumer items and services are kept relatively low. Again, however, this benefit comes at the expense of those trying to survive on the low wages paid by employers.

I believe that community membership and citizenship implies that we must bear some responsibility in moderating such distress, since it is beyond the immediate control of the harmed individuals. In our illustration, this could be done in a variety of ways. Concerned citizens might collectively lobby to ensure that unemployment insurance adequately covers those who are out of work but actively seeking employment. Individuals could generate grassroots support for policies that supplement or raise workers' low wages. Families might engage in direct assistance through their churches, synagogues, or community centers to help particular households get through a spell of unemployment. Regardless of the means, my point is that the nature of citizenship implies that we must assume some of the responsibility for easing the plight of those who are harmed by societal and economic forces that are beyond their control.

This has traditionally been the argument for spending public resources in order to maintain a social safety net.[9] To varying degrees, all industrialized countries assume that part of their societal responsibility is to ensure that such a safety net is in place. This argument is stated succinctly by the Australian Royal Commission on Human Relationships:

> Just as the child is vulnerable to the family, so are families vulnerable to the society of which they are a part. Malnutrition, poor housing, unemployment, discrimination are only a few of the pressures which can affect family life and well-being. Therefore society carries a responsibility to see that families can function effectively, particularly where the case of children is concerned. (1977: 63)

The example of unemployment is analogous to the argument I wish to make regarding our shared responsibility to address the ills of poverty. As detailed earlier in chapter 3, much of the explanation for poverty in America has to do with mechanisms beyond the control of any single individual. On a surface level, these factors manifest themselves in the characteristics of those who lose out at the game, while on a deeper level the causes lie in the fact that the game ensures that there will be losers in the first place. In the final analysis, poverty is generated primarily by the failure of our social, economic, and political systems to provide decent opportunities for all. As a result, the concept of shared responsibility in alleviating poverty becomes particularly relevant. It falls under the category of "duties, obligations, and functions" that is a component of citizenship and community membership.

Shared responsibility is thus a link that obligates and ties the nonpoor to the poor. As argued in prior chapters, the nonpoor have a self-interest in reducing poverty. Addressing poverty is also highly consistent with several core sets of values held by many Americans. What is developed here is a third reason for being concerned about impoverishment. Given the causes and characteristics of poverty, citizenship by its very nature implies that we must assume a shared responsibility for poverty and its alleviation.

Unfortunately, as Americans we tend to focus heavily on the attributes of the poor as the cause of their impoverishment, relieving ourselves of any shared responsibility for their situation. If individuals are solely responsible for their station in life, including poverty, it follows that we as community members are likely to feel little or no social obligation to help. In fact, by providing such help, we may only make the situation worse. Such is the conservative argument regarding the perceived failure of the welfare state to solve the problem of poverty (e.g., Murray, 1984; Olasky, 1992; Schwartz, 2000; Thompson, 1996).

This tendency to individualize problems is further exacerbated in a country as heterogenous as the United States. It becomes difficult to see our interconnectedness when people look different, act differently, or think differently. For example, race often forms a dividing line that separates individuals from one another in our society.[10] In the case of blacks and whites, such separation is seen in the high levels of racial residential segregation found within any city or neighborhood across the United States (Massey and Denton, 1993; U.S. Census Bureau, 2002f). This geographical racial divide weakens the interconnectedness between blacks and whites. We refer to problems as being in the *black* community, rather than within *our* community.

In addition, the United States has always extolled the qualities of individualism and self-reliance (Gans, 1988, 1995). Like heterogeneity, this often works against thinking of ourselves as interconnected, with shared responsibilities for one another. To rely on others for help is often interpreted as a sign of weakness. Individuals perceive that they should resist accepting assistance from others and should not be overly generous in providing such help to others.

Undue emphasis on individualism and self-reliance also prevents us from seeing beyond the individual to the broader dynamics that underlie social problems. As a result, the sources of problems are routinely reduced to individual rather than structural shortcomings. The previous discussion of unemployment is a good example. The inclination among many Americans is to view the unemployed as deficient, rather than to view the condition of unemployment as a deficiency of the economic structure.

Finally, individualism and self-reliance can result in feelings of hostility and insensitivity toward the plight of others, particularly the disadvantaged, which in turn works against the concept of shared responsibility. It obscures our ability to see communities broadly and collectively, and to see our connections with individuals and groups from all economic walks of life. As Larry May notes, "Since insensitivity includes the lack of awareness and critical appreciation of the needs and feelings of others, the more insensitive a person is, the less likely a person is to see correctly his or her place in a community of others" (1992: 69).

Occasionally we do conceptualize ourselves broadly within a "community of others." Unfortunately, it is usually the result of some major crisis, such as a natural catastrophe, war, terrorist act, or economic depression. In these cases, we tend to pull together as neighbors and citizens for the good of all. Typifying this sentiment, Ben Franklin commented during the signing of the Declaration of Independence, "We must all hang together, or most assuredly we shall all hang separately." Such a spirit can also occur during less monumental times, such as the holiday season or when a community's sports team makes a championship run. Under these conditions, there is a bond that often develops between individuals as a result of their membership in a particular community.[11]

It is this spirit, this sense of being a citizen of a larger community, that allows us to visualize our role within "a community of others." That role, I contend, includes sharing the responsibility for grievous ills such as poverty. This sense of shared responsibility ideally manifests itself through personal and government actions. As the National Conference of Catholic Bishops wrote in its pastoral letter on economic justice,

> The responsibility for alleviating the plight of the poor falls upon all members of society. As individuals, all citizens have a duty to assist the poor through acts of charity and personal commitment. But private charity and voluntary action are not sufficient. We also carry out our moral responsibility to assist and empower the poor by working collectively through government to establish just and effective public policies. (1986: 93)

One final point regarding shared responsibility. By failing to assume a shared and active role in addressing poverty, each of us indirectly becomes a part of the problem.[12] Through our collective insensitivity and inaction, we allow the status quo to continue. As Martin Luther King Jr. wrote, "All too many of those who live in affluent America ignore those who exist in poor America. In doing so, the affluent Americans will eventually have to face themselves with the question that Eichmann chose to ignore: How responsible am I for the well-being of my fellows? To ignore evil is to become an accomplice to it" (King, 1967a).

Seen in this light, the cause of poverty is turned on its head. Rather than various personal inadequacies attributed to the poor, a causal factor is found in the nonpoor's personal failure to be actively engaged in combating poverty, which in turn acts to maintain the status quo of poverty and economic disparity. Looking at the problem from this perspective, an underlying cause of and solution to poverty is our own sense of shared responsibility.

Wise Stewardship

A second important component of citizenship is that of stewardship. Like shared responsibility, stewardship implies taking into account the concerns and needs of one's fellow citizens. In this case, however, those citizens largely comprise the generations to come.[13]

Wise stewardship involves the careful management and care of the community and its surrounding environment. We generally think in these terms with respect to the physical environment. In this sense, we speak about being good stewards of the land. This involves carefully maintaining and conserving the environment so that it will be as pleasing and productive for those generations to come as it is for us today.

On the other hand, those who degrade the environment are failing to engage in good stewardship. Such individuals are using or destroying the benefits of the land for their own purposes, while leaving little in return for those to come. This violates the principle of reciprocity that underlies the concept of citizenship. Stewardship is a part of the obligation we have to our children's generation. Likewise, the next generation has an obligation to the following generation. The concept of reciprocity thus unfolds across the generations.

As mentioned, most of us are familiar with stewardship in terms of the physical environment. Yet stewardship applies to other aspects as well. Although we generally do not think in such terms, it includes our management of the social, economic, and political components of our communities (this is discussed at greater length in chapter 7), including the quality of schools, the level of crime, the viability of a city's infrastructure, the amount of financial debt, or the strength of community centers.

How we manage and maintain these elements of our environment is perhaps just as important to future generations as how we care for our physical environment. My argument here is that the existence of poverty seriously undermines our social environment and hence undercuts our ability to practice wise stewardship over our communities.[14]

As discussed in earlier chapters, impoverishment is directly and/or indirectly related to a host of debilitating conditions: a dramatic escalation in health and medical problems for children; increase in the likelihood of teenage pregnancy, high school dropout, and crime among adolescents; stunted economic productivity; destitution among the elderly.

These consequences of poverty are experienced firsthand by the poor and secondhand by the rest of us, as was argued in chapters 2 and 4. Poor neighborhoods become blighted, and the decay spills over into adjacent communities; public education deteriorates, affecting the quality of our workforce; the fear of crime causes the middle class to avoid urban areas altogether; the cost of building prisons becomes an albatross around our necks; and so on down a long list of negative effects on the larger society.

Perhaps one of the most serious consequences of poverty, along with a disproportionate growth of wealth at the top, is the bifurcation of our society. We are increasingly becoming a society of haves and have-nots. Over the past three decades, the gap between the opposite ends of the income and wealth distributions has been getting wider (Braun, 1997; Danziger and Gottschalk, 1995; Ellwood et al., 2000; Fischer and Hout, 2002; Keister and Moller, 2000; Morris and Western, 1999; U.S. Census Bureau, 2003b; Wolff, 1995). Those at the top have made substantial gains, those in the middle have been treading water, and those at the bottom have been sinking fast.

As one travels across the country, one sees situations that are typically thought of as third-world conditions. The life expectancy in some inner-city neighborhoods is lower than that in countries such as Bangladesh (McCord and Freeman, 1990). Yet at the same time, our medical system provides the finest care in the world for those who can afford it. Children with the greatest need for a good education often wind up in school systems that are struggling to acquire the bare essentials, while children who have countless advantages go to schools with state-of-the-art technology. Within the black population, one out of four men who reaches age 25 will have spent time in prison or on a suspended sentence, while three out of four of their white counterparts will have gone on to college (U.S. Census Bureau, 2002d).

One result of this increasing bifurcation of our society is what has been labeled the Brazilianization effect. The prosperous have been progressively isolating themselves from the poor and disadvantaged in society (Massey, 1996). The number of gated and walled communities has been growing at a rapid rate, as has the percentage of Americans in prison. Both of these trends have the effect of isolating and physically separating the haves from the have-nots. As F. Allan Hanson (1997a, 1997b) has argued, this has become the modern way in which more and more of the affluent deal with the social problem of poverty—by refusing to even see it. It is no coincidence that private security and prison construction are two of the top growth industries in the United States.

One community in California literally resembles a medieval town, with a wall, a moat, a drawbridge, and a device called a bollard that fires a three-foot metal cylinder into the bottom of unauthorized cars (Thurow, 1996). Large-scale walled and gated building projects have been going up across the country, particularly in Florida, California, Arizona, and Nevada. These developments are often broken into various "villages," with each village having its own gated entrance and walled perimeter. It is estimated that 5.9 percent of all American households live in a community surrounded by walls or fences, and that 3.4 percent reside in a gated community where access is controlled by a security guard or other means (Sanchez et al., 2003). These numbers are likely to rise sharply in the years ahead (see Blakely and Snyder, 1997, and Low, 2003, for an in-depth discussion of gated communities).

Robert Reich, in his book *The Work of Nations*, sketches a scenario of the America of the future:

> The fortunes of the most well-off and the least will thus continue
> to diverge. By 2020, the top fifth of American earners will
> account for more than 60 percent of all the income earned by

Americans; the bottom fifth, for 2 percent. [The top fifth] will withdraw into ever more isolated enclaves, within which they will pool their resources rather than share them with other Americans or invest them in ways that improve other Americans' productivity. . . . America's poorest citizens, meanwhile, will be isolated within their own enclaves of urban and rural desperation; an ever-larger proportion of their young men will fill the nation's prisons. The remainder of the American population, growing gradually poorer, will feel powerless to alter any of these trends. (1992: 302–303)

In particular, the very top of society has been reaping tremendous material rewards over the past thirty years, while the middle has remained stagnant and the poor have fallen further behind. The levels of income and wealth concentration have reached or surpassed those of the Gilded Age of the 1920s. For example, the top 10 percent of the U.S. population earned 41 percent of total income in 1998, up from 33 percent in 1980 (Picketty and Saez, 2001, 2003). The top 1 percent of the population (or 2.7 million Americans) received as much after-tax income as the bottom 100 million Americans (Kawachi and Kennedy, 2002). The richest one-hundredth of 1 percent of taxpayers (or about 13,000 families) earned nearly as much income in 1998 as the poorest 20 million households in the United States (Krugman, 2002). And finally, the 400 wealthiest taxpayers earned over 1 percent of all income in 2000, doubling their share since 1992, while at the same time paying a smaller percentage of their income in taxes (Internal Revenue Service, 2003).

The figures for wealth are even more startling. In 1998, the top 1 percent of American households held 38 percent of the entire wealth or net worth of the country, the top 5 percent held 59 percent, and the top 20 percent held 83 percent, while the bottom 80 percent of the population was in possession of only 17 percent of the total net worth in the country (Wolff, 2001).[15] Between 1983 and 1998, the top 20 percent of the population experienced 91 percent of the total gain that occurred in net worth. For example, the wealthiest 1 percent of American households saw their total net worth go from $7,175,000 in 1983 to $10,204,000 in 1998 (in 1998 dollars). On the other hand, the bottom 40 percent of households saw their net worth drop from $4,700 in 1983 to $1,100 in 1998.

Financial wealth is even more skewed. Financial wealth is a more liquid concept than net worth because it does not include the equity built up in owner-occupied housing.[16] In 1998, the top 1 percent of the population held 47 percent of the entire financial wealth in the country, the top 5 percent held 70 percent, and the top 20 percent held 91 percent, while the bottom 80 percent of the population controlled only 9 percent (Wolff, 2001).

A further indicator of the imbalanced wealth distribution in the United States is measured by the Gini coefficient. The Gini is an overall measure of the extent of inequality in society and ranges from 0 (indicating complete wealth equality) to 1 (indicating complete wealth inequality). In 1998, it had reached a level of .82 with respect to overall net worth and .89 in terms of financial wealth (Wolff, 2001). As with income inequality, each of these various indicators of wealth inequality has been climbing over the past thirty years, particularly during the 1980s and 1990s.

The gap between workers and CEOs has also been getting wider over the years. In 1970, the average worker's wage (in 1998 dollars) was $32,522. That same year, the average total pay of the top 100 CEOs was $1,255,000. By 1998, the average wage had risen slightly to $35,864, while the average total pay of the top 100 CEOs had jumped to a phenomenal $37,509,000 (Picketty and Saez, 2001). In other words, the average income of a top CEO in this country has gone from 39 times the average worker's salary in 1970, to more than 1,000 times what an average worker earns during the year.

Signs of such extreme wealth are not hard to find. Trophy houses of 10,000 or more square feet can be found sprouting up in affluent neighborhoods throughout the country. Consumption of particular luxury items has hit an all-time high. Exorbitant stock options and bailouts appear almost routine within the upper echelons of American business.

In some ways what has been happening is analogous to what has occurred for airline passengers who find themselves flying in first-class instead of coach. A very small number of passengers have reaped the rewards of riding in first class. The leg room is ample, the food is quite good, and the service is attentive. Yet for the large numbers who are riding in coach, the leg room has shrunk, the food now consists of pretzels and peanuts, and the service is stretched and overextended.

Debate exists over why levels of income and wealth inequality have been getting more extreme over the past twenty-five or thirty years. Factors often mentioned include changes in the economy (specifically the role of globalization, deindustrialization, and the higher demand placed upon skills and education), reductions in the rate of taxation at the upper income levels, demographic shifts in the labor force, and a relaxation of societal norms regarding the inappropriateness of sharp degrees of inequality.

No matter what the reasons, it is quite clear that the rising income and wealth inequality exerts a profound impact upon the overall health of the nation. A growing body of evidence suggests that widening income inequality (above and beyond the overall GDP of a country) negatively affects life expectancy, social cohesion, crime, political participation, and countless other indicators of well-being (Burtless and Jencks, 2002; Hout, 2003; Kawachi et al., 1999; Kawachi and Kennedy, 2002; Verba et al., 1995; Wilkinson, 1996). In addition, we have discussed in prior chapters the economic and social toll that poverty takes upon the rest of society. High levels of income inequality and poverty help to explain the paradox that the United States, while it is the wealthiest country in the world, lags behind many other countries in terms of key social indicators.

Ichiro Kawachi and Bruce Kennedy (2002) also point out that as the middle and lower class fall further behind in terms of relative economic well-being, the tendency is for them to become less generous toward supporting state initiatives to address these issues. As more citizens feel the pinch of economic vulnerability, they are hesitant to support taxation initiatives.

Increasing levels of wealth and income inequality are also steadily undermining the democratic process. The Center for Responsive Politics estimates that 80 percent of all political contributions come from less than 1 percent of the population (Collins et al., 1999). American democracy is rapidly becoming a pawn in the hands of wealthy individuals, corporations, and special interest groups. Partly as a result, fewer and fewer people are participating in the democratic process, often because they feel that such involvement is meaningless and futile.

In thinking about these conditions, we need to ask whether this is the type of society that we wish to leave our children. If the answer is yes, then we are practicing wise stewardship over our communities. If the answer is no, then we are failing in our obligations to the next generation.

I believe (and hope) that most of us would come to the conclusion that the conditions described do not represent the kind of social and economic environment we would like to see our children inherit. This being the case, we as citizens must attempt to reshape our country in ways more in keeping with the best interests of our children's futures. One of the single most important components in positively molding those futures is to reduce the extent and severity of poverty in America. Although many factors and elements are working to both undermine and to strengthen our communities, reducing poverty is fundamental to the creation of a society that is more viable, livable, and sustainable than the one we are currently creating. And that, after all, is what stewardship is all about.

Well-Traveled Roads

The three preceding chapters have asked the reader to consider the question, Why care? In other words, on what basis should Americans be concerned about the issue of poverty? Too few of us in academic circles adequately take this question on. Yet answering it with a clear voice is absolutely vital in providing the necessary climate for change.

My argument is that there are three compelling reasons for addressing the problem of poverty. First, it is in our self-interest to do so. Second, it is consistent with and essential to the fulfillment of several of our most important values. Third, it is part of our obligation and responsibility as citizens of wider communities. Self-interest, values, and responsibilities are three powerful criteria on which to base a concern for the poor and the condition of poverty. These are the threads that weave together the ties that bind.

Yet if such reasons are so compelling, why are not more Americans actively engaged? Assuredly, many are; unfortunately, many more are not. Several explanations for this were touched upon earlier, including a misunderstanding of the causes of poverty, our society's stress upon individuality and self-reliance, and the heterogeneity of the United States. Additional reasons are likely to be at work as well, such as different priorities, a lack of time, or a sense of futility and apathy. But perhaps the most important reason is the one that I have left until now to discuss.

Being concerned about either the poor or the condition of poverty is simply not consistent with the underlying ethos of a free-market capitalist economy. American society is driven by its unflinching support of free-market capitalism. It goes without saying that the influence of capitalism permeates our daily lives in immeasurable ways. As Americans, we tend to worship at the altar of competition, profit, consumption, wealth, and, too often, greed.

Profit and wealth have often been interpreted as signs of virtue, from the beginning of the country to the present day. For the Pilgrims (guided by Calvinism), prosperity and the accumulation of wealth were viewed as measures of God's blessing. These sentiments were more recently echoed with Gordon Gecko's famous line "Greed is good" in the movie *Wall Street*.

Fundamental to the workings of capitalism are the concepts of competition and profit. Free markets are based upon competition among the players, with the survival of the fittest the end result. Lester Thurow writes that "it is the duty of the economically fit to drive the unfit out of business and into economic extinction. 'Survival of the fittest' and inequalities in purchasing power are what capitalistic efficiency is all about" (1996: 242). Those who enter such competitions are fueled by the desire to make a profit, and to maximize profit at that. Profit therefore becomes the essential motivating factor that drives the behavior of individuals, corporations, and stockholders within such an economy.

Social commentators from Benjamin Franklin to modern-day pundits have reiterated the importance that Americans have attached to profit and economic success. Alexis de Tocqueville wrote in his treatise *Democracy in America*, "The love of wealth is therefore to be traced, as either a principal or accessory motive, at the bottom of all that the Americans do" ([1840] 1994: 229). More recently, Andrew Hacker notes that "in the end, Americans of every class feel the want—indeed the need—of incomes discernibly higher than the ones they currently have" (1997: 43).

The values of competition and profit are largely inconsistent with caring for the downtrodden or the poor. In fact, many free-market advocates argue that poverty is both just and inevitable. To the winners go the spoils; to the losers go the trappings of poverty. Such is the bottom line upon which capitalism flourishes. This paradigm implies that there is little reason to care about the poor and that such a concern can only make the market less efficient.[17] Patricia Arzabe notes that the paradigm of capitalism and continuous economic growth "considers poverty as a natural consequence of economic activity, as an externality. Thus, poverty is not considered an important problem of the system. It does not merit efforts for its solution" (2001: 35). Further, as Dr. Martin Luther King, Jr., observes, it encourages "smallhearted men to become cold and conscienceless so that, like Dives before Lazarus, they are unmoved by suffering, poverty-stricken humanity. The profit motive, when it is the sole basis of an economic system, encourages a cutthroat competition and selfish ambition that inspire men to be more I-centered than thou-centered" (1967b: 186).

Consequently, one of our most important and cherished beliefs—the belief in the free-market capitalist system—offers no compelling reason to consider the needs of the poor. This is certainly an obstacle to building a connection of concern between the nonpoor and the poor. My earlier appeals to enlightened self-interest, values, and citizenship simply do not hold water if one adheres to the free market as one's sole value.

Fortunately, most of us are motivated on the basis of more than one set of principles, beliefs, or emotions. We can be moved by both compassion and anger; believe in aspects of the Judeo-Christian ethic and the free market; follow the principles of both citizenship and self-interest. Each of these may be of greater or lesser importance depending upon our priorities, but we generally act out our lives influenced by a set of factors, rather than any single factor. Although the belief in the free market offers little reason to consider the plight of the poor, it is only one (albeit an important one) of many motivating factors and beliefs.

What I have been arguing in these last three chapters is that there are several other important aspects to our sense of self that should cause us to carefully consider the plight of the poor. Think of it in the following way. During one's life, there is a set of goals to be accomplished. These differ from person to person but might include things such as being professionally successful, acquiring financial security, leading an interesting and fulfilling life, raising a loving family, behaving in an ethical or spiritual manner, contributing to the community, serving one's country, and so on. Such goals can be thought of as destinations on the horizon. In order to arrive at those desired destinations, we travel along various roads. Depending upon their locations, the roads lead us through different types of terrain. For example, the bridges one may have to cross in order to be professionally successful can be quite different from the bridges one has to cross in order to facilitate the raising of a loving family.

If we are interested solely in the goal of facilitating a free-market capitalistic system, then we will bypass the valleys and communities along the way that are in poverty, much as our interstate highways now bypass small-town America. In all likelihood we will whisk by without concern, slowing down only to make an occasional stop, never straying far from the comfort of the interstate.

Yet what I have been arguing in the past three chapters is that in order to arrive at several of our other important destinations, we will have to approach the territory known as poverty. How we negotiate our passage will speak volumes about whether we will ultimately arrive at those destinations. Do we attempt to take a detour around the area? Do we roll up the windows and speed through as fast as possible? Or do we stop to lend an outstretched hand?

If we are interested in arriving at the destinations of enlightened self-interest, living up to our values, and responsible citizenship, I have argued that we must stop and lend a hand. We certainly do not have to remain for perpetuity, for there are many other stops to make along the routes to each journey's end. But we must slow down, get out of the car, and begin to help.

I briefly discussed in chapter 1 the community of East St. Louis, which is about as deep into the terrain of poverty as one can get. As a *St. Louis Post-Dispatch* reporter quoted by Jonathan Kozol noted,

> "The ultimate terror for white people is to leave the highway by mistake and find themselves in East St. Louis. People speak of getting lost in East St. Louis as a nightmare. The nightmare to me is that they never leave that highway so they never know what life is like for all the children here. They *ought* to get off that highway. The nightmare isn't in their heads. It's a real place. There are children living here." (Kozol, 1991: 18)

What I have tried to provide in this section of the book are several compelling reasons for why we must get off the highway and begin to lend a helping hand.

What kinds of actions and directions should we as individuals and as a society be pursuing? How might the status quo be changed? Where does one begin? These are the topics that we now turn to. In order to initiate a fundamental change in how America confronts the issue of poverty, a new way of thinking is needed. This is the subject of chapter 7.

Creating Fundamental Change

III

A New Paragdim

A New Paragdim

Progress is impossible without change; and those who cannot change their minds cannot change anything.

George Bernard Shaw

7

IN 1984, JOHN KENNETH GALBRAITH gave a commencement address titled "The Convenient Reverse Logic of Our Time" to the graduating students at American University. The central theme of Galbraith's talk was that, rather than moving from diagnosis to remedy in social policy, we have witnessed with greater frequency the rise of a reverse logic, moving from a preferred remedy to an appropriate diagnosis. As Galbraith explained,

Increasingly in recent times we have come first to identify the remedy that is most agreeable, most convenient, most in accord with major pecuniary or political interest, the one that reflects our available faculty for action; then we move from the remedy so available or desired back to a cause to which that remedy is relevant. (1986: 35)

Galbraith went on to illustrate with the example of poverty. Referring to poverty as "our most devastating social failure in this greatly affluent age and land" and "the heaviest burden on our social conscience," he noted that rather than devising social policies that would address the root causes of poverty, we have instead defined the causes of poverty in a way that is consistent with our preferred policy strategies. These strategies have included cutting back on the role and scope of the federal government, seeking policies that are relatively inexpensive, shifting responsibility to the state and local levels, stressing personal responsibility, and so on. Galbraith observed,

> From this need as to remedy we move back to the new cause of poverty. It is that the poor lack motivation—and they lack motivation because they are already unduly rewarded. That cause, once agreed upon, then calls for reduced expenditure on public services and less aid to the disadvantaged. So, in the recent past we have had, as an antipoverty measure, a broad curtailment of income and services to the poor. (1986: 36)

This tendency to view the nature of social problems in terms of a desired policy was anticipated one hundred years earlier by the French historian Albert Sorel, who observed, "There is an eternal dispute between those who imagine the world to suit their policy, and those who correct their policy to suit the realities of the world" (Platt, 1989: 258).

The argument in this final third of the book is that the old strategies for addressing poverty have rested on an imagined world that reflects a preferred set of myths, agendas, and policies, whereas a new approach to poverty alleviation must put in place a set of policies that reflects the realities of the world. These policies should be grounded in a new understanding of the nature and meaning of American poverty. This chapter is intended to provide the details of such a paradigm.

The premise for beginning here is a simple one—that how we view poverty is critical to guiding how we will address it. Part of America's ineffectiveness in reducing poverty during the past three decades stems from its skewed and incorrect perception of impoverishment. Imagine a doctor treating a patient on the basis of the wrong diagnosis. The chances are that the prescribed cure will have a negligible effect on the illness and perhaps make the patient worse. Such has been the case with U.S. poverty.

In short, we have followed a paradigm that has reflected a view of the world as many would like to see it, rather than being led by a paradigm that reflects the world as it really is. Fundamental change must therefore begin with a shifting of our understanding of poverty from one based upon the old ways of thinking to one based upon a new conceptualization.

I begin this chapter by briefly describing the major tenets of the old paradigm. Much of this will be quite familiar, since variations of it can be heard in political sound bites, mainstream policy research, the popular media, and informal discussions with one's neighbors. I then describe the foundations of a new paradigm for comprehending poverty. This paradigm is based upon several of the major themes found within the first two-thirds of this book and represents a sharp break from the old ways of viewing poverty. Finally, I conclude with several examples intended to illustrate that a paradigm shift in thinking can occur within a relatively short span.

The Old Paradigm

The old paradigm has been the dominant poverty perspective over a prolonged period of time. Indeed, aspects of it have been with us since the beginnings of the country. It is to a large extent a reflection and affirmation of both the free-market economic structure and the culture of individualism which have profoundly shaped the ideology of the United States. It has experienced ebbs and flows over time but appears to have been gaining in ascendency since the election of Ronald Reagan in 1980. At its core is the belief that both the causes and the solutions to poverty are to be found within the individual.

This paradigm begins with the key assumption that the American economic system generates abundant economic prosperity and well-being for all. The familiar phrases "rags to riches," "the land of opportunity," and "the American Dream" are emblematic of this. The assumption is not that everyone will be rich, but that with enough hard work and initiative, nearly everyone is capable of achieving and sustaining a modest and comfortable lifestyle. Given this assumption, poverty becomes understood largely as a result of individual failure.

According to this view, both the causes of and the solutions to poverty can be found within the context of the individual. The causes of poverty are seen primarily as individual inadequacies. There is a conservative and a liberal version of this. The conservative version of individual inadequacies tends to focus more heavily on personality characteristics. These include various character flaws, such as an absence of strong morals, failure to exert responsibility, laziness, an inability to save and plan for the future, a lack of intelligence, or addiction to alcohol and/or drugs (Gilder, 1981; Herrnstein and Murray, 1994; Schwartz, 2000). These are typified by Charles Murray's comments, noted at the beginning of chapter 2, in which he characterized poor unmarried women as rotten mothers who would rather party than take care of their children. As a result of these character flaws, individuals are thought to be unable to take advantage of the opportunities that are readily available. It is also believed that government policy exacerbates these problems when it puts in place social programs that do not encourage morality or work (Mead, 1986, 1992). As Robert Rector and William Lauber wrote in their Heritage Foundation report, *America's Failed $5.4 Trillion War on Poverty*,

> The welfare system has paid for non-work and non-marriage and
> has achieved massive increases in both. By undermining the
> work ethic and rewarding illegitimacy, the welfare system
> insidiously generates its own clientele. . . . Welfare bribes
> individuals into courses of behavior which in the long run are
> self-defeating to the individual, harmful to children, and increas-
> ingly a threat to society. (1995: 23)

Consequently, according to the conservative version of the old paradigm, badly designed social welfare programs can encourage people into making destructive decisions during their lives, such as dropping out of school, having children out of wedlock, not getting married, failing to take a low paying job, or engaging in crime.[1]

The liberal version of the old paradigm tends to focus more on the lack of marketable skills, training, and education, as well as on other characteristics that put the poor at a disadvantage in competing in the labor market. The focus is largely on the inadequate human capital that the poor have acquired. This, in addition to particular characteristics (such as being a single parent or having large numbers of children), hinders the ability of particular Americans to compete in the economy and thereby raises their risk of poverty. Rather than focusing on individual inadequacies as represented by character flaws, the liberal version views individuals as inadequate in terms of their skills, training, and education. As noted in chapter 3, the mainstream research community has basically reinforced this approach by focusing on individual and demographic attributes to explain behavior such as impoverishment.

What follows from either version is that the poor are by and large at fault for their poverty. This is the result of their not having enough fortitude and morality for getting ahead, making bad judgments in life, and/or failing to acquire the skills necessary to compete in today's economy. The concept of blame permeates the old paradigm.[2] The age-old distinction between the deserving and the undeserving poor, mentioned in chapter 6, is of course central to this—unless the working-age poor have a very good reason to explain their poverty (such as a debilitating illness not brought on by their own doing), they are seen as largely undeserving of help from others. Rather, they have only themselves to blame.

Closely connected to the issue of blame is the fact that the poor are viewed as different from mainstream Americans. They are frequently perceived as not being motivated enough, dropping out of high school, having children out of wedlock, failing to have the qualified skills for a higher paying job, and so forth (rather than as working steadily at low-paying jobs, trying to be good parents to their children, and paying taxes throughout their lives). Not only are the poor to blame for their impoverishment, but they are portrayed as not playing by the rules and therefore outside the mainstream American experience. These differences can be seen within the popular media, where the poor are often depicted as inner-city minority residents, women on welfare, street criminals, the homeless, or taken together, as synonymous with what has been labeled the underclass. Such images graphically convey a sense of their physical separation from middle America.

In addition to this physical separation, the human dimension of poverty is rarely discussed within the old paradigm, once again creating a distance between the poor and the rest of America. The pain of poverty is largely wiped away. Rather, poverty is viewed through the lens of individual inadequacy. Much of the empirical literature has also reinforced this superficiality. Poverty has routinely been reduced to a set of numbers and correlations.[3] The old paradigm tends to treat poverty in a one-dimensional fashion, either as an unflattering stereotype or as a set of regression coefficients.

Turning to solutions, the key according to the old framework is to address personal inadequacies. Again, there is a conservative and a more liberal version of this. The conservative view is that encouraging and rewarding individual initiative and responsibility is critical. The desired behaviors include working harder, staying married, and not having children out of wedlock. Social policy should reinforce and encourage such behavior. Indeed, the title of the 1996 welfare reform act was the Personal Responsibility and Work Opportunity Reconciliation Act.

On the other hand, cash assistance and generous welfare programs are believed not to be the answer because they may create disincentives for engaging in responsible behavior. Such was the argument made by Alexis de Tocqueville in his 1832 address to the Royal Academic Society of Cherbourg (1983), and such was the argument popularized 150 years later in Charles Murray's book *Losing Ground* (1984). As President George W. Bush noted, "Many are learning it is more rewarding to be a responsible citizen than a welfare client" (Bush, 2002). The distinction between responsibility on the one hand and the use of welfare on the other is critical from this perspective. Mainstream economic studies have also devoted considerable attention to the issue of incentives and disincentives within the welfare system, and, although the effects have been small, the fact that such a large body of work continues to focus on this question serves to legitimate the issue.

The liberal solution to poverty according to the old framework is to provide greater opportunities and access to job training and education, while demanding personal responsibility and motivation in return. The concept of the New Democrat epitomizes this view. As Bill Clinton stated in his 1992 Democratic National Convention acceptance speech in New York City, "We offer our people a new choice based on old values. We offer opportunity. We demand responsibility" (Clinton, 1992: 226). Or as former Senate Majority Leader Tom Daschle said ten years later regarding welfare reform, "As we demand responsibility, we need to provide greater opportunity" (Toner, 2002). The focus is thus on providing opportunities intended to upgrade the poor's limited human capital, with the strong expectation that individuals will make the most of these opportunities.

From the viewpoint of the old paradigm, our collective responsibility toward poverty is somewhat limited. Since poverty is viewed as the problem of the individual, it is up to the poor themselves to improve their condition. From the conservative view, society and those in authority should use their positions as a moral bully pulpit to encourage the poor to behave in responsible ways. Welfare programs and social policy should be structured in a manner that supports such behavior. Within the liberal version of the old paragigm, society should ensure that the poverty stricken have access to the means of building their education and skills. It is then up to the poor to take advantage of such opportunities.[4] As John Kingdon writes in describing this American approach,

> If unfortunate people were regarded as the victims of forces beyond their control, or simply down on their luck, then we could see our way clear to having government provide for them: "There but for the grace of God go I." But if, in the land of opportunity, they're responsible for their own condition, then self-help rather than government help is the appropriate prescription. At most, government programs should be designed to enhance opportunity, but nothing more. (1999: 37)

Ultimately, the old paradigm reflects and reinforces the myths and ideals of American society—that there are economic opportunities for all, that individualism and self-reliance are paramount, and that hard work is rewarded. Although poverty may be regrettable, it would be a mistake to call it unfair. It should not be surprising that the dominant paradigm of poverty is a reflection of the overall dominant ideology of America. While there are conservative and liberal versions of this paradigm, both reflect these ideals and myths.

It is particularly ironic (and indicative of its strength) that even those in poverty tend to adhere strongly to this paradigm. The example of Denise Turner in chapter 1 is typical. In my conversations with Denise, she repeatedly emphasized that hard work and effort would allow her to make it in spite of the formidable obstacles and hardships she had suffered. Surveys have consistently found that the poor tend to reiterate the mainstream values reflected in the old paradigm. Furthermore, those in poverty are often quick to characterize the overall situations of the poor and welfare recipients along the lines of the old paradigm, while carefully characterizing their own circumstance as different from this pejorative view (Rank, 1994). The paradox of believing in yet distancing oneself from the common stereotype is often the case for members of stigmatized groups (Goffman, 1963).

One of the reasons that American poverty is so severe is precisely the result of this mindset. The old paradigm offers little in the way of ideas for truly understanding and addressing poverty and, in fact, provides a justification for doing little. The one task that is undertaken is the never ending charge of reforming and analyzing welfare. Yet as we continue to modify the incentives and disincentives that are embedded in the social safety net, U.S. poverty remains the worst in the industrialized world. This appears to be a modern version of Nero fiddling while Rome burns. Fundamental change in confronting poverty must begin with a fundamental change in how poverty is viewed and understood. We now turn to what such a new paradigm might look like.

A New Paradigm

A new paradigm must be built not upon the myths of America but upon its realities. It should reflect a fuller appreciation of the meaning of poverty, rather than the one-dimensional view to which we are too often exposed. It must ultimately stimulate a fundamental shift in how we conceptualize and act toward the problem of poverty. Drawing on the various arguments and evidence presented in the first two-thirds of this book, I develop several themes that are intended to lay the foundation for such a paradigm.

Poverty Results from Structural Failings

The starting point for a new paradigm is the recognition that American poverty is largely the result of structural failings. As we discussed in chapter 3, there simply are not enough viable opportunities for all Americans. Individual deficiencies, such as the lack of human capital, help to explain who is more likely to be left out in the competition to locate and secure such opportunities, but it cannot explain why there is a shortage of opportunities in the first place. In order to answer that question, we must turn to the inability of the economic, political, and social structures to provide the supports and opportunities necessary to lift all Americans out of poverty.

The most obvious example of this is the mismatch between the number of decent-paying jobs and the pool of labor in search of such jobs. As was demonstrated in chapter 3, the failure of the labor market to lift all households out of poverty was substantial—between 9.4 and 32.7 percent of household heads were unable to raise their families out of poverty or near-poverty through their job earnings. Nearly one-third of household heads were in jobs that paid less than $10.00 an hour. It should be noted that these percentages do not include discouraged workers who have dropped out of the labor force or the approximately two million Americans incarcerated. The inability of the economy to produce enough viable job opportunities can also be seen in the levels of unemployment, which have ranged between 4 and 10 percent during the past forty years.

Exacerbating this situation is the fact that the American social safety net is extremely weak, resulting in sizable numbers of families who fall through its rather large holes. The United States has also failed to offer the types of universal coverage for child care, medical insurance, child allowances, or affordable housing that most other developed countries routinely provide. The result is an increasing number of families at risk of economic vulnerability and poverty.

Let us return to the analogy of musical chairs (introduced in chapter 3) to illustrate the relationship between these structural failures and the fact that those who experience poverty tend to have certain characteristics such as low levels of education or devalued skills. Picture a game of musical chairs in which there are ten players but only eight chairs available at any point in time. Those who are likely to lose out at this game tend to have characteristics that put them at a disadvantage in terms of competing for the available chairs (e.g., less education, fewer skills, head of single-parent families). However, given that the game is structured in a way such that two players are bound to lose, a deficiency in marketable attributes explains only who loses out, not why there are losers in the first place.

The critical mistake that has been made in the past by those who employ the old paradigm is that they have equated the question of who loses out at the game with the question of why the game produces losers in the first place. These are, in fact, distinct and separate questions. While deficiencies in human capital and other marketable characteristics help to explain who in the population is at a heightened risk of encountering poverty, the fact that poverty exists in the first place results not from these characteristics but from the lack of decent opportunities and supports in society. By focusing solely on individual characteristics, such as levels of education, we can shuffle people up or down in terms of their being more likely to land a job with good earnings, but we are still going to have somebody lose out if there are not enough decent-paying jobs to go around. In short, we are playing a large-scale version of musical chairs in which there are many more players than there are chairs.

The recognition of this dynamic represents a fundamental shift in think-ing from the old paradigm. It helps to explain why the social policies of the past two decades have been largely ineffective in reducing the rates of pov-erty. We have focused our attention and resources on either altering the incentives and disincentives for those playing the game or, in a very limited way, upgrading their skills and ability to compete in the game, while at the same time we have left the structure of the game untouched.

When the overall poverty rates in the United States do in fact go up or down, they do so primarily as a result of impacts on the structural level that increase or decrease the number of available chairs. In particular, the per-formance of the economy has historically been important. Why? Because when the economy is expanding, more opportunities (or chairs) are avail-able for the competing pool of labor and their families. The reverse occurs when the economy slows down and contracts. Consequently, during the 1930s and the early 1980s, when the economy was doing badly, poverty rates went up, while during periods of economic prosperity, such as the 1960s or the middle to late 1990s, the overall rates of poverty declined.

Changes in various social supports and the social safety net available to families also make a difference in terms of how well such households are able to avoid poverty or near-poverty. When such supports were increased through the War on Poverty initiatives in the 1960s, poverty rates declined. Likewise, when Social Security benefits were expanded during the 1960s and 1970s, poverty rates among the elderly declined precipitously. Conversely, when social supports have been weakened and eroded, as in the case of children's programs over the past 25 years, children's rates of poverty have gone up.[5]

The recognition of poverty as a structural failing also makes it quite clear why the United States has such high rates of poverty compared to other Western countries. These rates have nothing to do with Americans being less motivated or less skilled than citizens of other countries but have every-thing to do with the fact that our economy has been producing a plethora of low-wage jobs in the face of global competition and that our social policies have done little to support families compared to policies in European coun-tries. From this perspective, one of the keys to addressing poverty is to increase the labor market opportunities and social supports available to American households. Chapter 8 goes into detail regarding the specifics of such an approach.

In sum, a shift in thinking about the causes of poverty from an individually based explanation to a structurally based explanation allows us to distinguish and make sense of two specific questions. First, why does poverty exist? Second, who is more likely to experience poverty? The structural vulnerability explanation, with its musical chairs analogy, answers both questions. Poverty exists primarily because there is a shortage of viable economic opportunities and social supports for the entire population. Given this shortage, a certain percentage of the population is ensured of experiencing poverty. Individuals with a heightened risk of being on the short end of the economic stick will be those who are least able to effectively compete for the limited number of decent economic opportunities. This includes those with fewer marketable skills, less education, or ill health, as well as single parents, racial minorities, and residents in economically depressed areas. A new paradigm recognizes the fundamental distinction between understanding who loses out at the game and understanding how and why the game produces losers in the first place.

Poverty Is a Conditional State That Individuals Move In and Out Of

A second major premise underlying the new paradigm is the recognition of poverty as a conditional state that individuals move in and out of. Within the old way of thinking, we have talked and written about poor people. Yet the term *poor people* is in many respects a misnomer. As we have seen, individuals and households move in and out of the state of poverty, rather than remaining *poor people* throughout their lives. In addition, a majority of Americans experience impoverishment at some point during the life course.

Rather than framing the issue as one of poor people, our focus should be on the condition of poverty. This condition affects a very large percentage of the population at some point across the lifespan. The typical pattern is that individuals experience poverty for a year or two, get above the poverty line for an extended period of time, and then perhaps experience another spell at some later point. This was illustrated in chapter 2, as well as in the life course patterns discussed in chapter 4. The recognition of poverty as a conditional state into and out of which a majority of the population will move is fundamentally different from the static notion of poor people.

One way to illustrate this is with the concept of sickness. Most people are healthy for varying periods of time but periodically experience some kind of illness, such as a cold or the flu. In such cases, we would not define these individuals as sick people (even though they have experienced sickness) but rather would say that they are individuals who occasionally experience the condition of being ill. The appropriate focus is on recognizing the episodic nature of the condition, rather than defining the lives of such individuals in terms of the condition.

Certainly it may be the case that some people are more prone to sickness (just as some people are more prone to poverty). But even in these cases, we do not generally define such individuals as *sick people*. Only in the case of a chronic disease might we characterize such a person in terms of their illness.

The dynamics of poverty are much like those of sickness. Yet the old paradigm of poverty often lumps everyone who experiences poverty into the category of *poor people* or the *underclass*. The point I am making here does not deny that people experience periods in their lives when they are poor but argues that the label *poor people* reinforces a very static and unchanging image of who encounters poverty. Returning to our analogy, it would not make much sense to define everyone who at some point in the past has experienced a sickness as a sick person. But this appears to be what we do when we define those who have experienced poverty as poor people.

An additional consequence of such labeling is to solidify poverty as a dividing line that separates the population. The old paradigm strengthens the separation between the notions of poor and nonpoor. It fails to recognize the critical point that most Americans are actually both. Rather than pulling us together, the old paradigm pulls us apart.

Conversely, a new paradigm recognizes that poverty is a conditional state and an economic risk that many Americans will encounter. There is an awareness of the fluid nature of poverty and of the fact that a majority of Americans will experience poverty at some point during their lives. Individuals typically move between the states of being nonpoor and poor during their life course.

A new paradigm considers the condition of poverty, rather than those who occupy the condition, as harmful and deleterious. Poverty has the potential to undermine human well-being and development. It creates a number of problems for those who occupy its ranks. It can result in long-term consequences, depending upon the severity and the length of poverty experienced. This appears to be particularly true in the case of children's development. Children who grow up with extended bouts of severe poverty may experience permanent scars in terms of their health, educational attainment, or acquisition of skills and abilities.

Once again we can return to our illness analogy. On the one hand, ill health creates temporary pain and suffering for those who experience it. Yet individuals generally pass through such conditions, returning to a state of relatively good health. On the other hand, severe health problems such as a heart attack or stroke may produce more lingering damage. Here there may be permanent harm to the heart or brain that undermines the individual's future quality of life. The dynamics of poverty can be understood in a similar fashion. Severe poverty over a prolonged period of time may create permanent damage to individuals and their families.

A second important building block for a new paradigm is therefore the recognition of poverty as a conditional state that individuals move in and out of. It represents an economic risk that most Americans will encounter. The appropriate focus is upon the condition of poverty and the temporary and sometimes long-term effects that such a state has on the individuals who pass through it.

Poverty Constitutes Deprivation

A third component of the new paradigm broadens the scope and meaning of poverty from that of low income to the wider concept of deprivation. As we have seen in chapters 2, 4, 5, and 6, poverty acts to deprive individuals and families in a number of ways. A new conception of poverty must recognize that impoverishment represents more than just a shortage of income. This has recently been emphasized in the attention that European governments and scholars (particularly in England, France, and the Netherlands) have been placing upon the concept of social exclusion, or "the inability to participate in the activities of normal living" (Glennerster, 2002: 89; see Agulnik et al., 2002; Barnes et al., 2002; Bhalla and Lapeyre, 1999; Burchardt et al., 1999; United Kingdom Department of Social Security, 1999).

We have seen many illustrations of this point in prior chapters. Poverty undermines the quality of life for those in its ranks. As discussed in chapter 2, it results in serious compromises and struggles as people try to acquire basic resources such as food, clothing, shelter, health care, and transportation. These struggles produce considerable stress in the lives of the poverty-stricken and their families.

Poverty results in a reduction in the quality of one's health. Poverty is associated with a host of elevated health risks, including undernutrition, heart disease, dental problems, diabetes, lead poisoning, and mental illness. The result is a decline in one's physical well-being, culminating in a death rate for the poverty-stricken that is substantially higher than that for the affluent.

Another area of reduced capabilities lies in the stunted or diminished life chances for children and adults. Growing up in poverty-stricken neighborhoods can result in an inferior education. Both the quality and the quantity of education received are often substandard. There is also a greater exposure to other risks, such as crime. These risks in turn result in a lowered likelihood that students will acquire the skills necessary to compete effectively in the labor market.

In addition, poverty undercuts the ability of adults to build their economic assets, which can affect later life chances. The old saying that it takes money to earn money is certainly true and applies to financial and property assets as well. The ability to build equity in a house or a retirement fund is severely constricted by poverty.

Impoverishment is also closely associated with deprivation in the area of work. Those in poverty may be out of work or employed at part-time or dead-end jobs that simply do not pay enough to support a family. Such work is often physically demanding and intellectually taxing (for example, see Ehrenreich, 2001). Employment and work have historically been a central part of the American identity. The failure to have a job that allows one to support oneself and one's family is a major source of frustration.

Finally, poverty undermines the capability of individuals to fully partake of the freedoms, rights, and opportunities to which all citizens are theoretically entitled. As touched upon in chapter 5, poverty diminishes an American's ability to fully exercise specific rights, such as the right to a fair trial, or to participate in the democratic process.

A new paradigm of poverty must therefore recognize that impoverishment encompasses more than just low income. The lack of income is clearly a critical component of poverty and represents a convenient, logical, and pragmatic starting point and measuring stick. But we must go beyond thinking of poverty solely in terms of low income.[6] This involves incorporating a wider set of experiences and deprivations into our understanding. As Amartya Sen writes, "poverty must be seen as the deprivation of basic capabilities rather than merely as lowness of incomes, which is the standard criterion of identification of poverty" (1999: 87). He goes on to note,

> Policy debates have indeed been distorted by overemphasis on
> income poverty and income inequality, to the neglect of depriva-
> tions that relate to other variables, such as unemployment, ill
> health, lack of education, and social exclusion. Unfortunately, the
> identification of economic inequality with income inequality is
> fairly common in economics, and the two are often seen as
> effectively synonymous. If you tell someone that you are working
> on economic inequality, it is quite standardly assumed that you
> are studying income distribution. (108)

An example of bringing several aspects of deprivation to bear upon the measurement of poverty is the United Nations development of a human poverty index for industrialized countries (United Nations Development Programme, 2003). This index incorporates four measures: (1) deprivation in survival (the percentage of people not expected to survive to age 60); (2) deprivation in knowledge (the percentage of people ages 16–65 who are functionally illiterate); (3) deprivation in income (the percentage of the population below the income poverty line); and (4) social exclusion (the percentage of the total labor force that has been unemployed for twelve or more months). Such an index begins to reflect the wider meaning and scope of poverty.

It also reveals variations and differences that may not be apparent if we rely on a single measure of income poverty. For example, we have seen in chapter 2 that the United States does quite badly in comparisons of income poverty and inequality across developed nations. The United States tends to have the highest overall rates in the industrialized world. Yet if we examine deprivation in terms of long-term unemployment, the United States does exceedingly well. While European countries have much lower levels of income poverty and inequality than the United States, they also have significantly higher levels of long-term unemployment. A focus upon various measures of deprivation offers a more nuanced perspective on poverty. It suggests that there are different dimensions to poverty and that there may be some important variations across these dimensions.

Finally, conceptualizing poverty in terms of deprivation brings with it a more humane and accessible image. It is sometimes difficult to imagine what $18,392 really means (the poverty line for a family of four). It may be more intuitive to talk about long-term unemployment, illiteracy, or a shortened life expectancy. Broadening our focus to include deprivation brings a more human dimension and scale.

Poverty as an Injustice

Whereas the old paradigm's moral compass has been largely centered upon individual blame, the moral compass of a new paradigm rests upon the notion of injustice. There is a recognition that poverty constitutes an injustice of substantial magnitude. This view is based largely upon a juxtaposition of the first and third premises discussed earlier.

We have seen that poverty represents severe deprivation and hardship. This has been documented in countless studies, not to mention millions of human lives. The question of justice centers on whether such deprivation is deserved. From the perspective of the old paradigm, the answer is largely yes, with the blame for poverty lying with the poor themselves.

In contrast, the new paradigm views the condition of poverty as undeserved and unwarranted. As discussed in the first premise (and in greater detail in chapter 3), its roots can be traced back to the lack of economic opportunities and social supports. There simply are not enough decent-paying jobs and mechanisms in place (such as affordable health care, housing, or child care) to adequately support all American households. The condition of poverty represents an economic wrong that falls upon too many of our fellow citizens. What makes this injustice particularly grievous is the stark contrast between the wealth and abundance of America on the one hand and its levels of destitution on the other.

Let us employ Adam Smith's thought experiment of what this might look like to an "impartial spectator" (1759). Smith asks what an impartial spectator would make of a particular scenario—in this case the high levels of U.S. poverty within the context of vast material resources and wealth. As the impartial spectator delved into the current situation, he or she would soon learn that at any point in time more than one-third of the poor are children, and another 10 percent are elderly. Those of working age who encounter poverty have labored most of their lives but are often employed at jobs that do not pay enough to raise their families above the poverty line. Health care and child care assistance for such families are minimal. Those who are not working often suffer from physical disabilities or illnesses that prevent employment. In fact, nearly 40 percent of the poor between ages 25 and 64 have some type of disability. The impartial spectator would also see isolated cases of individuals who appear to have brought their poverty upon themselves. He or she would observe that these cases are often used to characterize the entire population that experiences poverty.

On the other hand, the impartial spectator would see the vast amounts of American prosperity and wealth. The standards of living for families in the upper portions of society surpass those of all other nations in the world. The impartial spectator would note that such families enjoy many tax benefits and public policies that further strengthen their economic position. He or she would be able to observe that, although many of these individuals work hard, much of their wealth has been inherited. Yet the impartial spectator would rarely hear this factor being invoked to characterize the affluent portion of the population. Rather, hard work and ingenuity are the key words used to account for their success. He or she would also note that there are scattered cases in which individuals have indeed risen from rags to riches.

The impartial spectator would soon learn that, in spite of the material resources of American society, and in spite of the assistance for the well-to-do, the U.S. government does the least of any nation in the industrialized world to help its economically vulnerable escape from poverty. Rather, it resorts to encouraging the poor to engage in moral and responsible behavior, while at the same time cutting back its social safety net and economic supports. While doing so, it argues that it is helping the most vulnerable in society to escape poverty.

What would an impartial spectator make of all this? I believe that the answer would be a moral outrage at the injustice of the situation. The impartial spectator would be able to see this for what it is—a masquerade that gives to the economically comfortable while taking away from those who have the least and then justifies the whole process in terms of virtue. The injustice of this situation would be abundantly clear.

A new paradigm acknowledges this. Injustice, rather than blame, becomes the moral ground on which such a perspective is based. Poverty is viewed as a societal injustice and an economic wrong. It is particularly glaring because it is both unnecessary and preventable. As mentioned in chapter 5, if the United States were an extremely impoverished country with a broken economy, widespread poverty would be regrettable but certainly understandable. Yet this is not the situation we face. The United States has both the means and the resources to address and substantially reduce its high levels of poverty. For reasons touched upon at various points in this book, the nation has chosen not to act. This inaction is simply unconscionable, given that we have the ability to confront such deprivation and human misery.

This type of injustice constitutes a strong impetus for change. It signals that a wrong is being committed that cries out for a remedy. The Revolutionary War, the abolitionist movement, women's suffrage, civil rights—all have been fueled by an understanding of the need and a passion to correct specific injustices that were taking place within particular historical times. The existence of poverty amid widespread prosperity must be seen in a similar light.

The new paradigm recognizes this and is premised on the idea that change is essential in addressing the injustices of poverty. This is in sharp contrast with the old paradigm, in which the moral focus is on individual blame. This has had the effect of simply reinforcing the current policy of doing little, resulting in continued rates of elevated poverty. A new paradigm allows us to actively engage and confront poverty, rather than comfortably settling for the status quo of widespread impoverishment.

The Condition of Poverty Affects and Undermines Us All

A final building block of a new paradigm is the recognition that poverty impacts and undermines us all. Indeed, the subtitle of this book—*Why American Poverty Affects Us All*—reflects this central theme. In the past, we have viewed poverty as primarily affecting those who experience it, and occasionally their proximate neighborhoods. The old paradigm has consistently failed to recognize the connections that all Americans have to poverty. This failure is epitomized by the distinction that we often implicitly make between *them* and *us*—that is, the poor versus the nonpoor.

The new paradigm breaks down this distinction by demonstrating that virtually all Americans are affected by poverty in one way or another. In chapter 4 I discussed several of the economic costs that are incurred by the entire population as a consequence of excessive poverty. Impoverishment produces severe health problems, inadequately educated children, and high rates of criminal activity. As a result, we pay more for health care, produce less productive workers, and divert needed resources into the building and maintaining of correctional facilities. In each of these cases, money is being spent on the back end of the problem rather than on the front end, which is assuredly a more expensive approach to take. To argue that we do not pay a steep price for our widespread poverty is putting our head in the sand.

It was also demonstrated in chapters 3 and 4 that a majority of the American population will encounter poverty and the welfare system at some point during their lifetimes, by age 75 three quarters of Americans will experience poverty or near poverty while two-thirds will utilize some type of safety net program by age 65. These numbers drive home the fact that poverty casts a very long shadow across the population. Rather than its being a question of *them*, poverty is clearly a question of *us*.

We are also connected to poverty in a somewhat different fashion as well. Its presence undermines us as a people and as a nation. It diminishes us all by tarnishing the integrity of our values. For example, the presence of widespread poverty juxtaposed against immense material prosperity appears to contradict much of what the Judeo-Christian ethic stands for. The Judeo-Christian ethic emphasizes that the barometer for a just and compassionate society lies in its treatment of the poor and vulnerable. As a nation and as a people, we appear to be badly failing at this test. Similarly, we have seen in chapter 5 that poverty impedes the ability of lower-income Americans to enjoy the full blessings of liberty, equality, and justice. The words "liberty and justice for all" ring hollow when a significant percentage of the population is economically and politically disenfranchised. This undermines every citizen, for it suggests that the American ideals we profess to believe in apply to some more than others. The very core of the American promise is compromised, diminishing us all.

Just as each of us is affected by poverty, each of us also has a responsibility for ending poverty. The concept of a collective responsibility was discussed in chapter 6. The new paradigm suggests that the alleviation of poverty will require a collective commitment from all Americans. This is in sharp contrast with the old paradigm, where the poor are basically left to fend for themselves. The new paradigm recognizes that poverty is an issue of public policy and requires a broad-based commitment. Within the old paradigm, the public's apathy toward the poor has been part of the problem. Within the new paradigm, the public's engagement in alleviating poverty is part of the solution.

A new paradigm suggests that we understand the condition of poverty within the wider context of an interconnected environment. This shift in thinking can be illustrated in the way we have begun to think about environmental protections. Until recently, we had failed to recognize the harm that befalls us all as a result of air, water, and ground pollution. These had been seen as having little consequence beyond the immediate location of the pollutants. However, mounting evidence suggests that this way of thinking about pollution is incorrect and dangerous. We have begun to understand the impact that pollution has within a wider environmental context. Pollution that occurs in one community may very well affect those in communities downwind or downstream. The use of coal in midwestern power plants results in acid rain in northeastern forests. The burning of fossil fuels or the use of chlorofluorocarbons can have a profound impact upon the world's climate, causing global warming or the loss of the atmospheric ozone layer. The physical environment is increasingly being understood as an interconnected system. What occurs in one part of the system may very well affect other parts.

As our awareness of these interconnections have increased, we have begun to realize that we all have a role to play in the solution. The increased popularity of recycling programs illustrates this. The very small individual act of bringing newspapers or aluminum cans to the curbside for a weekly pickup can have a large collective impact on environmental quality. At the same time, we have also realized the necessity of regulation and governmental controls to help curb pollution. Leaving the problem solely up to the individual polluters is no longer viable. Structural changes are increasingly needed in order to help alleviate levels of national and global pollution.

In a similar fashion, we must begin to understand poverty within the context of an interconnected environment. Here, however, our environment consists of the social, economic, and political institutions of society. Poverty must be understood as having profound ripple effects that denigrate and diminish those environments. This understanding also allows us to appreciate the fact that we all have a role to play in the alleviation of poverty. Individual actions over a sustained period of time can result in sizable changes. Yet as with our environmental problems, it is vital to recognize the importance that local, state, and federal governments must play in providing the resources, supports, and structure needed for a sustained effort.

Can the Shift Occur?

The question that naturally arises, of course, is whether such a shift in thinking can occur. Let us first take stock of what has been discussed so far. In the case of poverty, I have argued that the manner in which we have typically understood the issue has been both erroneous and a hindrance to constructive change. One of the motivations for this book has been to provide a new approach for understanding American poverty. This chapter has outlined several of the premises behind the formulation of a new paradigm.

The basic shift in such thinking begins by moving from a perspective that interprets poverty as an individual failing to one that recognizes the structural inadequacies that result in poverty. Second, the focus is upon poverty as a conditional state that individuals move in and out of, rather than on the static concept of poor people. Third, the human meaning of poverty is reinforced by going beyond the traditional emphasis on low income and adopting the broader concept of deprivation. Fourth, a new perspective points its moral compass toward injustice, rather than blame. There is a conviction that poverty amid American prosperity is a moral outrage. Finally, a new paradigm recognizes that we are all affected and undermined in countless ways by the existence of widespread poverty within our communities. Likewise, a new paradigm asserts that we are each a part of the answer.

It would be quite naive of me to suggest that this type of shift will occur overnight. It most certainly will not. The old paradigm and ways of thinking have been with us for a very long period of time, demonstrating a remarkably strong and lasting appeal. As Peter Edelman notes,

> Low-income people and their allies will have to articulate a bold
> new vision for poverty reduction and create the public will to
> realize it. This is a daunting task. Good antipoverty policy has
> never been a hallmark of the American social fabric. (2002: 20)

But it would also be wrong to ignore the fact that change does occur. What was once considered appropriate and in fashion, with time and evidence, can become antiquated. What was once considered just can one day be reviled as unjust. What was once considered truth can eventually be recognized as myth. Thus, while we should not underestimate the staying power of the old paradigm, neither should we be immobilized by its apparent strength.

Let me conclude by mentioning several examples that illustrate the fact that profound changes in individual and societal attitudes and behaviors can occur over relatively short periods of time. The first is that of the appropriateness of smoking, and in particular, smoking in public spaces. Over the past fifteen years, there has been a remarkable change in the societal norms and behaviors regarding smoking. As the dangers of cigarette (as well as cigar and pipe) smoking have become more apparent, and in particular the dangers of secondary smoke, significant changes have occurred in society. Nonsmoking sections in restaurants are universal, with a growing number of restaurants becoming smokefree. Smoking is now against the law in a number of public and retail spaces where people smoked frequently in the past. For example, when I lived in North Carolina during 1984 and 1985, smoking was commonplace in both supermarkets and department stores. Today, it is unheard of in such public spaces. Likewise, when I first moved into my current office building at Washington University, students routinely smoked in the hallways. Today, students must go outside the building in order to light up. It is hard to even imagine a student smoking inside the building, given the powerful norms and sanctions against doing so. The same is true for smoking aboard a passenger airliner. The point is that a profound change has occurred within a relatively short period of time in our attitudes toward the acceptability of smoking in enclosed public spaces.[7]

A second example of changing attitudes and behaviors is the remarkable transformation that took place, both morally and legally, regarding the legitimacy of civil rights for black Americans. Between the mid-1950s and the late 1960s, the civil rights movement revealed the hypocrisy of America's Jim Crow laws, its legally segregated school systems, its denial of voting rights, and a host of other inequities that brutally impacted upon black Americans. Opinions about the civil rights movement were transformed within a relatively short period of time.[8] At the beginnings of the movement, the asserted rights and claims were largely disregarded. By the end of the movement there was widespread recognition of the legitimacy of the demands made by those within the civil rights movement. Equally important, a host of significant legal changes were signed into law during the mid- to late 1960s that reflected the magnitude of this profound change. These included the Voting Rights Act, the Fair Housing Act, and the Civil Rights Act.

A final example of rapid changes taking place in how an issue is viewed and acted upon is that of the physical environment. Prior to 1960, public concern over the environment was limited and weak. Yet after publication of Rachel Carson's book *Silent Spring* (1962), concern for the environment increased dramatically during the 1960s and 1970s. The public began to see graphic examples of the consequences of unchecked pollution. Reflecting this concern, between 1969 and 1976, seventeen separate pieces of federal environmental legislation were passed, including the Clean Air Act of 1970, the Clean Water Act of 1972, and the establishment of the Environmental Protection Agency. Today, environmental protection is an issue that the public consistently places near the top of its overall concerns.

In each of these cases, the old ways of thinking had been dominant over extended stretches of time. Yet dramatic shifts occurred within relatively short time frames. A transformation took place in terms of how each of these social issues were viewed. As the dangers of the status quo became apparent, Americans realized the importance of paying closer attention to these concerns. By no means have we solved all of the problems or gone the necessary distance. Nevertheless, there has been a fundamental shift in the dominant paradigm applied to each of these social issues.[9]

Such a shift is now needed in the case of poverty. Widespread poverty amid prosperity must be seen as unacceptable. The status quo of an exceedingly high risk of poverty during the life course must be recognized as detrimental to us all. This chapter has sketched out a rough framework for what a new understanding into this issue might look like. Building on this paradigm, let us now turn to a particular set of strategies and policies designed to alleviate and reduce the risk of American poverty.

Future
Directions

8

True compassion is more than flinging a
coin to a beggar; it understands that an
edifice which produces beggars needs
restructuring.

Dr. Martin Luther King, Jr.

AT ITS HEART, social policy is a reflection of
interests, values, and goals. Whether the subject
is national security, welfare reform, or environmental protection, underlying values influence
the size and specifics of policy programs and
initiatives. These values derive from the concerns and priorities expressed by various players
in the political process, including the electorate,
interest and lobbying groups, political parties,
and individual legislators. Rather than occurring in a vacuum, public policy is shaped by
values.

An example of this is our current approach
to confronting poverty. As discussed in chapter 7,
the United States has taken a minimalist
strategy toward addressing poverty over the past
thirty years. The U.S. welfare state has been
marked by its limited scope and by its limited
ability to assist those in need of economic help.
This approach reflects several fundamental
beliefs and values. First is a faith that the
American free-market structure can provide

ample opportunities for all; government regulation of and interference with the free market are viewed as weakening its efficiency, resulting in higher levels of poverty. Second is a belief in rugged individualism; both the cause of and the solution to poverty are largely found in individual effort, hard work, and responsibility. Third, poverty is often viewed as an issue that pertains to disenfranchised groups, rather than the majority of the population; as a result, poverty reduction is not seen as a mainstream economic or social issue. Our current minimalist approach to dealing with poverty is a reflection of these fundamental beliefs and values.

A new approach for addressing poverty is rooted in a different set of values and beliefs. These have been touched upon throughout the prior chapters, particularly chapter 7. They include understanding that poverty is an issue of fundamental concern to all Americans, that each of us is directly and indirectly affected by America's high rate of poverty, and that reducing poverty is in all of our best interests. There is an added recognition that reliance upon the free market and rugged individualism has proven ineffective as a poverty-reduction strategy; rather, poverty is largely the result of structural inadequacies that fail to produce sufficient opportunities for all Americans. Strategies for reducing poverty should therefore focus on increasing the availability of such opportunities. Finally, there is a conviction that widespread poverty amid American prosperity is morally and ethically wrong and represents a societal injustice that should be set right. The economic and social deprivation endured by millions of Americans every day is indefensible, particularly in light of the country's vast material wealth. These represent the basic values that underlie the strategies for reducing poverty discussed in this chapter. Each individual strategy also reflects a more specific set of values.

Closely connected to the issue of values is the issue of priorities. Financial resources for the funding of public policies and programs are finite. How we choose to spend our federal, state, and local tax dollars requires setting priorities among a number of competing needs. Poverty reduction has historically been given low priority. The argument throughout this book is that much higher priority must be given to the issue. We currently spend and waste federal and state money that could be put to much better use on effective poverty alleviation. Such waste can be found in bloated military contracts, in the excessive tax breaks given to particular corporations and wealthy individuals, and in various pork barrel projects. In addition, a vast number of federal and state programs already benefit the middle and upper classes (Abramovitz, 2001; Sherraden, 1991). Balance and equity are called for in terms of helping lower-income Americans as well.

Several broad based strategies for reducing poverty are outlined in this chapter. To return to our earlier musical chairs analogy, they are primarily designed to provide more chairs (that is, opportunities and supports) for those who are in the game. In addition, they can be seen as investments in the development and well-being of individuals and families. The specific strategies include creating adequately paying jobs, increasing the access and availability of several key social goods, buffering the economic consequences of family change for children, building the assets of individuals and communities, and providing a sensible safety net for those who fall through the cracks. Together, the individual strategies outlined here reinforce one another. That is, the sum is greater than the parts. Taken together, I believe they have the potential to significantly reduce the extent and severity of poverty in the United States.

Creating Adequately Paying Jobs

We have seen that the lack of adequately paying jobs that can support a family is a fundamental problem tied to America's high rates of poverty. There simply are not enough decent-paying jobs to support all U.S. households. As was demonstrated in chapter 3, up to one-third of household heads in the labor market cannot raise their families out of poverty or near poverty through their job earnings. One of the keys to reducing poverty is therefore to produce a sufficient number of jobs and to ensure that full-time employment is able to lift a modestly sized family above the poverty line. As Bradley Schiller notes, "Jobs—in abundance and of good quality—are the most needed and most permanent solution to the poverty problem" (2004: 272).

There is a specific value that underlies this strategy. Americans who are working full-time, regardless of the nature of their job, deserve to be able to support themselves and a modestly sized family at a level above the poverty line. The underlying premise is the importance of making employment pay. Given the strong emphasis placed upon the value of work in America, it is incumbent upon us to make certain that we, in turn, value those who work. A fair exchange is one in which working full-time is associated with lifting a modestly sized family above the poverty line. As Oren Levin-Waldman argues,

> A society that prizes work as a core value ought to find positive inducements for these individuals to work and for them to do so with dignity. We as a society derive benefit from the work that all our members perform, even if this work should be considered "low- skilled." We as a society ought to be willing to pay the true costs of performing those tasks. The social safety net shouldn't necessarily entail government picking up the slack for the failure of firms to pay livable wages. Rather in the interest of ensuring that work and workers have dignity, government should ensure that jobs pay livable wages so that resorting to traditional public assistance programs will occur even less, and will ultimately become nonexistent. (2001: 178)

Too many Americans are currently working at jobs that will not lift a family out of poverty.

In addition, given the strong emphasis placed upon the importance of work, all Americans (and especially heads of households) have a right to a full-time job. The fact that the structure of the labor market leaves millions of Americans locked out of such a basic right is fundamentally wrong and inconsistent with our emphasis on the value of work. It is also incompatible with much of our recent social policy, particularly the welfare reform initiatives that emphasize work rather than welfare. As Timothy Bartik (2002) notes, a basic standard should stipulate that there is a sufficient full-time job available for every working-age head of household. Bartik estimates that an additional five to nine million more jobs are needed in order to reach this standard.

Two initiatives are proposed here that comprise an overall strategy for creating the necessary number of adequate paying jobs. The first is the transformation of the current array of existing jobs so that they can support a family. The second is the creation of enough jobs to employ those in need of work.

Supplementing and Raising the Wages of Existing Jobs

Let us start with the following benchmark—individuals who are employed full-time throughout the year (defined as working thirty-five hours per week over a fifty-two-week period, or 1,820 hours) should be able to generate earnings that will enable them to lift a family of three over the poverty threshold. Such a family might include a married couple with one child, a one-parent household with two children, or a three-generation household of mother, grandmother, and son. The 2002 poverty threshold for a family of three was set at $14,348. Consequently, in order to lift such a family above the poverty line, an individual needs to be earning at least $7.88 per hour.[1]

There are at least two ways of accomplishing this. One is to raise the minimum wage to such a level and then index it to inflation so that it will continue to lift a family of three over the poverty line in the future. A second approach is to provide a tax credit (such as the Earned Income Tax Credit) that supplements workers' wages so that their total income for the year lifts them above the poverty line. A fundamental difference between these two approaches is that the first places the burden and cost for increasing workers' wages largely on employers and industries, whereas the latter places it on the government. In either case, some of the costs will be passed along to us all, either as consumers or as taxpayers.

RAISING AND INDEXING THE MINIMUM WAGE The minimum wage went into effect in October 1938 at an initial level of $.25 an hour. The basic concept was that no employee should fall below a certain wage floor. There was an underlying value that workers should receive a fair wage for a fair day's work. However, unlike Social Security, the minimum wage has never been indexed to inflation; changes in the minimum wage must come through congressional legislation. Years often go by before Congress acts to adjust the minimum wage upward, causing it to lag behind the rising cost of living. For example, the minimum wage remained at $3.35 an hour between 1981 and 1989, substantially eroding its purchasing power. The current minimum wage in the United States stands at $5.15 an hour, a rate that went into effect in September 1997. An individual working full-time during the year (or 1,820 hours, using our earlier estimations) would earn a total of $9,373, far short of the $14,348 needed to lift a family of three above the poverty line.

Each time Congress does hold hearings with respect to raising the minimum wage, there is the inevitable political debate regarding the potential impact that such a raise will have on the economy, particularly on levels of unemployment. The argument has been that increasing the minimum wage leads employers to hire fewer workers, which in turn harms those looking for work in the low-wage sector of the economy. This assumes that if labor costs are higher, employers will be forced to trim their expenses by hiring fewer workers.

Empirical data have simply not borne this out. The best-known of these studies have been conducted by David Card and Alan Krueger (1995, 1998). They found no disemployment or substitution effects on workers in the fast-food industry in California and New Jersey when the state minimum wage rose from $3.35 to $4.25 in 1988 and from 4.25 to 5.05 in 1992.[2] Additional empirical research has resulted in parallel findings (Lang and Kahn, 1998; Levin-Waldman and McCarthy, 1998). In summarizing this body of work, Levin-Waldman states:

> Contrary to dire predictions, every time the minimum wage has been raised it has not had the negative effects it was theoretically supposed to have. This point has been noted in congressional testimony, and is often confirmed by the Labor Department. And it has certainly been highlighted by institutional economists in the past relying more on empiricism than on theory. (2001: 170)

Of course, raising the minimum wage from its current level of $5.15 an hour to our benchmark of $7.88 an hour would require a substantially bigger hike than prior raises in the minimum wage. The phase-in period might take place over several years in order to spread out the increase. Nevertheless, the negative impact is likely to be relatively modest. For example, Levin-Waldman (2000) found that 64 percent of small businesses said that they would not be adversely affected by an increase in the minimum wage from $5.15 to $7.25 an hour.

Another misplaced argument has been that most minimum wage earners are simply teenagers looking to earn a bit of spending money. According to this argument, raising the minimum wage would have only a slight impact on low-income families. Yet as Card and Krueger (1995) demonstrate, more than 70 percent of those who were affected by the minimum wage increases in 1990 and 1991 were adults, often women and minorities. Thirty-five percent of these workers were the sole wage earners in the family, compared with 41 percent for all workers. They provided 45 percent of the family's annual earnings, compared with 65 percent for all workers. The idea that the minimum wage affects primarily teenagers is erroneous.

In short, the positive impact of tying the minimum wage to the poverty level for a family of three and then indexing it to the rate of inflation would be substantial. First, it would establish a reasonable floor below which no full-time worker would fall. Second, it would allow such a worker to support a family of three above the official poverty line. Third, it would reinforce the value that Americans have consistently attached to work. Fourth, it would remove the political wrangling from the minimum wage debate. Fifth, it would address in a limited way the increasing inequities between CEOs who earn three or four hundred times what their average paid workers earn.

This approach also has the advantage of utilizing a currently existing policy. What is needed are two straightforward modifications—first, raising the wage to that of the poverty level for a family of three, and second, indexing it each year to the consumer price index so that it does not fall behind the rising cost of living. This approach is analogous to the manner in which Social Security payments operate each year. The overall strategy is therefore quite straightforward. The problem, as we have discussed earlier, is mustering the political will necessary to implement such a strategy.

In the not too distant past, however, the minimum wage approached and surpassed the level that we have been discussing here. The 1968 minimum wage (translated into 2000 dollars) would come out to $7.92 an hour (U.S. Bureau of the Census, 2002d). Thus, setting the minimum wage at a level that allows workers to support a family of three above the poverty threshold is certainly not unheard of or without precedent. And, in fact, the majority of Americans support such an increase in the minimum wage. Seventy-seven percent of Americans in a nationally representative sample were in favor of raising the minimum wage to $8.00 per hour. Furthermore, 79 percent favored regular increases in the minimum wage to keep up with inflation (Ms. Foundation for Women, 2002).

Finally, I should mention that throughout the country there has been a rise in what has become known as living wage campaigns (Moberg, 2000; Pollin, 2001; Pollin and Luce, 1998). The principles behind these campaigns are very similar to the principles behind the minimum wage debate.[3] In fact, one of the reasons that the living wage issue has arisen is precisely the failure of the minimum wage to keep up with inflation and to lift families out of poverty. Living wage statutes are being developed or have been enacted in hundreds of localities across the United States. They generally require taxpayer-subsidized employers (such as service contractors) to pay a wage that is substantially over the minimum wage (e.g., $8 or $9 an hour). These campaigns have been one of the most important grass-roots initiatives in seeking to redress the increasing prevalence of working poverty and escalating income inequality in the United States.

However, one of the problems with this approach is that it deals with low numbers of workers, in very specific geographical localities. It also leads opponents of a living wage to claim that localities that enact such statutes will have difficulty remaining competitive in the marketplace, because nearby localities will have lower labor costs. A more effective solution to the problem of low wages is federal legislation that would make the minimum wage equivalent to a living wage and that builds in the mechanisms to ensure that it keeps up with the rising costs of living. Although the current living wage campaigns are vitally important in raising the connection between low wages and poverty, and although they are making an important difference in the lives of workers who are affected by them, the raising and indexing of the minimum wage is a more effective and widespread solution for solving the problem of jobs that too often fail to economically support low- income families.

EARNED INCOME TAX CREDIT A second approach for supplementing and raising the earnings of low-income workers is through the tax structure, specifically through the use of tax credits. The primary example of such a credit is the Earned Income Tax Credit (EITC). The EITC was enacted in 1975 and underwent a significant expansion during the 1990s. In fact, it currently represents the largest cash antipoverty program in the United States and is frequently considered one of our more innovative economic policy ideas (see Ventry, 2002, for a historical and political background of the EITC).

The program is designed to provide a refundable tax credit to low-income workers, with the vast majority going to households with children. In 2002, a family with one child could qualify for the EITC if its earned income was below $29,201 (or $30,201 for married couples), while a family with two or more children could qualify if its household income was under $33,178 (or $34,178 for married couples). The maximum credit for a one-child family was $2,506; the benefit rose to $4,140 for a family with two or more children. The credit is normally received in a lump-sum payment as part of an overall tax refund for the previous year. Since it is a refundable credit, families receive the payment even if they do not owe any taxes.

Take the example of a family headed by a mother with two children. For the first $10,520 earned, she receives an additional 40 cents for each dollar made. If she earned $8,000 last year, she receives $3,200 from the EITC. If she earned $10,000, she receives a $4,000 EITC refund. For earnings between $10,520 to $13,520, the credit levels off at $4,140. Beyond $13,520, the credit is reduced by 21.06 percent, so that by $33,178 of earnings, no credit is received. For example, if our mother earns $20,000 for the year, her tax credit will be reduced to $2,775.

The goals of the EITC are to deliver economic relief at the low end of the earnings distribution and to furnish a strong work incentive. An individual cannot qualify for the EITC without earned income, and the impact is particularly strong at the lower levels. In our example, if the head of a household was earning $7.50 an hour (and her total earnings were under $10,000) the EITC would effectively raise her wage by an additional $3.00 an hour, to $10.50 an hour. The program thus provides a significant supplement to low earners, as well as an incentive to work. In 2002, it was estimated that 19 million Americans benefited from the EITC and that it pulled approximately 5 million individuals above the poverty line who otherwise would have fallen into poverty (Schiller, 2004). For families that remain in poverty, the EITC has helped to reduce the distance between their household income and the poverty line. It has also enabled families to purchase particular resources that can improve their economic and social mobility (e.g., school tuition, a car, or a new residence) or to meet daily expenses (Meyer and Holtz-Eakin, 2002; Romich and Weisner, 2002; Smeeding, Phillips, and O'Connor, 2000).

The EITC appeals to both liberals and conservatives. As Sheldon Danziger and Peter Gottschalk note, "It has retained bipartisan support because . . . it assists only those who work; it helps two-parent as well as single-parent families; it raises the employee's take-home pay without increasing the employer's labor costs" (1995: 158). In addition, it has helped to offset a trend since the early 1970s of declining real wages among low-skilled workers.

In order to make the EITC even more effective, its benefits should be expanded so that they provide greater assistance to low-income workers without children. As mentioned, the vast majority of the EITC benefits go to families with children. Yet there is no compelling reason why such benefits should not also be provided for individuals without children. Further work also needs to be done in order to increase the feasibility of receiving the EITC throughout the year, rather than as a lump sum during the tax season (although many families do prefer this way of receiving the EITC). Third, some households that qualify for the EITC fail to claim and take advantage of the tax credit. Better educating tax filers about the benefits of the EITC appears warranted. Fourth, state EITC programs should be encouraged as an additional anti-poverty component on top of the federal EITC benefits. Finally, consideration should also be given to modestly increasing the size of the credits currently given to families (although, as mentioned, considerable expansion occurred in the early 1990s and the federal program may currently be close to its optimal size; for example, see Liebman, 2002).

The policy of an expanded EITC, in conjunction with the raising and indexing of the minimum wage to the level of a living wage, would substantially help working men and women who, in spite of their efforts, are unable to get themselves and their families out of poverty or near-poverty. In addition, such policies begin to address (although in a very limited way) the increasing inequities and perceived unfairness of the American income distribution and wage structure. The fact that the gap between the highest- and lowest-paid workers in America has been growing rapidly over the past few decades and is currently the largest in the industrialized world calls out for simple standards of decency for those at the bottom of that distribution.

Speaking on the first year anniversary of the September 11 tragedy, the president of the Federal Reserve Bank of New York, William J. McDonough, noted that the growing income disparities violated both basic human morality and sound social policy. His remarks were made inside Trinity Church, which once lay in the shadows of the World Trade Center. His main theme was the importance in today's world of applying the commandment to love thy neighbor as thyself to include one's fellow worker. In this context, McDonough remarked,

> I believe there is one issue in particular which requires corrective action. A recent study shows that, twenty years ago, the average chief executive officer of a publicly traded company made forty-two times more than the average production worker. Perhaps one could justify that by the additional education required, the greater dedication, perhaps even the harder work. The same study shows that the average present day CEO makes over 400

times the average employee's income. It is hard to find somebody more convinced than I of the superiority of the American
economic system, but I can find nothing in economic theory that
justifies this development. I am old enough to have known both
the CEOs of twenty years ago and those of today. I can assure
you that we CEOs of today are not 10 times better than those of
twenty years ago. (2002)

Given this context, raising the living standards of those who are working
full-time so that they are able to lift themselves and a small family out of
poverty is without a doubt the morally and economically right thing to do. It
can be largely accomplished by adjusting the minimum wage and the Earned
Income Tax Credit.

Creating Enough Jobs

A second component of producing adequately paying jobs is ensuring that
there are enough jobs available for those in need of work. In many ways,
this is a much more difficult task than supplementing and raising the wages
of existing jobs. Nevertheless, it is essential that a sufficient number of jobs
be available to meet the demands of the existing labor pool.

As mentioned earlier, Timothy Bartik (2002) has estimated that during
the booming economic years of the late 1990s, between five and nine million more jobs were needed to provide each working-age poor household
with a full-time equivalent job. During recessions and economic downturns,
these numbers would obviously rise much higher. The fundamental question is how to create such jobs?

First, it should be noted that there has always been resistance to the idea
of full employment. For example, conventional wisdom has long held that
as levels of unemployment fall below 4, 5, or 6 percent, rates of inflation
will rise. This is referred to as the Phillips curve problem. As it becomes
harder for employers to find workers, they must pay higher wages in order
to attract employees. These higher costs are then passed on to the consumer
through higher product or service costs. As a result, inflation rises.

Recent trends suggest that this relationship may not be nearly as strong
as was once thought (Solow, 2002). The 1990s saw levels of unemployment
fall well below 5 percent, yet rates of inflation remained consistently low

during this period. However, it would undoubtedly be problematic with respect to inflation if rates of unemployment were to dip to extremely low levels such as 1 or 2 percent. With this caveat in mind, what can be done to stimulate the creation of more jobs?

Bartik (2001) notes that U.S. antipoverty policy in the past has focused heavily on labor supply policies (e.g., increasing individuals' human capital through job training programs or incentives to work through welfare reform), rather than on labor demand policies (increasing the number and quality of jobs). This approach has assumed that the labor market by itself will generate enough jobs to meet the needs of those seeking work—that, as the supply of labor increases, the labor market will in turn respond by generating more jobs to meet the demand. This does occur to some extent, but not nearly enough to meet the needs of the labor supply. According to Bartik (2002),

> when we push low-education persons into the labor market (the
> conservative approach) or train low-education persons and then
> push them into the labor market (the liberal approach), the
> private labor market will not create a sufficient number of jobs to
> employ all these labor market entrants. One possibility is that
> one-third to two-thirds of these labor market entrants will fail to
> obtain jobs. Alternatively, if more of the new entrants obtain
> jobs, their success will come at the expense of other low-
> education workers who will lose jobs, displaced because fewer
> job vacancies will be available. (105)

Consequently, although we need to make sure that job applicants have the skills and education necessary to perform the tasks needed, we must also make sure that enough jobs exist for those who are looking for work.

Various labor demand policies are therefore needed in order to generate a more robust rate of job growth. Several approaches can be taken. First, economic policy can seek in a broad way to stimulate job growth. These include fiscal policies such as increasing government expenditures, enhancing tax incentives for investment, or enacting consumer tax cuts. Monetary policy can provide a stimulus by making access to credit easier and cheaper (Schiller, 2004).

A second approach is to provide targeted wage subsidies to employers in order to stimulate job creation. As Lawrence Katz notes,

Wage subsidies to private employers have often been proposed by economists as a relatively flexible and efficient method to improve the earnings and employment of the less skilled. In a wage subsidy program, job creation and hiring decisions remain in the hands of private firms but the cost is partially borne by government. Firms are likely to respond to wage subsidies by increasing their utilization of workers in the targeted population. (1998: 22)

Although the details of such programs can vary considerably, the basic concept is that an employer receives a monetary subsidy for creating a position and/or hiring an individual (often from a targeted population) that the employer might not have hired without such an incentive. This approach could be aimed at businesses and industries that are potential employers of individuals from lower-income or lower-skill backgrounds. As an example, such an employer might receive a 50 percent subsidy on the first $15,000 of wages paid for every new position created. This could apply to the first year's wages; perhaps a subsidy of 25 percent might apply to the second year's wages. If the employer is willing to create a new position, he or she would be able to hire a worker at $15,000 but in effect have to pay out only $7,500 to that worker. The remaining $7,500 would be subsidized for the first year by the government. During the second year, the employer would receive $3,750 to offset the cost of the new worker's wages. In this fashion, the government would provide an incentive for employers to create job positions within the private economy, particularly jobs that would benefit lower-income households. The United States has experimented with several types of wage subsidy programs in the past, with modest results in terms of job creation (Bartik, 2001; Katz, 1998).

A third approach for creating jobs is through public service employment. The best-known example occurred during the Great Depression of the 1930s, when the federal government created programs such as the Works Progress Administration (WPA) and the Civilian Conservation Corps (CCC), which were designed to provide jobs for out-of-work Americans. Since that time, there have been a number of smaller attempts at establishing public service employment programs, often geared toward welfare recipients and youth. As David Ellwood and Elisabeth Welty (2000) note in their review of the effectiveness of public service employment programs, if done carefully and judiciously, they can help increase employment without displacing other workers, and they can produce genuinely valuable output. Such an approach appears particularly pertinent for welfare recipients who are nearing the end of their allotted time on the rolls. For those unable to find a job in the private sector, public service employment offers a solution to the problem of putting limits on the use of welfare while at the same time providing a viable alternative for those who want to work but who are unable to find a private sector job. In addition, public service workers can perform valuable services that are too often in short supply. These might range from contributing to community development projects, to assisting in the construction of affordable housing, to providing assistance for senior outreach programs.

Increasing the Accessibility of Key Social
and Public Goods

In some respects, the conditions of poverty and near-poverty are worse than the statistics would indicate. The reason for this is that several key social and public goods have become increasingly inaccessible for a number of American households. In particular, a quality education, health care, affordable housing, and child care either are out of reach or are obtained only at the cost of considerable economic expenditure and hardship. Yet these social goods are vital in building and maintaining healthy and productive citizens and families.

Virtually every other Western industrial society provides greater access and coverage to health care, affordable housing, and child care than does the United States (although it is also true that the social welfare states in many of these countries have been under increasing retrenchment pressure; Korp: 2003). They also do not display the wide fluctuations in educational quality that American children are subjected to at the primary and secondary levels. Why? The underlying reason is the belief that there are certain social and public goods that all individuals have a right to, and that making such resources accessible results in more productive citizens and societies in both the short and the long run. In addition, these countries recognize that such goods and services reduce the harshness of poverty and economic vulnerability.

Each of the four areas discussed in this section is complex and wide in its scope. Countless books and articles have been written on these subjects, accompanied by ongoing legislative debates. I touch upon only several key points and ideas in each of these areas, leaving it to the reader to further explore the specifics and nuances.

Quality Education

A quality education is one of the most vital assets that an individual can acquire. Indeed, a key motivation behind the introduction of public education in the mid-1800s was the importance of making education accessible to the general public, rather than to only the wealthy and privileged. Horace Mann, the well-known nineteenth-century educator, spoke of public education as the "great equalizer" and of school as a place where both disadvantaged and advantaged children would be taught under one roof. The expansion of and the greater access to public education have had a profound impact on the well-being of Americans and American society. They have contributed to an effective and productive workforce, a more informed citizenry, and countless other benefits.

Public education remains the avenue through which most Americans acquire their educational training. The vast majority of today's students attend public schools. In 1999, 89 percent of all primary and secondary students were enrolled in public schools, while 76 percent of students going on to college attended public institutions (U.S. Census Bureau, 2002d). As a result, public education remains the dominant vehicle for the vast majority of American students.

Unfortunately, as a result of the way that public education is funded at the primary and secondary levels, the quality of that education varies widely depending on the wealth of the community in which one resides. The bulk of U.S. school funding for elementary, middle, and high schools comes from the local tax base, primarily property taxes. School districts with a well-endowed property tax base generally have ample funding to operate quality public schools. This involves paying teachers competitive salaries, keeping student/teacher ratios relatively low, purchasing the necessary educational resources such as books for libraries or computer equipment for instruction, and so on.

On the other hand, schools in poor communities with diminished tax bases often are financially strapped. Teachers are frequently underpaid and overstressed, the physical facilities may be severely deteriorated and outdated, class sizes are often quite large, as well as many other disadvantages.

Students in these schools, predominately low-income and frequently of color, wind up being denied a quality education as a result. Linda Darling-Hammond and Laura Post write,

> Few Americans realize that the U.S. educational system is one of the most unequal in the industrialized world, and students routinely receive dramatically different learning opportunities based on their social status. In contrast to most European and Asian nations that fund schools centrally and equally, the wealthiest 10 percent of school districts in the United States spend nearly ten times more than the poorest 10 percent, and spending ratios of three to one are common within states. Poor and minority students are concentrated in the less well funded schools, most of them located in central cities and funded at levels substantially below those of neighboring suburban districts. (2000: 127)

As a result, many children receive an inferior education, dramatically reducing their ability to effectively compete in the labor market.

To deny children the fundamental right to a decent education is both morally wrong and bad social policy. It flies in the face of the American concept of equality of opportunity that was discussed in chapter 5. Countless studies have documented the immediate and lingering effects of disparate educational outcomes on later life. Improving public education for low-income children is absolutely essential.

Several steps are warranted. First, it is clear that although money in and of itself is not the complete answer, it nevertheless represents a large part of the solution. This is particularly the case for school districts that are unable to provide the necessary educational tools for their students (e.g., qualified teachers, educational materials). Evening out the vast financial differences that currently exist across school districts and then spending the additional money wisely by hiring qualified teachers and building strong curricula can make a significant difference. As Craig Jerald, a senior policy analyst at the Education Trust, put it, "The picture has become crystal clear. If you do both of those things you can really solve the problems" (Schemo, 2002).

Pressure should be brought to bear on the federal and state governments to even out the glaring disparities in school financing. Several states have begun to move in this direction, but many more need to follow their lead.

As noted, differences in spending per pupil can vary by thousands of dollars, with wealthy students blessed by countless social and economic advantages enjoying the most in terms of public per pupil spending, while students from poor backgrounds and possessing the fewest advantages, wind up receiving the least in terms of public tax dollars (see Rothman, 2000, for a further discussion of these issues at the state and local levels).

Beyond ensuring that all students have sufficient funding for their educations, we need to spend these funds wisely. A number of steps have been shown to be effective. These include spending money on the classroom (smaller class sizes, teacher development, educational materials), rather than on bureaucracy; hiring capable principals and well-qualified teachers trained in the subjects they are teaching; developing a challenging curriculum that imposes high expectations; involving parents in the education of their children; and establishing an orderly learning environment (Kahlenberg, 2001).

Finally, for low-income students to get the most out of their educational experience, there needs to be economic integration within the classroom. Schools in which the vast majority of children are in poverty have been shown to have a detrimental effect upon learning (Kahlenberg, 2002). As discussed in chapters 2 and 4, poverty puts an enormous strain on the lives of children, which spills over into their educational environment. This detriment is magnified in schools where most of the students are also in poverty, and frequently of color. Unfortunately, such schools have been increasing in frequency over the past decade (Frankenberg and Lee, 2002; Orfield and Gordon, 2001; Rusk, 2002). Research has demonstrated that students are much more likely to succeed educationally when they are in economically integrated environments, without lowering the performance of middle or upper-income children (Kahlenberg, 2002).

Although economic integration in the classroom can be extremely difficult to achieve given the long-established patterns of residential segregation by race and class, nevertheless it is critical. One approach is to allow parents the ability to choose among a variety of public schools and then to honor those preferences in a way that also contributes to economic integration within the particular schools (Willie and Alves, 1996). This idea of socioeconomic integration has been gaining ground in a number of communities across the country, from San Francisco, to La Crosse, Wisconsin, to Raleigh, North Carolina (see Century Foundation Task Force on the Common School, 2002, for examples).

Taken together, these steps will move us in the direction of improving the educational experience that low-income children receive. Although it is important that there are decent paying jobs available in the job market, it is also important that individuals have the necessary education and training to compete and succeed at those jobs. It is blatantly wrong that some American children, simply by virtue of their parents' economic standing, must settle for a substandard educational experience, while others receive a well-rounded education. All are American children, and all are entitled to a quality education.

Health Care

As with education, access to quality health care is largely dependent upon the size of one's wallet. For those who can afford it, America offers the finest medical care in the world. Those unable to absorb the increasing costs are frequently left out in the cold, without health care. As a result, more Americans are finding themselves either lacking in health insurance, with insufficient coverage, or with adequate coverage but only at a considerable expense. In 2002, 44 million Americans, or 15.2 percent of the population, lacked health insurance throughout the year. For those below the poverty line, nearly a third (30.4 percent) had no health coverage in spite of the Medicaid program, while 27.9 percent of those below 1.25 of the poverty line were without health insurance (U.S. Census Bureau, 2003d). During a thirty-six month period (1993 to 1996), 52.7 percent of those below the poverty line failed to have coverage continuously throughout, while 55.9 percent of those between 1.00 and 1.50 of the poverty line were not covered continuously (U.S. Census Bureau, 1998b). An estimated twenty million more Americans have inadequate health insurance to protect them from the expense of a major illness (Mullahy and Wolfe, 2001).

One of the reasons that Americans are lacking in health care coverage, particularly those in or near-poverty, is that their place of work does not provide health coverage. As we discussed earlier, an increasing number of low-wage and part-time jobs have been created during the past thirty years, and many of these jobs lack health benefits. Furthermore, for those who are under age 65 but out of work, health coverage is unlikely to be available except through the Medicaid program.

Access to health care is important in a variety of ways. Being able to address one's health needs is crucial in maintaining a productive life, both at work and at home. What, then, can be done to increase the health care access for those who find themselves left out?

The issue of reforming health care is enormously complex, as was demonstrated in the failed 1994 attempt at reform. This failure also demonstrated the power of various interest groups (e.g., the insurance industry, the American Medical Association) in shaping or preventing particular health care changes. Nevertheless, building a system around the fundamental principle of universal coverage is essential in providing decent-quality health care for all Americans. As noted earlier, the United States is far and away the exception among the industrialized countries in not offering universal coverage for its citizens. The question is not whether we have the needed funds to spend on health care. In fact, we spend more than twice the per capita amount on health care than that of the next nearest nation. Rather, the question is how best to spend these resources in order to ensure that all Americans have access to health care, while at the same time maintaining the overall quality of the system.

Universal coverage is essential in reforming the current health care system (for example, see the Physicians' Working Group for Single-Payer National Health Insurance, 2003). Unfortunately, this will not happen overnight. There are several important steps that can be taken in the meantime to increase the health care access of lower-income households. First, just as we have made the commitment in the 1960s to ensure universal coverage for the elderly, so too we should make the commitment for children. The Medicare program came into being in 1965 with the intention of providing health care coverage for all who were over age 65. Older Americans were felt to be a vulnerable and deserving population of universal health care.

The same argument can certainly be made for children. We have seen earlier that children are particularly vulnerable to poverty and its ill effects on health. Children are innocent victims of this overall process. As such, every child should have a right to decent quality health care, just as every elderly American has that right.

A very positive step toward this goal was taken with the introduction of the State Children's Health Insurance Program (CHIP), which was implemented across the various states in 1998. The CHIP program was an attempt to strengthen the existing coverage of low-income children. The idea has been to provide health coverage for lower-income children who normally would not qualify for Medicaid. In general, children living in households whose income is below 200 percent of the poverty line can receive health care through CHIP. Each state has the option of implementing CHIP as an expansion to its Medicaid program or running it as a separate program.

The major problem, however, with both the Medicaid and the CHIP programs is that not all eligible children are enrolled. For lower-income children in 2000 (below 200 percent of the poverty line), 32 percent had health coverage through a parent's employer, 42 percent had coverage through either Medicaid or CHIP, and 21 percent were uninsured. Among the uninsured, 60 percent were eligible for coverage through Medicaid, while an additional 24 percent were eligible through CHIP, leaving only one million children out of a total of 31.4 million low income children who were not eligible for any health care coverage (Kaiser Commission, 2002).

The issue is therefore one of ensuring that eligible children are enrolled in either the Medicaid or the CHIP program. A consensus exists that gains in enrollments can be achieved through simplifying and streamlining the enrollment process to make it easier for eligible families to enroll and stay enrolled and that communities and states should engage in outreach efforts to let families know that coverage is available and simple to secure (Mann et al., 2002). In addition, states around the country are beginning to consider expanding the CHIP program to include pregnant women, as well as the uninsured parents of children who qualify for CHIP coverage.

A second point of entry for expanding health care coverage to lower-income households is through an employer mandate that would require employers to provide some minimum level of health care coverage for their employees and families who did not have health coverage. Employers would provide access to health insurance either directly or indirectly by giving employees vouchers toward coverage (Mullahy and Wolfe, 2001). For smaller businesses, financial assistance could be provided at the federal level to absorb part of the costs such employers would have to bear.

A third avenue toward increasing the health care coverage of low-income households would be through the creation of a refundable tax credit to partially offset the cost that these households incur. Thus, a family that spent $2,100 during the year to purchase health insurance might receive $700 back from the federal government when it filed its federal income tax return. This approach is analogous to that of the Earned Income Tax Credit. It could also be designed so that the largest impact would be on households that fall below certain income levels (for example, 200 percent of the poverty line).

These three steps—making sure that eligible children are enrolled in either the Medicaid or the CHIP program; mandating that employers provide their employees with some type of health care coverage; and a refundable tax credit for individuals' health insurance expenses—would significantly increase the number of low-income Americans who have some type of health care coverage. In thinking about the importance of health care, along with education and decent-paying jobs, the late Senator Paul Wellstone, of Minnesota, noted in a campaign address shortly before his untimely death,

> If you want real welfare reform, focus on a good education, good health care, and a good job. If you want to reduce poverty, you focus on a good education, good health care, and a good job. If you want a stable middle class, you focus on a good education, good health care, and a good job. If you want to have citizens who can participate in democracy, you focus on a good education, good health care, and a good job. And if you want to end the violence, you could build a million new prisons and you could fill them all up, but you will never end this cycle of violence unless you invest in the health and the skill and the intellect and the character of our children—you focus on a good education, good health care, and a good job! (*St. Louis Post-Dispatch*, October 27, 2002)

In other words, these resources not only allow individuals to reduce their risk of economic vulnerability but also allow them to be productive citizens. Accessibility of health care is essential to this task.

Affordable Housing

Affordable housing represents another critical public good that has become harder to find in recent years, particularly for low-income households. The general rule of thumb is that households should spend no more than 30 percent of their income on housing (this is the standard definition of affordable housing). Yet the Joint Center for Housing Studies at Harvard University

(2003) estimates that, of the households in the bottom 20 percent of the U.S. income distribution, half were severely burdened by housing costs (that is, they were paying more than 50 percent of their total income on housing), while 23 percent were moderately burdened (they were expending between 30 and 50 percent of their income on housing). For low-income renters, the picture is even bleaker. Fifty-five percent were severely burdened by their rental costs, and one-quarter were moderately burdened; when one includes those who were living in structurally inadequate and/or overcrowded conditions, 82 percent of low-income renters had serious housing problems.

One of the reasons for this is that the cost of housing over the past twenty-five years has risen much more steeply than worker's wages. For example, the National Low Income Housing Coalition (2003) estimates that in order to afford the fair-market rent for an average two-bedroom apartment (that is, paying 30 percent of one's income for rent), a worker needs to be earning $15.21 an hour. As we have seen earlier, many heads of households are earning well below this. Wages have stagnated over the past twenty-five years, and the economy has been producing more jobs at the lower end of the wage scale. For example, the median wage of a retail salesperson in 1999 was $7.66 per hour, which is clearly insufficient to afford the rent on a two-bedroom apartment or to purchase a median-priced home in any major metropolitan area. In fact, even in the most "affordable" metropolitan areas, a retail salesperson would need at least double his salary to be able to purchase a median-priced home (Lipman, 2001). As former HUD secretary Andrew M. Cuomo observed, there are many "$6.00 an hour jobs in today's economy, but not much $6.00 an hour housing" (Housing and Development Reporter, 1998).

Furthermore, particular areas in the United States have especially severe shortages of affordable housing. In Massachusetts, one needs to be earning $22.40 an hour to be able to rent an adequate two-bedroom housing unit, while in San Francisco, one needs $34.13 an hour. As the bipartisan Millennial Housing Commission noted,

> there is simply not enough affordable housing. The inadequacy
> of supply increases dramatically as one moves down the ladder of
> family earnings. The challenge is most acute for rental housing
> in high-cost areas, and the most egregious problem is for the
> very poor. (2002: iv)

In addition to the proliferation of low-wage work, the private sector's failure to build an adequate stock of lower-end housing units and the federal government's decreasing expenditures on programs designed to address the housing needs of low-income families have made affordable housing even scarcer over the past two decades. The result is that more Americans, particularly those in the bottom quintile of the income distribution, are finding themselves without access to decent-quality affordable housing. Given these patterns, it is no wonder that homelessness has became such a visible issue over the past two decades.

The lack of affordable housing affects individuals in several ways. First, households that are already strapped for cash have much less to spend on food, clothing, health care, transportation, and other necessities because they are spending a significant amount of their income on housing. Second, not having decent, affordable, and stable housing has been shown to dramatically increase the levels of stress within families. Third, a household's lack of stable housing negatively affects children's development, in particular their academic performance and overall health. Finally, affordable and decent quality housing is critical in maintaining the vitality and sustainability of neighborhoods.

What can be done to strengthen low-income Americans' access to decent-quality affordable housing? Several approaches appear warranted. First, as indicated, there is a clear need to increase and rejuvenate the country's stock of affordable and modestly priced housing, through both new construction and the renovation of the existing housing stock. Tax incentives (such as the Low-Income Housing Tax Credit of 1986) should be strengthened to encourage the private market to build and renovate existing housing stock, and where private construction is not feasible, the federal and state governments need to become more directly involved in housing construction.

One idea for stimulating and funding such efforts is through the establishment of a national housing trust fund. This would be based upon the successful examples of various state, county, and city housing trust funds that are operating throughout the United States. The idea is to establish a national fund that would allow nonprofits and states to draw upon it in order to rehabilitate the existing housing stock and to construct new affordable housing. It would allow communities to define their housing needs and solutions and provide those communities with a dependable source of income to create more affordable housing opportunities. Such investments have been shown to be an important means for creating new jobs and stimulating further economic activity within local communities (Center for Community Change, 2001).

One source of revenue for such a trust fund would be to cap the home mortgage deduction at a lower level than is currently the case. Individuals are now able to deduct up to $1 million of interest on their itemized income tax returns. The question to ask ourselves is why should the federal government subsidize the building or buying of million-dollar homes. A more equitable approach would be to lower the home mortgage deduction to $500,000. This is still at least three times the median sales value of a new or existing home in the United States (U.S. Census Bureau, 2002d). If individuals want to buy or build a house for $800,000 or $1 million, they certainly can do so, but I fail to see a compelling reason why our country should subsidize this activity. Rather, the increased revenue that would be raised by lowering the home mortgage deduction could go into a national trust fund that would be used to assist lower-income renters and homeowners and to support the construction of affordable housing. A second source of funding could be the excess revenue from the Government National Mortgage Association (Ginnie Mae) and/or the Federal Housing Administration's (FHA) single-family insurance program. Both of these programs currently serve the housing needs of low-income families, yet their excess monies can be appropriated for other purposes. Directing this revenue into a national housing trust fund would ensure that it would address the needs for which these programs were designed.

A second avenue for increasing the accessibility of affordable housing to lower-income households is through the expansion and more effective use of housing vouchers. Approximately 1.5 million households use Section 8 housing vouchers in the country (Millennial Housing Commission, 2002). The program is designed to allow families with low incomes to rent private housing on the open market from those landlords that will accept the vouchers and whose rental units qualify for the program. Individuals pay no more than 30 percent of their income toward their rent, with the government making up the difference. The program has generally been considered a success in opening up the housing market to lower-income families. It allows individuals some flexibility and movement in terms of their housing decisions. Unfortunately, it has become increasingly difficult for families to find landlords willing to accept the vouchers. Policies should be put in place to encourage and increase landlord participation, and the program should be expanded and strengthened (see Millennial Housing Commission, 2002, for specific recommendations regarding improving the current system).

A third avenue for reducing the economic burden of housing costs is to provide some form of a refundable housing tax credit that would be directed to low-income households. Current tax policy allows homeowners to deduct the interest paid on their mortgages. This has helped millions of Americans by reducing the overall costs of owning a home. Yet in order to qualify for the deduction, households must itemize their income tax returns. The problem is that many low-income families do not itemize and therefore cannot take advantage of the deduction. Furthermore, the deduction is nonrefundable—it can be used only to reduce the overall amount of taxes owed. Consequently, if one's taxes are fairly low to begin with (as is the case for low-income earners), this deduction does not provide any economic relief.

What is needed is a refundable credit targeted to low-income homeowners and renters. An example is Wisconsin's Homestead Credit, which was designed to ease the impact of rent and property taxes on low-income households (Wisconsin Department of Revenue, 2003). The benefit can be taken either as an income tax credit or as a direct refund. The amount received depends on the income level of a household (for 2002 tax filers, household income had to be below $24,500 in order to qualify) and the amount paid in rent or property tax during the year. Larger credits and refunds go to those who have earned less but have paid more in housing costs. In this fashion, assistance is provided to both renters and homeowners at the lower end of the income distribution.

Finally, one cannot discuss the issue of housing and its accessibility without discussing the issue of race. Racial minorities (particularly African Americans) have historically been discriminated against in the housing market. Research has indicated that black and Hispanic renters are more likely to be excluded from housing made available to white renters, black and Hispanic home buyers learn about fewer available homes than white homebuyers, and blacks and Hispanics are more likely to be turned down for home loans than their white counterparts (Yinger, 1995; 2001). In each case, these effects are present even when any group differences in demographic or socioeconomic attributes are controlled for. The result of such housing market discrimination is higher rent burdens, poorer quality housing, and increased residential segregation for African Americans and Hispanic Americans.[4]

In order to address racial and ethnic discrimination in the housing market, there is a need for strong enforcement of antidiscrimination legislation such as the Fair Housing Act of 1968 and the Fair Housing Amendments Act of 1988, as well as enforcement of fair-lending legislation such as the Equal Credit Opportunity Act of 1974 and the Community Reinvestment Act of 1977. It is also critical to provide those agencies charged with enforcing antidiscriminatory legislation (such as the Department of Housing and Urban Development and the Justice Department) with the resources to do so properly. Lack of sufficient resources, often renders antidiscriminatory laws impotent.

Child Care

Good-quality and affordable child care represents a fourth public good in short supply. As most new parents quickly realize, finding child care that offers both of these attributes is a challenge. It is particularly challenging for lower-income working parents. Some turn to relatives such as grandparents to help watch younger children, others may use organized day care, still others rely on a family day care operation run out of a neighbor's home. The Census Bureau indicates that, for poor households that are making child care payments, their expenses on average are between 20 and 35 percent of their income (U.S. Census Bureau, 2000, 2002e). Families that were below the poverty line and paying for child care in 1997 had an average weekly expenditure of $52, while their average weekly pay was $260 (U.S. Census Bureau, 2002e). For many low-income working families, child care costs represent a major expense. This is particularly the case for welfare recipients. The cost of child care has been shown to be a significant barrier for women making the transition from welfare to work (Baum, 2002; Meyers et al., 2002).

At the same time, much of the child care offered today in the United States is of mediocre to poor quality. For example, a nationwide survey of 400 day care centers around the country was conducted in the mid 1990s. This involved observing the staff, facilities, and child care approaches practiced at centers and then rating them on several measures of overall child care quality. The result was that only 14 percent were considered of good quality, while 40 percent were given poor ratings (Helburn et al., 1995). Less formal types of child care, such as family day care homes or assistance by relatives, also tend to be of mediocre to poor quality (Kontos et al., 1995). Too often they consist of little more than custodial care, while lacking in intellectual or developmental stimulation. Such forms of child care are deleterious to all children but are particularly harmful to lower-income children. Cheryl Hayes and colleagues noted in their report for the National Research Council, "Poor-quality care, more than any single type of program or arrangement, threatens children's development, especially children from poor and minority families" (1990: 290).

Like education, health care, and housing, child care represents a huge policy issue that simply cannot be adequately covered here. A number of researchers and policy analysts have put forth directions and initiatives to consider in terms of reforming child care (see Bergmann, 1996; Blau, 2001; Kagan and Cohen, 1996; Zigler and Finn- Stevenson, 1999). As the National Research Council Report suggests, the overall goals of a revamped child care system should include quality within child care services and arrangements, improved accessibility to quality child care services for families, and enhanced affordability of child care services for low- and moderate-income families (Hayes et al., 1990).

Two initial steps can be taken to move toward these goals with respect to lower-income families. First, greater subsidies should be provided to support a family's use of quality child care programs and arrangements (Hayes et al., 1990). There are several types of subsidies currently available, but they are delivered primarily through the tax code as deductions and therefore fail to provide much relief to lower-income families. The Child Care and Development Block Grant program exists to help lower-income families with child care needs, but only one out of seven eligible children receives such assistance (Children's Defense Fund, 2002a). David Blau (2001) suggests a more targeted use of child care vouchers directed to lower-income families. Like housing vouchers, child care vouchers would allow lower-income families to seek out a variety of child care options and receive immediate reductions in their costs of child care. Vouchers could also be structured so that they would increase in value depending upon the quality of the child care used. For example, if a family were to utilize an unaccredited source of child care, it might receive a subsidy of 40 percent of the average cost of care; if it used a provider that was accredited and of good quality, it would receive a 60 percent subsidy, and if it utilized an accredited child care provider of excellent quality, it would receive an 80 percent subsidy. As Blau notes, this has the advantage of encouraging and rewarding families that seek higher-quality child care, and it provides an incentive for child care providers to offer higher-quality care in order to attract consumers.

A second step for increasing lower-income families' access to and the affordability of quality child care would be to expand the Head Start and Early Head Start programs. Head Start currently serves approximately one-third of eligible children ages 3–5 (Blau, 2001), while approximately 55,000 infants and toddlers are served by the Early Head Start Program from the more than two million eligible children (U.S. Department of Health and Human Services, 2002). Although they vary in design across localities, the programs are widely accepted as representing a high-quality experience for children. Head Start focuses on improving the learning skills, health, nutrition, and social competence of children.

Unfortunately, there are many eligible children not taking advantage of the programs. The reason for this is twofold. First, the programs lack the funding to include all such children. This can be directly resolved through increasing the federal funding for both the Head Start and Early Head Start programs. The second reason is that they operate as part-day programs. Having a child in a program only part of the day often does not mesh well with a working parent's schedule. An important step in increasing Head Start's accessibility would be to integrate it with community child care programs in order to provide extended-day care for children whose parents are employed (Hayes et al., 1990). More children would receive the benefit of the Head Start Program, and lower-income working parents would be able to meet their child care needs as well.

Buffering the Economic Consequences
of Family Changes

A third strategy for reducing American poverty is to buffer the economic consequences of family structural changes, in particular the detrimental impact of divorce and teenage pregnancy on the risk of poverty. An underlying value behind this (as well as the earlier strategies) is that the economic well-being of children should be a top priority. No child should suffer from poverty, regardless of the type of family that he or she is growing up in. Putting in place the previous job proposals helps all household heads support their children. Similarly, increasing the access to fundamental resources such as health care and housing helps all children and their families. But beyond these sets of policies, there are two particular events that put children at further economic risk—parental separation and/or divorce and, for girls, pregnancy during the teenage years. Policies that address the impact of such family structural changes on the economic well-being of children are discussed in this section.

A second value that underlies this section is the importance of parents' financial obligation to support their children. Social policy should be constructed in a way that reinforces this obligation. In the case of separation and divorce, it can ensure that noncustodial parents assist their children economically. In the case of teenage pregnancy, policy initiatives can be designed to reduce the occurrence of pregnancy among teens who are ill prepared to economically support a child.

Finally, there is a recognition that what constitutes "the family" has changed dramatically over the past three decades. Like it or not, there is much more variation today in the types of families that children reside in. Social policy must recognize and confront these realities, rather than try to ignore them or to turn back the clock to some imagined golden era (for example, see Coontz, 1992, 1997). Divorce is a part of everyday America, as is teenage pregnancy. We need to constructively deal with these potentially economically devastating events.[5]

Child Support Policies

American families have experienced substantial change over the past several decades. One of the most profound of these changes has been the rising incidence of divorce and single-parent families. It is estimated that half of all white children and two-thirds of all black children will spend some period of their childhood in a single-parent family (Teachman et al., 2000).

As a result, child support and its enforcement have become an increasing concern. As more and more children experience the separation and divorce of their parents, and as increasing numbers of children are born to single parents, the issue of noncustodial parents' financial responsibility takes on greater importance. The detrimental economic effects of divorce and single parenthood on women and their children has been extensively documented over the past two decades (McLanahan and Sandefur, 1994; McLanahan, 2002). This body of work has demonstrated that newly created female-headed households with children are at a significant risk of poverty. Within a year following divorce, a divorced woman's standard of living tends to fall by 30 to 35 percent, while a divorced man's standard of living rises between 10 and 15 percent on average (Cherlin, 1992).

One reason for the sharp decline in the economic well-being of households headed by divorced mothers is that they often fail to receive the court-ordered child support payments that are due them. In 1999, 45.9 percent of mothers received the full amount of court-ordered child support payments, 28.7 percent received only partial payment, and 25.4 percent received no payment (U.S. Census Bureau, 2002e). Of the $29.5 billion in child support payments due in 1999, $17.6 billion were actually received.[6]

Receiving the court-ordered amount of child support can make a significant difference in the ability of single-parent families to avoid poverty. Mothers who received the full amount of child support payments in 1999 had a poverty rate of 15.7 percent, those that received a partial amount had a poverty rate of 25.8 percent, and those who failed to receive any of their court-awarded child support had a poverty rate of 33.6 percent. Mothers who had not been awarded child support experienced a poverty rate of 36.2 percent (U.S. Census Bureau, 2002e).

Since the mid-1970s, a series of changes in federal laws has attempted to make child support enforcement more effective (Institute for Research on Poverty, 2000). This was particularly the case with the welfare reform changes passed in 1996. States are now required to operate a child support program that meets federal mandates (e.g., expanded efforts in income withholding, paternity establishment, enforcement of orders, and use of central registries). Failure to do so disqualifies a state from receiving grant monies under the Temporary Assistance for Needy Families program. Although these initiatives are at a beginning stage, evidence suggests that there has been an increase in the amount of child support received by divorced and never-married mothers (Sorenson and Halpern, 1999).

From a policy perspective, several options might be considered in order to make the child support system more effective. Irwin Garfinkel (1992) has argued that the current system could be strengthened into a child support assurance program that would provide far greater protection for mothers and their children. Such a system would contain three key elements. First, noncustodial parents would pay a set percentage of their income for child support. For example, noncustodial parents with one child might pay 15 percent of their income for child support. For two children, noncustodial parents would pay 22 percent of their income for child support, and so on. The amount taken out would be capped at some upper limit (e.g., 33 percent), as would the total amount of income to be taxed (e.g., $100,000). Such an approach would greatly simplify the current process of receiving court-ordered child support and would treat all noncustodial parents equally. The amount of child support transferred would be dependent upon the number of children that one had and the amount of earned income. All noncustodial parents would therefore be treated the same.

Second, the support payments would be automatically withheld from the noncustodial parent's paycheck in the same manner as Social Security payments. Using the formula given, a nonresident parent earning $3,000 a month would have $450 (or 15 percent of earnings) withheld and transferred each month to the custodial parent. This would effectively take the decision whether to pay child support out of the hands of the nonresident parent and would dramatically increase the amount of court-ordered child support payments that would find their way to American children. Just as we do not leave it up to workers to decide whether to pay into the Social Security system, similarly we should not leave it up to noncustodial parents to decide whether to make their court-ordered child support payments. Transferring these payments directly from the nonresidents' paycheck deals with this problem simply and effectively.

A third component of a revamped child support system would ensure that all children are guaranteed a minimum benefit level. Thus, if a noncustodial parent were not making enough income to meet this level, the government would then make up the difference. The exact amount of such a level can be debated, but for purposes of illustration let us assume that for one child this would be $3,000. In this case, if a noncustodial parent were earning $12,000 a year, and 15 percent of the parent's income was utilized to support that child, $1,800 would be transferred during the year for child support. However, this would fall short of the minimum level of $3,000, and therefore the government would make up the additional $1,200 in order to ensure the child's minimum level of $3,000 a year. In this fashion, children in single-parent households would not be allowed to fall below an economic floor in terms of financial support.

It should be noted that this system would apply to all parents who father or mother a child, regardless of whether they are married. The underlying value here is that if you become a parent, you have a financial obligation to your children. If two unwed teenagers have a child and that child lives with its mother, the father of the child still has a financial obligation to support his son or daughter. A certain percentage of income would be removed from the father's paycheck until his children reached the age of eighteen. In addition, the system would be applied equally to men and women. Although the vast majority of women have custody of their children, if the father has custody, then the mother would pay child support out of her paycheck.

This system has the potential to significantly reduce poverty among mothers and their children. Various simulations have resulted in a range of poverty reductions (Garfinkel, 1998). It also enforces and strengthens the parent's economic responsibility for child support, which can lead to federal and state savings by reducing welfare payments. Finally, it may lead to more responsible early sexual behavior by making it clear that parents will be held financially responsible for supporting their children until they reach the age of eighteen.

Preventing Teenage Pregnancies

A second family change leading to poverty is teenage pregnancy and early childbirth. Having a child at an early age and out of wedlock significantly increases the risk of poverty for both the mother and her child. It is estimated that 75 percent of all unmarried teen mothers will receive public assistance within five years of giving birth (Annie E. Casey Foundation, 1998). Having a child at an early age also leads to a much greater risk of dropping out of high school and having fewer marketable skills, which in turn has an impact on the mother's ability to work her way out of poverty. This can affect the education and skills that her child acquires and increases the risk that the child will in turn become a teen parent and therefore repeat the cycle (Haveman et al., 2001)

Although the teen pregnancy rate has been coming down over the past several years, the United States still remains at the top of the developed world in terms of the extent of teenage pregnancy. Approximately one million American teenagers become pregnant each year, with four out of five of these pregnancies being unintended (Henshaw, 1999; Kirby, 2001). Our teenage birth rates are twice as high as England's, four times as high as Germany's, six times as high as France's, and eight times as high as the Netherlands'. The elevated rate of U.S. teenage pregnancies takes its toll on society; one estimate places the financial burden at $7 billion a year (Maynard, 1997).

Significantly reducing the rate of teenage pregnancy will also reduce the extent of poverty, particularly among young Americans.[7] Research indicates that three critical components are necessary for such a reduction. First, it is essential that we provide medically accurate education regarding sexuality. Programs that are age appropriate and that contain balanced and realistic content about delaying sex until one is older and that promote safer sex practices for those who become sexually active have been shown to reduce the likelihood of teenage pregnancy (Planned Parenthood, 2002).

Second, providing access to contraception and family planning services can significantly reduce the rate of teenage pregnancy. A comparative study by the Alan Guttmacher Institute indicated that the major reason teen pregnancy and childbearing rates were so much higher in the United States than in Canada and several European countries was the different rates of contraceptive use. Sexually active teens in the United States were less likely to use contraception, and when they did, they were more likely to utilize less effective methods than their European and Canadian counterparts (Darroch et al., 2001). Having access to both family planning services and effective contraceptive methods has been shown to be critical in preventing teenage pregnancy.

Third, teens must be motivated to avoid pregnancy. This is particularly the case for teenagers who are residing in areas marked by high levels of concentrated poverty and bleak future prospects—in a world of negatives, having a child early is sometimes viewed as a positive. Developing real opportunities for such adolescents is therefore critical in providing a strong motivation to delay childbearing. These opportunities would encompass several of the earlier discussed topics such as adequately paying jobs and access to quality education, as well as opportunities for building both individual and community assets (to be discussed in the next section). As has been often noted, the best contraceptive is a real future.

Unfortunately, current U.S. policy has largely ignored these fundamental points, resulting in our high rates of teenage pregnancy. Children are exposed to the worst combination of messages. On one hand, they are bombarded with daily images from the media telling them that sex is exciting, fun, and spontaneous. On the other hand, they are frequently denied the education and tools to engage in responsible sexual behavior. They are told to "just say no." The result, of course, is the highest rate of teen pregnancy in the developed world. Public policy needs to be based upon the three principles outlined if we are to reduce our rates of teen pregnancy to the levels of our European and Canadian neighbors. Doing so will significantly reduce the number of Americans who fall into poverty at an early age.

An example of such an approach is the Children' Aid Society—Carrera Program, developed by Michael Carrera. The program combines education regarding sexuality, comprehensive health care that includes reproductive health services and information on contraception, and strong efforts to develop brighter futures for teens in the program. These include academic assessment, help with homework, tutoring, preparation for standardized exams, and assistance with college entrance applications. The program also helps to improve work prospects via a job club, assistance in finding employment, and career awareness. The program thus combines the three principles described.

A three-year evaluation of the twelve sites, located in poor neighborhoods nationwide, found that participants had significantly delayed the onset of sex, increased the use of condoms and other effective methods of contraception, and had one-third fewer pregnancies and births than those in the control group (Kirby, 2001). As one teenager explained, she had just assumed that she would become a teenage mother as her older sister had done. But after being in the program for three years, her expectations were changed.

> I wasn't thinking about college when I was young. But I changed when I was about 14. This program changed me. I have a life. I have things to do. I'm going to be a nurse. Will I have babies? No time soon. (Lewin, 2001)

The Children' Aid Society—Carrera Program illustrates that the principles discussed here can effectively reduce the high rates of teenage pregnancy and childbirth in this country and thereby reduce the risk of poverty for millions of adolescents and young adults.

Building Assets

Social policies are frequently designed to alleviate the current conditions of poverty. Indeed, the strategies of making work pay, providing access to key social goods, and enforcing child support are each aimed at improving the current economic conditions of individuals and families. This is understandable, given that poverty affects children and adults in the here and now. Yet approaches to poverty alleviation must also pay attention to longer-term processes and solutions. In particular, the accumulation of assets is crucial, both across the individual life course and within the communities in which Americans reside. The acquisition of such assets allows both individuals and communities to more effectively function and, for our purposes, to reduce their risk of poverty. These assets enable individuals to ride out periods of economic vulnerability. They also allow for the growth and strengthening of individual and community development. Assets build a stake in the future that income by itself often cannot provide. Unfortunately, the opportunities to acquire such assets have been in short supply for lower-income individuals and communities.

An underlying value behind the policies suggested here is that asset accumulation is valuable because of its role in fostering individual and community empowerment and self-determination. Assets are an important means by which individuals and communities are able to shape and improve their lives and neighborhoods. In addition, the asset policies discussed here are guided by a question of justice. A number of policies are in place that encourage asset accumulation for the middle and upper classes. It is only fair that comparable policies be developed for those with fewer resources. As Thomas Shapiro and Edward Wolff observe, "Current public policy offers substantial, highly regressive subsidies for wealth and property accumulation for relatively well-off individuals. In contrast, poverty policy has ignored asset building for resource-poor families" (2001: 6). The policies suggested here are an attempt to address this imbalance.

Individual Assets

There have been periods in our history when social policy was explicitly designed to foster asset accumulation for a large number of Americans, including those at the lower end of the income distribution (although racial groups such as African Americans and American Indians have routinely been excluded).[8] For example, the Homestead Act of 1862 allowed pioneers to lay their stake on 160 acres of land. As long as they remained and worked the land for five years, they became its owners. This policy enabled many families to build their futures and their children's futures. During the seventy-five-year duration of the Homestead program, 1.5 million households were given title to 246 million acres of land (Williams, 2000). In addition, the homestead itself represented a very tangible asset that could then be handed down to the next generation. By the time of the fourth generation, it is estimated that approximately 46 million Americans were descendants and beneficiaries of those who had homesteaded (Williams, 2000). The Homestead Act constituted a major asset-based policy in U.S. history that improved the lives of millions and played an important role in the economic development of the United States.

Another large-scale asset based policy was the G.I. Bill. Initiated in 1944, the original G.I. Bill provided $500 per year for college tuition and $50 a month for living expenses to veterans of World War II. This policy had a profound impact, opening the doors of higher education to those who needed such help in order to attend. At its peak in 1947, 49 percent of all students enrolled in higher education were supported by the G.I. Bill. Nearly 8 million veterans of the war received educational benefits through the bill. In addition, approximately 10 million veterans of World War II and the Korean War were able to use the G.I. loan program to purchase homes or start businesses (Shapiro, 2001). Once again, not only did this policy help millions of Americans, but it also was a sound investment in the country as a whole (Mettler, 2002).

Although the results are not as dramatic as these examples, policies continue to exist that encourage the development of assets. These policies are delivered primarily through the tax code (known as tax expenditures). For example, the ability to deduct the interest paid on a home mortgage when filing one's income tax return has enabled millions of Americans to lower their costs of owning a home. Partially as a result of this, the home has come to represent the major asset held by Americans—44 percent of all U.S. wealth is based in home equity (U.S. Census Bureau, 2001b). Governmental policy has clearly encouraged the accumulation of wealth via home ownership. Other examples of asset-building policies through the tax code include the lower tax rate on capital gains, the deduction allowed for contributions to individual retirement accounts (IRAs), and the exclusion of employer contributions to pension funds (Seidman, 2001). However, each of these types of asset policies primarily benefit the middle and upper classes. Christopher Howard (1997) has estimated that 88 percent of such tax expenditures go to families earning more than $50,000, while 44 percent go to those with household earnings over $100,000.

In contrast, a significant percentage of the population lacks assets, particularly financial assets such as savings or stocks. Oliver and Shapiro (1990) found that one-third of American households had no financial assets at all. Wolff (1998) has shown that families in the middle income quintile have financial assets that would maintain their standard of living without income for 1.2 months, while those in the bottom quintile would not be able to replace their income for any period of time. Carney and Gale (2001) report that 20 percent of all households have no basic transaction accounts (i.e., a savings or checking account) and that more than half of all households have less than $5,000 in financial assets. Those in the bottom 25 percent of the income distribution have virtually no financial assets whatsoever.

As Kathryn Edin (2001) and others have demonstrated, the accumulation of assets is largely dependent upon having an income surplus, along with the belief and faith that one's income will remain relatively stable from one month to the next. Given the nature of poverty and lower-income jobs, both of these requirements are often in short supply.[9]

What can be done to build the financial assets of those who have been left out? One innovative policy tool for building the assets of the poor has been the concept of Individual Development Accounts (or IDAs). This approach has been pioneered by Michael Sherraden (1991, 2001). Sherraden (1991) argues that government policy should provide incentives and resources that would allow low-income individuals and families to build their economic assets, much as it does for middle- and upper-class families. His assertion is that "asset accumulation and investment, rather than income and consumption, are the keys to leaving poverty" (1991: 294). Government policies should attempt to facilitate the building of individuals' and families' resources through asset accumulation.

To do this, Sherraden has formulated the concept of Individual Development Accounts, which allow poor individuals and families to participate in matched savings accounts, with the match being at least 1:1 and often much higher. Accumulated assets in these accounts can be used for a broad array of development purposes intended to strengthen a family's economic position, such as job training, education, starting a small business, or owning a home. The IDAs "can have multiple sources of matching deposits, including governments, corporations, foundations, community groups, and individual donors" (Sherraden, 2000: 161). IDAs are designed to provide a vehicle for lower-income families to save, and a financial incentive for them to do so. The savings themselves are intended to be used at a later time to further build and strengthen a household's assets and human capital.

The 1996 federal welfare reform legislation included a provision allowing states to use part of their block grant money to establish and fund IDAs. Both Presidents Bill Clinton and George W. Bush have demonstrated strong support for the concept, and more than forty states have some form of IDA policy. The concept is also gaining ground in countries such as Canada, Taiwan, and the United Kingdom. Evidence from a large demonstration project in the United States indicates that IDAs do indeed enable poor families to save and accumulate assets (Schreiner et al., 2002).[10]

Additional asset-based development policies should be developed. One recent example is the idea of a children's trust fund. Beginning at the child's birth, the government would contribute monetary funds on a regular basis into an account for each child. It would be universal in that all children would be entitled to such a fund, yet it would also be progressive in that lower-income families would receive proportionally a greater amount of resources than middle- or upper-income children. At age 18, children would be allowed to use their trust funds for particular purposes such as furthering their education, receiving technical training, or perhaps investing in a home a bit later in life. As Sherraden notes, such a policy has the potential to "reduce class divisions, increase opportunity, spark individual engagement and initiative, and increase both economic growth and active citizenship" (2002: 4). The idea of a children's trust fund has been adopted in the United Kingdom, and discussions are beginning to take place in the United States.

Another means of developing assets and broadening the base of wealth is through employee ownership plans. These include employee stock ownership plans, 401(k) plans, and broad-based stock option plans. The percentage of total corporate equity owned by nonmanagement employees has risen from less than 2 percent in 1987 to more than 8 percent in 2001 (representing approximately $800 billion). Currently, more than twenty million employees own stock in their companies through one of these above plans (National Center for Employee Ownership, 2002). Employee ownership plans represent yet another potential means for helping individuals build their assets, while at the same time raising the productivity of workers.

Community Assets

Just as individuals thrive with the acquisition and development of assets, so too do communities. Poor neighborhoods are often characterized by their lack of strong community assets, such as quality schools, decent housing, adequate infrastructure, economic opportunities, and available jobs. These, in turn, affect the life chances of residents in such communities. A trip to any poor inner-city or rural area makes this abundantly clear. What can be done to improve this situation?

A first step is to recognize and build on the abilities, strengths, and energy of residents within a neighborhood. Ultimately, the impetus to address neighborhood issues and problems must come from the neighbors themselves. Across the country, there has been a revitalization of grassroots community development and neighborhood organizations that have involved hundreds of thousands of residents (see Garr, 1995; Grogan and Proscio, 2000; Keating and Krumholz, 1999; Sirianni and Friedland, 2001; Von Hoffman, 2003; Warren, 2001; Williamson et al., 2002; Wright, 2001). They can be found from the low-income neighborhoods of the South Bronx in New York City, to the boot-heel region of southern Missouri, to Chinatown in San Francisco, California. As Paul Grogan and Tony Proscio note, residents in these communities,

> have used these organizations to invest in their assets rather than nurse old wounds. . . . They have built and renovated thousands of houses and apartments, recruited businesses into their neighborhoods, organized child-care centers and charter schools, and formed block watches and civic clubs. As individual groups, their achievements are sometimes laughably modest. In aggregate, they are becoming monumental. (2000: 4)

The rapid growth of nearly 4,000 community development corporations around the country is vivid evidence that residents in lower-income communities have been coming together to produce tangible and pragmatic improvements in the asset base of their neighborhoods.

One such example can be found fifteen minutes from my office here at Washington University. Located in North St. Louis, the Grace Hill Settlement House was founded in 1903 to help immigrant families settle into their new neighborhoods. Today, Grace Hill has evolved into a significant resource for the community. One of its most innovative programs is known as the MORE Time Dollar Exchange program (MORE standing for Member-Organized Resource Exchange). It is designed as a service barter system that allows neighbors to help one another and themselves. It works in the following way. For each hour that a resident gives to help someone else, that person is entitled to an hour of help from another resident. One person may build their "time dollars" by providing child care assistance and may in turn use their acquired time dollars to "purchase" a different service, perhaps a neighbor's home-fix-it skills. A computer network keeps track of the time dollars accumulated and used by each participating individual. The MORE system at Grace Hill is but one example of the multitude of grassroots innovations that are occurring across the country. This type of activity represents a beginning avenue through which the assets of lower-income communities are being built and strengthened.

Such activity and development frequently needs political capital and financial resources in order to accomplish specific community goals. Whether it be affordable housing, adequately supplied schools, or improved municipal services, additional resources are necessary. Therefore, a second step in revitalizing and strengthening the assets of lower-income neighborhoods is the development of coalitions and leadership from within such communities to exert political pressure and gain entry into the local and state decision-making process. Power can be obtained by organized money, but it can also be obtained by organized people. This is the principle that drives community development and grassroots organization efforts. When residents of communities are able to educate and organize themselves regarding specific issues of concern, they are better able to create positive change through the political process. Yet such a task is far from easy, especially in light of the daily turmoil of poverty.

Particular institutions are often needed to assist in this task. Historically, one of the most important has been religious organizations. They have provided the moral foundation for social justice, along with the organizational and resource capabilities necessary to foster and build community leadership skills. Other organizations exist as well. One in particular that has been instrumental in helping to develop such local leadership and coalition building is the Industrial Areas Foundation (IAF). The IAF was founded in 1940 by perhaps the most influential community organizer of the past century, Saul Alinsky. Since that time, the IAF has expanded considerably. There are currently more than sixty affiliated organizations in the U.S. network, along with affiliated organizations in Great Britain and South Africa. As Ernie Cortes, one of today's best-known and most effective organizers, notes, "The central role of the IAF organizations is to build the competence and confidence of ordinary citizens and taxpayers so that they can reorganize the relationship of power and politics in their communities, allowing them to reshape the physical and cultural face of their neighborhoods" (1996: 175). These groups may start with smaller issues and then work their way up. As Cortes describes,

> They begin with small, winnable issues—fixing a streetlight, putting up a stop sign. They move into larger concerns—making a school a safe and civil place for children to learn. Then they move to still larger issues—setting an agenda for a municipal improvement budget; strategizing with corporate leaders and members of the city council on economic growth policies; developing new initiatives in job training, health care, and public education. When ordinary people become engaged and begin to play large, public roles, they develop confidence in their own competence. (1996: 186–187)

Examples of such local organizations can be found throughout the country. The community-based group known as Communities Organized for Public Service (or COPS) has successfully mobilized low-income communities in and around San Antonio over the past thirty years. It has achieved major victories in influencing the power structure and acquiring municipal investments (such as storm sewers, adequate schools, and street repairs) that had long bypassed its communities. The Nehemiah Homes Project in Brooklyn and the Bronx has been able to acquire the necessary resources from the City of New York to build thousands of new single-family homes for working families. In the lower delta region, the Mississippi Choctaws have revitalized their community by building on their initial success in attracting federal and private investments. They have become one of the ten largest employers in Mississippi, with assets that include an industrial park, a major shopping center, and, more recently, a casino (this in a county that had been the state's poorest). Through effective political and economic leadership, the tribe has been able to transform its community from abject poverty into an economically vibrant environment. These and countless other examples demonstrate that effective community organizing and leadership can provide leverage and ultimately lead to a working relationship with larger political entities such as City Hall or the statehouse.

A third step in revitalizing economically distressed neighborhoods is attracting businesses and economic opportunities into such communities. The primary approach in the past has been to entice such movement through the creation of tax incentives targeted to businesses that choose to locate in a specified impoverished area. This has been the logic behind both the Enterprise Zone and Empowerment Zone programs, as well as the Tax Increment Financing (or TIF) programs found at the state level. In theory, the idea makes considerable sense. If economic opportunities are lacking in a particular community, why not increase the financial incentives so that it is to a business's advantage to locate in such an area? However, the limited amount of research that has been conducted on enterprise zones indicates that they are not a particularly effective way of stimulating job and economic opportunities (Ferguson, 2001). Providing tax incentives is simply not enough to overcome the reluctance of businesses to move into impoverished areas, and when they are used they often do not benefit those whom the programs were designed to help. The various TIF programs around the country have been able to stimulate some development and opportunities in economically depressed communities; however, the program also has tended to be abused by the decision makers who decide what communities are considered blighted. For example, here in St. Louis, TIF financing was used to help renovate a shopping mall containing a Nordstrom's and other exclusive stores in a community that very few would consider blighted.

More important is what we have just discussed—strengthening the assets of communities. In order to entice a business to move to a particular location, promoters must be able to demonstrate that the move will be profitable and to the business's advantage. Consequently, building communities that are attractive to investment is a step along this path. As Ronald Ferguson notes, "the main focus of local economic development strategies should be removing unnecessary barriers to business location and growth and getting the long-term fundamentals right with regard to infrastructure, taxation, regulation, and education" (2001: 442). Developing and building the assets of lower-income communities is vital if they are to attract economic opportunities. Gaining access to financial credit, such as through the Community Reinvestment Act, is also an important step in attracting such opportunities. If, in addition to this, the federal or state government is willing to provide further tax incentives for business to develop opportunities in lower-income communities, so much the better. But first the fundamentals must be in place. By seeing to this, communities that were once routinely bypassed by both the banking establishment and the private sector are now being seen as important investment opportunities in their own right (Grogan and Proscio, 2000).

Providing an Effective Safety Net

The previous strategies, if enacted, will do much to reduce the extent of poverty and hence the need for social welfare programs and a social safety net. Yet no matter how effective these policies are, some individuals and families will invariably fall between the cracks. Whether through the loss of a job, a sudden disability, or some other unanticipated event, there are times and situations in people's lives when a social safety net is needed.

Hyman Minsky (1986) also points out that free-market economies are prone to periods of instability, such as periodic recessions and economic downturns. Safety net programs help to serve as automatic stabilizers for the economy during these periods. That is, they grow during times of need and diminish during more prosperous times. For example, as rates of unemployment rise, more individuals draw on unemployment insurance to weather the temporary economic problems caused by the lack of jobs. As economic conditions improve, more people are able to find jobs and so no longer need unemployment insurance. In this fashion, safety net programs help to automatically stabilize the instability inherent within the economy.

A social safety net is therefore important in assisting individuals and families during times of need and in alleviating the economic instability associated with recessionary periods. In spite of this, the U.S. social safety net has become noticeably weaker over the past twenty-five years. Cash welfare programs have lost much of their purchasing power during the past three decades. The 1996 welfare reform changes transformed the entitlement status of AFDC into the nonentitlement TANF program. Other programs have lost considerable ground in terms of the number of people they reach. These include housing assistance, nutritional programs, and unemployment insurance. The one exception to this decline has been the increase in the number of low-income children who qualify for either Medicaid or the CHIP program. In short, the already weak U.S. safety net has gotten considerably weaker over the past 25 years.

One of the reasons for this is the tension between providing help to the needy on the one hand and not wanting to create disincentives to work or marriage on the other. The idea goes back hundreds of years. If a safety net is too generous, the argument goes, it will undermine the work ethic within the population, particularly for those at the lower end of the income distribution; why seek employment at a low-paying and difficult job if decent benefits are available from the social welfare state? Likewise, if benefits are made available to all, some fear that the institution of marriage will be weakened, along with the disincentives to out-of-wedlock childbearing.

Recent U.S. policy has focused heavily on avoiding the creation of work or marriage disincentives. This effort has become more pronounced in recent years as a result of the reduced attractiveness of work over the past three decades, as wages have stagnated, jobs provide fewer benefits, and so on. Therefore, in order to ensure that welfare is not a viable alternative, a safety net that was weak in the first place has been made even weaker. Public assistance benefits have been allowed to erode over recent years, time limits have been imposed on welfare recipients, work requirements have been made more stringent, and financial disincentives have been put in place to discourage childbearing while on welfare. The major thrust of recent American policy has emphasized work and marriage incentives, while largely ignoring the equally important issue of providing adequate assistance to the needy.

The approach here is quite different. Rather than making the social safety net less attractive, the previous four strategies focus on making work considerably more attractive, particularly at the bottom end of the income distribution. We have discussed the importance of ensuring that workers are paid a decent, livable wage. We have talked about increasing the accessibility of quality education, health care, affordable housing, and child care, all of which contribute to the ability and attractiveness of working within the economy. We have also discussed the concept of building assets through one's own contributions along with a government match, which again furthers the appeal and rewards of work.

Given this, an effective safety net that provides adequate protection against economic hardships is called for. By making jobs a more attractive option, the danger of creating work disincentives through the strengthening of the safety net is substantially reduced. Those who would be forced to turn to a social safety net program under our new set of policies would be truly those in need of assistance. They would include individuals who have temporarily lost a job, men or women who suffer from physical or mental disabilities, or older individuals who have depleted their resources. In these cases, a viable safety net is essential.

Two approaches could be taken toward achieving this goal. The first would be to strengthen the current array of programs that are directed to those in economic need. These programs include unemployment insurance, Workman's Compensation, Supplemental Security Income, Food Stamps, the TANF program, and General Assistance. Each of these programs could be evaluated to determine whether the resources allocated and the eligibility requirements are appropriate to meet the current needs.

Simply achieving greater participation levels in the current array of safety net programs would reduce the overall rate of poverty. For example, Sheila Zedlewski and colleagues (2002) estimate that, for those under age 65, full participation in the Food Stamp, SSI, EITC, and TANF programs could lift 3.8 million people out of poverty. Full participation would also reduce the rate of extreme poverty (those below 50 percent of the poverty line) by 70 percent. As with Medicaid and CHIP, simplifying and streamlining the enrollment process, along with increased outreach and educational efforts, could substantially raise participation levels in the programs.

A second approach would be to consolidate the vast number of U.S. social safety net programs into one overall program that would be directed to the needy. Eligibility would be guided by a series of criteria depending on the individual's circumstances. These would include the existence of conditions such as ill health or disability, unemployment, and so on. Those who qualified would be given a stipend to cover their basic needs. The monetary amount would be below the earnings of the lowest-paid workers under our new set of proposals, but still enough to provide a humane lifestyle. Periodic updates would allow for any needed changes in eligibility status.

The underlying recognition here is that there will always be individuals who fall through the cracks. A wise society makes sure that the need is genuine, but a decent society also makes sure that those in need are provided with enough resources to live humanely. Putting in place an effective yet compassionate social safety net ensures that such values are supported.

In summary, the strategies laid out in this chapter have the potential to move millions of Americans out of poverty and to prevent millions from falling into poverty. They are built on an understanding of poverty that is quite different from the common view that exists today. Such an understanding recognizes that much of American poverty is the result of failures within the economic and social structures of U.S. society. The strategies proposed here focus on moderating these structural failures. They include making sure that work exists and that it pays a living wage, increasing the availability of and access to key public resources such as education and health care, addressing the detrimental economic consequences of family change, building individual and community assets, and providing an effective social safety net. Taken as a whole, these policies can dramatically reduce the extent of poverty and economic vulnerability that currently exists in the United States.

Yet they also have the capacity to make America a more productive and livable society. All of these strategies are about investing in people and families. Making work pay invests in those employed at low-wage jobs. Increasing access to quality education and health care invests in children and families. Building assets is a direct investment in the lives of individuals and the communities they live in. Taken as a whole, the strategies discussed in this chapter are about alleviating poverty, but they are also about investing in Americans so that they are able to live up to their full potential. As a result, the initiatives outlined here are clearly beneficial to the majority of the American population.

Public Support

Two critical questions remain to be addressed: would the public support the initiatives proposed in this chapter, and how would we pay for them? With respect to the first question, evidence suggests (contrary to much of the political rhetoric) that there is substantial public backing for each of the policy ideas suggested here. A nationwide survey was conducted in 2001 to assess

Americans' attitudes and views regarding poverty (NPR/Kaiser Family Foundation/Kennedy School of Government, 2001). The survey was developed, conducted, and analyzed jointly by the Kennedy School of Government at Harvard University, National Public Radio, and the Kaiser Family Foundation. A nationally representative sample of 1,952 respondents age 18 or older was interviewed. The margin of error on most questions was plus or minus 2.2 percentage points.

With respect to our first strategy of creating adequately paying jobs, 85 percent of Americans said that they would support increasing the minimum wage; 80 percent supported an increase in tax credits for low-income workers; and 82 percent supported the expansion of government public employment programs. These percentages indicate overwhelming support within the American public for the concept of creating adequately paying jobs along the lines of the initiatives laid out earlier. As Hugh Heclo points out, "there is probably no more consistent and uniform finding in survey research than that the public values jobs and work for able-bodied poor adults" (1997: 143).

Our second major strategy focuses on providing greater access to and improving the affordability of several basic resources, including education, health care, housing, and child care. The Harvard survey indicated that 94 percent of Americans supported government actions to improve public schools in low-income areas. Eighty-three percent of respondents were in favor of spending more for medical care for poor people, 75 percent supported spending more on housing for low-income households, and 85 percent supported expanding subsidized day care. Americans are clearly in favor of the concept of increasing the poor's access to and the affordability of health care, housing, and child care.

Survey research has found solid support among the American public for the concepts of enforcing orders for child support and preventing teenage pregnancies (Bostrom, 2001). For example, 93 percent of Americans felt that teenage pregnancy in the United States was a serious problem, and 73 percent felt that, while teens should not be sexually active, those who were should have access to birth control (National Campaign to Prevent Teen Pregnancy, 2001).

The building of individual and community assets is a fourth strategy for which there is strong consensus. There has been support among both liberal and conservative lawmakers for policy initiatives such as IDAs that build individual assets, and strong support for programs that attempt to strengthen the assets within lower-income communities (Draut, 2002a). In many ways, policies designed to help build assets are as American as apple pie.

Finally, a solid majority of those surveyed in the Harvard study, although not as large as in the prior areas, support strengthening the social safety net. Fifty-four percent were in favor of increasing cash assistance for families, with 40 percent opposed; 61 percent supported making food stamps more available, with 35 percent opposed; and 57 percent supported guaranteeing everyone a minimum income, with 39 percent opposed.

The American public appears to overwhelmingly back the policies proposed in this chapter (for additional information on other attitude surveys that found very similar results, see Bostrom, 2001; Draut, 2002b). But would the public be willing to pay for such policies? The Harvard survey asked respondents this question in two different ways. They were first asked, "Would you be willing to pay more in taxes to pay for more of such government spending to help the poor?" Fifty-seven percent said yes, while 40 percent said no. However, when the question was phrased in a more direct way, the willingness of people to pay for such initiatives increased substantially. For example, respondents were asked, "Would you be willing to pay $200 a year more in taxes?" Seventy-eight percent said yes, while only 19 percent said no. In the year 2000, there were approximately 105 million American households (U.S. Census Bureau, 2002d). If each of these households paid $200 a year more in taxes, the government would raise an additional $21 billion to support poverty reduction initiatives.

However, rather than an across-the-board tax increase, there are other ways to provide financial support for these initiatives. Perhaps the most straightforward is to devote a greater amount of our current tax dollars to these initiatives. As discussed earlier, the question of priorities guides public policies. The argument throughout this book is that poverty is an issue that merits a higher priority. Devoting a greater percentage of tax revenues to effectively combating poverty is, in my opinion, a wise and prudent use of public resources. It is an investment in the development of individuals, families, and the nation.

In addition, American society has become increasingly unequal in terms of its income and wealth distribution. The gaps between the rich and poor, the powerful and the vulnerable, have been getting wider with each passing year. Over the past thirty years, the tax rates for upper-income households and corporations have been dramatically cut. It is time to revisit these issues. Countering this trend by instituting a degree of redistribution is, I believe, warranted. For example, removing the generous tax breaks for wealthy individuals and corporations is called for. Tightening up on tax loopholes would bring in other necessary revenue. Likewise, adjusting the current tax brackets so that those at the top pay a somewhat larger percentage of their earnings into the general coffers could provide some of the revenue needed to support the various initiatives offered in this chapter.

Ultimately, the issue is not, as former president George H. Bush put it, "that we have more will than wallet." Rather, we have the wallet, but do we have the will? This country could and should be doing much more when it comes to addressing the poverty and economic vulnerability that haunt millions of its citizens. Seventy-five percent of Americans agreed with the statement "This is a rich country which could afford to do more to help the poor than we do now" (Bostrom, 2001). It is nothing less than shameful that a country with such wealth, one that professes such high moral standards for itself and the rest of the world, chooses to do so little for those at the bottom. The social policies and programs discussed in this chapter can do much to correct this injustice. It is time to carry such initiatives forward.

From the Ground Up

> Never doubt that a small group of committed citizens can change the world. Indeed, it is the only thing that ever has.
>
> *Margaret Mead*

9

VISITORS TO Arlington National Cemetery encounter a number of powerful images—the solemn changing of the guard that takes place next to the Tomb of the Unknown Soldier, the eternal flame at the John F. Kennedy gravesite, the sheer number and symmetry of the thousands of white marble headstones for those who have served in the military. But for me, the most powerful image of all is the single cross on the side of a hill that marks the gravesite of Robert F. Kennedy. Part of this very simple but moving memorial is a quotation etched in granite at the foot of the hill. The quotation is taken from his 1966 "Day of Affirmation" address, which was given to students and faculty at the University of Cape Town in South Africa.

The basis of the speech was the belief that each individual can make a difference in creating a better world and a new order of things. The senator noted that there were powerful forces working against this ideal, with perhaps the most imposing being "the danger of futility; the belief there is nothing one man or one woman can do against the enormous array of the world's ills." Yet he went on to observe that it is the individual who has always made a difference in addressing the injustices of the world: "Few will have the greatness to bend history; but each of us can work to change a small portion of the events, and in the total of all these acts will be written the history of this generation." This is the overall context for the quote at the memorial, which reads,

> It is from numberless diverse acts of courage and belief that
> human history is shaped. Each time a man stands up for an
> ideal, or acts to improve the lot of others, or strikes out against
> injustice, he sends forth a tiny ripple of hope, and crossing each
> other from a million different centers of energy and daring those
> ripples build a current which can sweep down the mightiest
> walls of oppression and resistance.

As one looks at the single cross against the rising hill, these words seem to fit the spirit of the memorial exceedingly well. They are also quite appropriate for introducing this final chapter, where I touch upon the simple but powerful idea that each of us can make a difference in addressing the injustice of poverty.

Revisiting the Major Themes

Let me briefly restate the major themes and ideas found in this book. My purpose in writing *One Nation, Underprivileged* has been to provide a new way of thinking about the vexing problem of American poverty. One of the reasons for the high prevalence of U.S. poverty is not a lack of resources, but rather a lack of a national will to truly address the issue. I have argued that this is largely the result of a serious misunderstanding of American poverty. As a society, we have framed the cause of and the cure for poverty as predominately issues of individual motivation, while at the same time we have been largely unaware of poverty's wider ramifications. The result has been ineffective social policies, an acceptance of the status quo, and exceedingly high levels of poverty.

I have attempted to provide a framework that is built upon the realities of America, rather than the myths. We began by looking at the nature and causes of American poverty. The United States currently has the highest rate of poverty in the industrialized world. Such deprivation often leads to feelings of stress, pain, and suffering. Americans who experience poverty typically do so for one or two years, although for some, the time is much longer. Those who possess particular attributes such as low levels of education or less marketable skills, as well as persons of color and heads of single parent families, often have a more difficult time competing effectively in the labor market and are therefore more likely to encounter poverty.

However, as chapter 3 demonstrated, these attributes only explain who runs a greater risk of losing out at the game, rather than why the game produces losers in the first place. The argument was made that the economic structure of the United States simply does not produce enough decent-paying jobs for all who are in need of them. Similarly, the U.S. political and social structures fail to offer the types of supports and safety nets necessary to help avert the risk of poverty. The result is that, at various points in time, a significant percentage of the population is economically vulnerable to this risk.

The middle third of the book focused on the question of why each of us should be concerned about the issue of poverty. Too often these connections and links have been ignored. Yet poverty is an issue that affects us all. For some, it may involve seeing their tax dollars being spent on greater health care costs. For others, it may mean feeling unsafe when visiting particular neighborhoods, or deciding to avoid them altogether. For a majority of Americans, it results in experiencing impoverishment firsthand during their lifetimes. The notion that poverty is someone else's problem is mistaken. Rather than being an issue of *them*, poverty is clearly an issue of *us*.

Our connections with poverty are also apparent as we examine the value and belief systems that many Americans hold. The existence of widespread poverty amid prosperity flies in the face of what the Judeo-Christian ethic stands for, and it severely tarnishes America's ideological values, such as liberty, equality, and justice for all. If we truly believe in these values, we bear a strong moral obligation to address the troubling issue of impoverishment. Likewise, as citizens of wider communities, each of us carries a civic responsibility to become a part of the answer, rather than a part of the problem.

The final third of the book explored the means for creating a fundamental change that will reduce the extent of poverty in America. I have argued that such a change begins with establishing a paradigm for thinking about American poverty different from the one we have grown accustomed to. Chapter 7 outlined the tenets of such a paradigm. These included understanding the structural nature of poverty, the fact that poverty is a conditional state that individuals move in and out of, the wider meaning of poverty as deprivation, the moral and ethical injustice of poverty, and the fact that poverty affects us all. Chapter 8 then explored various policy initiatives and ideas that could significantly reduce the extent and harshness of American poverty. These fell under the broad categories of creating jobs that pay a living wage, increasing the accessibility of key public goods, buffering the economic consequences of family change, developing individual and community assets, and providing an effective social safety net.

The overall intent in these chapters has been to build upon solid evidence and strong arguments a new perspective for understanding poverty. The moral implication of this perspective is quite simple and clear—poverty amid plenty is wrong and unacceptable. It is a blight and embarrassment that should shame us all. As the age-old proverb wisely observes, "Poverty is no shame for those who have not. Poverty is a shame for those who have. A poor man shames us all." Given our abundant resources and wealth, it is a disgrace to have children who lack enough food to eat or seniors who are unable to afford their basic medications. These and the many other conditions of poverty are utterly wrong.

What Can One Person Do?

There is a final question then that clearly warrants discussion. It is the question of what each of us in our individual lives can do to move the country toward a more humanitarian and effective approach for addressing poverty. Societal problems often appear so intractable that we feel helpless or inept in bringing about any kind of positive change. Poverty can certainly be viewed in such a light. It is an enormous problem that has existed for centuries. Given such obstacles, can we individually make a difference, and, if so, in what ways? The answer to this question is unequivocally yes, with the manner being found in a variety of ways.

But first let us consider the alternative—to do nothing and remain uninvolved. This choice will surely lead to more of what we have encountered over the past thirty years. Poverty has become harsher, inequality has gotten wider, and social supports have diminished in strength. Doing nothing is clearly not a part of the answer. Rather, it appears to be a part of the problem.

It should be noted that the points I make here have been made by many others. As social reformers and activists have long observed, societal change begins with the informed actions of the individual. Such actions are the fundamental building blocks in sowing the seeds of change.

The question, then, is what each of us can do in our lives to move the country toward alleviating the severity of poverty. To begin, the chances are that those of you reading this book are already interested and concerned about the issue (and I hope that your interest and concern have been heightened by your reading these chapters). How can this concern be translated into positive action and change? I suggest at least three ways.

First, democracy begins with the discussion of ideas. Think about your numerous interactions during the course of a typical day, week, or month. Undoubtedly, these consist of many sorts of conversations with family members, friends, coworkers, acquaintances, students, persons in places of worship, and so on. In the process, various discussions occur across an array of topics. At times, we engage in conversations regarding relevant social topics. The opportunity to raise the consciousness of other individuals with respect to the issue of poverty presents itself to us all. Being able to effectively move individuals toward understanding the true nature and injustice of poverty is an important component of social change. As Paul Rogat Loeb notes in his book, *Soul of a Citizen: Living with Conviction in a Cynical Time,*

> Our actions don't always transform institutions directly. Change
> comes, to be sure, when we shift corporate or governmental
> policies, elect more accountable leaders, or create effective
> institutional alternatives. But it also comes when we stir the
> hearts of previously uninvolved citizens and help them take their
> own moral stands. It comes when we set in motion chains of
> concern that eventually help alter history. (1999: 101–102)

A number of the points in this book can be put to good use in raising the consciousness of others regarding the topic of poverty. For example, the fact that a majority of Americans will experience poverty at some point during their lives casts a dramatically different light upon the subject. It implies that the issue is not one of *them* but one of *us*. Getting our fellow citizens to realize this can create a shift in how the issue is perceived and acted upon. Pointing out the glaring physical inequalities across school districts can illustrate how children's opportunities vary radically depending on the wealth of their parents. As in an altered game of Monopoly, not all Americans are starting on an even playing field. Similarly, the analogy of musical chairs may allow others to visualize the process of poverty as a game with more players than chairs, as a result of which particular percentage of the population loses out. Again, such understanding can lead to a fundamental rethinking of the issue. Being able to confront and dismantle the familiar stereotypes surrounding poverty is critical.

As I have argued earlier, one of the reasons that America has had such high rates of poverty is not because of a lack of resources, but rather because of serious misunderstandings. This, in turn, has resulted in an overall lack of a national will to address the problem. Raising the consciousness of individual Americans is an important step in beginning to create a positive change from the status quo.

This task may not be quite as difficult as one might initially think. In the Harvard/NPR/Kaiser survey mentioned in the last chapter, respondents were asked how large a problem they felt poverty was in the United States. Fifty-five percent of Americans felt that poverty was a big problem, while 33 percent said that it was somewhat of a problem. The fact that 88 percent of Americans recognize poverty as a problem is an important starting point in discussing these issues.

Another starting point is that 36 percent of Americans reported that someone in their immediate family or another close relative was poor, while 48 percent of Americans said that they had a close friend who was poor. In addition, 33 percent responded that they or someone in their immediate family currently received welfare or public assistance benefits. This large number of Americans who have family or friends experiencing poverty or who rely on the social safety net is an important bridge for engaging in meaningful discussion.

Finally, when asked what was the more important cause of poverty—that people are not doing enough to help themselves out of poverty, or that circumstances beyond their control cause them to be poor—Americans were fairly evenly divided. Forty-eight percent responded that people were not doing enough, while 45 percent said that the more important reason was unfavorable circumstances. The fact that nearly half of Americans recognize the importance of wider circumstances in creating poverty represents an important base on which to begin building support for the arguments developed in this book.

A second avenue for exerting a positive impact is to support and/or to get directly involved in the multitude of antipoverty activities found across the country. Virtually every community has organizations and groups that are addressing aspects of poverty. These range from food pantries to after-school tutoring programs to affordable-housing construction projects. There are countless numbers of worthy groups that are making important differences in the lives of needy children and adults. Such groups can almost always use additional help.

There are also things that we can do on our own. A simple but powerful example took place during a birthday party for a friend of my daughter, who invited twenty or so of her classmates to a skating party. Rather than gifts, she asked her friends to bring an item that was on a wish list for an organization that takes care of neglected children. As a group they were able to donate many needed resources, such as clothes, toys, and school supplies. In addition, they all appeared to have a wonderful time at the skating party, and my daughter's friend still received several anticipated birthday presents from her family. This was an event that appeared to be a win-win situation all around.

Yet this gesture also had an impact upon raising the consciousness of the children and their parents to the plight of those who are less fortunate. The simple task of being concerned and doing something to address the needs of others is an important lesson from which we can all learn from. Many of the parents thought it was a terrific idea, and some of the children have carried on the tradition. In fact, my youngest daughter and her friend (whose birthdays are very close) were inspired by this example and combined their parties, asking their friends to bring a needed item for young children in a group home. There are countless other examples of creative gestures that individuals can make to help others who are less fortunate.

None of these actions by themselves are going to change the world. However, each can make an important difference in the lives of particular individuals. In addition, small efforts and gestures can collectively make a much larger difference. For example, the routine of taking one's newspapers, cans, and bottles to the curb for recycling, on an individual basis, has little impact on the environment. Collectively, however, this behavior can make a substantial difference. Similarly, individual efforts to assist the poverty-stricken, multiplied millions of times over, can collectively produce a substantial and significant impact.

This leads to a third level of involvement. We certainly need to deal with the here-and-now regarding the fallout from the conditions of poverty, and many of the groups and organizations that focus on poverty are dealing precisely with that. But we must also change the conditions that produce poverty in the first place. To return to our musical chairs analogy, we need to focus on creating more chairs for those who are participating in the game so that we produce fewer overall losers in the first place. Chapter 8 laid out several different ideas and policies that can produce such changes. These included ensuring that enough jobs are available and that such jobs are able to support families above the poverty line (by raising and indexing the minimum wage so that it represents a living wage, by expanding the Earned Income Tax Credit, and by promoting policies that encourage job growth), making sure that individuals have access to basic necessities (through increased health care coverage, creation of affordable housing, broadening the access to quality child care, strengthening the food and nutrition programs, and so on), and reducing the vast economic inequities between the top and the bottom within society (by diminishing the inequalities in educational quality across rich and poor communities, readjusting the structure of taxation, or developing asset-building policies for low-income families).

Moving the nation toward such policies implies involvement in the political arena. The issues of poverty, economic inequality, and injustice are infrequently discussed on a local, state, or national level. Becoming involved in the political process is essential for rectifying this situation. We are all aware of the impact that big money has on the political process. But groups of concerned citizens can also have an impact. Students who are engaged in lobbying and coalition building often tell me of their surprise when they learn that a relatively modest number of letters, telephone calls, or email messages can carry a substantial weight in the minds of legislators.

This is particularly the case when individuals effectively organize themselves in groups devoted to specific issues of concern. Such groups can be found in a wide array of settings, including local communities, churches, student groups, and national organizations. Many grassroots organizations are working on issues with the potential to add to the number of currently available chairs, including groups that focus on living wage campaigns, child and health care legislation, affordable housing, and asset-building initiatives.

In addition, what is needed is a national focus on the issues of poverty and economic inequality. These are topics that underlie and pull together many of the concerns that various groups are attempting to redress. Building coalitions across racial and gender lines, socioeconomic classes, community boundaries, and various interest groups is essential for developing a strong political focus upon the problem of poverty. This is a problem that will affect most Americans in one way or another. Understanding this and acting politically upon such information is critical. As Loeb observes,

> The lesson here is not to stop challenging injustices that arise
> from people's particular identities and backgrounds. But to
> promote human dignity, we need to build coalitions that are as
> broad as possible. In addition to the important task of staking
> out rights for specific marginalized groups, we also need to
> organize around issues that affect everyone, such as the unprec-
> edented gap between rich and poor, the corrupting influence of
> unaccountable wealth, the threats to our environment, and the
> general sense of powerlessness that pervades America today.
> (1999: 219)

A new political message is therefore called for. It must begin with the age-old assumption that we are only as strong as our weakest link. It asserts that the judgment of a society will depend not on how it treats its most powerful, privileged, and wealthy, but rather on how it treats its most vulnerable. It will invoke a spirit of cooperation, rather than one of greed. And it will place the concerns and needs of everyday Americans, rather than those of special-interest groups, at the top of its policy agenda. If we can begin to move the country toward such a political message, I foresee a dramatic reduction in the extent and severity of American poverty.

Concluding Note

Ultimately, then, the question we should ask ourselves is what kind of society we want to live in and create for our children. There are at least two paths that can be chosen. The first is the route that we are on now. As pointed out in chapter 6, this path will likely lead us to an increasing division between the haves and the have-nots. The top third of society will continue to prosper, the middle third will struggle, and the bottom third will fall further behind. The economic divisions in society are likely to get wider, rather than narrower. The privileged third will continue to physically separate itself further from the bottom two-thirds of society as social and economic conditions stagnate or deteriorate. Such patterns can be seen right now in the rise of gated communities, increased prison construction, growing private school enrollments, increased expenditures on private security, and so on. The United States will begin to reflect the bifurcation patterns typical of third-world countries. At the same time, we will continue to blame the less fortunate for their economic and social woes, while arguing that government should do less in terms of helping everyday Americans get ahead. This appears to be the path that we are traveling on now. We can chose to remain silent, go about our business, and continue down this slope.[1]

On the other hand, we can say no to such a scenario, with the awakening belief that this does not represent the type of country we want for ourselves or our children. We can collectively work for a new vision of America. This outlook melds the best of America—its creativity, freedoms, and energy—within a framework of concern, caring, and cooperation. It suggests that one day in the not-too-distant future, poverty will be viewed as utterly incomprehensible. Just as we no longer view legal discrimination or the dumping of raw pollutants into our rivers as acceptable, so too will poverty, hunger, and serious economic and social deprivation be seen as intolerable. They will be viewed as wrong and immoral, and just as we have been able to rectify problems in the past when we have put our minds to it, so too will we be able to seriously reduce the extent of poverty in the United States.

This is the vision that I have chosen to work for in the future. Of course, it will not occur overnight. It will be a long and difficult struggle. Yet as the Taoist philosopher Lao Tzu reminds us, "The journey of a thousand miles begins with one step." It begins with each of us understanding that we are all diminished as a result of poverty. That represents a first step. Acting upon this understanding becomes a next step. Creating social and political change is a further step. Each of our individual steps leads us closer toward a more livable and humane version of America. I believe the very soul of our nation depends upon creating such a change. Impossible? Perhaps, but as the former U.S. Supreme Court justice Louis Brandeis once observed, "Most of the things worth doing in the world had been declared impossible before they were done."

More than one hundred years ago, the damaging effects of American poverty were documented in Jacob Riis's landmark book *How the Other Half Lives* (1957, originally published 1890). Riis detailed in both words and photographs the impoverished conditions of tenement families in an area known as "the Bend" in New York City. At the conclusion of the book, he touched upon the dangers of having a large percentage of the population in poverty and the danger of the widening gap between the haves and the have-nots. In order to truly bridge such a gap, he observed, "I know of but one bridge that will carry us over safe, a bridge founded upon justice and built of human hearts" (226).

It is time that we begin to build such a bridge. Social justice and human compassion are indeed the building blocks for alleviating the disgraceful condition of widespread poverty found amid American prosperity. Such realities diminish us all. Rather than being seduced and sedated by the myths of America, we need to awaken to her realities. We must open our eyes to the falseness of the pervasive political message that claims we have no collective or governmental responsibilities for our fellow citizens. The deeper morality of social justice and human compassion inextricably link us together. To deny this is to deny what makes us human.

As we have touched upon earlier, the task of building such a bridge will be a difficult struggle. There are times when it appears very little is being accomplished. Yet as Riis observed regarding such feelings of discouragement, when nothing seemed to help,

I would go and look at a stone-cutter hammering away at his rock perhaps a hundred times without as much as a crack showing in it. Yet at the hundred and first blow it will split in two, and I knew it was not that blow that did it, but all that had gone before together. (1970: 163, originally published 1901)

Change can occur from the ground up. But we must begin, and we must persevere. Many Americans have been working toward the alleviation of poverty. Many more need to join their struggle. Uniting these efforts is a vision worth striving for—that one day in the not-too-distant future, we will look back on the widespread poverty that once blemished America and marvel at the sweeping changes that have occurred. No longer will there be children without enough to eat or parents unable to afford basic health care. That families once were forced to sleep on the streets will be an injustice of the past, as will working full-time but remaining economically destitute. The United States will become an innovator, rather than a laggard, in addressing and alleviating the scourge of poverty.

Such a dramatic change will have taken place not as a result of increasing profit margins. Nor will it have come about with more streamlined competitive practices. Rather, it will have occurred through the simple realization that impoverishment underprivileges us all. In that not-too-distant American future, we will wonder in astonishment how we ever allowed such dehumanization to exist.

Appendix A:

Sources

of Data

THROUGHOUT THE BOOK, data from a number of sources are utilized. This appendix describes several of these data sources. Each is based upon the methodology of the social survey. Social surveys are designed to obtain individual responses and information through a series of questions on various topics. Our concern in this book is with the issue of poverty, and hence the surveys that we turn to are widely recognized as having the best available national and cross-national data regarding individual and household income. In addition, the sample sizes in each of these data sets are large and randomly drawn, allowing us to generalize to the overall U.S. population with substantial confidence.

The Current Population Survey

The Current Population Survey (CPS) began in the late 1930s with the purpose of measuring the extent of unemployment and labor force participation in the country. Since 1940, the CPS has been administered on a monthly basis and is jointly sponsored by the U.S. Census Bureau and the U.S. Bureau of Labor Statistics. It constitutes the major source of labor force information for the U.S. population. Monthly unemployment figures that are reported in newspapers and other media outlets are those derived from the CPS. The CPS is a multistage stratified sample containing between 50,000 and 60,000 households monthly. These households are drawn from nearly 800 sample areas located in all fifty states.

In addition to information regarding monthly labor force participation, supplemental information is acquired at various times during the year. One of the most important of these supplements is what is known as the Annual Demographic Supplement (ADS), administered each March. The ADS began in 1947 and gathers demographic information including family characteristics, household composition, marital status, weeks worked, occupation, health insurance coverage, migration, and receipt of noncash benefits. It also collects data regarding household income for the previous calendar year (Current Population Survey, 2002).

One of the reasons this supplement is administered in March has been the assumption that more accurate income data can be obtained at this time of the year. March is the month before federal income tax returns are due, and many respondents would either have just prepared their income tax forms or would be about to do so. As a result, individuals may be more likely to accurately report their income for the previous year.

However, as in any survey, there is undoubtedly a certain amount of error introduced into the data. Some individuals may fail to recall specific information accurately, other individuals may misunderstand a particular question, mistakes may occur in the coding and entering of data, and so on. For an extended discussion regarding the data quality and methodology of the CPS, see Current Population Survey (2002).

On the basis of the information gathered in the March CPS, the U.S. Census Bureau reports its annual estimates of poverty for the nation. It should be noted that these estimates do not include homeless individuals living outside shelters (because the CPS is a household-based survey). The CPS also excludes individuals living in institutions such as prisons as well as armed forces personnel who reside on military bases.

Some of the data reported in chapter 2 comes from official reports and tabulations produced by the Census Bureau. Each September, the Census Bureau publishes its annual report, "Poverty in the United States." The Census Bureau also puts out at the same time its annual "Money Income in the United States," which uses the March CPS supplement to look at overall levels and patterns of income. Both of these reports provide the most accurate national information available regarding annual levels of poverty and income in the United States.

In addition, since 1995, the CPS has included a series of questions regarding food insecurity and hunger in several supplements. Sponsored by the Food and Nutrition Service of the United States Department of Agriculture, these have resulted in several reports that estimate national rates of food insecurity. This information is referred to in chapter 2.

The Survey of Income and Program Participation

A second major source of data and information regarding income and poverty has been the Survey of Income and Program Participation (SIPP). It is administered by the U.S. Census Bureau and has been ongoing since 1983. One of the drawbacks inherent in the Current Population Survey is that individuals are asked in March to recall their income for the previous year. Respondents may have difficulty remembering all of their sources of income, particularly those that are irregular or that are property income. The CPS also does not explicitly measure participation in government programs, nor does it collect data on assets and liabilities. Furthermore, the CPS constitutes a cross-sectional rather than a longitudinal design, and therefore individual and household changes cannot be measured.

The SIPP was developed to address some of these shortcomings. The original design called for a nationally representative sample of Americans who were fifteen years old or older selected from households in the civilian noninstitutionalized population. Interviewing began in October 1983. These households were then followed over a thirty-two month period, during which individuals were interviewed at four months intervals. Entirely new panels have subsequently been added every several years. Sampling is based on a multistage stratified sampling design (as is the case with the CPS).

Questions in the SIPP revolve largely around issues of income and assets, government program participation, demographic characteristics, and labor force participation. This information is generally measured on a monthly basis. For example, individuals are asked to report their income during each of the four months since the last interview. The interviews themselves take place both in respondents' homes and over the telephone.

The SIPP allows one to examine a number of changes that occur across time within households. These include monthly patterns of welfare participation, income fluctuations, labor force behaviors, and family structural changes.

The analysis in chapter 3 is based upon the 1996 Panel, in which there was an overall redesign to improve the quality of the SIPP's longitudinal estimates. The 1996 Panel included a large initial sample of 40,188 households (or 95,402 individuals) that were followed over a four-year period and interviewed every four months. The 1999 data from this panel are used in chapter 3 in order to estimate yearly working income, average hours worked per week, and poverty threshold levels.

As with the CPS, the U.S. Census Bureau issues a number of reports using the SIPP data. For an extended discussion of the history, methodology, and specific details of the SIPP data set, see Westat (2001).

The Panel Study of Income Dynamics

The Panel Study of Income Dynamics (PSID) represents a third major source of data utilized in this book. The PSID is a nationally representative, longitudinal sample of households and families interviewed annually since 1968. It has been administered by the Survey Research Center at the University of Michigan. One of its clear advantages over the CPS and SIPP data sets is the length of its longitudinal span. In fact, it currently constitutes the longest-running panel data set in the United States and the world. Data from the PSID are used to construct the series of life tables found in chapters 3 and 4 and in Appendix B. The PSID is ideal for this purpose because of its extremely long length, as well as the fact that it was specifically designed to track income dynamics and demographic changes over time.

As noted in chapter 4, the PSID initially interviewed approximately 4,800 U.S. households in 1968, obtaining detailed information on roughly 18,000 individuals in those households. These individuals are tracked annually, including children and adults who eventually break off from their original households to form new households (for example, children leaving home, adults after separations or divorce). Thus, the PSID is designed so that in any given year the sample is representative of the entire nonimmigrant U.S. population (beginning in 1999, interviews have been conducted biannually).

The PSID interviews a primary adult in each household to obtain information about each member of the family. From 1968 to 1972, these interviews were conducted face-to-face. Since 1973, the majority of interviews have been carried out by telephone. Consequently, recent PSID waves consist of approximately 92 percent telephone interviews and 8 percent face-to-face interviews (as a result of respondents not having a telephone or there being circumstances that make it unfeasible to do a telephone interview). The original response rate in 1968 was 76 percent. Since 1969, the annual response rates have ranged between 96.9 percent and 98.5 percent (Panel Study of Income Dynamics, 2003).

Although the PSID is without question the best available data set for the life table analyses presented in chapters 3 and 4 and in appendix B, it is not without drawbacks. In particular, the cumulative nonresponse rate and the lack of representativeness of the immigrant population are problematic. As a result of these drawbacks, a number of studies have analyzed the overall quality of data from the PSID. As Hill summarizes, "Taken as a whole, these different studies examine a variety of aspects of data quality; the general results are supportive of the PSID data being valid and not subject to major nonresponse bias" (1992: 31). For a more detailed discussion surrounding issues of data quality within the PSID, see Duncan and Hill (1989), Fitzgerald et al. (1998), Hill (1992), and Kim and Stafford (2000).

A series of life tables are constructed from the PSID in chapters 3 and 4 and appendix B. The life table is a technique that demographers and medical researchers often use. Although primarily found in mortality analysis, it can be applied to other areas of research as well (Namboodiri and Suchindran, 1987). The life table examines the extent to which specific events occur across intervals of time. In the analyses in chapters 3 and 4 and in appendix B, our time intervals were each year an individual ages. For any one of those years, we can calculate the probability that an event will occur (in this case, poverty, as well as the use of welfare programs) for those who have yet to experience the event. Furthermore, on the basis of these probabilities, we can also calculate the cumulative probabilities of an event's occurring across the life span. These cumulative probabilities represent the core of the life table analyses presented in chapters 3 and 4 and in appendix B.

To demonstrate the process of arriving at the specific probabilities, let us take the case of estimating the likelihood of falling below the official poverty line. For each wave (or year) of the study, we have information about the age of individuals and their total household income. From this information we can determine whether the household (and hence the individuals in the household) fell below the official poverty line. If they did not, this information is noted, and the individual is allowed to continue to the next year. If, on the other hand, they did experience poverty, this information is also noted, and the individual is then removed from any further analysis. In other words, once the event of poverty has occurred, the individual is no longer at risk of experiencing poverty for the first-observed time and is excluded from the calculations of probabilities at later age intervals. Each age interval therefore contains a large number of individuals who have not experienced poverty and a much smaller number of individuals who have. From these numbers the overall proportion of the population experiencing a first-observed spell of poverty at each specific age is calculated. Finally, from these age-specific proportions, we can generate the cumulative proportions that span the adult life cycle.

One of the consequences (and potential advantages) of this approach is that period effects are smoothed out within and across age intervals. For example, some of the approximately 10,000 individuals in the twenty-year-old group experienced their twentieth year in 1968, some in 1975, some in 1992, and so on. The advantage of this approach is that historical effects such as recessions do not unduly affect any particular age group or the hypothetical cohort as a whole (which can happen if one uses only one point in time to construct a life table). From 1968 to 1992, the overall rate of poverty was fairly stable, averaging between 11 percent and 15 percent (U.S. Census Bureau of the Census, 2003a). Likewise, between 1968 and 1997 the overall rate of welfare use (AFDC, Food Stamps, SSI, Medicaid, and other cash welfare) was also fairly constant (see Rank and Hirschl, 2002).

Individuals may contribute anywhere from one to twenty-five person-years in the poverty life tables and one to thirty person-years in the welfare life tables. For example, a woman in the PSID study who turned twenty in 1975 and then in 1979 experienced a year below the poverty line would have contributed five person-years within the analysis. In this case, she would be included in the estimates for ages 20, 21, 22, 23, and 24.

To extend the analysis beyond the twenty-five and thirty years of data points, individuals are allowed to enter the life tables during the ages at which they entered the study, rather than simply at age 20. For example, an individual who was age 30 in 1968 (the start of the PSID study) would have been included in the thirty-year-old age-specific probabilities and then followed accordingly (although obviously he or she would have been excluded from the twenty to twenty-nine age-specific probabilities). This procedure enables us to extend the life table probabilities out to age 75. It also allows us to use the full array of data found in the PSID, which ensures ample sample size for all age categories from which the estimated probabilities are derived.

A consequence of this approach, however, is that it introduces left-censoring into the analysis. Left censoring occurs for individuals who enter the study in midstream and for whom we do not have information as to whether the event (in this case, poverty) occurred prior to the age of entry. If the behavior of individuals who are left-censored is similar to individuals who we know are not left-censored (and therefore have yet to experience the event), then no bias is introduced into the life tables (Allison, 1984; Namboodiri and Suchindran, 1987). However, one could argue in the case of poverty that the behavior of left-censored individuals may be slightly different in that some of them undoubtedly have experienced poverty at an earlier point in their unobserved ages. On the basis of previous research, we can infer that individuals who have experienced poverty in the past are at a greater risk of experiencing poverty in the future compared with individuals who have not experienced poverty. As a result, the age-specific and cumulative estimates in the life table could be upwardly biased. The same argument would hold with respect to welfare use.

Fortunately, one can detect and correct for such bias using the following procedure. First, the life tables for the initial twenty-five years (ages 20–44) were constructed according to the previously described method. Then a second group of life tables was produced, but with the left-censored cases removed. By comparing the two, the pattern and extent of any bias resulting from left censoring could be examined. In general, the two sets of estimates were similar across the various life tables presented in this book, with the original probabilities tending to be slightly higher than those without the left-censored cases. From these comparisons, the overall amount and direction of bias could be determined within the original estimates. A correction factor then was used to adjust the age-specific life table probabilities accordingly. In this fashion, one could detect and correct for the fact that left censoring was present in the estimations. A similar procedure is used for analyses of the elderly in appendix B. In the estimations for children's poverty, left censoring is not present. Further details on these analyses can be found in Rank and Hirschl (1999b; 1999c).

In addition to the basic life table, what is known as a multivariate life table is also constructed. This allows us to examine the life table probabilities of individuals with various combinations of characteristics. These life table estimates are derived through calculating logit models at each age and then transforming the coefficients into age-specific probabilities. Once these age-specific probabilities have been calculated, one can easily compute the cumulative probabilities as described. For a more detailed discussion of this approach, see Guilkey and Rindfuss (1987).

The measure of poverty used in the life tables in chapters 3 and 4 and in appendix B is identical to that used by the Census Bureau in estimating the overall U.S. poverty rates (U.S. Bureau of the Census, 2003a). Total household income is the measuring stick for determining whether individuals fell below the poverty line. Households below specific income levels are considered poor. As discussed in chapter 2, these levels represent what is considered the least amount of income needed for a household to purchase a minimally adequate basket of goods (for example, food, clothing, and shelter) throughout the year. To account for inflation, the actual dollar amounts are adjusted each year in accordance with changes in the consumer price index. Thus, the dollar values pertaining to the specific poverty levels for households during the twenty-five waves of the PSID vary each year according to changes in the rate of inflation. The level itself also varies depending on household size.

As a whole, rates of poverty derived from the PSID tend to be somewhat lower than those derived from the Census Bureau's Current Population Survey. This is likely the result of a more complete accounting of income in the PSID (Duncan, 1984; Minarik, 1975).

The measure of welfare use in tables 4.5 and 4.6 is constructed from a series of questions asked by the PSID interviewers about whether the household has received any cash or in-kind public assistance at some point during the previous calendar years (1967–1996). Cash programs include AFDC, SSI, and other cash welfare such as General Assistance. In-kind programs consist of Food Stamps and Medicaid. From 1967 to 1996, Medicaid, Food Stamps, and AFDC were available in the United States (although the PSID began to ask questions about Medicaid receipt only in 1977). SSI was included in the PSID from 1975 on.

For each of the cash programs, respondents were asked, "Did you receive any income in [prior year] from [the specific program]?" Respondents who were married were also asked a set of questions about whether their spouse had received any income from these programs. With regard to Food Stamps, respondents were asked, "Did you (or anyone else in your family) use government food stamps at any time in [prior year]?" Finally, Medicaid use was assessed through the question, "Is anyone in your family living there covered by [Medicaid or Medical Assistance/Medi-Cal]?" Interviewers were instructed to be careful not to have respondents include Medicare in their answer regarding Medicaid receipt. These procedures ensured that respondents would not confuse one program with the other or combine them in their responses.

If a household received any public assistance, the individuals in the household were counted as receiving welfare. Earlier research has demonstrated that assistance from welfare programs is typically shared and benefits all members of a household (Edin and Lein, 1997; Rank, 1994; Seccombe, 1999). Cash programs and Food Stamps are obvious examples, but even if one family member receives Medicaid, the other members of the family typically benefit in that they do not have to absorb the costs of medical expenses for that individual.

It should be noted that the duration of a household's use of welfare during any given year can vary. Some, may have received benefits for the entire year, whereas others may have done so for only one or two months. In both cases, however, the individuals in those households would be counted as receiving welfare during the calendar year.

Information regarding means-tested program participation within the PSID has been shown to be quite accurate (reflecting positively on the ability of respondents to recall accurate information regarding welfare receipt). For example, Duncan and Hill (1989) compared the 1980 PSID estimates of income derived from cash public assistance programs with the official national figures for 1980 (taken from the Social Security Bulletin). Using the official figures as a benchmark, PSID respondents reported 92 percent of the income that they should be reporting from cash public assistance (including AFDC and General Assistance) and 84 percent of SSI income. Combining these public assistance programs, the PSID was able to account for 89 percent of all income that was received from the welfare system. Duncan and Hill postulate that the small difference between the PSID estimates and the official national figures may be the result of the exclusion of recent immigrants from the PSID sample. For our purposes, this reflects exceedingly well on the quality of the data, in that our focus is only upon individuals being able to recall whether they received a program or not, rather than the more difficult question of how much they received.

The Luxembourg Income Study

A fourth major source of poverty and income data is the Luxembourg Income Study (LIS). This project began in 1983 with the purpose of providing researchers with an enhanced ability for making cross-national comparisons with regard to income and other economic data. The LIS has been able to acquire survey data on individuals and households from a broad range of countries. It has then transformed this data in such a way that researchers can directly compare a number of economic variables across countries, including levels of poverty, income inequality, effectiveness of governmental transfer programs, and other demographic and economic indicators. The LIS has been under the joint sponsorship of the government of Luxembourg and the Center for Population, Poverty, and Policy Studies in Luxembourg.

Economic information from thirty countries is currently contained in the LIS database. For most of these countries, data are available across several different points in time. Nations included in the LIS study can be found in Europe, North America, the Far East, and Australia. In some cases, information goes back to the late 1960s; however, the bulk of the data were gathered in several waves during the 1980s and 1990s.

The LIS attempts to use the best available economic data within a particular country. In some cases, this may involve choosing from several data sources. In other cases, there may only be one such source. The surveys themselves differ widely from country to country. They are not uniform in terms of their nature or objective. Some are specifically designed to collect income data, while others may come from tax records, expenditure surveys, administrative records, or supplements to labor force surveys. For example, data for the United States are taken from the March Current Population Survey, which was discussed earlier. On the other hand, data for France and Norway are derived from income tax records.

The major accomplishment of the LIS study has been its ability to standardize and harmonize the variables found in these data sets so that researchers are able to make scientifically reasonable comparisons across countries. Once the data from a country have been acquired, particular variables of interest are transformed in a way that roughly standardizes them so that their meaning is similar across countries. As a result, researchers are able "to address important social issues without having to invest countless hours getting every variable that will be analyzed into a comparable format" (Smeeding, 2002b). Analyses using the LIS study are found in chapters 2 and 3. For further detail regarding the LIS, see Luxembourg Income Study (2000).

Appendix B:
Additional
Life Table
Analyses

THE LIFE TABLE ANALYSES presented in chapters 3 and 4 focus on the risk of poverty primarily among working-age adults. In this appendix, additional data are provided that illustrate the risk of poverty for both children and the elderly.

The Risk of Poverty across Childhood

Background

As discussed in chapter 2, children represent the age group most at risk of poverty since the late 1970s. Between one out of five and one out of six children falls below the poverty line at any point in time. In addition, young children under the age of six are at a particularly high risk of poverty. One reason is that young children typically have young parents. The wages that such parents are earning tend to be at the lowest levels of their work careers, putting them and their children at a greater risk of poverty. In addition, young children, because they require child care, may impose certain employment restrictions and costs on parents.

What is known about the longitudinal dynamics of poverty among children? Researchers who have focused on the dynamics of poverty among children have revealed patterns similar to the overall dynamics of poverty discussed in chapter 2. That is, most spells of poverty for children are relatively short (although somewhat longer than for adults), those who experience poverty often do so again in the future, and poverty can touch a fairly large percentage of the population (Ashworth et al., 1994; Blank, 1997; Bradbury et al., 2001b; Corcoran and Chaudry, 1997; Duncan and Rodgers, 1988, 1991).

For example, using the PSID from 1968 to 1982, Duncan and Rodgers (1988) found that for children younger than age 4 in 1968, one-third would experience poverty during a fifteen-year period, yet only one child in twenty would experience poverty for ten or more years. Ashworth and colleagues (1994) also utilized the PSID to calculate the incidence and duration of poverty during the first fifteen years of life. Their estimate was that 38 percent of children would face at least one year in poverty during this time, and approximately half of all children who were touched by poverty would experience three or fewer years of impoverishment.

As with cross-sectional data on poverty, longitudinal analyses have shown that a child's risk of poverty is particularly sensitive to race, family structure, and parental education (Ashworth et al., 1994; Blank, 1997; Corcoran, 2001; Corcoran and Chaudry, 1997; Gottschalk and Danziger, 2001; U.S. Bureau of the Census, 1998). Children who are nonwhite, who reside in single-parent families, or whose parents have low levels of education are more likely to experience poverty and to experience poverty over longer periods.

For example, in Duncan and Rodgers's study (1988), 79 percent of black children compared to 26 percent of nonblack children encountered poverty during the fifteen years of observation. Furthermore, 29 percent of black children experienced ten or more years of poverty, compared to only 1 percent of nonblack children. Ashworth et al. (1994) also found that 79 percent of black children experienced poverty at some point in a fifteen-year period, compared with 31 percent of white children.

Family structure has been shown to significantly impact the likelihood and duration of poverty among children. Duncan and Rodgers (1988) report that living with one parent rather than two parents throughout childhood increased the expected number of years of poverty for white children from 0.5 to 3.2 years and for black children from 3.0 to 7.3 years.

Parental education has been a third characteristic that is strongly associated with the dynamics of childhood poverty. Ashworth et al. (1994) report that 50 percent of children whose household heads had fewer than twelve years of education experienced poverty over a fifteen-year period, compared with 14 percent of children whose household heads had twelve or more years of education.

Like the research cited in chapter 2 on the overall dynamics of poverty, this research has added significantly to our longitudinal understanding of poverty among children. Such knowledge can be extended by calculating the probability of poverty at each age of childhood and across the entire span of childhood. Furthermore, we can examine how these probabilities vary by a child's race, the family structure in which she or he resides, and the level of parental education.

Life Table Analyses

Beginning with age 1 and continuing through age 17, table B.1 lists the cumulative percentages of children experiencing a first spell of poverty. The same calculations for the likelihood of near poverty (1.25 of the poverty line) and dire poverty (.50 of the poverty line) are included. Tables B.1, B.2, and B.3 are graphically divided into three sections that represent early childhood (ages 1–6 years), middle childhood (ages 7–12) and later childhood (ages 13–17).

Table B.1 shows that by age 6, 22.6 percent of American children have experienced a first spell of poverty. By age 12, 29.8 percent of children have been touched by poverty, and by the end of the formative years (age 17), more than one-third (34.1 percent) of U.S. children have experienced at least one year below the poverty line.

The middle column contains the probability of encountering poverty at the 1.25 level. By age 6, 29.3 percent of children have fallen below this level. By age 12, 36.6 percent have done so, and by age 17, 40.5 percent. Finally, the far right column contains the estimates for experiencing dire poverty, as measured by falling below one-half of the official poverty line. We can see that by age 6, 9.7 percent of children have experienced a year in dire poverty. By age 12, 14.8 percent have, and by age 17, 18.3 percent. The likelihood of experiencing extreme poverty is substantially less than that of falling below the official poverty or 1.25 of the poverty line. Nevertheless, extreme poverty is experienced by nearly one out of five children at some point during childhood.

TABLE B.1. The Cumulative Percent of Children
Who Experience Poverty

	Level of Poverty		
Age	Below 1.00 Poverty Line	Below 1.25 Poverty Line	Below .50 Poverty Line
1	10.6	15.1	3.5
2	14.8	20.0	5.1
3	17.3	23.0	6.7
4	19.5	25.6	7.7
5	21.4	27.6	8.9
6	22.6	29.3	9.7
7	24.0	30.6	10.6
8	25.3	32.1	11.6
9	26.7	33.8	12.6
10	27.8	34.8	13.4
11	28.8	35.9	14.3
12	29.8	36.6	14.8
13	30.8	37.4	15.4
14	32.1	38.3	16.2
15	32.8	39.2	16.7
16	33.4	39.9	17.5
17	34.1	40.5	18.3

Source: Panel Study of Income Dynamics, Rank and Hirschl
computations.

The life table analysis in table B.1 clearly reveals a substantial risk of poverty during the formative years. Rather than being an event that touches a limited proportion of children, the reach of poverty across childhood is quite broad, as is the reach of poverty across the adulthood years.

Table B.2 examines the impact of race, parental education, and family structure upon the risk of an initial spell of poverty during childhood. By age 6, 56.8 percent of black children have experienced at least one year of poverty, compared with 15 percent of white children (as was the case in the adult life tables in chapter 4, the sample size for children did not allow one to examine the life-course probabilities for additional racial or ethnic categories, such as Hispanics). By age 12, the percentages are 66.9 percent versus 21.5 percent; by age 17, 69.5 percent versus 25.9 percent. Black children at the age of one year have exceeded the risk of poverty that white children experience by the age of seventeen years.

The middle columns estimate the differences in the probability of experiencing poverty, depending on whether the head of household has fewer

TABLE B.2. The Cumulative Percent of Children Who Experience Poverty by Race, Education, and Marital Status of Household Head

Age	Race		Education		Marital Status	
	Black	White	< 12	≥ 12	Not Married	Married
1	31.3	5.8	25.4	5.4	38.8	4.9
2	40.7	8.8	33.7	8.1	50.2	7.4
3	46.4	10.7	38.9	9.9	56.9	8.9
4	50.7	12.4	43.3	11.3	61.1	10.4
5	54.5	14.0	46.2	12.9	65.1	11.7
6	56.8	15.0	48.9	13.6	67.6	12.5
7	59.5	16.0	50.9	14.8	70.2	13.3
8	61.3	17.1	52.7	15.9	72.1	14.2
9	63.1	18.6	54.4	17.3	73.8	15.4
10	64.3	19.7	56.1	18.3	75.3	16.2
11	65.3	20.6	57.4	19.1	76.5	17.0
12	66.9	21.5	58.4	20.1	77.6	17.8
13	68.0	22.3	59.2	21.0	78.2	18.7
14	68.5	23.7	61.2	22.0	79.3	19.9
15	68.7	24.5	61.8	22.8	79.4	20.8
16	69.2	25.2	62.0	23.6	80.0	21.3
17	69.5	25.9	62.7	24.2	80.5	21.9

Source: Panel Study of Income Dynamics, Rank and Hirschl computations.

than twelve years of education or twelve or more years of education. By age 17, 62.7 percent of children have encountered poverty who reside in less-educated households, compared to 24.2 percent of children who reside in more-educated households. Once again, the probability of experiencing a first spell of poverty at age 1 for children whose head of household has fewer than twelve years of education exceeds the seventeen-year risk for children whose head of household has twelve or more years of education.

Finally, just as racial and educational differences in the risk of poverty are substantial, so too are differences in family structure. In the right columns the sample is divided according to whether a child is residing in a married-couple household. The majority of nonmarried-couple households in the sample are female-headed families. It should be noted that we are not analyzing how the changes in family structure affect the likelihood of a first spell of poverty, only the effect that family structure has for children currently in a nonmarried or married-couple household. By age 6, 67.6 percent of children in nonmarried households have experiencing at least one year of poverty, compared to 12.5 percent of children in married households;

by age 12, 77.6 percent versus 17.8 percent; and by age 17, 80.5 percent versus 21.9 percent. As with race and education, children in nonmarried households who are one year old have exceeded the risk of poverty that children in married households experience during their entire seventeen years of childhood.

Table B.2 thus indicates that race, family structure, and education all have a profound impact on altering the risk of poverty across the childhood years. This is consistent with the prior research presented in chapter 2, the life table analyses in chapter 4, and the previous research on children's poverty, discussed earlier. Children who are black, who reside in nonmarried households, and/or whose household head has fewer than twelve years of education face a strong probability of experiencing at least one year below the poverty line during their childhoods. Their risk accumulates quickly during the first six years of childhood and then begins to level off during the middle and later stages of childhood. Consequently, most of these children are exposed to poverty early in childhood.

Table B.3 simultaneously assesses the impact of race, family structure, and parental education on the risk of experiencing a first spell of poverty during childhood (by using a multivariate life table analysis). Those with the smallest risk of poverty are found in the upper left portions of the table, while those with the largest risk are found in the lower right portions of the table. Several patterns are apparent in table B.3. First, the risk of poverty is dramatically altered by various combinations of characteristics. Whereas only 14.6 percent of children who are white, who reside in a married-couple household, and whose head has 12 or more years of education have experienced poverty (by age 17), 99.4 percent of children who are black, who reside in a nonmarried-couple household, and whose head has fewer than twelve years of education have experienced poverty during the same age period.

Second, each variable exerts a sizable independent effect on the probability of poverty among children. By contrasting profiles of children at risk of poverty in table B.3, one can see that education, marital status, and race all exert sizable independent effects on the cumulative likelihood of poverty. This is also indicated by the fact than in each of the seventeen individual logit models used to build table B.3, the variables of education, marital status, and race were significant at the .001 level.

Third, the impact of the three factors analyzed—being black, living in a nonmarried household, and having a household head with fewer than twelve

TABLE B.3. The Cumulative Percent of Children Who Experience Poverty by Various Combinations of Race, Education, and Marital Status of Household Heads

	Married		Not Married	
Age	≥ 12 Yrs. Educ.	< 12 Yrs. Educ.	≥ 12 Yrs. Educ.	< 12 Yrs. Educ.
White				
1	2.5	9.4	14.1	40.1
2	3.9	12.6	21.8	51.6
3	5.0	15.1	26.3	58.3
4	5.9	17.8	29.5	64.1
5	6.9	19.9	32.9	67.9
6	7.4	21.4	35.6	71.8
7	8.2	23.2	38.5	75.1
8	8.9	25.2	40.7	78.0
9	9.8	27.0	43.1	80.2
10	10.4	28.9	45.3	82.7
11	11.1	30.6	47.2	84.6
12	11.7	32.0	49.0	86.1
13	12.4	33.7	50.5	87.3
14	12.9	35.0	52.4	88.7
15	13.5	36.4	53.2	89.3
16	14.1	37.5	54.5	90.1
17	14.6	38.6	55.7	90.8
Black				
1	6.9	23.3	32.4	66.2
2	9.1	27.5	41.5	75.0
3	11.1	31.4	47.8	81.0
4	12.7	35.4	52.0	85.3
5	14.9	39.1	57.0	88.6
6	16.2	42.1	61.5	91.6
7	17.9	45.2	65.6	93.6
8	19.4	48.3	68.4	95.0
9	21.1	51.1	71.2	96.1
10	22.5	53.8	73.7	97.0
11	23.8	56.4	75.7	97.7
12	25.4	58.8	78.1	98.2
13	26.8	61.2	79.6	98.5
14	27.9	62.9	81.3	98.9
15	29.6	65.4	82.4	99.1
16	30.9	67.1	83.8	99.2
17	32.2	68.6	85.0	99.4

Source: Panel Study of Income Dynamics, Rank and Hirschl computations.

years of education—is additive on the risk of poverty. Possessing one of these characteristics raises the chances of experiencing poverty (by age 17) two to four times (compared with children who possess none of these characteristics). Having two of these attributes raises the likelihood of poverty five to six times, and having all three results in a sevenfold increase in the likelihood of ever experiencing poverty during childhood. In short, table B.3 illustrates that various combinations of racial, family structural, and educational attributes profoundly influence the chances that American children will experience poverty during childhood.

The Risk of Poverty across the Elderly Years

Background

As noted in chapter 2, the poverty rates for the elderly have declined dramatically over the past four decades. This remarkable reduction in the overall risk of poverty for the elderly population has been credited primarily to the increasing generosity of Social Security, along with the introduction of the Medicare program in 1965 (Bok, 1996; Hurd, 1989). Ironically, as a result of this success, some policymakers and social scientists have begun to question whether public policy may have gone too far in favoring elderly adults (Lee and Haaga, 2002; Preston, 1984). Yet before concluding that elders' risk of poverty is minimal, we need to ascertain the longitudinal likelihood of poverty for the elderly. Several studies have focused on this question.

Using the Retirement History Study (covering the period 1968–1978 and starting with individuals ages 58–63), Holden, Burkhauser, and Myers (1986) found that 29.7 percent of the elderly would experience poverty during this ten-year period, compared to a peak yearly poverty rate of 13.9 percent. In addition, 80 percent of poor widows were able to escape poverty after six years, as were 88 percent of married couples. Holden and colleagues also noted that many of those escaping from poverty would again fall below the poverty line in the near future—after six years, 53 percent of widows and 35 percent of married couples were again poor (also see Burkhauser, Holden, and Feaster, 1988; Holden and Smeeding, 1990).

Using the PSID data, Coe (1988) found that for those age 65 and over, the likelihood of exiting from poverty was quite high within the first three years of impoverishment, but fell dramatically after that. A majority of poverty spells among the elderly were relatively short—65 percent lasted three years or less—whereas a minority of the elderly, 26.1 percent, endured poverty spells that lasted ten or more years. As with children's patterns of poverty, the dynamics of poverty spells for the elderly largely mirror the overall findings of poverty dynamics for the general population.

A second major research focus has examined the impact of widowhood on impoverishment (Bound, et al., 1991; Dodge, 1995; Holden, Burkhauser, and Feaster, 1988; Hungerford, 2001; McLaughlin and Holden, 1993; Smith and Zick, 1986; Vartanian and McNamara, 2002; Zick and Smith, 1986, 1991). This body of work has revealed that widows face a greater risk of poverty than married couples. For example, Hungerford (2001) found that women were nearly twice as likely to experience poverty a year after their husband's death than during the year prior to his death. In addition, women who were poor prior to widowhood became even poorer with widowhood. Likewise, Zick and Smith (1986) found that, five years following the death of a spouse, two out of five widows had experienced at least one year below the poverty line, compared with one in ten married couples. This has led some academics to argue that poverty after age 65 is primarily a woman's problem (Barusch, 1994; Warlick, 1985). Yet research also indicates that widowers experience a risk of poverty similar to that of widows (Smith and Zick, 1986; Zick and Smith, 1986; 1991). It may be that gender increases the probability of poverty because women face a greater likelihood of experiencing the death of a spouse.

Life Table Analyses

Table B.4 examines the cumulative percentage of the elderly who will experience various levels of poverty between the ages of sixty and ninety. Looking first at the occurrence of poverty at the 1.00 level, by age 70, 17.9 percent of the elderly U.S. population have spent a year below the poverty line. By age 80, 28.7 percent of the population have experienced poverty, and of those surviving up to age 90, 40.4 percent have experienced poverty. What this analysis reveals is that, rather than being an event occurring to a small minority of the elderly U.S. population, poverty is an experience that touches a sizable number of elderly Americans at some point.

It is estimated that those who reach age 60 have an average life expectancy of twenty-one years (National Center for Health Statistics, 1997). Thus, the average length of time for which these individuals are at risk of poverty is from ages 60–81. We can therefore estimate that nearly 30 percent of sixty-year-olds will experience poverty at some point during their final years (the

TABLE B.4. The Cumulative Percent of the Elderly Who
Experience Poverty

| | Level of Poverty | | |
Age	Below 1.00 Poverty Line	Below 1.25 Poverty Line	Below .50 Poverty Line
60	5.4	8.5	1.6
65	12.2	15.8	4.1
70	17.9	22.2	5.4
75	23.3	29.1	7.1
80	28.7	34.7	10.5
85	35.3	42.4	12.2
90	40.4	47.7	14.7

Source: Panel Study of Income Dynamics, Rank and Hirschl
computations.

exact percentage from the full life table analysis is 29.7 percent; see Rank
and Hirschl, 1999b).

The estimates for experiencing poverty at the 1.25 level are found in the
middle column. This is especially pertinent in that a number of older Americans have incomes that are just above the official poverty line (indeed, if one
compares the Census Bureau's 1.00 and 1.25 estimates of poverty, elderly
adults have the largest percentage increase of any age group). By age 70, 22.2
percent of the elderly have fallen below 1.25 of the poverty line; by age 80,
slightly over one-third, and by age 90, nearly one-half (47.7 percent). Again,
extrapolating from the average life expectancy of an additional twenty-one
years for those age 60, 36.4 percent of sixty-year-olds will experience poverty at the 1.25 level at some point during their final years.

The right column contains the percentage of elderly adults who experience dire poverty. Here we find that the risk of acute poverty among the
elderly is quite low. The cumulative percentage by age 70 is 5.4 percent; 10.5
percent by age 80; and 14.7 percent by age 90. Although more than one-third
of the elderly have experienced a year below the official poverty line by the
time they reach age 85, only 12.2 percent have experienced extreme poverty.
These findings are consistent with those of McLauglin and Jensen (1993)
who found that:

> while elderly persons cluster at the lower end of the income
> distribution (i.e., have comparatively high poverty and near
> poverty rates), they are less likely to be in deep poverty than

individuals younger than 65. This could be due to Social Security benefits, which offer minimal but stable income for many elderly families, and to Supplemental Security Income, which offers a safety net not normally accessible to younger people. (48)

Table B.4 thus indicates that poverty (but not dire poverty) is an event that can touch a surprisingly high percentage of elderly Americans. This pattern has long been masked by the fact that the overall poverty rate for elders is fairly low. That is, in any given year the likelihood of poverty is relatively modest. However, this likelihood quickly accumulates over time, and a sizable percentage of individuals experience poverty or near-poverty conditions at some point during their later years of life.

In table B.5, the impact of race, education, marital status, and gender on the odds of poverty is illustrated. The analysis in both tables B.5 and B.6 extends only out to age 85 because the sample sizes are too small beyond that point for particular demographic groups.

As was the case for children, we find that race, education, and marital status all exert a strong influence on the odds of the elderly experiencing poverty. Between the ages of sixty and eighty-five, 64.6 percent of blacks have encountered poverty, as have 32.7 percent of whites; 48.4 percent of those with fewer than twelve years of education have been poor, as have 20.5 percent of those with twelve or more years of education; and 51.2 percent of those who are not married have been poor, as have 24.9 percent of those who are married. On the other hand, gender does not appear to exert

TABLE B.5. The Cumulative Percent of the Elderly Who Experience Poverty by Race, Education, Gender, and Marital Status

	Race		Education		Marital Status		Gender	
Age	Black	White	< 12	≥ 12	Not Married	Married	Female	Male
60	14.3	4.4	8.7	2.5	11.1	3.6	6.3	4.2
65	30.6	10.3	19.3	6.0	24.9	7.7	14.5	9.4
70	45.4	15.0	27.5	9.0	32.9	11.9	20.5	14.6
75	54.7	20.2	34.3	12.8	39.4	15.8	26.1	19.6
80	59.4	25.8	41.0	16.0	45.1	19.9	32.0	24.3
85	64.6	32.7	48.4	20.5	51.2	24.9	38.3	31.1

Source: Panel Study of Income Dynamics, Rank and Hirschl computations.

a strong influence on the odds of poverty during the later years. This is similar to the patterns described in chapter 4.

Table B.6 examines the risk of poverty in a multivariate context. Like table B.3, table B.6 is structured so that those with lowest risk of poverty are in the upper left portions of the table, while those with the greatest risk are in the lower right portions of the table. Several patterns are apparent. First, the likelihood of poverty is dramatically altered by the various combinations of characteristics. Whereas only 13 percent of white, married women with twelve or more years of education experience poverty by age 85, 88.1 per-

TABLE B.6. The Cumulative Percent of the Elderly Who Experience Poverty by Various Combinations of Race, Gender, Education, and Marital Status

| Age | ≥ 12 Years Education | | < 12 Years Education | |
	Married	Not Married	Married	Not Married
White Females				
60	1.8	4.8	5.4	13.8
65	4.0	11.7	12.7	32.3
70	5.7	15.8	19.3	41.7
75	8.2	20.7	24.9	48.8
80	10.7	25.4	30.8	56.9
85	13.0	28.6	37.4	63.1
White Males				
60	1.5	4.2	4.7	12.1
65	3.7	10.7	11.0	29.3
70	5.6	16.0	16.4	40.2
75	8.5	21.8	22.4	48.8
80	11.6	27.3	28.5	57.7
85	14.1	30.9	35.4	64.4
Black Males				
60	3.7	9.7	10.8	25.3
65	8.5	22.1	24.6	52.6
70	13.9	34.9	39.7	72.3
75	19.0	44.1	49.0	80.9
80	21.5	47.6	53.7	84.4
85	24.5	50.9	59.8	87.7
Black Females				
60	4.3	11.1	12.3	28.3
65	9.7	24.5	28.9	57.0
70	15.5	35.9	48.7	75.6
75	20.1	43.3	56.4	81.9
80	22.4	46.5	60.7	85.1
85	25.2	49.6	66.2	88.1

Source: Panel Study of Income Dynamics, Rank and Hirschl computations.

cent of black, unmarried women with fewer than twelve years of education experience poverty by the same age.

Second, education, race, and marital status all have sizable independent effects on the rate of poverty among the elderly. These varying effects can be seen by contrasting differing profiles of individuals at risk of poverty. A white, married man with twelve or more years of education has a cumulative level of poverty by age 85 of 14.1 percent. In contrast, his unmarried counterpart's cumulative level is 30.9 percent; his less than twelve years of education counterpart's level is 35.4 percent; and his black counterpart's level of poverty is 24.5 percent. Marital status, education, and race independently exert sizable effects on the cumulative likelihood of poverty. This is also indicated by the fact that in virtually all of the 26 individual logit models used to construct table B.6, the variables of marital status, education, and race were significant at the .01 level.

Furthermore, the effect on the risk of poverty of being unmarried, of having less than 12 years of education, and of being black are additive (as was the case for children). For both women and men, possessing one of these characteristics more than doubles the cumulative risk of poverty by age 85. Possessing any two of these characteristics increases the cumulative risk four to five times, while possessing all three characteristics results in a six- to sevenfold increase in the risk of poverty by age 85.

Finally, once these three variables are accounted for, the effect of gender is inconsequential. For example, comparing the cumulative proportions for white men and women with similar marital status and educational attainment reveals a basically identical pattern of poverty. The same is true for black men and women. Although race, education, and marital status exert sizable independent effects on the probability of poverty among the elderly, gender does not. Rather than a direct effect, gender undoubtedly asserts itself indirectly through the fact that women are more likely than men to experience widowhood (and hence inherit the status of being unmarried). Women are also more likely to have fewer than twelve years of education because they faced educational barriers. Gender therefore appears to exert itself not as a direct effect but rather as an indirect effect through marital status and education.

In conclusion, elderly adults are generally portrayed as representing a demographic group with a relatively low likelihood of poverty. This perspective, when based upon cross-sectional data (such as that from the U.S.

Census Bureau), is essentially correct. However, the life table analysis presented here indicates that poverty is an event that can touch a surprisingly high percentage of elderly Americans at some point. As individuals get older, they deplete more of their resources and assets. Medical costs are also likely to escalate. As a result, the risk of poverty grows over time. This pattern has long been masked by the fact that the overall poverty rate for elders is fairly low; that is, in any given year the occurrence of poverty is relatively modest. However, such occurrences quickly accumulate over time, resulting in a sizable percentage of individuals who experience poverty or near-poverty conditions at some point during their later years of life.

Notes

1. Even more jarring was the death of a homeless woman at a bus stop across the street from the Department of Housing and Urban Development. Inside, officials were debating the budget to be allocated for programs on the homeless. One HUD employee looking out a window toward the scene "grew sardonic counting seven police cars, two police motorcycles, a fire truck and an ambulance. 'It's just strange to see how many resources a person gets after they die—not a fraction of that beforehand,' she said" (DeParle, 1993).

2. And of course these paradoxes are quite apparent on a worldwide basis. As Amartya Sen begins his book, *Development as Freedom*, "We live in a world of unprecedented opulence, of a kind that would have been hard even to imagine a century or two ago. . . . And yet we also live in a world with remarkable deprivation, destitution and oppression" (1999: xi).

3. A different twist was provided by Bob Dylan, who followed in Woody Guthrie's footsteps. Dylan wrote, "This land is your land & this land is my land—sure—but the world is run by those that never listen to music anyway" (1971: 88).

4. See Jim Cullen's book *The American Dream* (2003) for a brief history of how the concept of the American Dream has evolved.

5. Although occasionally groups such as the media, politicians, or lawyers are scapegoated as well. See Gans (1995), Gilens (1999), Handler and Hasenfeld (1991), Katz (2001), Mitchell (1998), Sidel (1996), and Sklar (1995) for a discussion of the issue of scapegoating and the poor.

6. For further details regarding Harrington's work and life, see Maurice Isserman's biography, *The Other American: The Life of Michael Harrington* (2000).

7. Assembly series, Washington University, tape transcription, March 23, 1989, St. Louis, Missouri.

Chapter 2

1. Planned Parenthood Federation of America Symposium, "Examining America's Social Ills: Is the 'Illegitimacy' Argument Offtrack?" Tape transcription, May 24, 1994, Washington, DC.

2. For a discussion involving the role of think tanks in promoting political and ideological agendas, see James Allen Smith's *The Idea Brokers: Think Tanks and the Rise of the New Policy Elite* (1993) or Jean Stefanic and Richard Delgado's *No Mercy: How Conservative Think Tanks and Foundations Changed America's Social Agenda* (1996). One of the most scathing characterizations that I have come across regarding the far right wing agenda and the role of think tanks in promoting that agenda were remarks by Representative David Obey, of Wisconsin,

> They pass meaningless resolutions that praise God, motherhood and country but don't do anything. They stick it to little people, because little people don't have access to information and can't fight back. They rely on a huge tub of money that flows into their party coffers to drown out objections. They have a huge juggernaut of private foundation money organized by the right-wing economic elite and they pour money into these so-called think tanks to pretend that independent research verifies their world view. (Weiner, 1999)

3. For various perspectives on the war on poverty, and the broader initiative of the Great Society, see Brauer (1982), Gillette (1996), Goodwin (1988), Haveman (1987), Lemann (1989), Unger (1996), and Zarefsky (1986).

4. Orshansky considered four food plans developed by the Department of Agriculture to calculate what a minimal diet would cost to purchase. The most frugal, entitled the Economy Food Plan, was eventually chosen. Orshansky also calculated the poverty thresholds using the somewhat more

generous Low-Cost Food Plan; however, these were never adapted. As Howard Glennerster notes,

> When Orshansky came to settle on her minimum food budget, she chose the very lowest of the food budgets on offer from the work of the Department of Agriculture. It was meant for those in emergency need. Her reasons, as she explained afterward, were political. She wanted a base that could not be challenged for its generosity, just as Rowntree did in 1901. She remains appalled that it has been set in aspic ever since. (2002: 86–87)

5. There is considerable argument as to whether these levels are set too low, too high, or just right. Those who argue that they are set too high point to a failure of the official measure to take into account benefits accrued from in-kind programs (e.g., Food Stamps, Medicaid). Those who argue that the poverty levels are set too low note that certain costs, such as housing or child care, have escalated dramatically since the poverty lines were first established.

6. In order to better gauge what these various household costs are across the country, the Self-Sufficiency project started by Diana Pearce at the University of Washington has provided estimates regarding the costs of housing, food, child care, transportation, health care, and miscellaneous expenses in different localities around the country. Researchers calculate how much income is needed to support various-size families in these localities. For example, in 2002 it was determined that in order to adequately support the needs of a family consisting of two adults and two children in St. Louis, the adults would need to be earning $33,551 a year, or $2,796 a month (Pearce and Brooks, 2002).

7. Indeed, the Gallup poll has asked the following question over the past fifty years: "What is the smallest amount of money a family of four (husband, wife, and two children) needs each week to get along in this community?" The average amounts given by respondents have been substantially higher than what the weekly poverty level for a family of four would be. In addition, in 1989, the Gallup Organization asked respondents in four monthly samples the following question: "People who have income below a certain level can be considered poor. That level is called the 'poverty line.' What amount of weekly income would you use as a poverty line for a family of four (husband, wife, and two children) in this community?" The results were that individuals set the poverty line 23 percent higher than the official

poverty line for a family of four. See Vaughn (1993) and O'Hare et al. (1990) for an extensive discussion of this issue. The bottom line is that Americans' subjective opinions of what constitutes poverty is significantly more generous than the official measurement of poverty.

8. Although I have chosen to focus on a family of four for my comparison, the percentages are roughly the same regardless of household size.

9. The reason for this is that during the 1950s and 1960s, increases in income were well above the overall rates of inflation, whereas the poverty thresholds simply kept up with the levels of inflation. This resulted in a growth in the gap between the two during times of real wage growth.

10. The amount that individuals have been getting from Social Security has been well above what they and their employer put into it. For example, the average person who retired in 1980 received back within four years of retirement everything that the worker and the employer had paid into Social Security (Kollman, 1995).

11. In figure 2.2, the percentages for white and black families were not available for 1968 and 1969. In addition, data for black families were not available from 1959 through 1967. However, the percentages for these years can be estimated by first knowing the size of the total population and the white population during each of these years. The difference between these two serves as the approximate size of the black population. Knowing this fact then allows us to estimate what the black rates were during these years, given the total rate and white rate. In figure 2.1, data were not available for the elderly during the years of 1960–1965.

12. This short-term pattern is also found if one measures poverty on a monthly rather than on a yearly basis (U.S. Census Bureau, 2003c).

13. The racial group with the highest levels of poverty is that of American Indians who live on reservations. It is estimated by the Bureau of Indian Affairs that at least half of the 1.3 million American Indians who live on reservations are poor, with unemployment rates running at approximately 50 percent.

14. Hispanic is a category of ethnicity rather than race. Consequently, Hispanics can be either white or black, although the vast majority count themselves as white.

15. Paul Jargowsky (2003) found that the percent of poor individuals living in highly impoverished neighborhoods (those with poverty rates in

excess of 40 percent) declined from 15 percent in 1990, to 10 percent in 2000. The percent of impoverished whites living in such neighborhoods declined from 7.1 to 5.9 percent, for African Americans the decline was from 30.4 to 18.6 percent, and for Hispanics the decline was from 21.5 to 13.8 percent. See Kingsley and Pettit (2003) for further analyses of the decline in concentrated poverty during the 1990s. These results indicate that the vast majority of the poor do not live in neighborhoods characterized by extremely high concentrations of poverty.

16. The 1990 Americans with Disabilities Act defined disability as a substantial limitation in a major life activity. In the Census Bureau analysis, individuals were classified as disabled if they met any of nine separate criteria. These included items such as using a wheelchair or cane, having difficulty seeing or hearing, or having a learning disability. Severe disability was defined as meeting the criteria on several of the more severe measures among these nine (U.S. Bureau of the Census, 2001a).

17. The analysis was also conducted using 40 percent of the median income as a poverty measure. The results were identical in terms of the relative position of the United States versus the other nations.

18. On the other hand, poverty in the United States compared to that found in Third World countries is obviously less harsh. However, we rarely compare our social and economic well-being to individuals and families in Third World countries; our comparison group tends to be other industrialized developed nations.

19. Furthermore, the United States remains near the top when this is broken down by poverty within one- and two-parent households (Smeeding, 1997a).

20. As one adopts more stringent measures of relative or absolute poverty, the United States performs progressively worse vis-à-vis other countries (Smeeding, 1997a). For further comparative work on poverty, see Bradbury et al. (2001a), Jesuit and Smeeding (2002), Oyen et al. (1996), and United Nations Development Programme (2000).

21. Additional work that has focused on comparisons across nations (using somewhat different measures of poverty) has basically found a very similar story. For example, the United Nations has developed a human poverty index for industrialized countries (United Nations Development Programme, 2003) that incorporates four measures of well-being (discussed in chapter 7).

The United States ranked worst on the human poverty index when compared to the other sixteen industrialized countries, even though its GDP ranking was first.

22. As I suggested in the final chapter of *Living on the Edge*, it is perhaps psychologically easier to deal with poverty by removing its human face and misery, just as it may be psychologically easier to blame the individual for their impoverishment rather than to face the more disturbing thought that poverty results from the social and economic structures from which the nonpoor benefit.

23. There are a number of excellent accounts that provide depth and insight into the human condition of living in poverty, including Berrick (1995), Edin and Lein (1997), Kozol (1988), and Shirk et al. (1999).

24. Food insecurity is defined as households who "were uncertain of having, or unable to acquire, enough food to meet basic needs for all household members because they had insufficient money and other resources for food" (Nord et al., 2003: 4).

25. For example, research has indicated that the poor are more likely to be exposed to environmental pollution and hazards (Bullard, 1990; Perlin et al., 2001). Sources of such pollution (e.g., factories, waste dumps, coal plants) tend to be found in lower-income geographical areas. As a result, those who live nearby are more likely to be exposed to higher levels of pollution, which can often have an adverse effect upon health.

26. This and the quotes on pages 42, 43, 46, and 47 are from women who were interviewed for *Living on the Edge*, but whose specific quotes were not reported in the book.

27. See Tyler et al. (1997) for an extended discussion of the literature regarding relative deprivation.

Chapter 3

1. In recent times, these debates have often divided into one of three ideological camps. Most common has been the emphasis on poverty as an individual failing. From this perspective, specific attributes of impoverished individuals have brought about their poverty. These range from the lack of an industrious work ethic or virtuous morality, to low levels of education or competitive labor market skills. A second perspective has emphasized the importance of cultural factors in maintaining poverty. The argument here

is that individuals growing up in poverty-stricken neighborhoods cope and adjust to their environment, often in dysfunctional ways, resulting in the creation and perpetuation of an economic underclass. A third approach has interpreted poverty as the result of failings at the structural level, such as the inability of the economy to produce enough decent paying jobs (see Rank, 2001, for a review of these approaches).

2. In contrast to the high rates of poverty and low-wage work in the United States, the U.S. rates of unemployment have been substantially below those of most European countries (where unemployment has typically averaged between 6 and 12 percent). However, an analysis by Bruce Western and Katherine Beckett (1999) demonstrates that the relatively low U.S. unemployment rates are partially a result of the extremely high rates of incarceration found in America. Removing a large number of American men from the labor force through incarceration keeps unemployment rates artificially low. When this factor is taken into account and adjusted for, the U.S. rates of unemployment fall more into line with those of Europe. As the authors write,

> In the short run, large prison and jail populations conceal a high level of joblessness. If included in labor market statistics, the population of incarcerated men would contribute about two percentage points to the U.S. male unemployment rate by the mid-1990's. . . . Challenging claims of "Eurosclerosis" and the successful deregulation of the U.S. labor market, our estimates of labor inactivity among U.S. men consistently exceed average European unemployment rates between 1975 and 1994. State intervention in the labor market through the penal system thus contributes to a falsely optimistic picture of U.S. labor market performance in comparison to Europe. (1999: 1052)

A similar argument can be made with respect to the measurement of poverty. The official U.S. poverty measure does not include the incarcerated. Inclusion of this population raises the overall poverty rate (in 1997) between 9 and 15 percent (Irvine and Xu, 2002), further widening the poverty gap between the United States and other Western industrialized nations.

3. For single persons and one-parent families, the head of the family is simply the adult in the family. For married couples, the husband is designated the head of family.

4. Of course, for married couples, there are two potential wage earners. The analysis here focuses on the ability of the job held by the husband to raise his family above the poverty threshold.

5. Given the dismal track record of averting poverty in the United States, it is particularly ironic that President George W. Bush would announce, "Across the globe, free markets and trade have helped defeat poverty, and taught men and women the habits of liberty" (Madrick, 2003).

6. In addition, when compared to other industrialized nations, the United States tends to direct a much smaller percentage of its GDP toward helping poorer countries.

7. This process can also be found within the childhood years. Peter Gottschalk and Sheldon Danziger (2001) examined the extent of income mobility for U.S. children using the PSID data. They found that the level of household income early in childhood strongly predicted the level of household income later in childhood. For example, they compared the economic status of a group of children between the ages of birth and five years in the early 1980s, and again ten years later. They found that of those children who fell into the lowest income quintile in the early 1980s, 87.6 percent of them remained either there or in the second lowest quintile ten years later. Likewise, for those children who began childhood in the top income quintile, 88.7 percent remained in the top two quintiles 10 years later.

8. Although Dalton Conley's (1999) analysis of the PSID data points to the importance of differences in wealth in understanding much of the black/white differences found in society. Conley writes:

> Many of the behaviors and circumstances that we have come to so closely associate with blackness or whiteness are really more attributable to the class structure of American society. It just happens that this class structure overlays very well onto skin color, which is a lot more visible than someone's investment portfolio. By saying that class "just happens" to map onto skin color, I do not mean to imply that this fact is the result of random chance. The consolidation of race and class is the fundamental problem to which this work and thousands that have preceded it point. (1999: 23)

9. McMurrer and Sawhill write, "Recent estimates suggest that no more than 10 to 15 percent of differences in earnings or income is associated with differences in cognitive ability" (1998: 76).

10. An interesting visual example of this can be found in the *7 Up* documentary series that has been directed by Michael Apted. Fourteen children were initially interviewed in England in 1963, when they were seven years old. The series has since reinterviewed the children at seven-year intervals, with the latest film being *42 Up*. The impact of social class in shaping these children's lives can be seen quite literally as they age in front of our eyes.

11. In addition, see Wilson's *The Truly Disadvantaged* (1987) for a further description of this process. Elijah Anderson's (1990, 1999) work has also examined this dynamic and its effects on inner-city neighborhoods. See Small and Newman (2001) for a review of this line of research. For a historical review of the underclass from the civil war to the present, see Jacqueline Jones's *The Dispossessed* (1992).

12. Or see Maril (2000) for a description of this process as it applies to Oklahoma.

13. Since around 1970, a growing percentage of the jobs produced by the U.S. economy have been at a lower wage level (Ellwood et al., 2000). Much discussion has ensued on the reasons for this pattern. Many have argued that competitive pressures from globalization, along with the shift to a service economy, have resulted in the growing numbers of low-wage jobs (for example, see Bluestone and Harrison, 1982, 1988; Castells, 1998; Greider, 1997).

14. Although paths A and B, and C and D, answer different questions, there is also a connection between the two. For example, as the lack of job opportunities grow in society (path C), the bar will be raised in terms of the human capital requirements needed to compete for the remaining viable jobs (path A). On the other hand, a greater availability of job opportunities will likely lower the bar in terms of human capital requirements. Consequently, changes in paths C and D may very well result in changes in paths A and B; similarly, changes in paths A and B may result in changes in paths C and D. For example, as the population becomes more educated and skilled, an argument can be made that this results in a more innovative and creative workforce, resulting in greater economic opportunities.

15. Of course, it must be stressed that any explanation or theory is an oversimplification of the reality. Take, for example, the well-established connection between smoking and lung cancer. Many of us undoubtedly know someone who has chained-smoked all of his or her life, yet has never developed lung cancer. Such cases do not fit the causal pattern of cigarette smoking leading to lung cancer. However, if thousands of cases were examined, we would find that the likelihood of developing lung cancer is substantially higher for heavy smokers than for nonsmokers. The key here, of course, is the concept of probability or risk. For those who smoke, the risk of developing the disease is significantly raised. That does not mean, however, that every smoker will develop lung cancer.

Similarly, there are many cases of poverty that do not fit the model outlined in figure 3.1. For example, we might point to an individual raised in an extremely poor family who failed to receive a high school diploma, yet overcame such obstacles and amassed a fortune in his or her lifetime. However, if we look at thousands of cases, the chances are that we will find that many more severely disadvantaged individuals will experience poverty during their lifetimes than will individuals with college degrees who were raised by wealthy parents.

Chapter 4

1. The profession of social work, however, has maintained a fairly strong allegiance to the value of social justice throughout its history. In particular, there has been an emphasis upon the moral injustice of poverty, and the use of the social sciences to address this wrong.

2. See Hill (1992) for an extended description of the PSID.

3. The poverty tables utilize the waves from 1968 to 1992, while the welfare tables employ the waves from 1968 to 1997.

4. For additional analyses involving the life-course risk of poverty and welfare use, see Rank and Hirschl (1999a; 1999b; 1999c; 2001a; 2001b; 2001c; and 2002).

5. One of the issues raised regarding the official measurement of poverty is that it may include individuals who sometimes might not be considered poor in a traditional sense, particularly full-time students. As a result, the life table probabilities were reestimated after removal of full-time students from the analysis. The results were virtually identical to those in table 4.1.

6. Leisering and Leibfried (1999) in their life-course analysis of poverty and welfare use in Germany find a very similar finding with respect to gender. When they analyzed poverty and welfare use within the context of the life course, there was little to no gender effect for the same reasons posited here.

7. Participation by the U.S. population varies from program to program. For example, using the Survey of Income and Program Participation (SIPP) data, the U.S. Census Bureau (1999b) estimated that in an average month in 1994, 11.3 percent of the American population received Medicaid, 9.7 percent Food Stamps, 5.5 percent AFDC or General Assistance, 4.7 percent Housing Assistance, and 2.0 percent SSI. The percentage of the U.S. population receiving any means-tested welfare program in an average month in 1994 was 15.2 percent.

8. For an informative history of lead poisoning in the United States, see Christian Warren's book, *A Brush with Death: A Social History of Lead Poisoning* (2000).

9. These were conducted by several well-known economic and poverty researchers using data from the Panel Study of Income Dynamics and the New Jersey Income Maintenance Experiment.

10. In addition, Cohen estimates that the overall social cost of not obtaining a high school education is between $291,000 and $466,000 (Cohen, 1996).

11. For other discussions regarding the costs of crime, see Kavka (1994), Reiss and Roth (1993), and U.S. Department of Justice (1994).

12. These percentages are based upon using the 2000 census population counts for the nation. In reflecting upon the historically high rates of U.S. incarceration, Saul Alinsky notes at the end of his book *Rules for Radicals*, "we have made a mockery of being our brother's keeper by being his jail keeper" (1971: 196).

13. Although the evidence is very strong, for a discussion and debate regarding alternative explanations, see chapter 5 in Currie (1985), chapter 3 in Jencks (1992), and chapter 3 in Reiss and Roth (1993).

14. In addition, there is evidence that a worsening of overall economic indicators, such as unemployment, can significantly increase the overall rate of crime. For example, the 1984 Joint Economic Committee of Congress found that a one-tenth increase in unemployment (i.e., going from 10 percent to 11 percent unemployment) was associated with an additional 400,000

arrests per year. For further research on this topic, see Cantor and Land (1985), Chiricos (1987), Devine et al. (1988), Kang et al. (1991), and Land et al. (1995). Likewise, those nations with the least amount of economic inequality (e.g. Denmark, the Netherlands, Norway), tend to have the lowest rates of crime, while those with the greatest levels of economic inequality (e.g., the United States) tend to have the highest rates of crime (Currie, 1985).

15. See U.S. National Advisory Commission on Civil Disorders (1968) and Harris and Wilkins (1988) for an in-depth discussion of these issues.

16. From *Politics* (1990, originally 4th century B.C.).

17. In addition, see Greenwood et al. (1996) for an estimate of the financial advantage of diverting children from crime.

18. And of course these are interconnected. For example, poverty results in health problems in children, such as undernutrition. This, in turn, leads to problems in children's ability to concentrate and learn, impacting detrimentally upon their education. A stunted education narrows the range of opportunities, which then results in a greater propensity to engage in crime. An example of this is the connection that Needleman et al. (2002) have found between lead poisoning as a child and an increased risk of engaging in delinquency and crime as an adolescent.

19. This issue is revisited in more detail in chapter 6.

Chapter 5

1. Or as Carl Degler writes, "The metaphor of the melting pot is unfortunate and misleading. A more accurate analogy would be salad bowl, for, though the salad is an entity, the lettuce can still be distinguished from the chicory, the tomatoes from the cabbage" (1970: 296).

2. Most of the Apocryphal/Deuterocanonical Books are included in the Orthodox and Catholic Bibles, but not in the Jewish and Protestant Bibles.

3. In this section, all quotations taken from the Old and New Testaments are from the HarperCollins Study Bible (New Revised Standard Version Bible, 1993), with the location of the passages in parentheses.

4. The word *poor* can be translated and used in a number of different ways. For an analysis of this issue, refer to the Anchor Bible Dictionary's (Freedman, 1992) discussion regarding the words *poor* and *poverty*.

5. This theme is also found within the Torah (Leviticus 19.18). When asked for a summary of the Torah, Rabbi Hillel responded, "What is hate-

ful to you, do not do to your neighbor; that is the whole Torah, while the rest is commentary thereon; go and learn it" (Wattles, 1996: 42). See chapter 4 in *The Golden Rule* (1996) by Jeffrey Wattles, for an extended discussion of this.

6. This is similar to the concept of the Golden Rule. For an in-depth analysis of the Golden Rule in various historical, theological, and philosophical contexts, see Wattles (1996).

7. Interestingly, this exact saying does not appear in the Gospels, although Luke 6.38 is very similar in content.

8. For further theological interpretations regarding poverty and the Judeo-Christian ethic see Blank (1992), Carlson-Thies and Skillen (1996), Copeland (1994), De Vries (1998); Gushee (1999); Hamill (2002), Hehir (1991), Meeks (1989), National Conference of Catholic Bishops (1986), Shank (1995), United Church of Christ (1989), and Weinfeld (1995).

An interesting example of applying the Judeo-Christian ethic to the policy arena has been the movement to reform the Alabama tax code, led by Susan Pace Hamill. Hamill (2002) has argued that Alabama's tax system places an inordinate burden upon the poor, while taxing the wealthy at a much lower rate. She pointed out that this was in direct violation of what the Judeo-Christian ethic stands for. The Republican governor of the state, Bob Riley, concurred: "I've spent a lot of time reading the New Testament, and it has three philosophies: Love God, love each other, and take care of the least among you" (Horrigan, 2003). A reform initiative that would have changed the tax code was subsequently defeated by the voters of Alabama in September 2003.

9. It is interesting that many of these statements also invoke the name of God, linking these principles in some respects, with the Judeo-Christian ethic to which most of the founders of this country subscribed.

10. One of the fundamental distinctions regarding liberty was made by Isaiah Berlin (1958) in his essay "Two Concepts of Liberty." Berlin distinguished between two kinds of freedom: negative and positive, often described as freedom *from* versus freedom *to*. According to Berlin, negative freedom represented the freedom from, for example, political tyranny. Positive freedom represented the ability to engage in various individual pursuits. As is clear in the Webster's definition, both notions of freedom are undermined by poverty, although positive freedom is perhaps most diminished for the poverty stricken in America.

11. In addition, see Phillipe Van Parijs's book *Real Freedom for All* (1995) for a discussion of how the lack of opportunities and inequalities undermines the realities of freedom within capitalist societies.

12. *Freedom from want* was portrayed in the Rockwell painting as a family sitting down to a Thanksgiving dinner. The paintings first appeared in the *Saturday Evening Post* in early 1943. A brief essay accompanied each of the four freedom paintings. As Foner notes,

> For *Freedom from Want*, the editors chose an unknown Filipino
> poet, Carlos Bulosan, who had emigrated to the United States at
> the age of sixteen. . . . Bulosan wrote of those Americans still
> outside the social mainstream—migrant workers, cannery
> operatives, black victims of segregation—for whom freedom
> meant having enough to eat, sending their children to school,
> and being able to "share the promise and fruits of American
> life." (1998: 227)

13. Indeed, substantial research evidence indicates that the entire criminal justice process (from the likelihood of arrest to the length of sentencing) is strongly influenced by the socioeconomic status of the individual in question (e.g., Reiman, 2001).

14. The lack of adequate access to the legal system was the justification for establishing the Legal Services Corporation in 1974.

15. For a discussion of both voting and employment as critical components of citizenship and for ways the poor are, in effect, less than full citizens as a result of their lack of access to them, see Shklar (1991).

16. For further discussions of the scales of justice, see issues of the *Law Library Journal* for May 1959, May 1971, summer 1980, and winter 1990.

17. It should be noted that other conceptions of justice exist as well (for example, see the six-volume collection *Equality and Justice,* edited by Peter Vallentryne, 2003). However, the notion of justice as balance (with balance being framed in terms of deserving and undeserving) has strongly influenced the American interpretation of this moral principle. Therefore, the question we are asking is, within this framework, to what extent poverty is just. Of course, one could also ask to what extent the wealthy "deserve" their wealth.

18. See Sen (1992) for an extended discussion of the concept of "equality of what." In other words, the key distinction in thinking about equality is always the question of what. In the case of America, equality has generally

been interpreted as equality of opportunity. See Sen (1997) for a more technical discussion of these issues.

19. For an analysis of the conceptual underpinnings behind equal opportunity theory, see Mithaug (1996).

Chapter 6

1. In Alexandre Dumas's *The Three Musketeers*, D'Artagnan asks his compatriots, "All for one, one for all, that is our device, is it not?" Although the expression has become clichéd, it nevertheless captures a powerful concept that is reflected in this chapter. D'Artagnan is in fact expressing the social contract that we have with one another, particularly in times of need. Such a contract is the glue that ties the Musketeers together, and it is the glue that binds us together as well.

2. As John Donne wrote in 1624, "No man is an island, entire of itself; every man is a piece of the continent, a part of the main. If a clod be washed away by the sea, Europe is the less, as well as if a promontory were, as well as if a manor of thy friend's or of thine own were: any man's death diminishes me, because I am involved in mankind, and therefore never send to know for whom the bell tolls; it tolls for thee."

3. See Hart and Honore (1959) and Feinberg (1970) for illuminating discussions regarding the relationship of causality to responsibility.

4. This is analogous to the free rider problem as elucidated by Mancur Olson (1965).

5. Many other such examples could be given. For example, we expect that our government will provide us with various services and entitlements, yet too often we are reluctant to pay for such benefits through taxation. The political promise of cutting taxes without touching social programs that benefit the middle class is ever popular. In short, we expect governmental assistance without personal cost. Such an imbalance in reciprocity again belies the concept of citizenship.

6. Of course, most entitlements and government assistance are directed not at the poor but at the middle and upper classes (Abramovitz, 2001; Shapiro and Wolff, 2001). Likewise, corporations and businesses have been receiving significant amounts of benefits from the local, state, and federal governments, while at the same time they have increasingly failed to honor the social contract with their workers (Reich, 2002).

7. The evaluation of individual responsibility within the context of having control over one's situation and choices is an important distinction that goes back to the beginnings of philosophical discourse on this subject. For example, see the Aristotle's *Nicomachean Ethics*, Books III and V.

8. For several pertinent philosophical discussions of shared and community responsibility, see Goodwin (1985), May (1996), and Smiley (1992).

9. For example, see Beveridge (1942), Mill (1848), and Titmuss (1958).

10. The issue of race has a long history of being used to divide poor whites and blacks so that that they fail to see their common interests. As Lyndon Johnson explained to an aide in 1960, "I'll tell you what's at the bottom of it. If you can convince the lowest white man that he's better than the best colored man, he won't notice you picking his pocket. Hell, give him somebody to look down on, and he'll empty his pockets for you" (Dallek, 1991: 584).

11. For a discussion of the spirit of community or the lack thereof, see Etzioni (1996) and Putnam (2000).

12. This argument is analogous to the problem of omissions within moral philosophy.

13. A similar concept is that of trusteeship. See Baier (1984) for a discussion of our obligations to future generations.

14. A strong argument can also be made that poverty harms the physical environment. The most obvious examples lie in third world countries, where destructive environmental practices such as deforestation and slash-and-burn agriculture are engaged in by impoverished farmers in order to survive.

15. Net worth refers to the current value of all one's marketable assets minus the current value of debts. Assets include items such as the equity built up in owner-occupied housing, savings and checking accounts, the gross value of other real estate owned by the household, stocks, mutual funds, IRAs, and so on. Debt includes the sum of mortgage debt, consumer debt, educational loans, loans from financial institutions, medical bills, auto loans, and so on. Financial worth is the same as net worth but does not include the equity that one has built up in owner-occupied housing.

16. The major asset that most middle-income individuals have is the equity they have built up in their homes (U.S. Census Bureau, 2001b), and therefore the figures for financial worth are more skewed than those for net worth.

17. Although certainly not all believers in the free market would accept this statement. For example, both Adam Smith and Andrew Carnegie felt

that enlightened self-interest, support for the poor, and capitalism went hand in hand.

Chapter 7

1. A recent example of this logic is the syndicated columnist Mona Charen's claim that the food and nutrition safety net programs have led to obesity among the poor. As she writes,

> Yet every year, the United States spends billions encouraging lower-income people to eat more. Twenty million Americans collect food stamps, which encourages over-consumption. . . . And so we continue to push food at those who need a lot less of it. (Charen, 2003)

2. This is much more the case within the conservative version of the old paradigm. The liberal version recognizes to a greater extent that certain opportunities (such as a decent education) must also be made available.

3. This is not to say that numbers and empirical work are unimportant. On the contrary, I view them as highly important, as indicated by the extensive empirical analyses presented in earlier chapters. However, my point is that empirical work represents only one aspect of poverty. It is essential to understand and appreciate the human meaning, as well, and to let that inform one's work. As I have argued before, such an understanding calls for a variety of approaches to studying poverty, including a range of qualitative methodologies (Rank, 1992, 1998, 2001).

4. For various discussions regarding the ideology, fundamental themes, and perceived role of government in America, see Dietze (1993), Kingdon (1999), and Lipset (1996). And of course, one of the most insightful perspectives is also one of the earliest, Alexis de Tocqueville's *Democracy in America*, in which it appears that he first introduced the term *individualism* (McCloskey and Zaller, 1984).

5. However, one must always exert caution in making these types of one-to-one arguments at the macro level. Various factors may be operating in society to raise or lower the overall poverty rates. Simply because two trends are occurring at the same time by no means proves that one is causing the other to occur.

6. As mentioned in chapter 2, there has been much discussion with respect to revising the manner in which poverty is measured in the United States. Yet these discussions have almost exclusively focused upon better ways of measuring low income, not the wider concept of deprivation that has been proposed here.

7. Other societal changes with respect to particular public health issues come to mind. For example, several decades ago, the use of seat belts in automobiles was uncommon. Today it is routine. The same is true for the use of bicycle and motorcycle helmets.

8. Although it should be emphasized that the fight for civil rights had a long-standing history prior to the 1950s.

9. For examples of rapid popular cultural changes, see Malcolm Gladwell's book, *The Tipping Point* (2000).

Chapter 8

1. Selecting the official poverty line for a family of three as a benchmark for tying the minimum wage to is, of course, somewhat arbitrary. Other benchmarks could certainly be substituted. However, my feeling is that it is a reasonable and moderately conservative place to begin this discussion. In addition, the definition of what constitutes full-time work is somewhat arbitrary. I have used a standard benchmark of thirty-five hours per week, across fifty-two weeks. This was also the definition used in chapter 3 when we examined the earnings capability of full-time employment to lift families out of poverty.

2. Substitution effects occur when employers who have to pay higher wages, hire workers with greater skills, rather than the lower-skilled workers they might have hired at lower wages.

3. The concept of a living wage goes back to the turn of the twentieth century and the Progressive era. For example, Father John A. Ryan's book *A Living Wage* was published in 1906. Social reformers argued that the level of wages workers received should be guided not simply by the law of supply and demand but also by social and moral considerations such as the need to support one's family (Foner, 1998).

4. See Charles (2003) for a review of the literature with respect to housing discrimination and residential segregation.

5. This of course is a fundamental split between conservatives and liberals. Do we attempt to return the family to some earlier, and often ideal-

ized form (the more conservative approach), or do we attempt to deal with the economic realities of the family today (the more liberal or progressive approach)? A conservative approach to these issues often focuses on increasing the incentives for marriage and the disincentives to form other types of families. A progressive approach attempts to construct policies that deal with the economic realities of the family today. This ideological split harkens back to the comments by John Kenneth Gailbraith and Albert Sorel presented at the start of chapter 7.

6. The bulk of child support goes to women, since 85 percent of all custodial parents are mothers (U.S. Bureau of the Census, 2002e). Of custodial parents who are fathers and who have been awarded child support, 37.7 percent received full payment, 27.2 percent received partial payment, and 35.1 percent received no payment. Of the $2.8 billion due in child support to fathers, $1.4 billion was received in 1999.

7. For a somewhat different assessment, see Frank Furstenberg (2003). Furstenberg has directed a long-term study of Baltimore women who gave birth during their teen years. They were re-interviewed at several points across the life course. He writes,

> The findings of the Baltimore Study strongly suggest that the
> long-term costs of teenage childbearing, at least among Black
> families, were only modest. No doubt, some of the women would
> have achieved more and at an earlier age had they been able to
> delay their first birth, but because of their poor circumstances
> before pregnancy, they still would have encountered many of the
> same economic and social barriers to rising up to the middle
> class. (2003: 31)

8. Promises have been made to both African Americans and American Indians regarding the hope of acquiring assets. For example, after the Emancipation Proclamation, there was much talk and expectation among the freed slaves that Southern property would be redistributed after the Civil War in the form of "forty acres and a mule." Such a policy would have had a major impact upon the asset-building capacity of a group that had been denied the most basic of human rights. Unfortunately, it was never adopted.

9. One device that lower-income families are able to use in terms of building their assets is the earlier discussed refund from the Earned Income

Tax Credit. As Edin (2001), Smeeding, Phillips, and O'Connor (2000), and others have shown, the EITC refund is sometimes used to make the down payment on a house or pay college tuition.

10. A well-known example of asset building in less-developed countries is that undertaken by the Grameen Bank in Bangladesh. Begun in 1983 by Muhammad Yunus, the bank has provided small loans and credit to more than two million families for self-employment purposes throughout rural Bangladesh. It has employed sound financial principles that have helped poor families to build their assets by developing small businesses. At the same time, the bank has been rewarded with a loan repayment rate of nearly 100 percent (for further details, see Yunus, 1999).

Chapter 9

1. For an interesting account of what America might look like by following this path, see an essay by the philosopher Richard Rorty (1999). Rorty takes the perspective of someone looking back at America from the year 2096. He begins by observing,

> Our long, hesitant, painful recovery, over the last five decades, from the breakdown of democratic institutions during the Dark Years (2014–2044) has changed our political vocabulary, as well as our sense of the relation between the moral order and the economic order. Just as twentieth-century Americans had trouble imagining how their pre–Civil War ancestors could have stomached slavery, so we at the end of the twenty-first century have trouble imagining how our great-grandparents could have legally permitted a CEO to get 20 times more than her lowest paid employees. We cannot understand how Americans a hundred years ago could have tolerated the horrific contrast between a childhood spent in the suburbs and one spent in the ghettos. Such inequalities seem to us evident moral abominations, but the vast majority of our ancestors took them to be regrettable necessities. (1999: 243)

Bibliography

Abramovitz, Mimi. 2001. "Everyone Is Still on Welfare: The Role of Redistribution in Social Policy." *Social Work* 46: 297–308.

Agulnik, Phil, et al. 2002. *Understanding Social Exclusion*. New York: Oxford University Press.

Alaimo, Katherine, Christine M. Olson, and Edward A. Frongillo Jr. 2001. "Food Insufficiency and American School-Aged Children's Cognitive, Academic, and Psycho-social Development. *Pediatrics* 108: 44–53.

Alaimo, Katherine et al., 2001. "Food Insuffi½ciency, Family Income, and Health in US Preschool and School-Aged Children." *American Journal of Public Health* 91: 781–786.

Alinsky, Saul D. 1971. *Rules for Radicals: A Practical Primer for Realistic Radicals*. New York: Random House.

Allison, Paul A. 1984. *Event History Analysis*. Beverly Hills, CA: Sage.

Allwitt, Linda F., and Thomas D. Donley. 1997. "Retail Stores in Poor Urban Neighborhoods." *Journal of Consumer Affairs* 31: 139–164.

American Heritage College Dictionary, 3rd Edition. New York: Houghton Mifflin.

Anderson, Elijah. 1990. *StreetWise: Race, Class, and Change in an Urban Community*. Chicago: University of Chicago Press.

———. 1999. *Code of the Street: Decency, Violence, and the Moral Life of the Inner City*. New York: Norton.

Andreason, Alan R. 1993. "Revisiting the Disadvantaged: Old Lessons and New Problems." *Journal of Public Policy and Marketing* 12: 270–275.

Andrews, Robert. 1993. *The Columbia Dictionary of Quotations*. New York: Columbia University Press.

Annie E. Casey Foundation. 1998. *When Teens Have Sex: Issues and Trends*. Baltimore, MD: Annie F. Casey Foundation.

Appelbaum, Eileen, Annette Bernhardt and Richard J. Murnane. 2003. *Low-wage America: How Employers Are Reshaping Opportunity in the Workplace*. New York: Russell Sage Foundation.

Arendt, Hannah. 1963. *On Revolution*. New York: Viking.

Aristotle. 1925. *Nicomachean Ethics*. New York: Oxford University Press.

———. 1990. *Politics*. Cambridge, MA: Harvard University Press.

Arzabe, Patricia Helena Massa. 2001. "Human Rights: A New Paradigm." *The Poverty of Rights: Human Rights and the Eradication of Poverty*. Edited by Willem Van Genugten and Camilo Perez-Bustillo. London: Zed Books. Pp. 29–48.

Ashworth, Karl, Martha Hill, and Robert Walker. 1994. "Patterns of Childhood Poverty: New Challenges of Policy." *Journal of Policy Analysis and Management* 13: 658–680.

Aughinbaugh, Alison. 2000. "Reapplication and Extension: Intergenerational Mobility in the United States." *Labour Economics* 7: 785–796.

Australian Royal Commission on Human Relationships. 1977. *Final Report*. Canberra: Australian Government Publishing Service.

Avruch, Sheila and Alicia Puente Cackley. 1995. "Saving Achieved by Giving WIC Benefits to Women Prenatally." *Public Health Report* 110: 27–34.

Bachman, Jerald G., Lloyd D. Johnston, and Patrick M. O'Malley. 1991. *Monitoring the Future, 1990*. Ann Arbor, MI: Institute for Social Research, University of Michigan.

Baier, Annette. 1984. "For the Sake of Future Generations." *Earthbound: New Introductory Essays in Environmental Ethics*. Edited by Tom Regan. Philadelphia: Temple University Press. Pp. 214–246.

Bane, Mary Jo, and David T. Ellwood. 1986. "Slipping into and out of Poverty: The Dynamics of Spells." *Journal of Human Resources* 21: 1–23.

———. 1994. *Welfare Realities: From Rhetoric to Reform*. Cambridge, MA: Harvard University Press.

Barnes, Matt, et al. 2002. *Poverty and Social Exclusion in Europe*. Cheltenham, UK: Edward Elgar.

Bartik, Timothy H. 2001. *Jobs for the Poor: Can Labor Demand Policies Help?* New York: Russell Sage Foundation.

———. 2002. "Poverty, Jobs, and Subsidized Employment." *Challenge* 45: 100–111.

Barusch, Amanda S. 1994. *Older Women in Poverty: Private Lives and Public Policies.* New York: Springer.

Baum, Charles L. 2002. "A Dynamic Analysis of the Effect of Child Care Costs on the Work Decisions of Low-Income Mothers with Infants." *Demography* 39: 139–164.

Becker, Gary S. 1981. *A Treatise on the Family.* Cambridge, MA: Harvard University Press.

———. 1993. *Human Capital: A Theoretical and Empirical Analysis with Special Reference to Education.* Chicago: University of Chicago Press.

Beeghley, Leonard. 2000. *The Structure of Social Stratification in the United States.* Boston: Allyn and Bacon.

Bergmann, Barbara. 1996. *Saving Our Children: What the United States Can Learn from France.* New York: Russell Sage Foundation.

Berlin, Isaiah. 1958. *Two Concepts of Liberty.* Oxford, UK: Clarendon Press.

Berrick, Jill Duerr. 1995. *Faces of Poverty: Portraits of Women and Children on Welfare.* New York: Oxford University Press.

Beveridge, William. 1942. *Social Insurance and Allied Services: Report.* New York: Macmillan.

Bhalla, A. S., and Frederic Lapeyre. 1999. *Poverty and Exclusion in a Global World.* New York: St. Martin's.

Bhattacharya, Jayanta et al., 2002. "Heat or Eat? Cold Weather Shocks and Nutrition in Poor American Families." Paper presented at the USDA Food Assistance Research Development Grants Workshop, Northwestern University, Evanston, Illinois, April 19.

Billings, Dwight B., and Kathleen M. Blee. 2000. *The Road to Poverty: The Making of Wealth and Hardship in Appalachia.* Cambridge, UK: Cambridge University Press.

Blakely, Edward J., and Mary Gail Snyder. 1997. *Fortress America: Gated Communities in the United States.* Washington, DC: Brookings Institution Press.

Blank, Rebecca M. 1992. *Do Justice: Linking Christian Faith and Modern Economic Life.* Cleveland, OH: United Church Press.

———. 1997. *It Takes a Nation: A New Agenda for Fighting Poverty.*
Princeton, NJ: Princeton University Press.

Blau, David M. 2001. *The Child Care Problem: An Economic Analysis.* New
York: Russell Sage Foundation.

Blau, Francine D., Marianne A. Ferber, and Anne E. Winkler. 2002. *The
Economics of Women, Men, and Work.* Upper Saddle River, NJ:
Prentice Hall.

Blau, Judith R., and Peter M. Blau. 1982. "The Cost of Inequality: Metropolitan Structure and Violent Crime." *American Sociological Review*
47: 114–129.

Bluestone, Barry, and Bennett Harrison. 1982. *The Deindustrializaton of
America: Plant Closings, Community Abandonment, and the Disman-
tling of Basic Industry.* New York: Basic Books.

———. 1988. *The Great U-Turn: Corporate Restructuring and the Polariz-
ing of America.* New York: Basic Books.

Boisjoly, Johanne, Katherine M. Harris, and Greg J. Duncan. 1998.
"Trends, Events, and Duration of Initial Welfare Spells." *Social
Service Review* 72: 466–492.

Bok, Derek. 1996. *The State of the Nation: Government and the Quest for a
Better Society.* Cambridge, MA: Harvard University Press.

Booth, Charles. 1892. *Life and Labour of the People of London, First Series:
Poverty.* London: Macmillan.

Bostrom, Meg. 2001. "Achieving the American Dream: A Meta-Analysis
of Public Opinion Concerning Poverty, Upward Mobility, and
Related Issues." Paper prepared for the Ford Foundation project
"Making Work Pay for Families Today."

Bound, John et al., 1991. "Poverty Dynamics in Widowhood." *Journal of
Gerontology: Social Sciences* 46: S115–S124.

Bourgois, Philippe. 1995. *In Search of Respect: Selling Crack in El Barrio.*
New York: Cambridge University Press.

Bradbury, Bruce, Stephen P. Jenkins, and John Micklewright. 2001a. *The
Dynamics of Child Poverty in Industrialised Countries.* Cambridge, UK:
Cambridge University Press.

———. 2001b. "The Dynamics of Child Poverty in Seven Industrialised
Nations." *The Dynamics of Child Poverty in Industrialised Countries.*
Edited by Bruce Bradbury, Stephen P. Jenkins, and John Mickle-
wright. Cambridge, UK: Cambridge University Press. Pp. 92–132.

Bradley, Robert H., and Robert F. Corwyn. 2002. "Socioeconomic Status and Child Development." *Annual Review of Psychology* 53: 371–379.

Brauer, Carl M. 1989. "Kennedy, Johnson, and the War on Poverty." *Journal of American History* 69: 98–119.

Braun, Denny. 1997. *The Rich Get Richer: The Rise of Income Inequality in the United States and the World*. Chicago: Nelson-Hall.

Brooks-Gunn, Jeanne, Greg J. Duncan, and J. Lawrence Aber. 1997. *Neighborhood Poverty: Context and Consequences for Children*. New York: Russell Sage Foundation.

Brown, J. Larry, and Ernesto Pollitt. 1996. "Malnutrition, Poverty, and Intellectual Development." *Scientific American* 274: 38–43.

Bullard, Robert D. 1990. *Dumping in Dixie*. Boulder, CO: Westview Press.

Burchardt, T., J. Le Grand, and D. Piachaud. 1999. "Social Exclusion in Britain, 1991–1995." *Social Policy and Administration* 33: 227–244.

Burkhauser, Richard V., J. S. Butler, and Karen C. Holden. 1991. "How the Death of a Spouse Affects Economic Well-Being after Retirement: A Hazard Model Approach." *Social Science Quarterly* 72: 504–519.

Burkhauser, Richard V., Karen C. Holden, and Daniel Feaster. 1988. "Incidence, Timing, and Events Associated with Poverty: A Dynamic View of Poverty in Retirement." *Journal of Gerontology: Social Sciences* 43: S46–S52.

Burkhauser, Richard V., Karen C. Holden, and Daniel A. Myers. 1986. "Marital Disruption and Poverty: The Role of Survey Procedures in Artificially Creating Poverty." *Demography* 23: 621–631.

Burtless, Gary, and Christopher Jencks. 2002. "American Inequality and Its Consequences." *Luxembourg Income Study Working Paper Series*, No. 339, Maxwell School of Citizenship and Public Affairs, Syracuse University, Syracuse, New York.

Bush, George W. 2002. "President Announces Welfare Reform Agenda." Speech at St. Luke's Catholic Church, February 26, Washington, DC.

Cantor, David, and Kenneth C. Land. 1985. "Unemployment and Crime Rates in the Post–World War II United States: A Theoretical and Empirical Analysis." *American Sociological Review* 50: 317–332.

Caplovitz, David. 1963. *The Poor Pay More: Consumer Practices of Low-Income Families*. Glencoe, IL: Free Press.

Card, David, and Rebecca M. Blank. 2002. *Finding Jobs: Work and Welfare Reform*. New York: Russell Sage Foundation.

Card, David, and Alan B. Krueger. 1995. *Myth and Measurement: The New Economics of the Minimum Wage*. Princeton, NJ: Princeton University Press.

———. 1998. "A Reanalysis of the Effect of the New Jersey Minimum Wage Increase on the Fast-Food Industry with Representative Payroll Data." Working Paper No. 6386. National Bureau of Economic Research.

Carlson-Thies, Stanley, and James W. Skillen. 1996. *Welfare in America: Christian Perspectives on a Policy in Crisis*. Grand Raids, MI: William B. Eerdmans.

Carney, Stacie, and William G. Gale. 2001. "Asset Accumulation among Low-Income Households." *Assets for the Poor: The Benefits of Spreading Asset Ownership*. Edited by Thomas M. Shapiro and Edward N. Wolff. New York: Russell Sage Foundation. Pp. 165–205.

Caskey, John P. 1994. *Fringe Banking: Check-Cashing Outlets, Pawnshops, and the Poor*. New York: Russell Sage Foundation.

Castells, Manuel. 1998. *End of the Millennium*. Malden, MA: Blackwell.

Center for Community Change. 2001. *Home Sweet Home: Why America Needs a National Housing Trust Fund*. Washington, DC: Center for Community Change.

Century Foundation Task Force on the Common School. 2002. *Divided We Fail: Coming Together through Public School Choice*. New York: Century Foundation Press.

Charen, Mona. 2003. "America's Poor are Getting Fat and Lazy on Government Handouts." *St. Louis Post-Dispatch*, January 27, Section B, p. 7.

Charles, Camille Zubrinsky. 2003. "The Dynamics of Racial Residential Segregation." *Annual Review of Sociology* 29: 167–207.

Cherlin, Andrew J. 1992. *Marriage, Divorce, Remarriage*. Cambridge, MA: Harvard University Press.

Children's Defense Fund. 2002a. "Low-Income Families Bear the Burden of State Child Care Cutbacks." September 5. Washington, DC: Children's Defense Fund.

———. 2002b. "Increase Investments in Head Start." Washington, DC: Children's Defense Fund.

Chiricos, Theodore G. 1987. "Rates of Crime and Unemployment: An Analysis of Aggregate Research Evidence." *Social Problems* 34: 187–212.

Chung, Chanjin, and Samuel L. Myers Jr. 1999. "Do the Poor Pay More for Food? An Analysis of Grocery Store Availability and Food Price Disparities." *Journal of Consumer Affairs* 33: 276–291.

Clinton, Bill. 1992. "A New Covenant." *Putting People First*. Bill Clinton and Al Gore. New York: Times Books. Pp. 217–232.

Cloward, Richard A., and Lloyd E. Ohlin. 1960. *Delinquency and Opportunity: A Theory of Delinquent Gangs*. New York: Free Press.

Coe, Richard D. 1988. "A Longitudinal Examination of Poverty in the Elderly Years." *Gerontologist* 28: 540–544.

Cohen, Albert K. 1955. *Delinquent Boys*. Glencoe, IL: Free Press.

Cohen, Barbara E., Martha R. Burt, and Margaret M. Schulte. 1993. "Hunger and Food Insecurity among the Elderly." Project Report. Washington, DC: Urban Institute.

Cohen, Mark A. 1996. "The Monetary Value of Saving a High-Risk Youth." Working Paper, Owen Graduate School of Management, Vanderbilt University, Nashville, TN.

———. 1998. "The Monetary Value of Saving a High Risk Youth." *Journal of Quantitative Criminology* 14: 5–33.

Cohen, Mark A., Ted R. Miller, and Brian Wiersema. 1996. "Victim Costs and Consequences: A New Look." National Institute of Justice Research Report, NCJ-155282, February.

Collins, Chuck, Chris Hartman, and Holly Sklar. 1999. *Divided Decade: Economic Disparity at the Century's Turn*. Boston, MA: United for a Fair Economy.

Commission on Violence and Youth. 1993. *Violence and Youth: Psychology's Response. Summary Report of the APA Commission on Violence and Youth*. Washington, DC: American Psychological Association.

Conley, Dalton. 1999. *Being Black, Living in the Red: Race, Wealth, and Social Policy in America*. Berkeley: University of California Press.

Coontz, Stephanie. 1992. *The Way We Never Were: American Families and the Nostalgia Trap*. New York: Basic Books.

———. 1997. *The Way We Really Are: Coming to Terms with America's Changing Families*. New York: Basic Books.

Copeland, Warren R. 1994. *And the Poor Get Welfare: The Ethics of Poverty in the United States*. Nashville, TN: Abingdon Press.

Corcoran, Mary. 1995. "Rags to Rags: Poverty and Mobility in the United States." *Annual Review of Sociology* 21: 237–267.

————. 2002. "Mobility, Persistence, and the Consequences of Poverty for Children: Child and Adult Outcomes." *Understanding Poverty.* Edited by Sheldon H. Danziger and Robert H. Haveman. Cambridge, MA: Harvard University Press. Pp. 127–161.

Corcoran, Mary E., and Ajay Chaudry. 1997. "The Dynamics of Childhood Poverty." *The Future of Children* 7: 40–54.

Corcoran, Mary et al., 1992. "The Association between Men's Economic Status and Their Family and Community Origins." *Journal of Human Resources* 27: 575–601.

Cortes, Ernesto, Jr. 1996. "Reweaving the Fabric: The Iron Rule and the IAF Strategy for Power and Politics." *Reducing Poverty in America: Views and Approaches.* Edited by Michael R. Darby. Thousand Oaks, CA: Sage. Pp. 175–198.

Cottle, Thomas J. 2001. *Hardest Times: The Trauma of Long Term Unemployment.* Westport, CT: Praeger.

Cullen, Jim. 2003. *The American Dream: A Short History of an Idea That Shaped a Nation.* New York: Oxford University Press.

Current Population Survey. 2002. "Design and Methodology." Current Population Survey, Technical Paper 63RV. Washington, DC: U.S. Government Printing Office.

Currie, Elliott. 1985. *Confronting Crime: An American Challenge.* New York: Pantheon.

Dahrendorf, Ralf. 1999. "Foreword." *Time and Poverty in Western Welfare States: United Germany in Perspective.* Edited by Lutz Leisering and Stephan Leibfried. Cambridge, UK: Cambridge University Press. Pp. ix–xi.

Dallek, Robert. 1991. *Lone Star Rising: Lyndon Johnson and His Times, 1908–1960.* New York: Oxford University Press.

Danziger, Sheldon, and Peter Gottschalk. 1995. *America Unequal.* New York: Russell Sage Foundation.

Danziger, Sheldon, and Robert H. Haveman. 2001. *Understanding Poverty.* New York: Russell Sage Foundation.

Darling-Hammond, Linda, and Laura Post. 2000. "Inequality in Teaching and Schooling: Supporting High-Quality Teaching and Leadership in Low-Income Schools." *A Notion at Risk: Preserving Public Education as an Engine for Social Mobility.* Edited by Richard D. Kalenberg. New York: Century Foundation Press. Pp. 127–167.

Darroch, Jacqueline E., et al. 2001. "Teenage Social and Reproductive Behavior in Developed Countries: Can More Progress Be Made?" Occasional Report No. 3, November. New York: Alan Guttmacher Institute.

Degler, Carl N. 1970. *Out of Our Past: The Forces That Shaped Modern America*. New York: Harper and Row.

De Parle, Jason. 1993. "Homelessness Hitting Home: A Death on HUD's Doorstep." *New York Times*, November 30, Section A, p. 1.

De Vries, Barend A. 1998. *Champions of the Poor: The Economic Consequences of Judeo-Christian Values*. Washington, DC: Georgetown University Press.

Devine, Joel A., and James D. Wright. 1993. *The Greatest of Evils: Urban Poverty and the American Underclass*. New York: Aldine de Gruyter.

Dietze, Gottfried. 1993. *American Democracy: Aspects of Practical Liberalism*. Baltimore, MD: Johns Hopkins University Press.

Dodge, Hiroko H. 1995. "Movements out of Poverty among Elderly Widows." *Journal of Gerontology: Social Sciences* 50B: S240–S249.

Drake, Brett, and Shanta Pandey. 1996. "Unraveling the Relationship between Neighborhood Poverty and Child Maltreatment." *Child Abuse and Neglect* 20: 1003–1018.

Draut, Tamara. 2002a. "New Opportunities? Public Opinion on Poverty, Income Inequality and Public Policy: 1996–2002." Paper prepared for Demos: A Network for Ideas and Action, New York.

———. 2002b. "Crossing Divides: New Common Ground on Poverty and Economic Security." Paper prepared for Demos: A Network for Ideas and Action, New York.

Du Bois, W. E. B. 1899. *The Philadelphia Negro*. Philadelphia: University of Pennsylvania Press.

———. 1983. *Black Reconstruction in America: An Essay toward a History of the Part Which Black Folk Played in the Attempt to Reconstruct Democracy in America, 1860–1880*. New York: Atheneum. Originally published in 1935.

Dunbar, Leslie. 1988. *The Common Interest: How Our Social-Welfare Policies Don't Work, and What We Can Do about Them*. New York: Pantheon.

Duncan, Cynthia M. 1992. "Persistent Poverty in Appalachia: Scarce
    Work and Rigid Stratification." *Rural Poverty in America*. Edited by
    Cynthia M. Duncan. New York: Auburn House. Pp. 111–133.

Duncan, Greg J. 1984. *Years of Poverty, Years of Plenty: The Changing
    Economic Fortunes of American Workers and Families*. Ann Arbor, MI:
    Institute for Social Research.

———. 1988. "The Volatility of Family Income over the Life Course."
    Life-Span Development and Behavior, Vol. 9. Edited by Paul B. Baltes,
    David L. Featherman, and Richard M. Lerner. Hillsdale, NJ:
    Lawrence Erlbaum. Pp. 317–358.

Duncan, Greg J., and Jeanne Brooks-Gunn. 1997. *Consequences of Grow-
    ing Up Poor*. New York: Russell Sage Foundation.

Duncan, Greg J., Kathleen Mullan Harris, and Johanne Boisjoly. 2000.
    "Time Limits and Welfare Reform: New Estimates of the Number
    and Characteristics of Affected Families." *Social Service Review* 74:
    55–75.

Duncan, Greg J., and Daniel H. Hill. 1989. "Assessing the Quality of
    Household Panel Data: The Case of the Panel Study of Income
    Dynamics." *Journal of Business and Economic Statistics* 7: 441–452.

Duncan, Greg J., and P. Lindsay Chase-Lansdale. 2002. *For Better and for
    Worse: Welfare Reform and the Well-Being of Children and Families*.
    New York: Russell Sage Foundation.

Duncan, Greg J., and Willard L. Rodgers. 1988. "Longitudinal Aspects of
    Childhood Poverty." *Journal of Marriage and the Family* 50: 1007–
    1021.

———. 1991. "Has Children's Poverty Become More Persistent?"
    American Sociological Review 56: 538–550.

Duncan, Greg J., et al. 1995. "Poverty and Social-Assistance Dynamics in
    the United States, Canada, and Europe." *Poverty, Inequality and the
    Future of Social Policy: Western States in the New World Order*. Edited
    by Katherine McFate, Roger Lawson, and William Julius Wilson.
    New York: Russell Sage Foundation. Pp. 67–108.

Duncan, Greg J., et al. 1998. "How Much Does Childhood Poverty Affect
    the Life Chances of Children?" *American Sociological Review* 63: 406–
    423.

Duncan, Otis Dudley. 1968. "Inheritance of Poverty or Inheritance of
    Race?" *On Understanding Poverty: Perspective from the Social Sciences*.

Edited by Daniel Patrick Moynihan. New York: Basic Books. Pp. 85–109.

Dylan, Bob. 1971. *Tarantula.* New York: Macmillan.

Edelman, Marian Wright. 1992. "Vanishing Dreams of America's Young Families." *Challenge* May–June: 13–19.

Edelman, Peter. 2001. "Searching for America's Heart: RFK and the Renewal of Hope." Boston: Houghton Mifflin.

————. 2002. "Reforming Welfare—Take Two." *Nation* (February 4), 16–20.

Edin, Kathryn. 2001. "More than Money: The Role of Assets in the Survival Strategies and Material Well-Being of the Poor." *Assets for the Poor: The Benefits of Spreading Asset Ownership.* Edited by Thomas M. Shapiro and Edward N. Wolff. New York: Russell Sage Foundation. Pp. 206–231.

Edin, Kathryn, and Christopher Jencks. 1992. "Reforming Welfare." *Rethinking Social Policy: Race, Poverty, and the Underclass.* Edited by Christopher Jencks. Cambridge, MA: Harvard University Press. Pp. 204–235.

Edin, Kathryn, and Laura Lein. 1997. *Making Ends Meet: How Single Mothers Survive Welfare and Low-Wage Work.* New York: Russell Sage Foundation.

Edwards, Mark Evan, Robert Plotnick, and Marieka Klawitter. 2001. "Do Attitudes and Personality Characteristics Affect Socioeconomic Outcomes? The Case of Welfare Use by Young Women." *Social Science Quarterly* 82: 827–843.

Ehrenreich, Barbara. 2001. *Nickel and Dimed: On (Not) Getting by in America.* New York: Metropolitan Books.

Elder, Glen H., Jr. 1995. "The Life Course Paradigm: Social Change and Individual Development." *Examining Lives in Context: Perspectives on the Ecology of Human Development.* Edited by Phyllis Moen, Glen H. Elder, Jr., and Kurt Luescher. New York: American Psychological Association. Pp. 101–140.

Ellwood, David T., and Elisabeth D. Welty. 2000. "Public Service Employment and Mandatory Work: A Policy Whose Time Has Come and Gone and Come Again?" *Finding Jobs: Work and Welfare Reform.* Edited by David E. Card and Rebecca M. Blank. New York: Russell Sage Foundation. Pp. 299–372.

Ellwood, David T. et al. 2000. *A Working Nation: Workers, Work, and Government in the New Economy.* New York: Russell Sage Foundation.

Esping-Andersen, Gosta. 1990. *The Three Worlds of Welfare Capitalism.* Princeton, NJ: Princeton University Press.

Etzioni, Amitai. 1996. *The New Golden Rule: Community and Morality in a Democratic Society.* New York: Basic Books.

Failinger, Marie A., and Larry May. 1984. "Litigating against Poverty: Legal Services and Group Representation." *Ohio State Law Journal* 45: 2–56.

Farley, Reynolds. 1996. *The New American Reality: Who We Are, How We Got Here, Where We Are Going.* New York: Russell Sage Foundation.

Feagin, Joe R. 1975. *Subordinating the Poor: Welfare and American Beliefs.* Englewood Cliffs, NJ: Prentice Hall.

———. 2000. *Racist America: Roots, Current Realities, and Future Reparations.* New York: Routledge.

Federal Bureau of Investigation. 1996. *Uniform Crime Reports for the United States 1995.* Washington, DC: U.S. Government Printing Office.

Feinberg, Joel. 1970. *Doing and Deserving: Essays in the Theory of Responsibility.* Princeton, NJ: Princeton University Press.

Ferguson, Ronald F. 2001. "Community Revitalization, Jobs and the Well-Being of the Inner-City Poor." *Understanding Poverty.* Edited by Sheldon H. Danziger and Robert H. Haveman. New York: Russell Sage Foundation. Pp. 417–443.

Fischer, Claude S., and Michael Hout. 2002. "Differences among Americans in Living Standards across the Twentieth Century." Survey Research Working Paper, University of California, Berkeley.

Fischer, Claude S., et al. 1996. *Inequality by Design: Cracking the Bell Curve Myth.* Princeton, NJ: Princeton University Press.

Fisher, Gordon M. 1992. "The Development and History of the Poverty Thresholds." *Social Security Bulletin* 55: 3–14.

Fitzgerald, John, Peter Gottschalk, and Robert Moffitt. 1998. "An Analysis of Sample Attrition in Panel Data: The Michigan Panel Study of Income Dynamics." *Journal of Human Resources* 33: 251–299.

Foner, Eric. 1998. *The Story of American Freedom.* New York: Norton.

Food Research and Action Center. 1991. *Community Childhood Hunger*

Identification Project: A Survey of Childhood Hunger in the United States. Washington, DC: Food Research and Action Center.

Foreign Policy. 2003. "Ranking the Rich." *Foreign Policy*, May/June.

Fowles, Richard, and Mary Merva. 1996. "Wage Inequality and Criminal Activity: An Extreme Bounds Analysis for the United States, 1975–1990." *Criminology* 34: 163–182.

Frankenberg, Erica, and Chungmei Lee. 2002. "Race in American Public Schools: Rapidly Resegregating School Districts." Report for The Civil Rights Project, Harvard University, Cambridge, MA.

Freedman, David Noel. 1992. *The Anchor Bible Dictionary.* New York: Doubleday.

Freeman, Richard B. 1996. "Why Do So Many Young Americans Commit Crimes and What Might We Do About It?" *Journal of Economic Perspectives* 10: 22–45.

Furstenberg, Frank F. 2003. "Teenage Childbearing as a Public Issue and Private Concern." *Annual Review of Sociology* 29: 23–39.

Gaffaney, Timothy J. 2000. *Freedom for the Poor: Welfare and the Foundations of Democratic Citizenship.* Boulder, CO: Westview Press.

Galbraith, John Kenneth. 1986. *A View from the Stands: Of People, Politics, Military Power and the Arts.* Boston, MA: Houghton Mifflin.

Gale, William G., and John Karl Scholz. 1994. "Intergenerational Transfers and the Accumulation of Wealth." *Journal of Economic Perspectives* 8: 145–160.

Gallup, Poll [Online]. 2003. www.gallup.com/poll/topics/crime.asp[Jan. 9, 2003].

Gans, Herbert J. 1988. *Middle American Individualism: The Future of Liberal Democracy.* New York: Free Press.

————. 1995. *The War against the Poor: The Underclass and Antipoverty Policy.* New York: Basic Books.

Garfinkel, Irwin. 1992. *Assuring Child Support.* New York: Russell Sage Foundation.

————. 1998. *Fathers under Fire.* New York: Russell Sage Foundation.

Garr, Robin. 1995. *Reinvesting in America: The Grassroots Movements That Are Feeding the Hungry, Housing the Homeless, and Putting Americans Back to Work.* Reading, MA: Addison-Wesley.

Gelles, Richard J. 1993. "Poverty and Violence towards Children." *American Behavioral Scientist* 35: 258–274.

Geronimus, Arline T., et al. 2001. "Inequality in Life Expectancy, Functional Status, and Active Life Expectancy across Selected Black and White Populations in the United States." *Demography* 38: 227–251.

Gilder, George. 1981. *Wealth and Poverty*. New York: Basic Books.

Gilens, Martin. 1999. *Why Americans Hate Welfare: Race, Media, and the Politics of Antipoverty Policy*. Chicago: University of Chicago Press.

Gillette, Michael L. 1996. *Launching the War on Poverty: An Oral History*. New York: Twayne.

Gladwell, Malcolm. 2000. *The Tipping Point: How Little Things Can Make a Big Difference*. Boston: Little, Brown.

Glennerster, Howard. 2002. "United States Poverty Studies and Poverty Measurement: The Past Twenty-Five Years." *Social Service Review* 76: 83–107.

Glickman, Dan. 1997. "Remarks of Secretary Dan Glickman at the FRAC Annual Dinner." Food Research and Action Center, Washington, DC, June 17.

Goffman, Erving. 1963. *Stigma: Notes on the Management of Spoiled Identity*. Englewood Cliffs, NJ: Prentice Hall.

Gokhale, Jagdeesh, and Lawrence J. Kotlikoff. 2002. "Simulating the Transmission of Wealth Inequality." *American Economic Review* 92: 265–269.

Goodwin, Leonard. 1972. *Do the Poor Want to Work? A Social-Psychological Study of Work Orientations*. Washington, DC: Brookings Institution.

———. 1983. *Causes and Cures of Welfare: New Evidence on the Social Psychology of the Poor*. Lexington, MA: Lexington Books.

Goodwin, Richard N. 1988. *Remembering America: A Voice from the Sixties*. New York: Harper and Row.

Goodwin, Robert. 1985. *Protecting the Vulnerable: A Reanalysis of Our Social Responsibilities*. Chicago: University of Chicago Press.

Gottschalk, Peter, and Sheldon Danziger. 2001. "Income Mobility and Exits from Poverty of American Children, 1970–1992." *The Dynamics of Child Poverty in Industrialised Countries*. Edited by Bruce Bradbury, Stephen P. Jenkins and John Micklewright. Cambridge, UK: Cambridge University Press. Pp. 135–153.

Gottschalk, Peter, Sara McLanahan, and Gary D. Sandefur. 1994. "The Dynamics and Intergenerational Transmission of Poverty and Welfare Participation." *Confronting Poverty: Prescriptions for Change.*

Edited by Sheldon H. Danziger, Gary D. Sandefur, and Daniel H. Weinberg. Cambridge, MA: Harvard University Press. Pp. 85–108.

Greenwood, Peter, et al. 1996. *Diverting Children from a Life of Crime: Measuring Costs and Benefits.* Santa Monica, CA: Rand Corporation.

Greider, William. 1997. *One World, Ready or Not: The Manic Logic of Global Capitalism.* New York: Simon and Schuster.

Grogan, Paul S., and Tony Proscio. 2000. *Comeback Cities: A Blueprint for Urban Neighborhood Revival.* Boulder, CO: Westview Press.

Gueron, Judith M., and Edward Pauly. 1991. *From Welfare to Work.* New York: Russell Sage Foundation.

Guilkey, David K., and Ronald R. Rindfuss. 1987. "Logistic Regression Multivariate Life Tables: A Communicable Approach." *Sociological Methods and Research* 16: 276–300.

Gushee, David P. 1999. *Toward a Just and Caring Society: Christian Responses to Poverty in America.* Grand Rapids, MI: Baker Books.

Hacker, Andrew. 1997. *Money: Who Has How Much and Why.* New York: Simon and Schuster.

Hagan, John, and Ruth D. Peterson. 1995. *Crime and Inequality.* Stanford, CA: Stanford University Press.

Halle, David. 1984. *America's Working Man: Work, Home, and Politics among Blue-Collar Property Owners.* Chicago: University of Chicago Press.

Hamill, Susan Pace. 2002. "An Argument for Tax Reform Based on Judeo-Christian Ethics." *Alabama Law Review* 54: 1–96.

Handler, Joel F., and Yeheskel Hasenfeld. 1991. *The Moral Construction of Poverty: Welfare Reform in America.* Newbury Park, CA: Sage.

Hanson, F. Allan. 1997a. "Why Don't We Care about the Poor Anyway?" *Humanist* 57: 11–14.

———. 1997b. "How Poverty Lost Its Meaning." *Cato Journal* 17: 189–209.

Harkness, Joseph, Sandra J. Newman, and Barbara J. Lipman. 2002. "Housing America's Working Families: A Further Exploration." *New Century Housing* 3: 1–39.

Harrington, Michael. 1962. *The Other America: Poverty in the United States.* New York: Macmillan.

Harris, Fred R., and Roger W. Wilkins. 1988. *Quiet Riots: Race and Poverty in the United States.* New York: Pantheon.

Harris, Katherine Mullen. 1996. "Life after Welfare: Women, Work and Repeat Dependency." *American Sociological Review* 61: 407–426.

Hart, H. L. A., and A. M. Honore. 1959. *Causation in the Law.* Oxford: Clarendon Press.

Hartwell, R. M. 1986. "The Long Debate on Poverty." Paper presented at the Political Economy Seminar Series, Washington University, St. Louis, Missouri.

Harvey, Philip. 2000. "Combating Joblessness: An Analysis of the Principal Strategies that Have Influenced the Development of American Employment and Social Welfare Law During the 20th Century." *Berkeley Journal of Employment and Labor Law* 21: 677–758.

Haveman, Robert. 1987. *Poverty Policy and Poverty Research: The Great Society and the Social Sciences.* Madison: University of Wisconsin Press.

———. 1988. *Starting Even: An Equal Opportunity Program to Combat the Nation's New Poverty.* New York: Simon and Schuster.

Haveman, Robert, Barbara Wolfe, and Karen Pence. 2001. "Intergenerational Effects of Nonmarital and Early Childbearing." *Out of Wedlock: Causes and Consequences of Nonmarital Fertility.* Edited by Lawrence L. Wu and Barbara Wolfe. New York: Russell Sage Foundation. Pp. 287–316.

Hayes, Cheryl D., John L. Palmer, and Martha J. Zaslow. 1990. *Who Cares for America's Children: Child Care Policy for the 1900s.* Washington, DC: National Academy Press.

Heclo, Hugh. 1997. "Values Underpinning Poverty Programs for Children." *The Future of Children* 7: 141–148.

Hehir, J. Bryan. 1991. "Catholic Theology and Economic Justice." *Eden Journal* 1: 18–27.

Helburn, Suzanne W. 1995. "Cost, Quality, and Child Outcomes in Child Care Centers: Technical Report." Department of Economics, University of Colorado.

Henshaw, S. K. 1999. *Special Report: U.S. Teenage Pregnancy Statistics with Comparative Statistics for Women Aged 20–24.* New York: Alan Guttmacher Institute.

Herrnstein, Richard J., and Charles Murray. 1994. *The Bell Curve: Intelligence and Class Structure in American Life.* New York: Free Press.

Hill, Martha S. 1992. *The Panel Study of Income Dynamics: A User's Guide.* Newbury Park, CA: Sage.

Holden, Karen C., Richard V. Burkhauser, and Daniel A. Myers. 1986. "Income Transitions at Older Stages of Life: The Dynamics of Poverty." *Gerontologist* 26: 292–297.

Holden, Karen C., and Timothy M. Smeeding. 1990. "The Poor, the Rich, and the Insecure Elderly Caught in Between." *Milbank Quarterly* 68: 191–219.

Horan, Patrick, and Patricia Austin. 1974. "The Social Bases of Welfare Stigma." *Social Problems* 21: 648–657.

Horrington, Kevin. 2003. "Alabama Asks Itself WWJJ (What Would Jesus Tax)?" *St. Louis Post-Dispatch*, August 2, Section B, p. 3.

Housing and Development Reporter. 1998. "Current Developments." West Group, May 4, p. 808.

Hout, Michael. 2003. "Money and Morale: What Growing Inequality Is Doing to Americans' Views of Themselves and Others." *Survey Research Center Working Paper*, University of California, Berkeley, California.

Howard, Christopher. 1997. *The Hidden Welfare State: Tax Expenditures and Social Policy in the United States.* Princeton, NJ: Princeton University Press.

Howell, Joseph T. 1972. *Hard Living on Clay Street: Portraits of Blue Collar Families.* New York: Anchor Books.

Hull House. 1895. *Hull House Maps and Papers.* New York: Thomas Y. Crowell.

Hungerford, Thomas L. 2001. "The Economic Consequences of Widowhood on Elderly Women in the United States and Germany." *Gerontologist* 41: 103–110.

Hunter, Robert. 1904. *Poverty.* New York: Macmillan.

Hurd, Michael D. 1989. "The Economic Status of the Elderly." *Science* 244: 659–664.

Institute for Research on Poverty. 1998. "Revising the Poverty Measure." *Focus* 19: 1–55.

Institute for Research on Poverty. 2000. "Child Support Enforcement Policy and Low-Income Families." *Focus* 21: 1–86.

Internal Revenue Service. 2003. "Statistics of Income Bulletin." Publication 1136 (Revised 6–03).

Irvine, Ian, and Kuan Xu. 2002. "Crime, Punishment and the Measurement of Poverty in the United States, 1979–1997." *Luxembourg Income*

Study Working Paper Series, No. 333, Maxwell School of Citizenship and Public Affairs, Syracuse University, Syracuse, New York.

Isserman, Maurice. 2000. *The Other American: The Life of Michael Harrington*. New York: Public Affairs.

Jankowski, Martin Sanchez. 1995. "Ethnography, Inequality, and Crime in the Low-Income Community." *Crime and Inequality*. Edited by John Hagen and Ruth D. Peterson. Stanford, CA: Stanford University Press. Pp. 80–94.

Jargowsky, Paul A. 1997. *Poverty and Place: Ghettos, Barrios, and the American City*. New York: Russell Sage Foundation.

———. 2003. "Stunning Progress, Hidden Problems: The Dramatic Decline of Concentrated Poverty in the 1990s." *The Living Cities Census Series*, May, The Brookings Institution, Washington, DC.

Jaynes, Gerald David, and Robin M. Williams. 1989. *A Common Destiny: Black and American Society*. Washington, DC: National Academy Press.

Jencks, Christopher. 1979. *Who Get Ahead: The Determinants of Economic Success in America*. New York: Basic Books.

———. 1992. *Rethinking Social Policy: Race, Poverty, and the Underclass*. Cambridge, MA: Harvard University Press.

———. 2002. "Does Inequality Matter?" *Daedalus* 131: 49–65.

Jesuit, David, and Timothy M. Smeeding. 2002. "Poverty Levels in the Developed World." *Luxembourg Income Study Working Paper Series*, No. 321, Maxwell School of Citizenship and Public Affairs, Syracuse University, Syracuse, New York.

Johnson, Lyndon B. 1965a. "President Lyndon B. Johnson's Annual Message to the Congress on the State of the Union, January 8, 1964." *Public Papers of the Presidents of the United States: Lyndon B. Johnson, 1963–64*. Volume 1, entry 91, pp. 112–118. Washington, DC: U.S. Government Printing Office.

———. 1965b. "The President's Inaugural Address, January 20, 1965." *Public Papers of the Presidents of the United States: Lyndon B. Johnson, 1965*. Volume I, entry 27, pp. 71–74. Washington, DC: U.S. Government Printing Office.

Joint Center for Housing Studies. 2003. *The State of the Nation's Housing*. Cambridge, MA: John F. Kennedy School of Government, Harvard University.

Jones, Jacqueline. 1992. *The Dispossessed: America's Underclasses from the Civil War to the Present*. New York: Basic Books.

Kagan, Sharon L., and Nancy Cohen. 1996. *Reinventing Early Care and Education: A Vision for a Quality System*. San Francisco: Jossey-Bass.

Kahlenberg, Richard D. 2001. *All Together Now: Creating Middle-Class Schools through Public School Choice*. Washington, DC: Brookings Institution Press.

———. 2002. "Economic School Integration: An Update." Century Foundation Issue Brief Series, Century Foundation, New York.

Kaiser Commission. 2002. "Enrolling Uninsured Low-Income Children in Medicaid and CHIP." Kaiser Commission on Medicaid and the Uninsured, Key Facts, May.

Kangas, Olli. 2000. "Distributive Justice and Social Policy." *Luxembourg Income Study Working Paper Series*, No. 221. Maxwell School of Citizenship and Public Affairs, Syracuse University, Syracuse, New York.

Katz, Lawrence F. 1998. "Wage Subsidies for the Disadvantaged." *Generating Jobs: How to Increase Demand for Less-Skilled Workers*. Edited by Richard B. Freeman and Peter Gottschalk. New York: Russell Sage Foundation. Pp. 21–53.

Katz, Michael B. 1989. *The Undeserving Poor: From the War on Poverty to the War on Welfare*. New York: Pantheon.

———. 1995. *Improving Poor People: The Welfare State, the "Underclass," and Urban Schools as History*. Princeton, NJ: Princeton University Press.

———. 1996. *In the Shadow of the Poorhouse: A Social History of Welfare in America*. New York: Basic Books.

———. 2001. *The Price of Citizenship: Redefining the American Welfare State*. New York: Metropolitan Books.

Kaufman, Phil. R. 1999. "Rural Poor Have Less Access to Supermarkets, Large Grocery Stores." *Rural Development* 13: 19–25.

Kavka, Gregory S. 1994. "The Costs of Crimes: Coleman Amended." *Ethics* 104: 582–592.

Kawachi, Ichiro, and Bruce P. Kennedy. 2002. *The Health of Nations: Why Inequality Is Harmful to Your Health*. New York: New Press.

Kawachi, Ichiro, Bruce P. Kennedy, and Richard G. Wilkinson. 1999. *The Society and Population Health Reader: Income Inequality and Health*. New York: New Press.

Keating, Dennis W., and Norman Krumholz. 1999. *Rebuilding Urban Neighborhoods: Achievements, Opportunities, and Limits.* Thousand Oaks, CA: Sage.

Keister, Lisa A., and Stephanie Moller. 2000. "Wealth Inequality in the United States." *Annual Review of Sociology* 26: 63–81.

Kim, Myoung, Jim Ohls, and Rhonda Cohen. 2001. *Hunger in America 2001: National Report Prepared for America's Second Harvest.* Princeton, NJ: Mathematical Policy Research.

Kim, Yong S., and Frank P. Stafford. 2000. "The Quality of the PSID Income Data in the 1990s and Beyond." Panel Study of Income Dynamics Working Paper, University of Michigan, Ann Arbor.

King, Martin Luther, Jr. 1967. *Where Do We Go from Here: Chaos or Community?* New York: Harper and Row.

———. 1967b. "Hearings Before the Subcommittee on Executive Reorganization of the Committee on Government Operations, United States Senate, Eighty-Ninth Congress, Second Session, December 14 and 15, 1966, Part 14." Washington, DC: U.S. Government Printing Office.

Kingdon, John W. 1999. *America the Unusual.* New York: St. Martin's.

Kingsley, G. Thomas, and Kathryn L. S. Pettit. 2003. "Concentrated Poverty: A Change in Course." *The Neighborhood Change in Urban America Series*, May, The Urban Institute, Washington, DC.

Kirby, Douglas. 2001. *Emerging Answers: Research Findings on Programs to Reduce Teen Pregnancy.* Washington, DC: National Campaign to Prevent Teen Pregnancy.

Klerman, Lorraine, and M. B. Parker. 1991. *Alive and Well? A Research and Policy Review of Health Programs for Poor Young Children.* New York: National Center for Children in Poverty.

Kluegel, James R., and Eliot R. Smith. 1986. *Beliefs about Inequality: Americans' Views of What Is and What Ought to Be.* New York: Aldine de Gruyter.

Kollman, Geoffrey. 1995. "Social Security: The Relationship of Taxes and Benefits for Past, Present and Future Retirees." *CRS Report for Congress.* Washington, DC: Library of Congress, Congressional Research Service, January 9.

Kontos, Susan, et al. 1995. *Quality in Family Child Care and Relative Care.* New York: Teachers College Press.

Korenman, Sanders, and Jane E. Miller. 1997. "Effects of Long-Term Poverty on Physical Health of Children in the National Longitudinal Survey of Youth." *Consequences of Growing Up Poor.* Edited by Greg J. Duncan and Jeanne Brooks-Gunn. New York: Russell Sage Foundation, Pp. 70–99.

Korpi, Walter. 2003. "Welfare-State Regress in Western Europe: Politics, Institutions, Globilization, and Europeanization." *Annual Review of Sociology* 29: 589–609.

Kozol, Jonathan. 1988. *Rachel and Her Children: Homeless Families in America.* New York: Fawcett Columbine.

———. 1991. *Savage Inequalities: Children in America's Schools.* New York: Crown.

Krueger, Alan B. 2002. "Economic Scene; The Apple Falls Close to the Tree, Even in the Land of Opportunity." *New York Times,* November 14, Section C, p. 2.

Krugman, Paul. 2002. "For Richer." *New York Times,* October 20. Section 6, p. 62.

Land, Kenneth C., David Cantor, and Stephen T. Russell. 1995. "Unemployment and Crime Rate Fluctuations in the Post-World War II United States." *Crime and Inequality.* Edited by John Hagan and Ruth D. Peterson. Stanford, CA: Stanford University Press. Pp. 55–79.

Lang, Kevin, and Shulamit Kahn. 1998. "The Effect of Minimum-Wage Laws on the Distribution of Employment: Theory and Evidence." *Journal of Public Economics* 69: 67–82.

Lee, Jung Sun, and Edward A. Frongillo, Jr. 2001. "Nutritional and Health Consequences Are Associated with Food Insecurity among U.S. Elderly Persons." *Journal of Nutrition* 131: 1503–1509.

Lee, Ronald, and John Haaga. 2002. "Government Spending in an Older America." *Population Reference Bureau Reports on America* 3: 1–16.

Leidenfrost, Nancy B. 1993. "An Examination of the Impact of Poverty on Health." Report prepared for the Extension Service, U.S. Department of Agriculture.

Leidenfrost, Nancy B., and Jennifer L. Wilkins. 1994. *Food Security in the United States: A Guidebook for Public Issues Education.* Cooperative Extension System. United States Department of Agriculture, Washington, DC.

Leisering, Lutz, and Stephan Leibfried. 1999. *Time and Poverty in Western Welfare States: United Germany in Perspective.* Cambridge, UK: Cambridge University Press.

Lemann, Nicholas. 1988. "The Unfinished War—Parts I and II." *Atlantic Monthly,* December, pp. 37–56, and January 1989, pp. 53–68.

Levin-Waldman, Oren M. 2000. "The Minimum Wage Can Be Raised: Lessons from the 1999 Levy Institute Survey of Small Business." *Challenge* (January–February): 86–96.

———. 2001. *The Case of the Minimum Wage: Competing Policy Models.* Albany: State University of New York Press.

Levin-Waldman, Oren M., and George W. McCarthy. 1998. "Small Business and the Minimum Wage." *Policy Note 3.* Jerome Levy Economics Institute.

Lewin, Tamar. 2001. "Program Finds Success in Reducing Teenage Pregnancies." *New York Times,* May 30, Section A, p. 16.

Lichter, Daniel T., and Martha L. Crowley. 2002. "Poverty in America: Beyond Welfare Reform." *Population Bulletin* 57: 1–36.

Lieberson, Stanley. 1994. "Understanding Ascriptive Stratification: Some Issues and Principles." *Social Stratification: Class, Race, and Gender in Sociological Perspective.* Edited by David B. Grusky. Boulder, CO: Westview Press. Pp. 649–658.

Liebman, Jeffrey B. 2002. "The Optimal Design of the Earned Income Tax Credit." *Making Work Pay: The Earned Income Tax Credit and Its Impact on America's Families.* Edited by Bruce D. Meyer and Douglas Holtz-Eakin. New York: Russell Sage Foundation. Pp. 196–234.

Lipman, Barbara J. 2001. "Paycheck to Paycheck: Working Families and the Cost of Housing in America." *New Century Housing* 2: 1–52.

Lipset, Seymour Martin. 1996. *American Exceptionalism: A Double-Edged Sword.* New York: Norton.

Loeb, Paul Rogat. 1999. *Soul of a Citizen: Living with Conviction in a Cynical Time.* New York: St. Martin's Griffen.

Low, Setha. 2003. *Behind the Gates: Life, Security, and the Pursuit of Happiness in Fortress America.* New York: Routledge.

Luxembourg Income Study. 2000. *LIS Quick Reference Guide.* Syracuse,

NY: Maxwell School of Citizenship and Public Affairs, Syracuse University.

MacLeod, Darrel Montero, and Alan Speer. 1999. "America's Changing Attitudes toward Welfare and Welfare Recipients, 1938–1995." *Journal of Sociology and Social Welfare* 26: 175–186.

McCloskey, Herbert, and John Zaller. 1984. *The American Ethos: Public Attitudes toward Capitalism and Democracy*. Cambridge, MA: Harvard University Press.

McCord, Collin, and Harold P. Freeman. 1990. "Excess Mortality in Harlem." *New England Journal of Medicine* 322 (Jan 18): 173–177.

McCormick, Marie C., et al. 1992. "The Health and Developmental Status of Very-Low-Birth-Weight Children at School Age." *Journal of the American Medical Association* 267 (April 22–29): 2204–2208.

McDonough, William J. 2002. "Remarks by William J. McDonough, President and Chief Executive Officer, Federal Reserve Bank of New York." Service at Trinity Church, September 11 Commemoration, New York City, September 11.

McGovern, George. 2001. *The Third Freedom: Ending Hunger in Our Time*. New York: Simon and Schuster.

McLanahan, Sara. 2002. "Life without Father: What Happens to the Children." *Contexts* 1: 35–44.

McLanahan, Sara, and Gary Sandefur. 1994. *Growing Up with a Single Parent: What Hurts, What Helps*. Cambridge, MA: Harvard University Press.

McLanahan, Sara, Annemette Sorensen, and Dorothy Watson. 1989. "Sex Differences in Poverty: 1950–1980." *Signs* 15: 102–122.

McLaughlin, Diane K., and Leif Jensen. 1993. "Poverty among Older Americans: The Plight of Nonmetropolitan Elders." *Journal of Gerontology: Social Sciences* 48: S44–S54.

McLaughlin, Diane K., and Karen C. Holden. 1993. "Nonmetropolitan Elderly Women: A Portrait of Economic Vulnerability." *Journal of Applied Gerontology* 12: 320–334.

McLeod, Jane D., and Michael J. Shanahan. 1993. "Poverty, Parenting, and Children's Mental Health." *American Sociological Review* 58: 351–366.

McMurrer, Daniel P., and Isabel V. Sawhill. 1997. "The Declining Importance of Class." *Opportunity in America*, Urban Institute Series, No. 4, April.

———. 1998. *Getting Ahead: Economic and Social Mobility in America.* Washington, DC: Urban Institute Press.

Madrick, Jeff. 2003. "Economic Sense; Looking Beyond Free Trade as a Solution to Helping the Developing World." *New York Times,* June 12, Section C, p. 2.

Maguire, Kathleen, and Ann L. Pastore. 2001. *Sourcebook of Criminal Justice Statistics 2000.* Washington, DC: U.S. Government Printing Office.

Mann, Cindy, et al. 2002. "Reaching Uninsured Children through Medicaid: If You Build It Right They Will Come." Kaiser Commission on Medicaid and the Uninsured, June.

March of Dimes. 2002. www.modimes.org/health library.

Maril, Robert Lee. 2000. *Waltzing with the Ghost of Tom Joad: Poverty, Myth, and Low-Wage Labor in Oklahoma.* Norman: University of Oklahoma Press.

Martinez, Ramiro, Jr. 1996. "Latinos and Lethal Violence: The Impact of Poverty and Inequality." *Social Problems* 43: 131–145.

Massey, Douglas S. 1996. "The Age of Extremes: Concentrated Affluence and Poverty in the Twenty-First Century." *Demography* 33: 395–412.

Massey, Douglas S., and Nancy A. Denton. 1993. *American Apartheid: Segregation and the Making of the Underclass.* Cambridge, MA: Harvard University Press.

May, Larry. 1992. *Sharing Responsibility.* Chicago: University of Chicago Press.

———. 1996. *The Socially Responsive Self: Social Theory and Professional Ethics.* Chicago: University of Chicago Press.

Mayer, Karl Ulrich, and Nancy B. Tuma. 1990. "Life Course Research and Event History Analysis: An Overview." *Event History Analysis in Life Course Research.* Edited by Karl Ulrich Mayer and Nancy B. Tuma. Madison: University of Wisconsin Press. Pp. 3–20.

Mayer, Susan E. 1995. "A Comparison of Poverty and Living Conditions in the United States, Canada, Sweden, and Germany." *Poverty, Inequality and the Future of Social Policy: Western States in the New World Order.* Edited by Katherine McFate, Roger Lawson, and William Julius Wilson. New York: Russell Sage Foundation. Pp. 109–151.

———. 1997. *What Money Can't Buy: Family Income and Children's Life Chances.* Cambridge, MA: Harvard University Press.

Maynard, Rebecca A. 1997. *Kids Having Kids: Economic Costs and Social Consequences of Teen Pregnancy*. Washington, DC: Urban Institute Press.

Mazumder, Bhashkar. 2001. "Earnings Mobility in the U.S.: A New Look at Intergenerational Inequality." *Federal Reserve Board of Chicago Working Paper*, WP2001–18.

Mead, Lawrence. 1986. *Beyond Entitlement: The Social Obligations of Citizenship*. New York: Free Press.

————. 1992. *The New Politics of Poverty: The Nonworking Poor in America*. New York: Basic Books.

Meeks, M. Douglas. 1989. *God the Economist: The Doctrine of God and Political Economy*. Minneapolis, MN: Fortress Press.

Meeks, Wayne A. 1993. "Introduction to the HarperCollins Study Bible." In *The HarperCollins Study Bible: New Revised Standard Version*. New York: HarperCollins. Pp. xvii–xxiv.

Merton, Robert. 1938. "Social Structure and Anomie." *American Sociological Review* 3: 672–682.

Mettler, Suzanne. 2002. "Bringing the State Back into Civic Engagement." *American Political Science Review* 96: 351–365.

Meyer, Bruce D., and Douglas Holtz-Eakin. 2002. *Making Work Pay: The Earned Income Tax Credit and Its Impact on America's Families*. New York: Russell Sage Foundation.

Meyers, Marcia K., Theresa Hintze, and Douglas A. Wolf. 2002. "Child Care Subsidies and the Employment of Welfare Recipients." *Demography* 39: 165–179.

Mill, John Stuart. 1848. *Principles of Political Economy with Some of Their Applications to Social Philosophy*. Boston, MA: Little and J. Brown.

Millennial Housing Commission. 2002. *Meeting Our Nation's Housing Challenges*. Washington, DC: Bipartisan Millennial Housing Commission.

Mills, C. Wright. 1959. *The Sociological Imagination*. New York: Oxford University Press.

Millsap, Mary Ann, Marc Moss, and Beth Gamse. 1993. *The Chapter 1 Implementation Study: Final Report*. Washington, DC: U.S. Department of Education, Office of Policy and Planning.

Minarik, Joseph. 1975. "New Evidence on the Poverty Count." In American Statistical Association, *Proceedings of the Social Statistics Section* (1975): 544–559.

Minsky, Hyman P. 1986. *Stabilizing an Unstable Economy.* New Haven, CT: Yale University Press.

Mitchell, Lawrence E. 1998. *Stacked Deck: A Story of Selfishness in America.* Philadelphia: Temple University Press.

Mithaug, Dennis E. 1996. *Equal Opportunity Theory.* Thousand Oaks, CA: Sage.

Moberg, David. 2000. "Martha Jernegons' New Shoes." *American Prospect* 11, no. 15 (June 19–July 3).

Moffitt, Robert. 1992. "Incentive Effects of the U.S. Welfare System: A Review." *Journal of Economic Literature* 30: 1–61.

Morris, Martina, and Bruce Western. 1999. "Inequality in Earnings at the Close of the Twentieth Century." *Annual Review of Sociology* 25: 623–657.

Moss, Philip, and Chris Tilly, 2001. *Stories Employers Tell: Race, Skill, and Hiring in America.* New York: Russell Sage Foundation.

Ms. Foundation for Women. 2002. "Economic Stimulus, Welfare, and Minimum Wage." Presentation on a Nationwide Survey of 800 Likely Voters, January 12–14.

Mullahy, John, and Barbara L. Wolfe. 2001. "Health Policies for the Non-elderly Poor." *Understanding Poverty.* Edited by Sheldon H. Danziger and Robert H. Haveman. New York: Russell Sage Foundation. Pp. 278–313.

Mulligan, Casey B. 1997. *Parental Priorities and Economic Inequality.* Chicago: University of Chicago Press.

Munger, Frank. 2002. *Laboring below the Line: The New Ethnography of Poverty, Low-Wage Work, and Survival in the Global Economy.* New York: Russell Sage Foundation.

Murray, Charles. 1984. *Losing Ground: American Social Policy 1950–1980.* New York: Basic Books.

———. 1993. "Society Cannot Tolerate Illegitimacy." *St. Louis Post-Dispatch,* December 20, Section B, p. 7.

Namboodiri, Krishnan, and C. M. Suchindran. 1987. "Life Table Techniques and Their Applications." Orlando, FL: Academic Press.

National Campaign to Prevent Teen Pregnancy. 2001. *With One Voice: America's Adults and Teens Sound Off about Teen Pregnancy: A*

National Survey. Washington, DC: National Campaign to Prevent Teen Pregnancy.

National Center for Employee Ownership. 2002. "A Comprehensive Overview of Employee Ownership." National Center for Employee Ownership, www.nceo.org.

National Center for Health Statistics. 1997. "Report of Final Mortality Statistics, 1995." *Monthy Vital Statistics Report* 45: 1–80.

National Conference of Catholic Bishops. 1986. *Economic Justice for All: Pastoral Letter on Catholic Social Teaching and the U.S. Economy.* Washington, DC: United States Catholic Conference.

National Low Income Housing Coalition. 2003. *Out of Reach 2003: America's Housing Wage Climbs.* Washington, DC: National Low Income Housing Coalition.

National Research Council. 1993. *Losing Generations: Adolescents in High-Risk Settings.* Washington, DC: National Academy Press.

————. 1995. *Measuring Poverty: A New Approach.* Washington, DC: National Academy Press.

Needleman, Herbert K. 1994. "The Current Status of Childhood Lead Toxicity." *Advances in Pediatrics* 40: 125–139.

Needleman, Herbert L., et al. 2002. "Bone Lead Levels in Adjudicated Delinquents: A Case Control Study." *Neurotoxicology and Teratology* 24: 711–717.

New Revised Standard Version Bible. 1993. *The HarperCollins Study Bible.* New York: HarperCollins.

Newman, Katherine. 1999. *No Shame in My Game: The Working Poor in the Inner City.* New York: Knopf.

NPR/Kaiser Family Foundation/Kennedy School of Government. 2001. "National Survey on Poverty in America." April. Menlo Park, CA: Henry J. Kaiser Family Foundation.

Noble, Charles. 1997. *Welfare as We Knew It: A Political History of the American Welfare State.* New York: Oxford University Press.

Nord, Mark, et al. 2003. "Household Food Security in the United States, 2002." Food Assistance and Nutrition Research Report No. 35. Washington, DC: U.S. Department of Agriculture.

Nussbaum, Martha C. 1995. *Poetic Justice: The Literary Imagination and Public Life.* Boston: Beacon Press.

O'Connor, Alice. 2001. *Poverty Knowledge: Social Science, Social Policy, and the Poor in Twentieth-Century U.S. History*. Princeton, NJ: Princeton University Press.

O'Hare, William P., et al. 1990. *Real Life Poverty in America: Where the American Public Would Set the Poverty Line*. Washington, DC: Center on Budget and Policy Priorities and the Families USA Foundation.

Olasky, Marvin. 1992. *The Tragedy of American Compassion*. Washington, DC: Regnery.

Oliver, Melvin L., and Thomas M. Shapiro. 1990. "Wealth of a Nation: A Reassessment of Asset Inequality in America Shows at Least One-Third of Households Are Asset Poor." *American Journal of Economics and Sociology* 49: 129–151.

———. 1995. *Black Wealth/White Wealth: A New Perspective on Racial Inequality*. New York: Routledge.

Olson, Erik J. 1994. "No Room at the Inn: A Snapshot of an American Emergency Room." *Stanford Law Review* 46: 449–501.

Olson, Mancur, Jr. 1965. *The Logic of Collective Action: Public Goods and the Theory of Groups*. Cambridge, MA: Harvard University Press.

Orfield, Gary. 1993. *The Growth of Segregation in American Schools: Changing Patterns of Separation and Poverty since 1968*. Alexandria, VA: National School Boards Association.

Orfield, Gary, and Nora Gordon. 2001. *Schools More Separate: Consequences of a Decade of Resegregation*. Cambridge, MA: Harvard Civil Rights Project.

Orfield, Gary, and John T. Yun. 1999. *Resegregation in American Schools*. Cambridge, MA: Harvard Civil Rights Project.

Organization for Economic Cooperation and Development. 1999. *Social Expenditure Database 1980–1996*. Paris: Organization for Economic Cooperation and Development.

Orshansky, Mollie. 1965. "Counting the Poor: Another Look at the Poverty Profile." *Social Security Bulletin* 28: 3–29.

Oyen, Else, S. M. Miller, and Syed Abdus Samad. 1996. *Poverty: A Global Review*. Oslo: Scandinavian University Press.

Ozawa, Martha N., and Rebecca Y. Kim. 1998. "The Declining Economic Fortunes of Children in Comparison to Adults and Elderly People." *Social Work Research* 22: 14–30.

Panel Study of Income Dynamics. 2003. *On-line User's Guide*. Ann Arbor: University of Michigan.

Pappas, Gregory, et al. 1993. "The Increasing Disparity in Mortality between Socioeconomic Groups in the United States, 1960 and 1986." *New England Journal of Medicine* 329: 103–115.

Parker, Robert Nash. 1989. "Poverty, Subculture of Violence, and Type of Homicide." *Social Forces* 67: 983–1007.

Patterson, James T. 2000. *America's Struggle against Poverty in the Twentieth Century.* Cambridge, MA: Harvard University Press.

Pear, Robert. 1995. "House Backs Bill Undoing Decades of Welfare Policy." *New York Times*, March 25, Section A, p. 1.

Pearce, Diana. 1978. "The Feminization of Poverty: Women, Work and Welfare." *Urban and Social Change Review* 3: 1–4.

Pearce, Diana, and Jennifer Brooks. 2002. "The Self-Sufficiency Standard for Missouri." Prepared for the Friends of the Missouri Women's Council, November.

Perlin S. A., D. Wong, and K. Sexton. 2001. "Residential Proximity to Industrial Sources of Air Pollution: Interrelationships among Race, Poverty, and Age." *Journal of the Air and Waste Management Association* 51: 406–421.

Phillips, Meredith, and Tiffani Chin. 2003. "School Inequality: What Do We Know?" Paper prepared for the Russell Sage Foundation's Social Dimensions of Inequality Program, Russell Sage Foundation, New York.

Physicians' Working Group for Single-Payer National Health Insurance. 2003. "Proposal of the Physicians' Working Group for Single-Payer National Health Insurance." *Journal of the American Medical Association* 290: 798–805.

Pickering, George W. 1988. "Social Ethics in the American Context." *Issues of Justice: Social Sources and Religious Meanings.* Edited by Roger D. Hatch and Warren R. Copeland. Macon, GA: Mercer University Press. Pp. 29–56.

Picketty, Thomas, and Emmanuel Saez. 2001. "Income Inequality in the United States, 1913–1998." National Bureau of Economic Research, Working Paper 8467, Cambridge, MA.

———. 2003. "Income Inequality in the United States, 1913–1998." *Quarterly Journal of Economics* 118: 1–39.

Planned Parenthood Federation of America. 2002. "Reducing Teenage Pregnancy." Fact Sheet.

Platt, Suzy. 1989. *Respectfully Quoted: A Dictionary of Quotations Requested from the Congressional Research Service.* Washington, DC: U.S. Library of Congress.

Pollin, Robert. 2001. "Time for a Living Wage: Interview with Robert Pollin." *Challenge* 44: 6–18.

Pollin, Robert, and Stephanie Luce. 1998. *The Living Wage: Building a Fair Economy.* New York: New Press.

Poppendieck, Janet. 1997. "The USA: Hunger in the Land of Plenty." *First World Hunger: Food Security and Welfare Politics.* Edited by Graham Riches. New York: St. Martin's. Pp. 134–164.

———. 1998. *Sweet Charity?: Emergency Food and the End of Entitlement.* New York: Viking.

President's Commission on Law Enforcement and Administration of Justice. 1967. *The Challenge of Crime in a Free Society: A Report by the President's Commission on Law Enforcement and Administration of Justice.* Washington, DC: U.S. Government Printing Office.

Preston, Samuel H. 1984. "Children and the Elderly: Divergent Paths for America's Dependents." *Demography* 21: 435–457.

Pugh, Margaret. 1998. *Barriers to Work: Spatial Divide between Jobs and Welfare Recipients in Metropolitan Areas.* Washington, DC: Center on Urban and Metropolitan Policy, Brookings Institution.

Putnam, Robert D. 2000. *Bowling Alone: The Collapse and Revival of American Community.* New York: Simon and Schuster.

Quadagno, Jill. 1994. *The Color of Welfare: How Racism Undermined the War on Poverty.* New York: Oxford University Press.

Rainwater, Lee, and Timothy M. Smeeding. 1995. "Doing Poorly: The Real Income of American Children in a Comparative Perspective." *Luxembourg Income Study Working Paper Series*, No. 127, Maxwell School of Citizenship and Public Affairs, Syracuse University, Syracuse, New York.

———. 2003. *Poor Kids in a Rich Country: America's Children in Comparative Perspective.* New York: Russell Sage Foundation.

Rank, Mark R. 1988. "Racial Differences in Length of Welfare Use." *Social Forces* 66: 1080–1101.

———. 1989. "Fertility among Women on Welfare: Incidence and Determinants." *American Sociological Review* 54: 296–304.

———. 1994. *Living on the Edge: The Realities of Welfare in America.* New York: Columbia University Press.

————. 1997. "The Ties That Bind: Rebuilding Our Social Obligations to the Economically Vulnerable." Paper presented at the International Conference on Socio-Economics, Montreal, Canada, July 5–7.

————. 2000. "Socialization of Socioeconomic Status." *Handbook of Family Development and Intervention*. Edited by William C. Nichols, Mary Anne Pace-Nichols, Dorothy S. Becvar, and Augustus Y. Napier. New York: Wiley. Pp. 129–142.

————. 2001. "The Effect of Poverty on America's Families: Assessing our Research Knowledge." *Journal of Family Issues* 22: 882–903.

Rank, Mark R., and Li-Chen Cheng. 1995. "Welfare Use across Generations: How Important Are the Ties That Bind?" *Journal of Marriage and the Family* 57: 673–684.

Rank, Mark R., and Thomas A. Hirschl. 1999a. "The Likelihood of Poverty across the American Adult Life Span." *Social Work* 44: 201–216.

————. 1999b. "Estimating the Proportion of Americans Ever Experiencing Poverty during their Elderly Years." *Journal of Gerontology: Social Sciences* 54B: S184–S193.

————. 1999c. "The Economic Risk of Childhood in America: Estimating the Probability of Poverty across the Formative Years." *Journal of Marriage and the Family* 61: 1058–1067.

————. 2001a. "The Occurrence of Poverty across the Life Cycle: Evidence from the PSID." *Journal of Policy Analysis and Management* 20: 737–755.

————. 2001b. "Rags or Riches? Estimating the Probabilities of Poverty and Affluence across the Adult American Life Span." *Social Science Quarterly* 82: 651–669.

————. 2001c. "The Measurement of Long Term Risks across the Life Course." *Social Science Quarterly* 82: 680–686.

————. 2002. "Welfare Use as a Life Course Event: Toward a New Understanding of the U.S. Safety Net." *Social Work* 47: 237–248.

Raphael, Steven, and Michael Stoll. 2000. "Can Boosting Car Ownership Rates Narrow Inter-Racial Employment Gaps?" Paper presented at the Center on Urban and Metropolitan Policy, Brookings Institution, Washington, DC, July.

Rawls, John. 1971. *A Theory of Justice*. Cambridge, MA: Harvard University Press.

———. 1993. *Political Liberalism*. New York: Columbia University Press.

———. 2001. *Justice as Fairness: A Restatement*. Cambridge, MA: Harvard University Press.

Rector, Robert, and William Lauber. 1995. *America's Failed $5.4 Trillion War on Poverty*. Washington, DC: Heritage Foundation.

Reich, Robert B. 1992. *The Work of Nations*. New York: Vintage.

———. 2002. *I'll Be Short: Essentials for a Decent Working Society*. Boston: Beacon Press.

Reid, L. L. 2000. "The Consequences of Food Insecurity for Child Well-Being: An Analysis of Children's School Achievement, Psychological Well-Being, and Health." JCPR Working Paper No. 137, Joint Center for Poverty Research, Northwestern University/University of Chicago.

Reiman, Jeffrey. 2001. *The Rich Get Richer and the Poor Get Prison: Ideology, Class, and Criminal Justice*. Boston: Allyn and Bacon.

Reiss, Albert J., Jr., and Jeffrey A. Roth. 1993. *Understanding and Preventing Violence*. Washington, DC: National Academy Press.

Richardson, Jeanita A. 2002. "Poor, Powerless and Poisoned: The Social Injustice of Childhood Lead Poisoning." *Journal of Children and Poverty* 8: 141–157.

Riis, Jacob A. 1957. *How the Other Half Lives: Studies among the Tenements of New York*. New York: Hill and Wang. Originally published 1890.

———. 1970. *The Making of an American*. London: MacMillan. Originally published 1901.

Ritakallio, Veli-Matti. 2001. "Trends of Poverty and Income Inequality in Cross-National Comparison." *Luxembourg Income Study Working Paper*, No. 272, Maxwell School of Citizenship and Public Affairs, Syracuse University, Syracuse, New York.

Rodgers, Joan R. 1995. "An Empirical Study of Intergenerational Transmission of Poverty in the United States." *Social Science Quarterly* 76: 178–194.

Rogowski, Jeannette. 1999. "Measuring the Cost of Neonatal and Perinatal Care." *Pediatrics* 103: 329–335.

Romich, Jennifer L., and Thomas S. Weisner. 2002. "How Families View and Use the Earned Income Tax Credit: Advanced Payment Versus Lump-Sum Delivery." *Making Work Pay: The Earned Income*

Tax Credit and Its Impact on America's Families. Edited by Bruce D. Meyer and Douglass Holtz-Eakin. New York: Russell Sage Foundation, Pp. 366–392.

Rorty, Richard. 1999. "Looking Backward from the Year 2096." *Philosophy and Social Hope.* New York: Penguin. Pp. 243–251.

Rosenfeld, Richard, 2002. "Crime Decline in Context." *Contexts* 1: 25–34.

Rothman, Nancy L., Rita J. Lourie, and John Gaughan. 2002. "Lead Awareness: North Philly Style." *American Journal of Public Health* 92: 739–741.

Rothman, Richard. 2000. "Equalizing Education Resources on Behalf of Disadvantaged Children." *A Notion at Risk: Preserving Public Education as an Engine for Social Mobility.* Edited by Richard D. Kahlenberg. New York: Century Foundation Press. Pp. 31–92.

Rowntree, B. Seebohm. 1901. *Poverty: A Study of Town Life.* London: Macmillan.

Rubin, Lillian B. 1992. *Worlds of Pain: Life in the Working-Class Family.* New York: Basic Books.

———. 1994. *Families on the Faultline: America's Working Class Speaks about the Family, the Economy, Race, and Ethnicity.* New York: HarperCollins.

Ruggles, Patricia. 1990. *Drawing the Line: Alternative Poverty Measures and Their Implications for Public Policy.* Washington, DC: Urban Institute Press.

———. 1992. "Measuring Poverty." *Focus* 14: 1–9.

Rusk, David. 2002. "Trends in School Segregation." Background Paper for the Report of the Century Foundation Task Force on the Common School, *Divided We Fail: Coming Together Through Public School Choice.* New York: Century Foundation Press.

Sampson, Robert J., and William Julius Wilson. 1995. "Toward a Theory of Race, Crime and Urban Inequality." *Crime and Inequality.* Edited by John Hagen and Ruth D. Peterson. Stanford, CA: Stanford University Press. Pp. 37–54.

Sanchez, Thomas W., Robert E. Long, and Dawn Phavale. 2003. "Security versus Status: First Look at AHS's Gated Community Data." Paper presented at the Fannie Mae Foundation Research Seminar Series, June 20.

Sandefur, Gary D., and Steven T. Cook. 1998. "Permanent Exits from

Public Assistance: The Impact of Duration, Family, and Work."
Social Forces 77: 763–786.

Schemo, Diana Jean. 2002. "Neediest Schools Receive Less Money,
Report Finds." *New York Times*, August 9, Section A, p. 10.

Schiller, Bradley R. 2004. *The Economics of Poverty and Discrimination*.
Upper Saddle River, NJ: Prentice Hall.

Schreiner, Mark, Margaret Clancy, and Michael Sherraden. 2002. *Saving
Performance in the American Dream Demonstration: A National
Demonstration of Individual Development Accounts*. Center for Social
Development, Washington University, St. Louis, Missouri.

Schwartz, Joel. 2000. *Fighting Poverty with Virtue: Moral Reform and
America's Urban Poor, 1825–2000*. Bloomington: Indiana University
Press.

Schwartz-Nobel, Loretta. 2002. *Growing Up Empty: The Hunger Epidemic
in America*. New York: HarperCollins.

Seccombe, Karen. 1999. *So You Think I Drive a Cadillac? Welfare Recipients' Perspectives on the System and Its Reform*. Needham Heights, MA:
Allyn and Bacon.

———. 2000. "Families in Poverty in the 1990s: Trends, Causes, Consequences, and Lessons Learned." *Journal of Marriage and the Family*
62: 1094–1113.

Sedlak, Andrea J., and Diane D. Broadhurst. 1996. *Third National Incidence Study of Child Abuse and Neglect: Final Report*. Washington, DC:
U.S. Department of Health and Human Services.

Seidman, Laurence S. 2001. "Assets and the Tax Code." *Assets for the Poor:
The Benefits of Spreading Asset Ownership*. Edited by Thomas M.
Shapiro and Edward N. Wolff. New York: Russell Sage Foundation.
Pp. 324–356.

Sen, Amartya. 1992. *Inequality Reexamined*. New York: Russell Sage
Foundation.

———. 1997. *On Economic Inequality*. Oxford, UK: Clarendon Press.

———. 1999. *Development as Freedom*. New York: Knopf.

Settersten, Richard A., and Karl Ulrich Mayer. 1997. "The Measurement
of Age, Age Structuring, and the Life Course." *Annual Review of
Sociology* 23: 233–261.

Shah-Canning, D., J. J. Alpert, and H. Bauchner. 1996. "Care-Seeking

Patterns of Inner-City Family Using an Emergency Room: A Three-Decade Comparison." *Medical Care* 34: 1171–1179.

Shank, Harold. 1995. "A Challenge to Suburban Evangelical Churches: Theological Perspectives on Poverty in America." *Journal of Interdisciplinary Studies* 7: 119–134.

Shapiro, Thomas M. 2001. "The Importance of Assets." *Assets for the Poor: The Benefits of Spreading Asset Ownership.* Edited by Thomas M. Shapiro and Edward N. Wolff. New York: Russell Sage Foundation. Pp. 11–33.

———. 2004. *The Hidden Cost of Being African American: How Wealth Perpetuates Inequality.* New York: Oxford University Press.

Shapiro, Thomas M., and Heather Beth Johnson. 2000. "Assets, Race, and Educational Choices." Center for Social Development Working Paper, No. 00-7, Washington University, St. Louis, MO.

Shapiro, Thomas M., and Edward N. Wolff. 2001. *Assets for the Poor: The Benefits of Spreading Asset Ownership.* New York: Russell Sage Foundation.

Sherman, Arloc. 1994. *Wasting America's Future: The Children's Defense Fund Report on the Costs of Child Poverty.* Boston: Beacon Press.

Sherraden, Michael. 1991. *Assets and the Poor: A New American Welfare Policy.* Armonk, NY: M. E. Sharpe.

———. 2000. "From Research to Policy: Lessons from Individual Development Accounts. *Journal of Consumer Affairs* 34: 159–181.

———. 2001. "Asset-Building Policy and Programs for the Poor." *Assets for the Poor: The Benefits of Spreading Asset Ownership.* Edited by Thomas M. Shapiro and Edward N. Wolff. New York: Russell Sage Foundation. Pp. 302–323.

Shirk, Martha, Neil G. Bennett, and J. Lawrence Aber. 1999. *Lives on the Line: American Families and the Struggle to Make Ends Meet.* Boulder, CO: Westview Press.

Shklar, Judith N. 1991. *American Citizenship: The Quest for Inclusion.* Cambridge, MA: Harvard University Press.

Short, James F., Jr. 1997. *Poverty, Ethnicity, and Violent Crime.* Boulder, CO: Westview Press.

Shryer, Tracy. 1994. "19 Children Found Living in Roach-Infested Apartment." *Los Angeles Times.* February 3, Section A, p. 10.

Sidel, Ruth. 1996. *Keeping Women and Children Last: America's War on the Poor*. New York: Penguin.

Simon, Thomas W. 1995. *Democracy and Social Injustice: Law, Politics, and Philosophy*. Lanham, MD: Rowman and Littlefield.

Sirianni, Carmen, and Lewis Friedland. 2001. *Civic Innovation in America: Community Empowerment, Public Policy, and the Movement for Civic Renewal*. Berkeley: University of California Press.

Sklar, Holly. 1995. *Chaos or Community? Seeking Solutions, Not Scapegoats for Bad Economics*. Boston: South End Press.

Skogan, Wesley. 1990. *Disorder and Decline: Crime and the Spiral of Decay in American Neighborhoods*. New York: Free Press.

Skogan, Wesley, and Michael G. Maxfield. 1981. *Coping with Crime: Individual and Neighborhood Reactions*. Beverly Hills, CA: Sage.

Small, Mario Luis, and Katherine Newman. 2001. "Urban Poverty after *The Truly Disadvantaged*: The Rediscovery of the Family, the Neighborhood, and Culture." *Annual Review of Sociology* 27: 23–45.

Smeeding, Timothy M. 1997a. "Financial Poverty in Developed Countries: The Evidence from LIS. Final Report to the United Nations Development Programme." *Luxembourg Income Study Working Paper Series*, No. 155, Maxwell School of Citizenship and Public Affairs, Syracuse University, Syracuse, New York.

———. 1997b. "American Income Inequality in a Cross-National Perspective: Why Are We So Different?" *Luxembourg Income Study Working Paper Series*, No. 157, Maxwell School of Citizenship and Public Affairs, Syracuse University, Syracuse, New York.

———. 2000. "Changing Income Inequality in OECD Countries: Updated Results from the Luxembourg Income Study (LIS)." *Luxembourg Income Study Working Paper Series*, No. 252, Maxwell School of Citizenship and Public Affairs, Syracuse University, Syracuse, New York.

———. 2002a. "Real Standards of Living and Public Suport for Children: A Cross-National Comparison." *Luxembourg Income Study Working Paper Series*, No. 345, Maxwell School of Citizenship and Public Affairs, Syracuse University, Syracuse, New York.

———. 2002b. "The LIS/LES Project: Overview and Recent Development." *Luxembourg Income Study Working Paper Series*, No. 294, Maxwell School of Citizenship and Public Affairs, Syracuse University, Syracuse, New York.

Smeeding, Timothy M., Katherin Ross Phillips, and Michael A. O'Connor. 2000. "The EITC: Expectation, Knowledge, Use, and Economic and Social Mobility." *National Tax Journal* 53: 1187–1209.

Smeeding, Timothy M., and Lee Rainwater. 2001. "Comparing Living Standards across Countries: Real Incomes at the Top, the Bottom, and the Middle." Paper presented at the conference, "What Has Happened to the Quality of Life in America and Other Advanced Nations?" Levy Institute, Bard College, Annandale-on Hudson, New York, June.

Smeeding, Timothy M., Lee Rainwater, and Gary Burtless. 2000. "United States Poverty in a Cross-National Context." *Luxembourg Income Study Working Paper Series*, No. 244, Maxwell School of Citizenship and Public Affairs, Syracuse University, Syracuse, New York.

———. 2001. "U.S. Poverty in a Cross-National Context." *Understanding Poverty*. Edited by Sheldon H. Danziger and Robert H. Haveman. Cambridge, MA: Harvard University Press. Pp. 162–189.

Smiley, Marion. 1992. *Moral Responsibility and the Boundaries of Community: Power and Accountability from a Pragmatic Point of View*. Chicago: University of Chicago Press.

Smith, Adam. 1776. *An Inquiry into the Nature and Causes of Wealth of Nations*. London: W. Strahan and T. Cadell.

———. 1976. *The Theory of Moral Sentiments*. Oxford, UK: Clarendon Press. Originally published in 1759.

Smith, Christopher E. 1991. *Courts and the Poor*. Chicago: Nelson-Hall.

Smith, James Allen. 1991. *The Idea Brokers: Think Tanks and the Rise of the New Policy Elite*. New York: Free Press.

Smith, Judith, R., Jeanne Brooks-Gunn, and Pamela K. Klebanov. 1997. "Consequences of Living in Poverty for Young Children's Cognitive and Verbal Ability and Early School Achievement." *Consequences of Growing Up Poor*. Edited by Greg J. Duncan and Jeanne Brooks-Gunn. New York: Russell Sage Foundation. Pp. 132–189.

Smith, Ken R., and Cathleen D. Zick. 1986. "The Incidence of Poverty among the Recently Widowed: Mediating Factors in the Life Course." *Journal of Marriage and the Family* 48: 619–630.

Smith, Kevin B., and Lorene H. Stone. 1989. "Rags, Riches, and Boot-straps: Beliefs about the Causes of Wealth and Poverty." *Sociological Quarterly* 30: 93–107.

Solon, Gary. 1989. "Intergenerational Income Mobility in the United States." *Institute for Research on Poverty Discussion Paper*, No. 894–89, University of Wisconsin-Madison.

———. 1992. "Intergenerational Income Mobility in the United States." *American Economic Review* 82: 393–408.

Solow, Robert. 2002. "Why Were the Nineties So Good? Could It Happen Again?" *Focus* 22: 1–7.

Sorenson, Elaine, and Ariel Halpern. 1999, "Child Support Enforcement: How Well Is It Doing?" *Urban Institute Discussion Paper*, No. 99-11, Urban Institute, Washington, DC.

Stefanic, Jean, and Richard Delgado. 1996. *No Mercy: How Conservative Think Tanks and Foundations Changed America's Social Agenda.* Philadelphia: Temple University Press.

Stevens, Ann Huff. 1994. "The Dynamics of Poverty Spells: Updating Bane and Ellwood." *American Economic Review* 84: 34–37.

———. 1999. "Climbing out of Poverty, Falling Back in: Measuring the Persistence of Poverty over Multiple Spells." *Journal of Human Resources* 34: 557–588.

Sweet, James A., and Larry L. Bumpass. 1986. *American Families and Households.* New York: Russell Sage Foundation.

Sycheva, Valentina S. 1997. "Measuring the Poverty Level: A History of the Issue." *Sociological Research* 36: 45–59.

Teachman, Jay D., Lucky M. Tedrow, and Kyle D. Crowder. 2000. "The Changing Demography of America's Families." *Journal of Marriage and the Family* 62: 1234–1246.

Thompson, Tommy. 1996. *Power to the People: An American State at Work.* New York: HarperCollins.

Thurow, Lester C. 1996. *The Future of Capitalism: How Today's Economic Forces Shape Tomorrow's World.* New York: William Morrow.

Titmuss, Richard M. 1958. *Essays on "The Welfare State."* London: Allen and Unwin.

Tocqueville, Alexis de. 1983. "Memoir on Pauperism." *Public Interest* 70: 102–120.

———. 1994. *Democracy in America*, vol. 2. New York: Knopf. Originally published 1840.

Toner, Robin. 2002. "Rallies in Capital Protest Bush Welfare Proposals." *New York Times*, March 6, Section A, p. 17.

Tonry, Michael. 1995. *Malign Neglect: Race, Crime, and Punishment in America*. New York: Oxford University Press.

Tropman, John E. 1998. *Does America Hate the Poor? The Other American Dilemma: Lessons for the 21st Century from the 1960s and the 1970s*. Westport, CT: Praeger.

Turk, Austin. 1969. *Criminality and the Legal Order*. Chicago: Rand McNally.

Tyler, Tom R., et al. 1997. *Social Justice in a Diverse Society*. Boulder, CO: Westview Press.

Unger, Irwin. 1996. *The Best of Intentions: The Triumphs and Failures of the Great Society under Kennedy, Johnson and Nixon*. New York: Doubleday.

United Church of Christ. 1989. *Christian Faith: Economic Life and Justice*. Cleveland, OH: Office for Church and Society.

United Kingdom Department of Social Security. 1999. *Opportunity for All: Tackling Poverty and Social Exclusion*. 1st Poverty Report, Cm. 4445. London: HMSO.

United Nations Development Programme. 2000. *UNDP Poverty Report 2000*. New York: United Nations Publications.

————. 2003. *Human Development Report 2003*. New York: Oxford University Press.

U.S. Bureau of the Census. 1992. "Studies in Household and Family Formation." Current Population Reports, Series P-23-179. Washington, DC: U.S. Government Printing Office.

————. 1996. "Who Stays Poor? Who Doesn't?" Current Population Reports, Series P70-55. Washington, DC: U.S. Government Printing Office.

————. 1998a. "Trap Door? Revolving Door? Or Both?" Current Population Reports, Series P60-201. Washington, DC: U.S. Government Printing Office.

————. 1998b. "Who Loses Coverage and for How Long?" Current Population Reports, Series P70-64. Washington, DC: U.S. Government Printing Office.

————. 1999a. "Experimental Poverty Measures: 1990 to 1997." Current Population Reports, Series P60-205. Washington, DC: U.S. Government Printing Office.

————. 1999b. "Dynamics of Economic Well-being: Program Participation, Who Gets Assistance?" Current Population Reports, Series P70-69. Washington, DC: U.S. Government Printing Office.

————. 2000. "Who's Minding the Kids? Child Care Arrangements." Current Population Reports, Series P70-70. Washington, DC: U.S. Government Printing Office.

————. 2001a. "Americans with Disabilities." Current Population Reports, Series P70-73. Washington, DC: U.S. Government Printing Office.

————. 2001b. "Did You Know? Homes Account for 44 Percent of All Wealth." Current Population Reports, Series P70-75. Washington, DC: U.S. Government Printing Office.

————. 2002a. "Poverty in the United States: 2001." Current Population Reports, Series P60-219. Washington, DC: U.S. Government Printing Office.

————. 2002b. "Money Income in the United States: 2001." Current Population Reports, Series P60-218. Washington, DC: U.S. Government Printing Office.

————. 2002c. "Health Insurance Coverage: 2001." Current Population Reports, Series P60-220. Washington, DC: U.S. Government Printing Office.

————. 2002d. *Statistical Abstract of the United States: 2002.* Washington, DC: U.S. Government Printing Office.

————. 2002e. "Who's Minding the Kids? Child Care Arrangements: Spring 1997." Current Population Reports, Series P70-86. Washington, DC: U.S. Government Printing Office.

————. 2002f. "Custodial Mothers and Fathers and Their Child Support: 1999." Current Population Reports, Series P60-217. Washington, DC: U.S. Government Printing Office.

————. 2002g. "Racial and Ethnic Residential Segregation in the United States: 1980–2000." CNESR-3. Washington, DC: U.S. Government Printing Office.

————. 2003a. "Poverty in the United States: 2002." Current Population Reports, Series P60-222. Washington, DC: U.S. Government Printing Office.

————. 2003b. "Money Income in the United States: 2002." Current Population Reports, Series P60–221. Washington, DC: U.S. Government Printing Office.

————. 2003c. "Dynamics of Economic Well-Being: Poverty 1996–1999." Current Population Reports, Series P70-91. Washington, DC: U.S. Government Printing Office.

————. 2003d. "Health Insurance Coverage in the United States: 2002." Current Population Reports, Series P60-223. Washington, DC: U.S. Government Printing Office.

U.S. Department of Health and Human Services. 2002. *Making a Difference in the Lives of Infants and Toddlers and Their Families: The Impacts of Early Head Start.* Princeton, NJ: Mathematica Policy Research.

U.S. Department of Justice. 1994. "The Costs of Crime to Victims." Bureau of Justice Statistics Crime Data Brief, February, NCJ-145865.

————. 2000. *Sourcebook Of Criminal Justice Statistics, 2000.* Bureau of Justice Statistics, NCJ 190251.

————. 2002. "Justice Expenditure and Employment in the United States, 1999." Bureau of Justice Statistics Bulletin, February, NCJ 191746.

————. 2003a. "Prisoners in 2002." Bureau of Justice Statistics Bulletin, July, NCJ 200248.

————. 2003b. "Probation and Parole in the United States, 2002." Bureau of Justice Statistics Bulletin, August, NCJ 2001135.

U.S. House of Representatives. *2000 Green Book: Overview of Entitlement Programs.* Washington, DC: U.S. Government Printing Office.

U.S. National Advisory Commission on Civil Disorders. 1968. *Report.* New York: Bantam Books.

U.S. Public Health Service. 1988. *Surgeon General's Report on Nutrition and Health.* Washington, DC: U.S. Government Printing Office.

Vallentryne, Peter. 2003. *Equality and Justice.* New York: Routledge.

Van Parijs, Philippe. 1995. *Real Freedom for All: What (If Anything) Can Justify Capitalism?* Oxford, UK: Clarendon Press.

Vartanian, Thomas P., and Justine M. McNamara. 2002. "Older Women in Poverty: The Impact of Midlife Factors." *Journal of Marriage and the Family* 64: 532–548.

Vaughan, Denton R. 1993. "Exploring the Use of the Public's Views to Set Income Poverty Thresholds and Adjust Them over Time." *Social Security Bulletin* 56: 22–46.

Ventry, Dennis J. 2002. "The Collision of Tax and Welfare Politics: The Political History of the Earned Income Tax Credits." *Making Work Pay: The Earned Income Tax Credit and Its Impact on American Families.* Edited by Bruce D. Meyer and Douglas Holtz-Eakin. New York: Russell Sage Foundation. Pp. 15–66.

Verba, Sidney. 2001. "Political Equality: What Is It? Why Do We Want It?" Paper prepared for the Russell Sage Foundation's Social Dimensions of Inequality Program.

Verba, Sidney, Kay Lehman Schlozman, and Henry Brady. 1995. *Voice and Equality: Civic Voluntarism in American Politics.* Cambridge, MA: Harvard University Press.

Von Hoffman, Alexander, 2003. *House by House: The Rebirth of America's Urban Neighborhoods.* New York: Oxford University Press.

Vosler, Nancy. 1996. *New Approaches to Family Practice: Confronting Economic Stress.* Thousand Oaks, CA: Sage.

Voydanoff, Patricia. 1990. Economic Distress and Family Relations: A Review of the Eighties." *Journal of Marriage and the Family* 52: 1099–1115.

Wachtel, Howard M. 1971. "Looking at Poverty from a Radical Perspective." *Review of Radical Political Economics* 3: 1–19.

Walker, Robert. 1994. *Poverty Dynamics: Issues and Examples.* Aldershot, UK: Avebury.

Walmsley, Roy. 2003. *World Prison Population List.* London: Home Office.

Walzer, Michael. 1990. "What Does It Mean to Be an 'American'?" *Social Research* 57: 591–614.

———. 1992. *What It Means to Be an American.* New York: Marsilio.

Warlick, Jennifer L. 1985. Why Is Poverty after 65 a Woman's Problem?" *Journal of Gerontology* 40: 751–757.

Warren, Christian. 2000. A Brush with Death: A Social History of Lead Poisoning. Baltimore, MD: Johns Hopkins University Press.

Warren, Mark R. 2001. *Dry Bones Rattling: Community Building to Revitalize American Democracy.* Princeton, NJ: Princeton University Press.

Wattles, Jeffrey. 1996. *The Golden Rule.* New York: Oxford University Press.

Weaver, R. Kent, Robert Y. Shapiro, and Lawrence R. Jacobs. 1995. "Trends: Welfare." *Public Opinion Quarterly* 59: 606–627.

Webster's Encyclopedic Unabridged Dictionary of the English Language. 1996. New York: Gramercy Books.

Weiner, Tim. 1999. "Public Lives; A Congressman's Lament on the State of Democracy." *New York Times,* October 4, Section A, p. 14.

Weinfeld, Moshe. 1995. *Social Justice in Ancient Israel and in the Ancient Near East.* Minneapolis, MN: Fortress Press.

Westat. 2001. *Survey of Income and Program Participation Users' Guide, Third Edition*. Rockville, MD: Westat.

Western, Bruce, and Katherine Beckett. 1999. "How Unregulated Is the U.S. Labor Market? The Penal System as a Labor Market Institution." *American Journal of Sociology* 104: 1030–1060.

Western, Bruce, Meredith Kleykamp, and Jake Rosenfeld. 2003. "Crime, Punishment, and American Inequality." Paper prepared for Russell Sage Foundation's Social Dimensions of Inequality Program.

White, Lynn, and Stacy J. Rogers. 2000. "Economic Circumstances and Family Outcomes: A Review of the 1990s." *Journal of Marriage and the Family* 62: 1035–1051.

Wilkinson, Richard G. 1996. *Unhealthy Societies: The Afflictions of Inequality*. London: Routledge.

Williams, David R., and Chiquita Collins. 1995. "U.S. Socioeconomic and Racial Differences in Health: Patterns and Explanations." *Annual Review of Sociology* 21: 349–386.

Williams, Kirk R. 1984. "Economic Sources of Homicide: Reestimating the Effects of Poverty and Inequality." *American Sociological Review* 49: 283–289.

Williams, Trina. 2000. "The Homestead Act: A Major Asset-Building Policy in American History." Working Paper 00-9, Center for Social Development, Washington University, St. Louis, MO.

Williamson, Thad, David Imbroscio, and Gar Alperovitz. 2002. *Making a Place for Community: Local Democracy in a Global Era*. New York: Routledge.

Willie, Charles, and Michael Alves. 1996. *Controlled Choice: A New Approach to School Desegregated Education and School Improvement*. Providence, RI: Education Alliance Press and the New England Desegregation Assistance Center, Brown University.

Wilson, William Julius. 1987. *The Truly Disadvantaged: The Inner City, the Underclass, and Public Policy*. Chicago: University of Chicago Press.

———. 1996. *When Work Disappears: The World of the New Urban Poor*. New York: Knopf.

Wisconsin Department of Revenue. 2003. "Homestead Credit." Madison: Wisconsin Department of Revenue.

Wolfe, Alan. 1989. *Whose Keeper? Social Science and Moral Obligation*. Berkeley: University of California Press.

————. 1998. *One Nation, After All.* New York: Viking.

Wolfe, Barbara L. 1994. "Reform of Health Care for the Nonelderly Poor." *Confronting Poverty: Prescriptions for Change.* Edited by Sheldon H. Danziger, Gary D. Sandefur, and Daniel H. Weinberg. Cambridge, MA: Harvard University Press. Pp. 253–288.

Wolff, Edward N. 1995. *Top Heavy: A Study of the Increasing Inequality of Wealth in America.* New York: Twentieth Century Fund Press.

————. 1998. "Recent Trends in the Size Distribution of Household Wealth." *Journal of Economic Perspectives* 12: 131–150.

————. 2001. "Recent Trends in Wealth Ownership, from 1983 to 1998." *Assets for the Poor: The Benefits of Spreading Asset Ownership.* Edited by Thomas M. Shapiro and Edward N. Wolff. New York: Russell Sage Foundation. Pp. 34–73.

Wright, David J. 2001. *It Takes a Neighborhood: Strategies to Prevent Urban Decline.* Albany, NY: Rockefeller Institute Press.

Yankelovich, Daniel. 1994. "How Changes in the Economy Are Reshaping American Values." *Values and Public Policy.* Edited by Henry J. Aaron, Thomas E. Mann, and Timothy Taylor. Washington, DC: Brookings Institution. Pp. 16–53.

Yinger, John. 1995. *Closed Doors, Opportunities Lost: The Continuing Costs of Housing Discrimination.* New York: Russell Sage Foundation.

————. 2001. "Housing Discrimination and Residential Segregation as Causes of Poverty." *Understanding Poverty.* Edited by Sheldon H. Danziger and Robert H. Haveman. New York: Russell Sage Foundation. Pp. 359–391.

Yunus, Muhammad. 1999. *Banker to the Poor: Micro-Lending and the Battle against World Poverty.* New York: PublicAffairs.

Zarefsky, David. 1986. *President Johnson's War on Poverty: Rhetoric and History.* University: University of Alabama Press.

Zedlewski, Sheila R., Linda Giannarelli, Joyce Morton, and Laura Wheaton. 2002. "Extreme Poverty Rising, Existing Government Programs Could Do More." Urban Institute, New Federalism, Series B, No. B-45, April.

Zick, Cathleen D., and Ken R. Smith. 1986. "Immediate and Delayed Effects of Widowhood on Poverty: Patterns from the 1970s." *Gerontologist* 26: 669–675.

———. 1991. "Patterns of Economic Change Surrounding the Death of a Spouse." *Journal of Gerontology: Social Sciences* 46: S310–S320.

Zigler, Edward, and Matia Finn-Stevenson. 1999. *Schools of the Twenty-First Century: Linking Child Care and Education.* Boulder, CO: Westview Press.

Zimmerman, David J. 1992. "Regression toward Mediocrity in Economic Review." *American Economic Review* 82: 409–429.

Index

Adams, John, 86–87, 143

adolescents. *See* teen pregnancy

ADS. *See* Annual Demographic Supplement

African Americans. *See* blacks

Aid to Families with Dependent Children (AFDC), 102, 104, 236, 262, 263. *See also* social safety net; welfare

Alan Guttmacher Institute, 225

Alinsky, Saul, 233, 291n.12

American civic principles
democracy, 133, 142–44, 162, 247
equality, 133, 140–42, 144, 208, 294n.18
justice, 133, 137–40, 144, 294n.17
liberty, 133–37, 144, 293n.10

American Dream, 3, 12, 142, 171, 281n.4. *See also* American civic principles; American traditional values

American Dream, The (Cullen), 281n.4

American Enterprise Institute, 20

American Indians, 284n.13, 299n.8

American traditional values
individualism, 11–12, 155, 156, 163, 171, 175, 194, 297n.5
land of opportunity, 12, 171, 175
as obstacle to understanding poverty, 11–13, 163–65
profit and competition, 163–65, 254
self-reliance, 12, 155, 156, 163, 175

America's Second Harvest, 38

Anderson, Elijah, 289n.11

Annual Demographic Supplement (ADS), 256

Apted, Michael, 289n.10

Arendt, Hannah, 145

Aristotle, 119, 296n.7

Arzabe, Patricia, 164

assets. *See* asset building for communities; asset building for individuals; community assets; individual assets

asset building for communities
Communities Organized for Public Service (COPS), 233
Community Reinvestment Act, 235
empowerment zones, 234
enterprise zones, 234
Grace Hill Settlement House, 232
Industrial Areas Foundation (IAF), 233
MORE Time Dollar Exchange program, 232
Nehemiah Homes Project, 233
Tax Increment Financing (TIF), 234

asset building for individuals
children's trust fund, 230
employee ownership plans, 230
G.I. Bill, 228
Grameen Bank, 300n.10
home mortgage deduction, 216, 228
Homestead Act, 228
Individual Development Accounts (IDAs), 229–30, 239

Australian Royal Commission on Human Relationships, 154

Bartik, Timothy, 53, 55, 196, 203, 204

Beckett, Katherine, 287n.2

Beeghley, Leonard, 137

Bell Curve, The (Herrnstein and Murray), 17

Berlin, Isaiah, 293n.10

Bible, 124–32, 292nn.2–4. *See also under* Judeo-Christian ethic

Billings, Dwight, 78

Bill of Rights, 135. *See also* American civic principles

English Poor Laws (1601), 138, 148
Enterprise Zone program, 234. *See also under* asset building for communities
environmental awareness, 157–58, 188, 191, 286n.25, 296n.14
equality, 133, 140–42, 144, 208, 294n.18. *See also under* American civic principles
Equality and Justice (Vallentryne), 294n.17

Families on the Faultline (Rubin), 44, 69
family structure
  as related to poverty, 27, 29, 270–74
  addressing the economic consequences of, 220–26
  See also female-headed families
Farley, Reynolds, 100
Federal Housing Administration (FHA), 216
Federal Reserve Board, 153
female-headed families, 27–28, 222
  life course poverty risk, 97, 270–74
  policies for helping, 221–26
  stress of, 44
  See also family structure
Ferguson, Ronald, 234
FHA. *See* Federal Housing Administration
Foner, Eric, 134, 294n.12
food
  food insecurity, 38, 286n.24
  heat-or-eat dilemma, 43, 118
  high cost of, 41
  hunger, 38, 114
  lack of adequate diet, 38–39
  as measurement for poverty, 22–23, 282–83n.4
Food Stamps, 23, 102, 103, 104, 106, 237, 262, 263, 283n.5, 297n.1. *See also* food; social safety net; welfare
foster care system, 19
Franklin, Benjamin, 12, 49, 156
freedom. *See* liberty

free-market capitalism, 20, 109, 153, 163, 165, 235
Furstenberg, Frank, 299n.7

Galbraith, John Kenneth, 169–70, 299n.5
Gale, William, 72
Gans, Herbert, 11
Garfinkel, Irwin, 222
gated communities, 159, 252
gender, 140
  feminization of poverty, 100–101
  impact on acquisition of human capital, 74
  life course poverty risk, 95, 97–101, 291n.6
General Assistance, 102, 262. *See also* social safety net; welfare
Gettysburg Address, 132–33. *See also* American civic principles
G.I. Bill, 228. *See also under* asset building for individuals
Gini coefficient, 161
Ginnie Mae. *See* Government National Mortgage Association
Gladwell, Malcolm, 298n.9
Glennerster, Howard, 25, 283n.4
Glickman, Dan, 39
Golden Rule, 292–93nn.5–6. *See also under* Judeo-Christian ethic
Golden Rule, The (Wattles), 292–93nn.5–6
Gottschalk, Peter, 288n.7
Government National Mortgage Association (Ginnie Mae), 216. *See also under* asset building for communities; housing
Grameen Bank (Bangladesh), 300n.10. *See also under* asset building for communities
Great Depression, 64, 76, 134, 205
Great Society, 135, 282n.3
Grogan, Paul, 231
Guthrie, Woody, 5

iron deficiency, 113. *See also* health
Isserman, Maurice, 282n.6

Jargowsky, Paul, 284n.15
Jefferson, Thomas, 86, 123
Jerald, Craig, 208
Jesus, 129–31. *See also* Judeo-Christian ethic
jobs. *See* employment
Johnson, Lyndon B., 20, 22, 119, 135, 140, 296n.10
Jones, Jacqueline, 289n.11
Judeo-Christian ethic, 123–32, 165, 187, 245, 293nn.8–9
  Bible, 124–32, 292nn.2–4
  Golden Rule, 292–93nn.5–6
  New Testament, 124, 125, 129–32, 293n.8
  Old Testament, 124, 125–29
  Texts of Judaism, 124, 125–29
  Torah, 124, 292–93n.5
justice, 133, 137–40, 144, 294n.17
  as balance, 137–38, 294n.17
  Themis or Lady Justice, 138, 294n.16
  See also under American civic principles

Katz, Lawrence, 204
Kawachi, Ichiro, 162
Kennedy, Bruce, 162
Kennedy, John F., 13, 243
Kennedy, Robert F., 243–44
Kerner Commission, 119
King, Martin Luther, Jr., 15, 157, 164, 193
Kingdon, John, 175
Kozol, Jonathan, 166
Krueger, Alan, 198

labor market. *See* employment
Lao Tzu, 252
Latinos. *See* Hispanics
Lauber, William, 172
lead poisoning, 112–13, 114–15, 182, 291n.8, 292n.18. *See also* children; health
Leidenfrost, Nancy, 40

Levin-Waldman, Oren, 196, 198
liberty, 133–37, 144, 293n.10
  Four Freedoms, 134–35, 294n.12
  See also under American civic principles
life course. *See under* female-headed families; gender; poverty; race; social safety net
Lincoln, Abraham, 132
LIS. *See* Luxembourg Income Study
Living on the Edge (Rank), 6, 8, 38, 48, 68, 133, 286n.22, 286n.26
Living Wage, A (Ryan), 298n.3
living wage initiatives, 199–200, 298n.3
lobbying, 143
Loeb, Paul Rogat, 247, 251
Losing Ground (Murray), 17, 174
low-birthweight babies, 112
Luxembourg Income Study (LIS), 33–35, 61, 264–65

Mann, Horace, 207
marriage, 43–44, 236. *See also* family structure
Major Barbara (Shaw), 119
May, Larry, 152, 156
McDonough, William J., 202
McLeod, Jane, 46
McMurrer, Daniel, 72, 73
Mead, Margaret, 243
Medicaid, 23, 40, 102, 103, 104, 106, 210, 212, 213, 236, 237, 262, 263, 283n.5, 291n.7. *See also* health; health insurance; social safety net; welfare
Medicare, 27, 40, 211, 274. *See also* health insurance
Meeks, Wayne, 124
mental health, 44, 46, 112
Mica, John, 36–37
Middle American Individualism (Gans), 11
Mills, C. Wright, 64
minimum wage, 197–200, 298n.1. *See also* employment

Minsky, Hyman, 235

Mississippi Choctaws, 233–34

Mitchell, Lawrence, 12

mortgages, 216, 217, 228. *See also* housing

Moses, 125–26

Murray, Charles, 17–20, 45, 172, 174

National Conference of Catholic Bishops, 126, 131, 156

national housing trust fund, 215–16. *See also under* housing

Native Americans. *See* American Indians

Newman, Katherine, 77

New Testament, 124, 125, 129–32, 293n.8. *See also under* Judeo-Christian ethic

Nicomachean Ethics (Aristotle), 296n.7

No Mercy (Stefanic), 282n.2

Nussbaum, Martha, 37

Obey, David, 282n.2

O'Connor, Alice, 50

older adults. *See* elderly

Old Testament, 124, 125–29. *See also under* Judeo-Christian ethic

On the Social Contract (Rousseau), 145

orphanages, 18, 19

Orshansky, Molly, 22–23, 25, 282–83n.4

Other America, The (Harrington), 14

Other American, The (Isserman), 282n.6

Panel Study of Income Dynamics (PSID), 29, 63, 90–91, 102, 258–64, 268, 274, 290n.2, 291n.9

Pearce, Diana, 283n.6

Personal Responsibility and Work Opportunity Reconciliation Act (1996), 148, 174. *See also* social safety net; welfare

Phillips curve problem, 153, 203

Pledge of Allegiance, 132, 133, 144

Poetic Justice (Nussbaum), 37

Politics (Aristotle), 292n.16

pollution. *See* environmental awareness

Poor Richard's Almanac (Franklin), 12, 49

Post, Laura, 208

poverty

causes of, 49–50, 148, 248

changes possible by each individual, 246–51

characteristics associated with, 30–32

among children, 25–28, 33, 34, 35, 38, 40, 45–47, 110, 121, 151, 178, 181, 221, 267–74

as conditional state, 179–81

data sources, 255–65

definition of, 21–22, 38, 61

demographic composition of, 30–32

as deprivation, 181–84, 194, 245, 246

as doing without, 38–42

among elderly, 25–27, 33, 34, 38, 151, 274–80

Galbraith on, 169–70

human meaning of, 36–48, 189, 297n.3

as individual failing, 49–53, 64, 79, 107, 148, 171–74, 286–87n.1

as injustice, 184–86, 194

international comparisons, 33–36, 61–62, 285nn.17–21

length and frequency of, 28–29, 52

life-course analysis of, 62–65, 67, 89–101, 267–80, 291n.6

as life-course event, 89–91

likelihood of, 92–95

measurement of, 20–25, 282–83n.4, 287n.2, 290n.5, 298n.6

Murray on, 17

new paradigm of, 176–89

old paradigm of, 171–76

risk across American life course, 88–109

as shared responsibility, 152–57

societal costs of, 109–21

stress of, 42–45

as structural failing, 49–82, 148, 176–79, 194, 246, 287n.1

threshold, 23–25